Soucek, Branko.

Neural and concurrent real-time systems

$39.95

DATE			

Neural and Concurrent Real-Time Systems

Sixth-Generation Computer Technology Series

Branko Souček, Editor
University of Zagreb

Neural and Massively Parallel Computers: The Sixth Generation
Branko Souček and Marina Souček

Neural and Concurrent Real-Time Systems: The Sixth Generation
Branko Souček

Neural and Concurrent Real-Time Systems

The Sixth Generation

BRANKO SOUČEK
Department of Mathematics
University of Zagreb

WILEY

A Wiley-Interscience Publication

JOHN WILEY & SONS

New York / Chichester / Brisbane / Toronto / Singapore

Library of Congress Cataloging in Publication Data:

Souček, Branko.
Neural and concurrent real-time systems: the sixth generation/
Branko Souček.
p. cm.
"A Wiley-Interscience publication."
Includes bibliographies and index.
ISBN 0-471-50889-6
1. Neural computers. 2. Real-time data processing. I. Title.
QA76.5.S6572 1989
006.3—dc19 89-5682
CIP

Printed in the United States of America

10 9 8 7 6 5 4 3 2 1

To Sneška
and
our son, Branko

CONTENTS

PREFACE

Thanks to advances in artificial neural networks, expert systems, and concurrent processors, it is now possible to build *intelligent* real-time systems, which belong to the sixth-generation technology. Intelligent real-time systems described in this book cover the following applications: intelligent instruments, data acquisition, signal and speech processing, computer vision and graphics, process control and manufacturing inspection, intelligent robots, decision-making systems, on-line simulators, transputer-based superclusters, flexible factory cells, and compter integrated manufacturing.

The built-in neural and concurrent processors and knowledge bases provide these systems with a set of new features: learning and self-organization, fuzzy reasoning, very high-speed signal processing and process control, real-time recognition and classification of patterns in signals and images, high reliability due to the dispersed storage, and a very high performance/price ratio. As a result, intelligent real-time systems present a rapidly growing technology.

The book is divided into two parts:

Part I: INTELLIGENT PROCESSES (Chapters 1 to 5)
Part II: INTELLIGENT SYSTEMS (Chapters 6 to 11)

Chapter 1 gives an overview of signal processing. Histogram measurement principles are reviewed first; different methods for the correlation analysis are explained next. Computer programs are shown to calculate power spectra for periodic and nonperiodic signals. Chapter 2 reviews the processes needed to understand real-time systems: sampling and quantizing theorems, analog-to-digital conversion, and servicing and queueing involving serial and parallel components.

Chapter 3 describes mapping, adaptation, and learning in neural networks. Neural networks of very fine and medium granularity are presented: field computers, back-propagation networks, high-order units, alternating projection networks, and stochastic cells. Chapter 4 gives concrete examples of neural networks in real-time applications. Examples cover signal processing, noise cancellation, EKG, sonar, speech, phonetic typewriter, image recognition, object classification, manufacturing inspection, feedback process control, and robot manipulators. Neural networks open the road toward new learning, control, and robots, avoiding analytical system design.

Chapter 5 deals with coarse grain intelligent processes: artificial genetic selection, forward-backward chaining of knowledge schemas, and frames. Examples include expert systems for fault diagnosis, factory cell simulation and knowledge-based robots and process control.

Chapter 6 gives an overview of computers in instrumentation and in-process control. The basic techniques explained are: input/output transfer, interrupts, direct-memory access, interfacing, real-time clock, channels, pools, and semaphores. Real-time operating systems, schedulers and monitors are also explained and widely used real-time computers, buses, and networks are illustrated.

Chapter 7 describes newly developed neural chips and systems. Structures realizing 20 billion multiply/adds per second equivalent to 40,000 MIPS are shown. Neurocomputers with 10 million processing elements are presented. Digital and analog neural chips are described and compared. The chapter ends with the description of high-speed neural coprocessors. Chapter 8 defines the concurrent system as a set of relatively independent processes, connected to each other through synchronized messages. Functional features of the transputer family of chips and the OCCAM language are described. Real-time programming is explained, including timers, scheduling, interrupts, and polling.

Chapter 9 concentrates on concurrent system design and applications. Concrete examples of parallel system design and real-time programming, based on transputers and OCCAM, are presented. Examples range from simple units, speech, vision and graphics, to multi-user flight simulators and flexible manufacturing cells.

Chapter 10 deals with the upper level transputer-based concurrent systems: computing surface, cluster and superclusters. These systems achieve the power of supercomputers for a tenth of the cost of other systems. Superclusters can expand infinitely, with overall throughput going up in proportion to the number of processors. Application specific topologies can be configured with the network configuration unit.

Chapter 11 outlines the market for neural, concurrent, and intelligent real-time systems. A whole new industry and business has been born. Intelligent systems and services represent the infrastructure for a highly efficient and clean economy of the 1990s. The suggestions of Nobel Laureates, devoting time and energy in intelligence research, are discussed.

The book has been written as a textbook for students, as well as a reference for practicing engineers and scientists. A minimal undergraduate-level background is assumed, although many fundamentals are reviewed. The treatment is kept as straightforward as possible emphasizing functions, systems, and applications. A comprehensive list of manufacturers at the end of the book includes addresses, products, and services (neural, concurrent, intelligent, real-time systems). Readers interested in other related topics of neural and concurrent processing should combine this book with B. Souček and M. Souček, *Neural and Massively Parallel Computers: The Sixth Generation,* Wiley, New York, 1988. These two books are independent volumes, with only a slight overlap.

Zagreb, Yugoslavia
September 1989

BRANKO SOUČEK

ACKNOWLEDGMENTS

I acknowledge the encouragement, stimulating atmosphere, discussions, and support received from my teachers, friends, and colleagues. Here, I can only name a few:

P. Brajak, I. Bratko, A. D. Carlson, F. Cellier, B. Furht, S. R. Hameroff, F. J. Hill, F. Jović, G. A. Korn, D. Koruga, H. Kraljević, R. H. Mattson, V. Milutinović, B. Ostojić, P. Papić, G. R. Peterson, M. Petrinović, S. Prešern, J. W. Rozenblit, A. Scott, P. Šuhel, T. Triffet, D. Vrsalović, B. P. Zeigler, A. Železnikar.

I thank the following institutions where I performed the experiments with neural, concurrent, and real time systems:

Department of Mathematics, University of Zagreb

Department of Electrical and Computer Engineering, University of Arizona

Department of Neurobiology and Behavior, State University of New York at Stony Brook

Brookhaven National Laboratory

Institute Rudjer Bošković

To write a book like this one, it was necessary to borrow some data from the manuals of computer/system manufacturers. I should like to thank the following companies for giving permission to adapt material from their publications:

AI Wave, Inc.
Global Holonetic Corporation
Hecht-Nielsen Neurocomputer Corporation
INMOS Group of Companies
Intellicorp
Nestor, Inc.
Oxford Computer
Paracom
Parsytec
Syntonic Systems, Inc.
TRW

Special thanks to John Wiley's editors and reviewers and to Mrs. B. Grdović and Mrs. V. Zlatić for assistance during preparation of the manuscript for the publisher. I am grateful to Mrs. L. Van Horn for an outstanding job in supervising the copyediting of the manuscript.

Neural and Concurrent Real-Time Systems

PART I

Intelligent Processes

Signal Processing
Sampling, Quantizing, Servicing, and Queueing
Mapping, Adaptation, and Learning in Neural Networks
Neural Networks in Real-Time Applications
Knowledge Chaining in Real-Time Applications

CHAPTER 1

Signal Processing

INTRODUCTION AND SURVEY

A substantial increase in data collection efficiency can be achieved if data can be sorted on the basis of some parameter. In this case, hundreds or thousands of pieces of data, instead of being individually recorded, can be accumulated into one counting location. Each value of the parameter should have its own counting location. A histogram accumulated in this way presents the probability distribution function of the measured parameter. This kind of data collection is used in numerous experiments and can be readily done with a laboratory computer. Data collecting and sorting systems are usually called *analyzers*.

This chapter describes basic data analysis techniques. Probability distribution measurement principles are reviewed first, and the most important analysis techniques are described next. Different kinds of data analyzers are widely used in physics, chemistry, biomedicine, and engineering (pulse-height analyzers, time-of-flight analyzers, Mossbauer-effect analyzers, neuron activity analysis, industrial product testing, communication signal analysis, etc.).

A simple yet efficient tool for analyzing random data through statistical averaging is the correlation function, which describes the time dependencies of a random data record. The correlation function can be measured with special instruments or a laboratory computer. In this chapter, we describe the basic definition and properties of the correlation function and explain two methods for calculating it. It is shown that the classical method, although good for analysis of random amplitudes, produces meaningless results if used to analyze random intervals. Both computer-simulated and experimental data have been used to check the correlation algorithms. A modified method for interval analysis is explained, and computer programs for both methods are discussed.

The most obvious presentation of the signal is in the time domain: the amplitude of the signal is displayed as a function of time. Another important presentation of the signal is in the frequency domain. For this purpose a Fourier series is used. The signal waveform may be expanded into a series of sine waves. By finding the amplitudes of these sine waves, we form the power spectra. The power spectral density function describes the general frequency composition of the data. The frequency composition of the data, in turn, bears important relationships to the basic characteristics of the physical or biomedical system involved.

In this chapter the Fourier series expansion is explained. Computer programs are used to calculate Fourier coefficients for a periodic signal and the power spectra for a nonperiodic signal. Also, some typical, frequently occurring waveforms are analyzed, and their power spectra are displayed and discussed. The chapter concludes with a discussion of special machines for measuring the power spectra and their variation with time. Such sonograms are widely used in acoustic communication for speech study and for animal communication study.

1.1. AMPLITUDE AND LATENCY HISTOGRAMS

In analyzing nature, one finds that many results indicate that the subjects of measurements belong to the class of random physical phenomena. *Randomness* means that the data are nonperiodic, exhibit no explicit time trend, bias, or regularity, and cannot be precisely defined for all time by any simple analytic function. Many random processes belong to the class of stationary processes. *Stationary* means that certain statistical properties of the data do not change with time.

Three main types of statistical analyses should be carried out for random and stationary data:

1. Amplitude probability density functions,
2. Correlation functions, and
3. Power spectral density functions.

These functions describe a random process, much like the amplitude, waveform, and Fourier frequency spectrum describe a deterministic process. This chapter deals with methods for measuring the amplitude probability density function (pdf).

Five important examples of processes that could occur in practice, singly or in combinations, will now be considered:

1. Sine waves,
2. Narrow-band noise,
3. Wide-band noise,
4. Discrete random pulses, and
5. Discrete random time intervals.

For each of these waveforms we develop the pdf. Five waveforms are pictured in Figure 1.1.

The sine wave in Figure 1.1*a* is completely described by the equation

$$x(t) = A \sin(2\pi f_0 t + \theta) \tag{1.1}$$

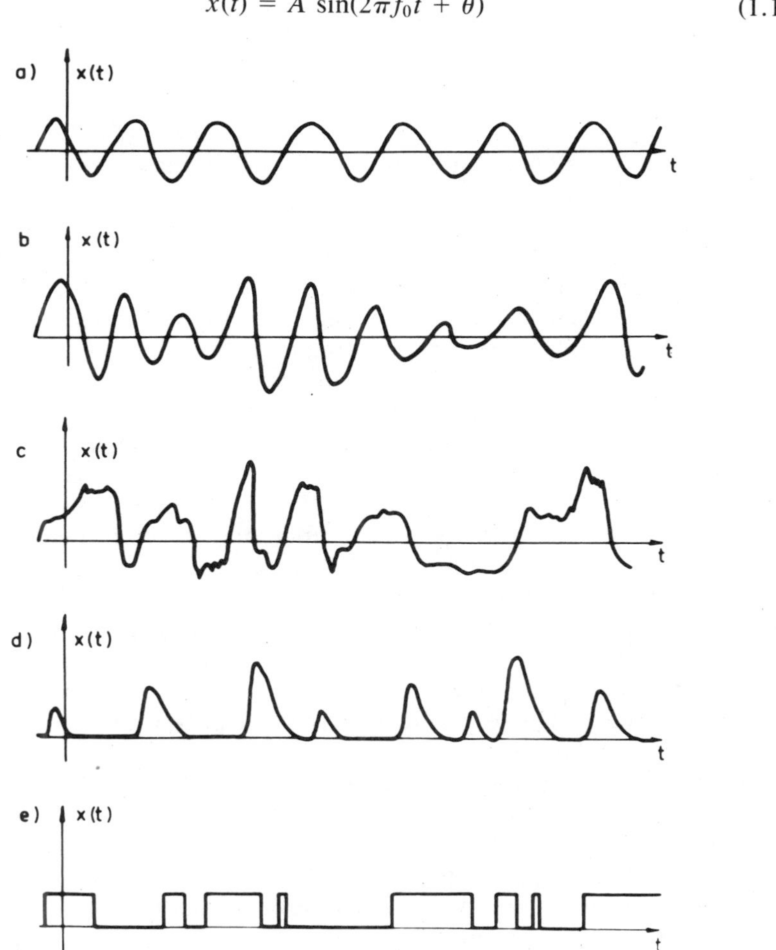

Figure 1.1 *Five special time histories: (a) sine wave; (b) narrow-band noise; (c) wide-band noise; (d) discrete random pulses; (e) discrete random intervals.*

where $x(t)$ is the instantaneous amplitude A is the maximum amplitude, f_0 is the center frequency, and θ is the initial phase angle.

Narrow-band noise (Figure 1.1*b*) is more difficult to represent analytically. It can sometimes be considered as a combination of a sine wave and noise:

$$x(t) = A(t) \sin[2\pi f_0 t + \theta(t)] \tag{1.2}$$

where the amplitude and phase now vary (relatively slowly) randomly with time. The frequency spread associated with $x(t)$ is assumed to be small compared with f_0.

Another possible representation for narrow-band noise is the additive type

$$x(t) = s(t) + n(t) \tag{1.2a}$$

Here $s(t)$ is the fixed sine wave, as described by Equation 1.1. This wave is mixed with a random noise $n(t)$ of a relatively narrow frequency spectrum and with the central frequency close to f_0.

In practice, we can obtain narrow-band noise by passing a random noise through a narrow-band filter. If the noise is mixed with a useful signal, this method can be used to improve the signal-to-noise ratio (SNR), provided that the two are not inside the same frequency band.

For wide-band noise no analytical representation is possible. All frequencies are theoretically possible in the record. The proportion of time spent in any frequency band is variable. Knowledge of instantaneous amplitude values associated with any narrow frequency band generally gives no information about the amplitudes associated with an adjacent narrow frequency band. A typical wide-band noise representation is given in Figure 1.1*c*.

Discrete random pulses (Figure 1.1*d*) and discrete random time intervals (Figure 1.1*e*) are often produced in nuclear and biomedical experiments. Generally there is no way to describe such waveforms by simple analytical expressions.

The pdfs to be described will be applied to instantaneous amplitude values for the first three processes in Figure 1.1 for the peak values of pulses in the fourth process and for the duration of pulses in the last process. Similar pdfs can be developed for other parameters of interest.

Pictures of appropriate pdfs for a sine wave, narrow-band noise, and wide-band noise, where the mean value is assumed to be zero, are shown in Figures 1.2*a*, *b*, *c*, respectively. The sine wave instantaneous amplitudes are distributed between $x = \pm A$, the most probable amplitudes where the sine wave spends most of its time. The pdf in Figure 1.2*b* is double-peaked, with a minimum at $x = 0$ and tails rapidly approaching zero. The pdf in Figure 1.2*c* is the well-known normal (Gaussian) type, with tails asymptotic to the x axis as $x \rightarrow \pm\infty$.

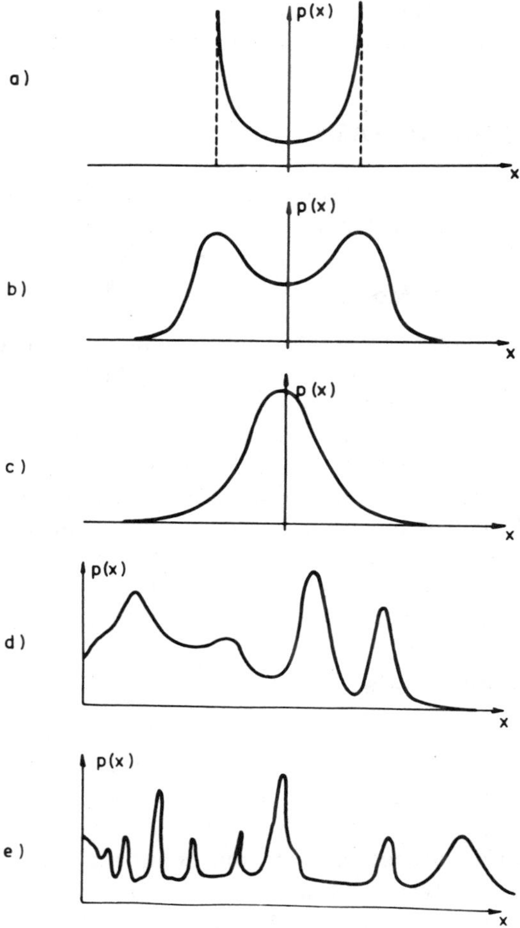

Figure 1.2 *Probability density functions:* (*a*) *sine wave;* (*b*) *narrow-band noise;* (*c*) *wide-band noise;* (*d*) *discrete random events;* (*e*) *discrete random time intervals.*

Figure 1.2*d* shows the pdf of the peak values for discrete random pulses obtained from radioactive ^{60}Co. Figure 1.2*e* shows the captured gamma ray events versus time of flight. Such "spectra" give an insight into the nuclear process under consideration.

If we know the pdf, we can compute the probability that the amplitude values will lie in any specified range, and this parameter may be significant for particular applications. For example, one may be interested in estimating the probability of excessively high amplitudes as an indication of an abnormal condition in an electroencephalogram data analysis, predicting structural failures under random vibration, or in discovering clipping or nonlinearities of a system. Of special importance is its application to nuclear pulse spectrometry. Although most measuring systems are developed primarily for nuclear fields, they can usually be used for other applications.

1.2. MEASURING HISTOGRAMS

A computer analyzer can have different modes of operation, the most important being single-parameter, sample-voltage, multiplex, and multiparameter.

1.2.1. Single-Parameter Mode

The input to the analyzer is a train of pulses, such as that generated by a nuclear detector. The analog-to-digital converter (ADC) changes each pulse amplitude into a binary word that is sent to the computer. In the computer, the binary word represents a memory address. Each time a given memory-address word is received from the ADC, the memory location is incremented by 1. The transformation from pulse amplitude to memory channel is demonstrated in Figure 1.3*a*. The pulse amplitude is projected horizontally onto the conversion gain slope, then vertically into the appropriate memory channel. The pulse arrival time is dictated by the physical source of the pulses. Each pulse initiates analog-to-digital conversion and data accumulation.

1.2.2. Sample-Voltage Mode

Sample-voltage mode analysis should be used for continuous waveforms. The ADC is controlled by the external sample clock, which determines the sampling rate. When the sample is taken, the amplitude at the sample time is digitized and becomes a memory address. The memory word contents corresponding to the address are increased by one count and become accumulated data. The sampling analysis of a sine wave is shown in Figure 1.3*b*. The accumulated value in each memory location is proportional to the probability density at that amplitude.

1.2.3. Multiplex Mode

In multiplex mode, few ADCs can be connected to the same computer and operate under multiplex scanner control. Hence, few independent measurements can be carried out at the same time. Each converter has its device address and responds only to that address for which it was programmed. Data can be transferred between converters and memory in the scanning programmed mode or on the basis of an interrupt request.

1.2.4. Multiparameter Mode

In multiparameter mode, two or more inputs are processed to form two- or higher-dimensional pdfs. For example, two-parameter pulse-height analysis

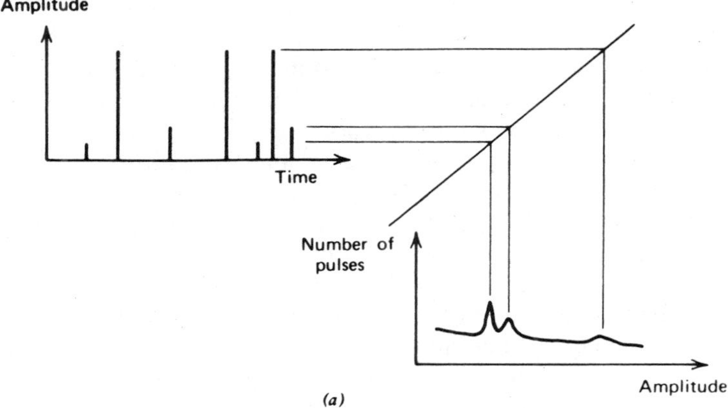

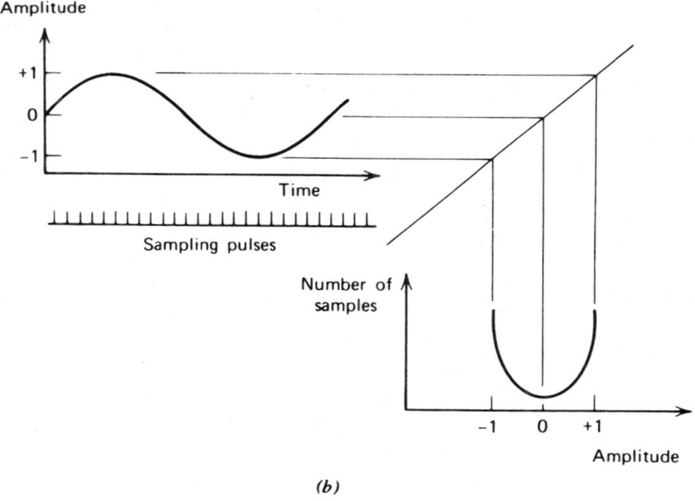

Figure 1.3 *(a) Transformation from pulse amplitude to memory channel. (b) Sampling analysis of a sine wave.*

is a coincidence analysis of two pulses from separate detectors occurring in the same time interval. The output of one converter becomes the X parameter, the output of the other becomes the Y parameter, and the number of times each XY combination occurs becomes the Z parameter of a three-dimensional field.

The predominant technique for the quantization of pulse height (voltage or charge) derives from a method originated by Wilkinson[1] in 1950. It consists of first converting the height into a time interval and then counting clock pulses to measure that interval. The count is then a direct proportion of the original pulse height to the precision of clock intervals, within the accuracy of the pulse-to-time converter. After conversion, the obtained information is used to address the memory.

The first memories were acoustic delay line (Hutchinson and Scarrot[2]). Later, electrostatic memories and magnetic drums appeared. Ferrite-core memories first came into use in 1955. Now real-time computers are directly connected to the ADCs and work as multichannel analyzers. A major advantage of the computer-oriented stored-program system is that both the sequencing of the functions and their detailed makeup can be readily altered by programming to meet the individual requirements of any situation. The first computer analyzer systems were published in 1962 to 1963. Figure 1.4 shows a typical pulse-height analyzer using the Wilkinson-type converter directly connected to the computer equipped with a cathode ray tube (CRT) display.

Pulse-to-time conversion is accomplished by charging a capacitor to a voltage proportional to the maximum excursion of the signal pulse, and then discharging it linearly in time by using a constant current. The counting of clock pulses is started at the beginning of the rundown and stopped when the capacitor voltage reaches zero. Those pulses are counted in an ADC register, which is used to address the computer memory.

The computer displays the data on the CRT. The x coordinate comes from memory address A_x, but the y coordinate is the contents of the A_x address. The flow diagram of the display program consists of an inner loop for point display and an outer loop for picture display. After the abscissa has reached its maximum value x_{max}, the x value is reset (that is, $x = 0$), and the picture display starts again.

During the display of every point, interrupt is possible. The display program is interrupted with the appearance of new data, and the computer jumps to another interrupt program. The computer saves the accumulator (ACC) contents and commences the datum transfer, that is, the taking of a new item. The ADC transfers the register contents (it has a new item accepted at the end of analog-to-digital conversion) to the ACC. Afterward these contents are used as memory address. The contents of that location are incremented, which means that a new descriptor is stored together with some others. Later, the computer restores the ACC contents, clears the ADC register, and tests to see if a sufficient number of data have been taken. If so, the computer continues displaying the collected data. If not, a new interrupt is made possible, and the display continues waiting for new data.

Figures 1.5*a*, *b*, *c* show the measurement progression of 1024-channel ^{60}Co spectra, using a laboratory computer.[3] The spectrum is increased with time by an increasing number of input data.

Table 1.1 is a program in real-time BASIC to sample the sine wave and display the amplitude histogram. The results are presented in Figure 1.6.

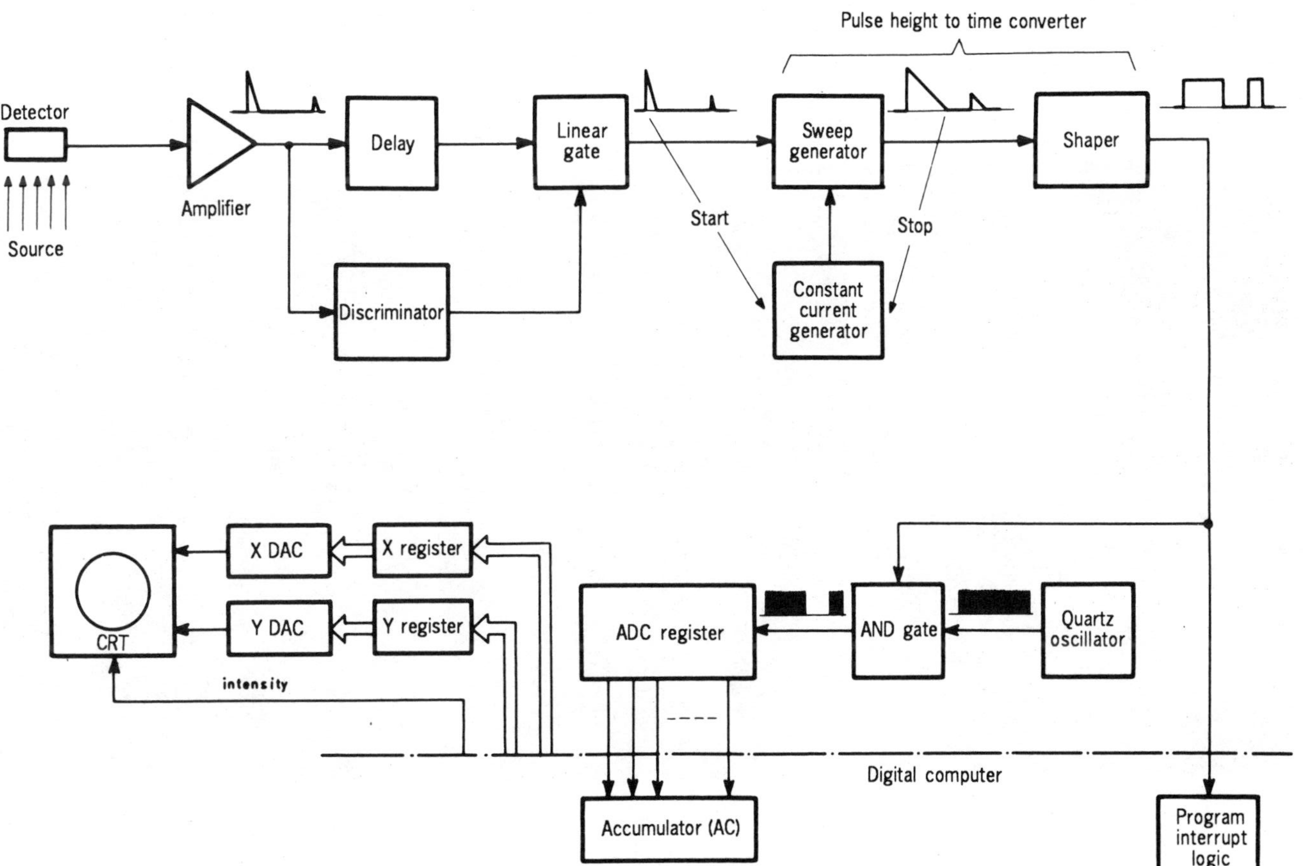

Figure 1.4 *Typical pulse-height analyzer system using amplitude-to-time-to digital converter directly connected to the computer. The probability distribution is displayed on the CRT scope.*

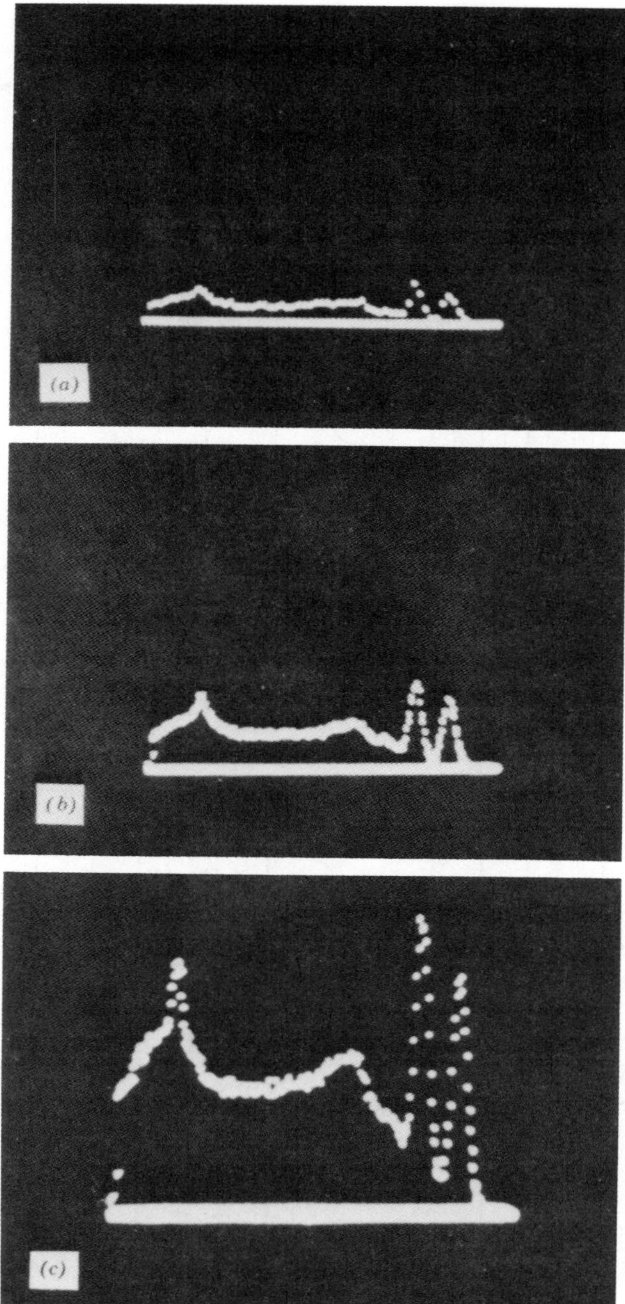

Figure 1.5 *Course of measurement of the probability distribution, as displayed on CRT after 1, 3, and 10 time intervals.*

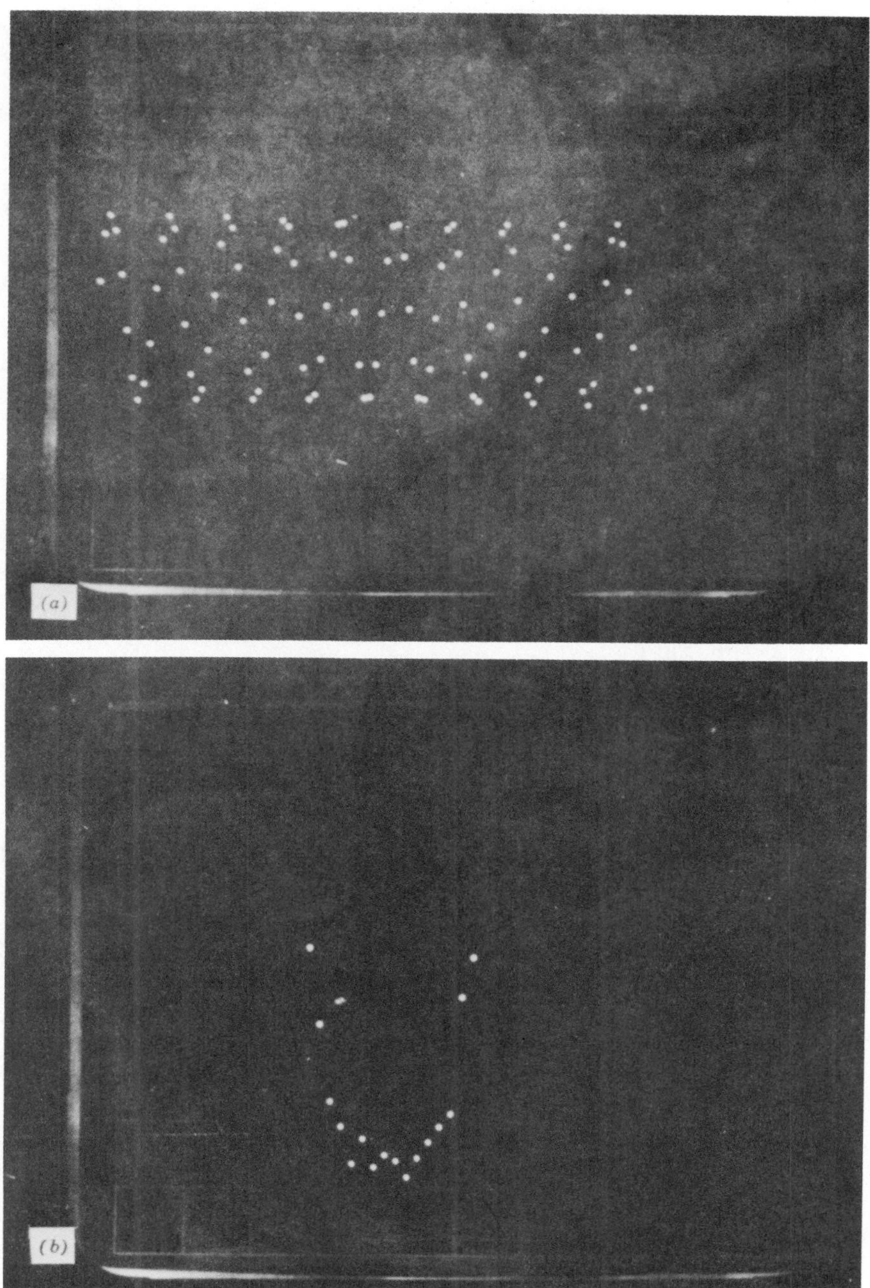

Figure 1.6 *Real-time experiment programmed in BASIC language: (a) sampling and display of the sine voltage; (b) measured amplitude probability distribution.*

TABLE 1.1

```
LIST
10 REM REAL-TIME HISTOGRAM MEASUREMENT
20 REM SAMPLE DATA FROM CHANNEL TWO
30 REM AT A RATE OF 10 MILLISECONDS
35 FEM SIGNAL FREQUENCY IS 10 Hz
40 REM HISTOGRAM ARRAY H, DATA ARRAY D
50 DIM H(50),D(100)
60 FOR K=1 to 50
70 H(K)=0
80 NEXT K
100 REM INITIALIZE CLOCK
110 SET RATE 3,10
120 REM SAMPLE 100 DATA POINTS FOR DISPLAY
130 FOR I=1 TO 100
140 WAITC
150 D(I)=ADC(2)
160 NEXT I
170 FOR I=1 TO 100
180 X=.01*I
185 Y=.5+.5*D(I)
190 PLOT X,Y
195 DELAY
198 NEXT I
200 INPUT A
205 CLEAR
210 REM SAMPLE DATA FOR HISTOGRAM
220 FOR I=1 TO 1000
230 WAITC
240 S=ADC(2)
250 S1=.5+.5*S
260 K=INT(50*S1)
270 H(K)=H(K)+1
280 NEXT I
300 REM DISPLAY HISTOGRAM
310 FOR K=1 TO 50
320 X=K/50
330 Y=5.000000E-03*H(K)
340 PLOT X,Y
350 DELAY
360 NEXT K
400 STOP
```

1.3. AMPLITUDE CORRELATION

1.3.1. Definitions

The correlation function describes the general dependence of the data values at one time on the values at another time. Correlation is usually applied to random data analysis, and it can be used to detect periodic signals buried in noise. Also, correlation provides a measure of similarity between two waveforms. Two correlation functions are generally used: autocorrelation and cross-correlation. *Autocorrelation* measures the similarity of a signal to a time-delayed version of itself, whereas *cross-correlation* measures the degree of similarity of one waveform (source, input, stimulus) to a second waveform (output, response).

The mathematical definition of the autocorrelation function $R_{xy}(C)$ is

$$R_{xx}(C) = \lim_{T\to\infty} \frac{1}{T} \int_0^T x(t)x(t + C)\, dt \tag{1.3}$$

Figure 1.7 shows a small part of a random waveform. Equation 1.3 takes the product of $x(t)$ at time t and $x(t + C)$ at time $t + C$. This operation is repeated for every value of t, $0 < t < T$. The integral sums all products, and $1/T$ is the average over the observation time T. The resulting average product approaches an exact autocorrelation function as $T \to \infty$.

The mathematical definition of the cross-correlation function $R_{xy}(C)$ is

$$R_{xy}(C) = \lim_{T\to\infty} \frac{1}{T} \int_0^T x(t)y(t + C)\, dt \tag{1.4}$$

The only difference between Equations 1.3 and 1.4 is that in the cross-correlation calculation the signal $x(t)$ is multiplied by a time-delayed version of a second signal $y(t)$, rather than a time-delayed version of itself.

1.3.2. Properties and Applications of the Correlation Function

Figure 1.8 shows a typical plot of $R_{xx}(C)$ versus time displacement C for sine waves, sine waves plus random noise, narrow-band random noise, and wide-band random noise. The autocorrelation function has the following properties:

1. Autocorrelation is an even function with a maximum at $C = 0$. Because even functions are symmetrical around $C = 0$, we need to compute the correlation function only for positive values of C.

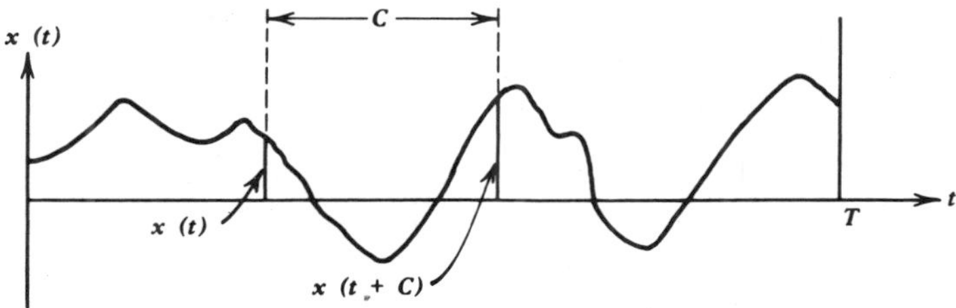

Figure 1.7 *Random waveform. To form autocorrelation function for the lag* C, *the product* x(t)x(t + c) *is formed for every value of* t.

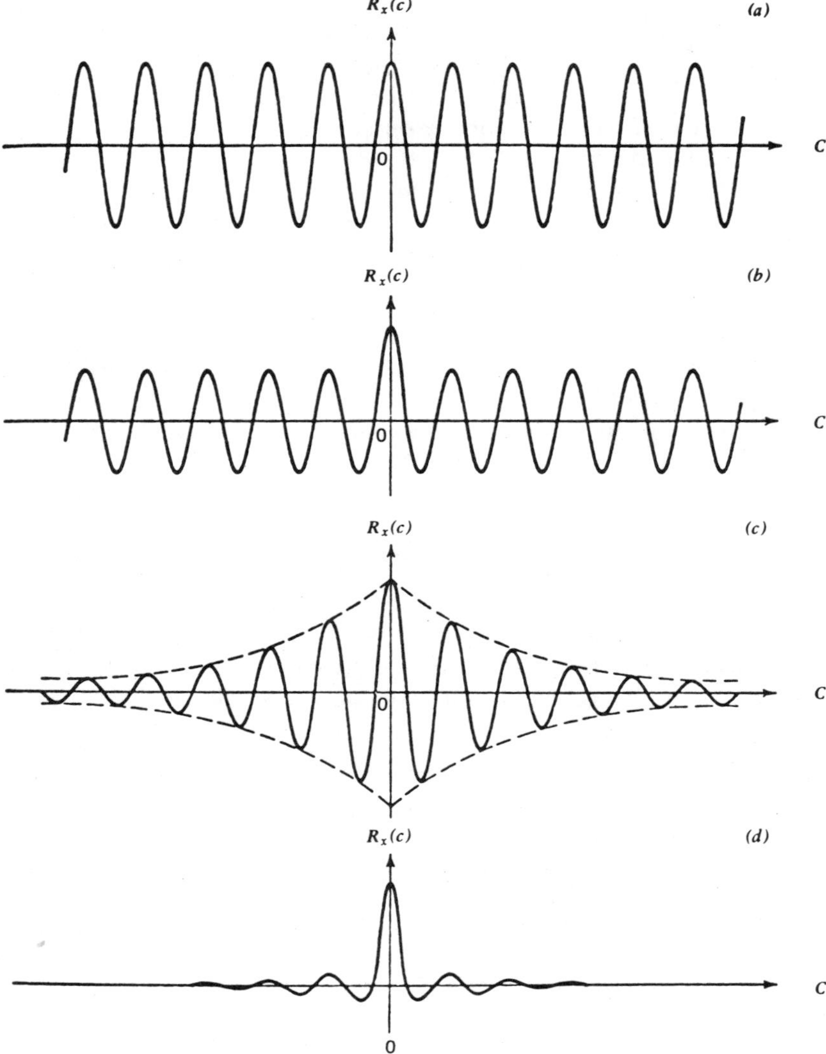

Figure 1.8 *Autocorrelation functions for some typical signals:* (a) *sine wave;* (b) *sine wave plus random noise;* (c) *narrow-band random noise;* (d) *wide-band random noise.*

2. The maximal value $R_{xx}(0)$ of $R_{xx}(C)$ is equal to the mean value of the time function. For display purposes it is convenient to normalize the maximum value to 1 by displaying the function $R_{xx}(C)/R_{xx}(0)$.
3. The value of the correlation function at $C > \infty$ is equal to the square of the mean value of the time function.
4. If the time function contains periodic components, then $R_{xx}(C)$ has components having the same period (Figure 1.8).

5. If the time function contains only random components, then $R_{xx}(C)$ will exponentially approach zero as C increases (Figure 1.8*d*).
6. If the time function is composed of two or more components, then $R_{xx}(C)$ is the sum of the correlation functions of each component. Figure 1.8*b* presents the correlation function for a sine wave plus random noise; it was obtained by summing the functions displayed in Figures 1.8*a*, *d*.
7. The cross-correlation function also has properties 3 to 6. However, it is not necessarily an even function. The maximum value of $R_{xx}(C)$ will occur for that value of the time shift C for which the signals x and y are most alike.

Typical applications for correlation include

1. Determining the transmission path and propagation delay of electrical, mechanical, acoustical, or seismic waves;
2. Detecting a very weak signal buried deep in noise;
3. Indicating epilepsy through comparison of electroencephalograms from the two halves of the brain;
4. Measuring the impulse-response function of complex systems in the presence of noise;
5. Studying Parkinson's disease and analyzing tremor frequency; and
6. Communication and speech research.

Equation 1.3 has been modified and programmed for digital computers to calculate autocorrelation functions for different signals. The program is presented in Table 1.2. To apply digital computing techniques, we have modified Equation 1.3 as follows: The signal is sampled at regular time intervals $I = 1, 2, \ldots, T$, producing digital data $x(1), x(2), \ldots, x(T)$. The function is integrated for $I = 0$ to $I = T$. The parameter T is the number of sampled values used for the calculation. Large values of T are needed for accuracy.

Statements 20 to 100 are used to allocate space for the sampled data X and the correlation function R, and to enter the parameters of the program: $M =$ number of data available; $C1 =$ number of desired correlation intervals; and $T =$ number of samples to be used for the calculation. The values is $T = M - C1$, to make sure that every sample will have a chance to be multiplied with another sample $C1$ positions farther down the array.

This program can be used for real data generated by an external source. To show the features of the correlation function, we shall simulate a few typical waveforms, using an auxiliary computer program. Statements 120 to 220 generate a sine wave plus noise with amplitudes S_1 and N_1, respectively. Statements 230 to 310 will produce the display of the generated waveforms. Figures 1.9*a* to 1.12*a* show four waveforms, for four different SNRs, displayed on the scope.

TABLE 1.2

```
LIST
20 REM CORRELATION,AMPLITUDES
30 DIM D(100)
40 USE D
50 DIM X(300)
60 DIM R(50)
70 PRINT "#OF DATA"
80 INPUT M
90 PRINT "#OF CORR"
100 INPUT C1
110 T=M-C1
111 REM
112 REM
115 REM
120 REM INPUT OR SIMULATION OF DATA
130 REM SIMULATE SINE PLUS NOISE
135 REM SINE AMPL.=S1,NOISE AMPL.=N1
140 PRINT "ENTER S1,N1"
150 INPUT S1,N1
155 F=0
160 FOR I=1 TO M
170 E=RND(1)+RND(2)+RND(3)-1.5
180 F=.5*F+E
190 S=SIN(.5*I)
200 X(I)=S1*S+N1*F
220 NEXT I
230 PRINT "DISPLAY DATA"
240 FOR I=1 TO C1
250 Z=I/C1
260 W=.5+X(I)/3
270 PLOT Z,W
280 DELAY
290 NEXT I
300 INPUT V
310 CLEAR
311 REM
312 REM
315 REM
400 REM CORRELATION LOOP
410 REM CORRELATION LAG IS C
415 FOR C=0 to C1
420 R(C)=0
430 FOR I=1 TO T
440 R(C)=R(C)+X(I)*X(I+C)
450 NEXT I
460 R(C)=R(C)/T
470 NEXT C
500 PRINT "DISPLAY CORRELATION"
510 FOR C=0 TO C1
520 Z=C/C1
530 W=R(C)/R(0)
540 W=.5+W/5
550 PLOT Z,W
560 DELAY
570 NEXT C
600 STOP
```

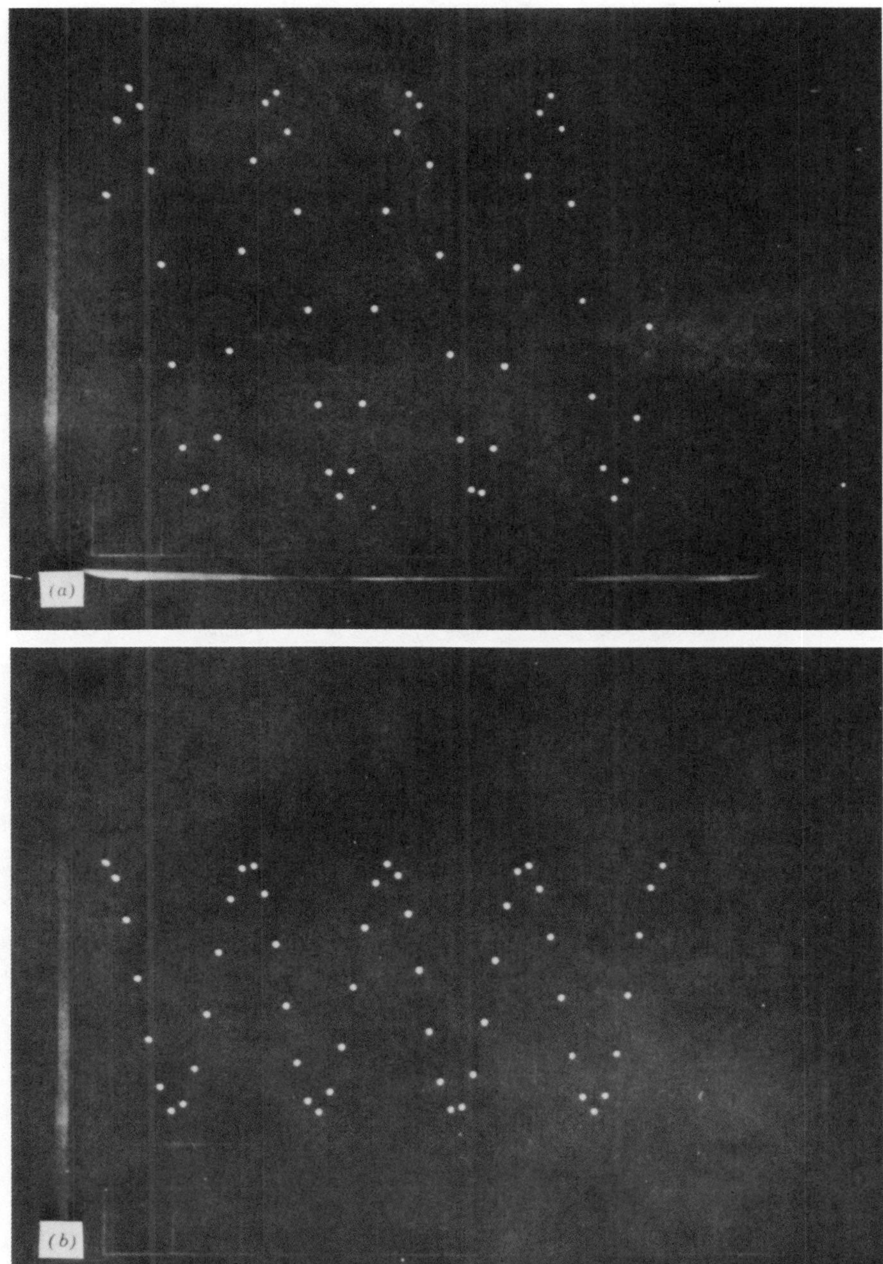

Figure 1.9 (*a*) *Sine wave signal as a function of time.* (*b*) *Its autocorrelation function as a function of the time lag* C.

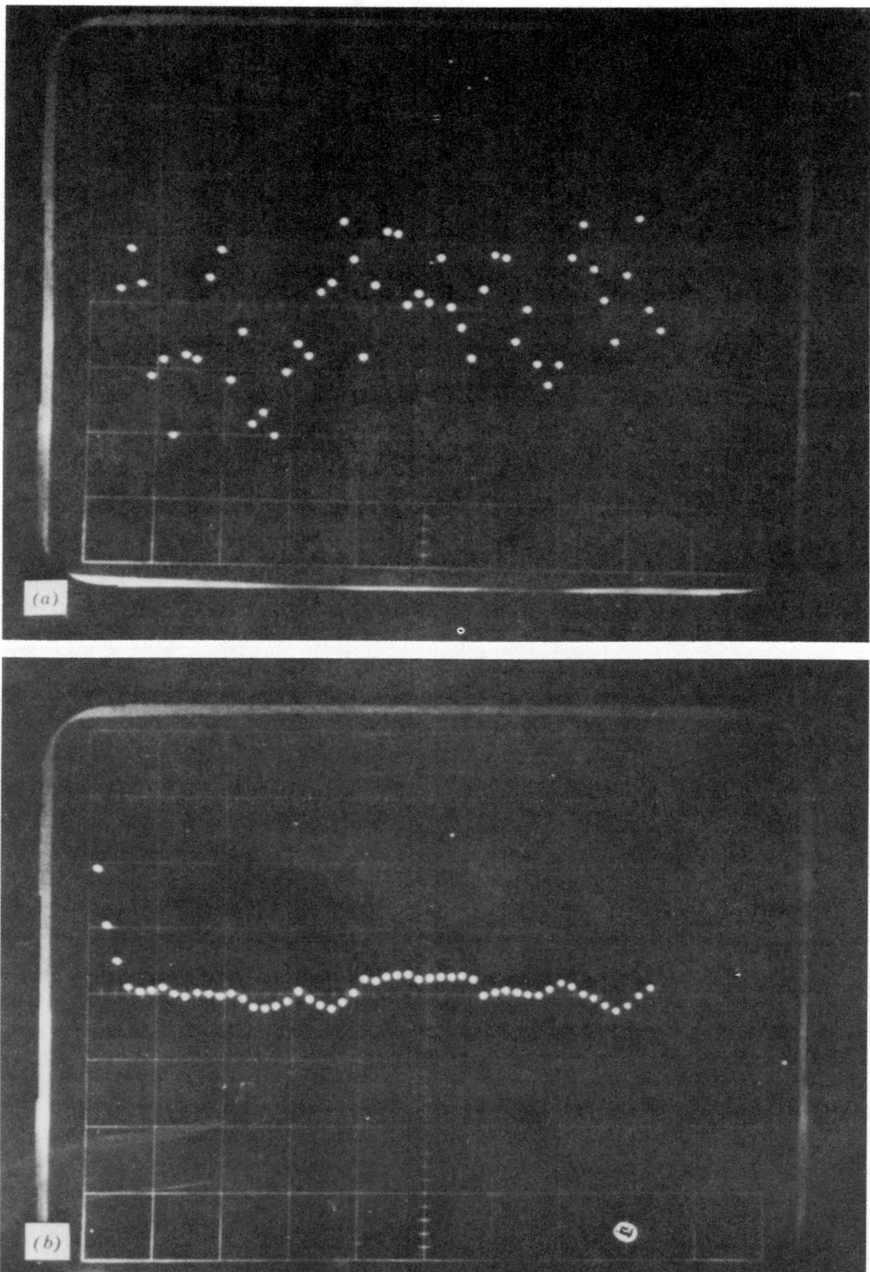

Figure 1.10 *(a) Random noise signal as a function of time. (b) Its autocorrelation function as a function of the time lag C.*

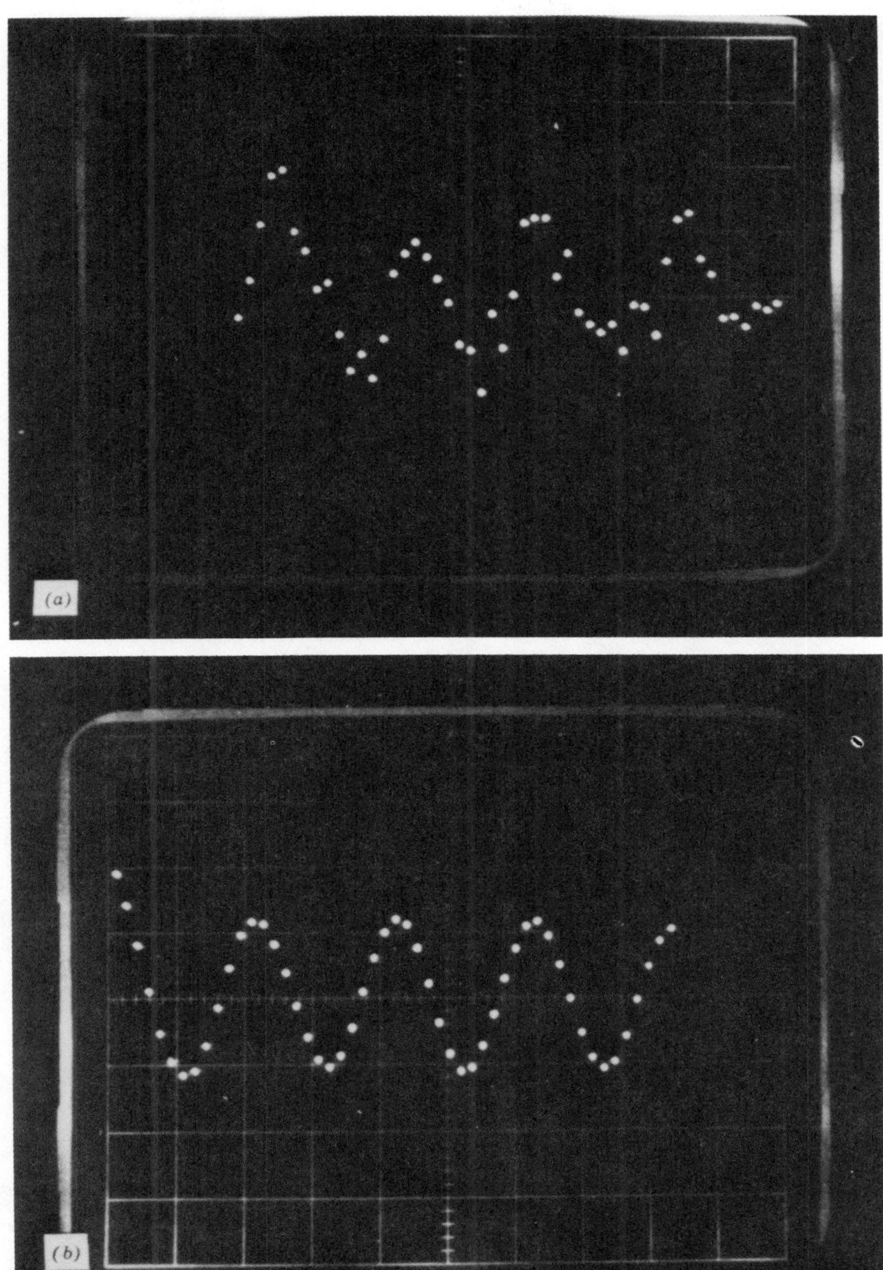

Figure 1.11 *Sine wave plus random noise:* (*a*) *signal as a function of time;* (*b*) *its autocorrelation function as a function of the time lag* C.

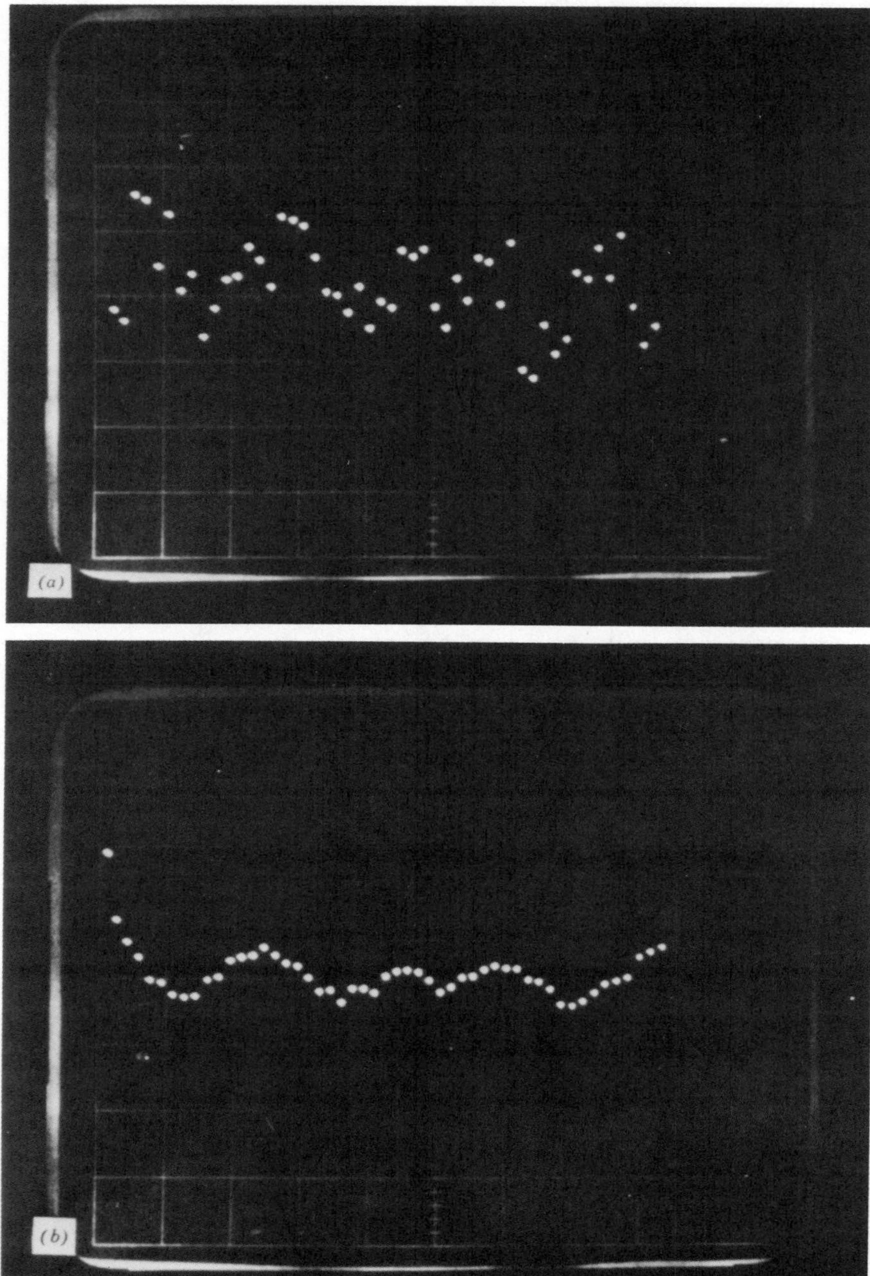

Figure 1.12 *Sine wave plus random noise: (a) signal as a function of time; (b) its autocorrelation function as a function of the time lag C.*

The actual correlation function calculation is programmed with statements 410 to 470. For each value of the time lag C, the autocorrelation is computed from the expression $x(I)x(I + C)$, and the products are added together for $0 \leq I \leq T$. Statements 510 to 600 display the calculated correlation function. Figures 1.9*b* to 1.12*b* show four autocorrelation functions for the four waveforms presented in Figures 1.9*a* to 1.12*a*.

Figure 1.9 is a sine wave and its autocorrelation function. As expected, the correlation function is periodic with the same period as the signal.

Figure 1.10 shows random noise and its autocorrelation. This time the correlation function is exponential and approaches zero for large values of C.

Figures 1.11 and 1.12 show a mixture of a sine wave and noise. Because the signal is composed of two components, the autocorrelation function is the sum of the autocorrelation functions of each component.

Figure 1.12 shows how correlation can be used to find a periodic signal buried in noise. The periodic signal is small and cannot be observed directly (Figure 1.12*a*). However, the correlation function clearly shows the periodic component (Figure 1.12*b*).

1.4. INTERVAL CORRELATION

1.4.1. Simulated Data

In biological and biomedical signals, the basic information is frequently carried in the form of a time interval (interspike latency, or response interval). One typical train of spikes is presented in Figure 1.13.

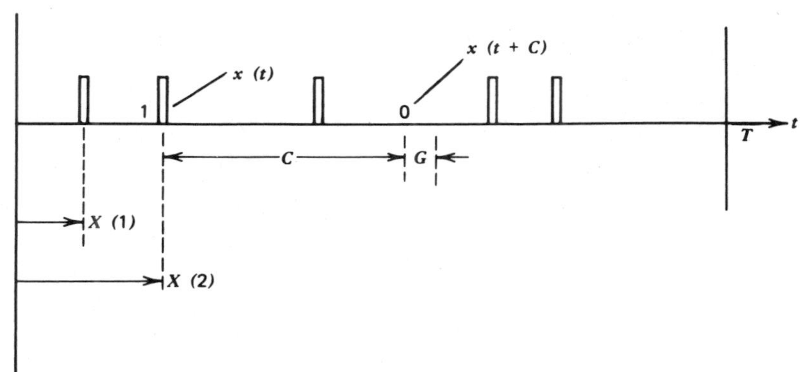

Figure 1.13 *Random interspike intervals. To form the autocorrelation function for the lag C, the product* x(t)x(t + c) *is formed for each spike. The product could take only the values 0 or 1.*

In this case, one has to be careful in calculating the correlation function. Direct substitution of data values, $x1$, $x2$, . . . into Equation 1.3 might lead to totally wrong conclusions. Another approach is needed to measure and calculate the correlation function for the signal in which the information carrier is the time interval. The correct procedure could be explained in the following way, starting from Equation 1.3 and Figure 1.13.

The signal in Figure 1.13 presents a train of spikes with random interspike intervals. Usually the amplitudes of the spikes are not of interest to the experimenter, whose only concern is to find out the properties of the interspike intervals. Hence, we normalize all amplitudes to 1.

For a given time lag C, the product from Equation 1.3 can have only one of two values: $x(t)x(t + C) = 1$, if the second spike is found inside the window G at a distance C from the first spike; or $x(t)x(t + C) = 0$, if there is no second spike inside the window G at a distance C from the first spike.

To calculate the correlation function for a given lag C, we apply the foregoing procedure to all spikes in the train. By adding together the partial products thus formed, we obtain the correlation function. The program for the latency correlation, based on this procedure, is shown in Table 1.3.

Statements 30 to 114 allocate the space and initialize the parameters of the program. Statements 120 to 230 simulate a random train of intervals. Each interval is composed of two components: a constant period of duration $S1$, and a random period with mean duration $N1$. Statement 210 generates random numbers, following the Poisson interval distribution. Statement 220 adds the intervals, which means that the interval x is always measured relative to the beginning of the interval train, as shown in the bottom part of Figure 1.13.

Statements 240 to 320 produce the scope display. The ordinate of the display is the interval x, measured relative to zero, whereas the abscissa is a serial number of the interval. Figures 1.14, 1.15, and 1.16*a* show three interval displays for three different ratios of constant period and random period.

TABLE 1.3

```
LIST
20 REM CORRELATION,INTERVALS
30 DIM D(100)
40 USE D
50 DIM X(300)
60 DIM R(50)
70 PRINT "#OF DATA"
80 INPUT M
90 PRINT "OF CORR"
100 INPUT C1
110 T=M-C1
112 PRINT "TIME WINDOW G=1"
114 G=1
116 REM
118 REM
```

TABLE 1.3 *(Continued)*

```
119 REM
120 REM INPUT OR SIMULATE DATA
130 REM SIMULATION
140 REM INTERVAL=CONSTANT PERIOD+RANDOM PERIOD
150 REM CONSTANT AMPLITUDE=S1,RANDOM AMPL.=N1
160 PRINT "ENTER S1,N1"
170 INPUT S1,N1
180 X(1)=0
190 FOR I=2 TO M
200 E=RND(1)
210 F=-LOG (1-E)
220 X(I)=X(I-1)+S1+N1*F
230 NEXT I
240 PRINT "DISPLAY INTERVALS"
250 FOR I=1 TO C1
260 Z=I/C1
270 W=1.000000E-03*X(I)
280 PLOT Z,W
290 DELAY
300 NEXT I
310 INPUT V
320 CLEAR
350 REM
351 REM
352 REM
400 REM CORRELATION LOOP
410 REM CORRELATION LAG IS C
418 FOR C=0 to C1
420 R(C)=0
422 P=C
424 Q=C+.95*G
430 FOR I=1 TO T
435 K1=3+INT(.1*C)
440 FOR K=0 TO K1
450 IF X(I+K)>=(X(I)+P)GO TO 470
460 NEXT K
465 GO TO 500
470 IF X(I+K)>(X(I)+Q)GO TO 500
480 R(C)=R(C)+1
500 NEXT I
510 R(C)=R(C)/T
520 NEXT C
600 PRINT "DISPLAY CORRELATION"
610 FOR C=0 TO C1
620 Z=C/C1
630 W=.5+.2*R(C)
640 PLOT Z,W
650 DELAY
660 NEXT C
700 STOP
```

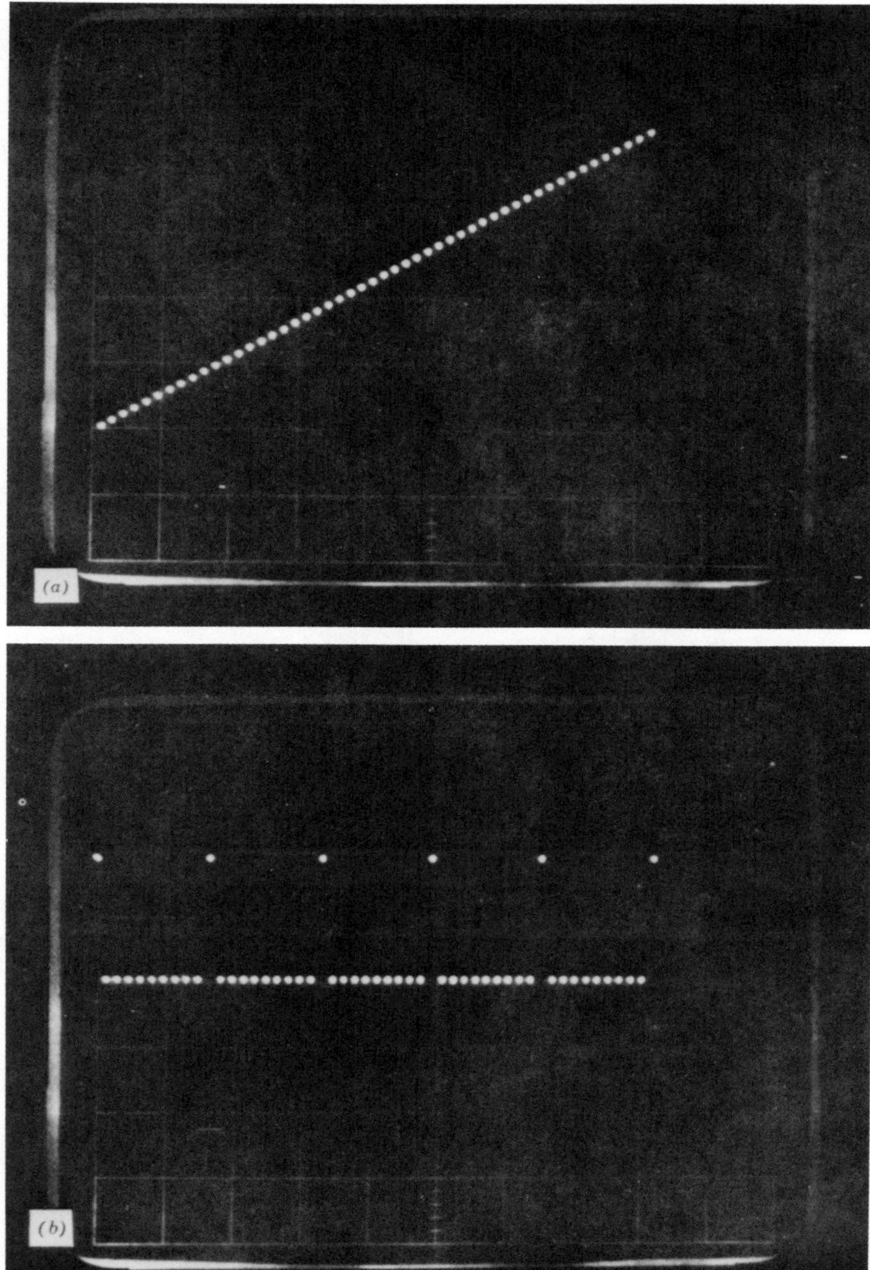

Figure 1.14 *Intervals composed only of constant period, of 10 time units:* (a) *Spike arrival instants* x *measured relative to time* t = *0 and displayed as a function of the serial number of the spike;* (b) *autocorrelation function (Note the period of 10 time units).*

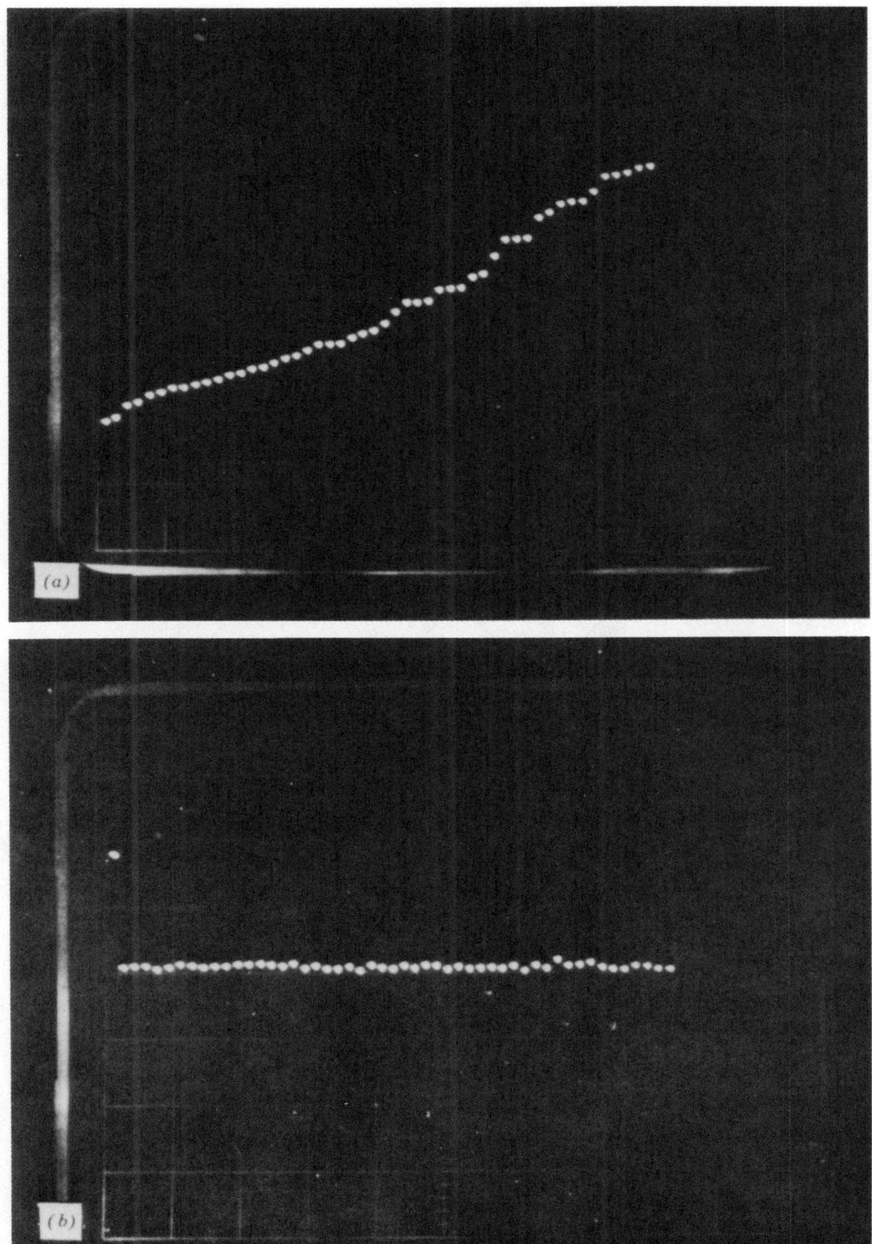

Figure 1.15 *Intervals composed only of the random component:* (a) *spike arrival instants* x *measured relative to time* t = 0 *and displayed as a function of the serial number of the spike;* (b) *autocorrelation function.*

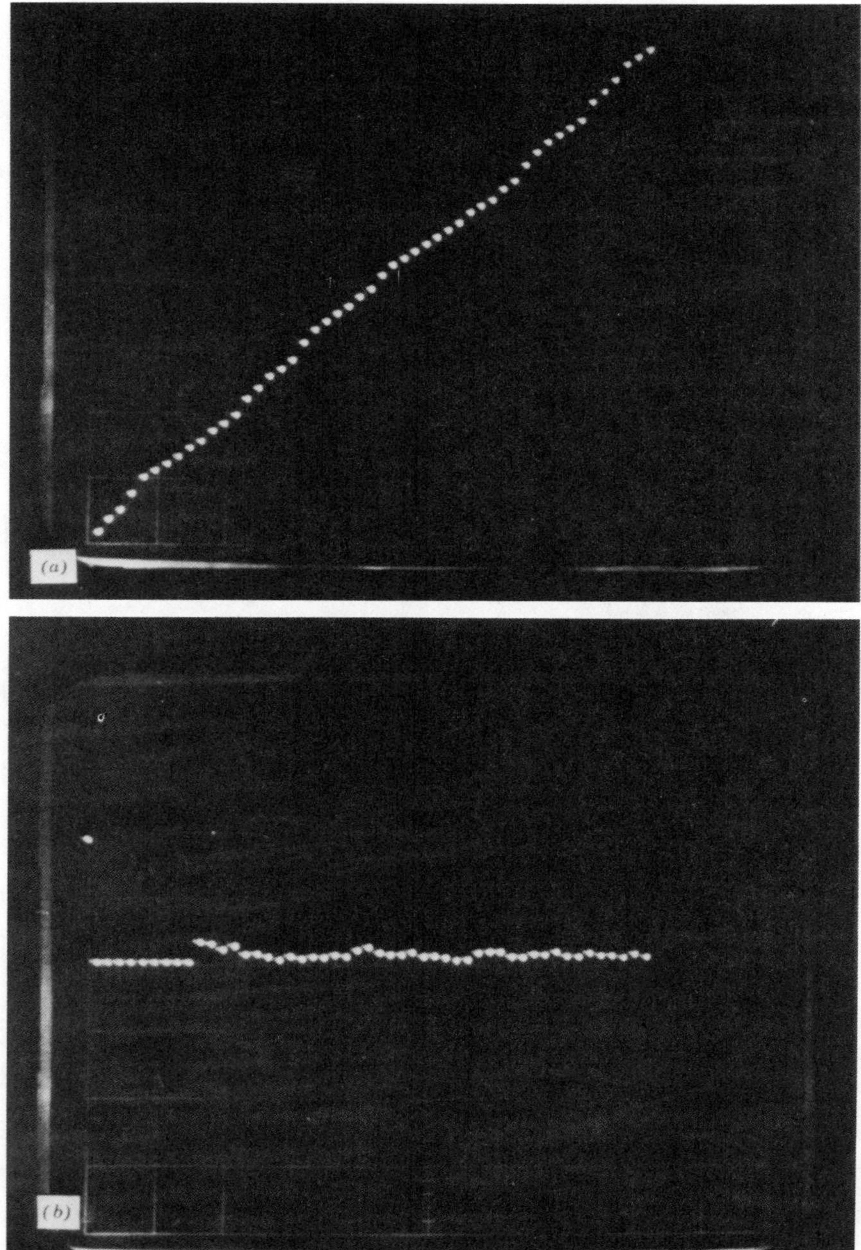

Figure 1.16 *Mixture of constant period and random period:* (a) *spike arrival instants;* (b) *autocorrelation function.*

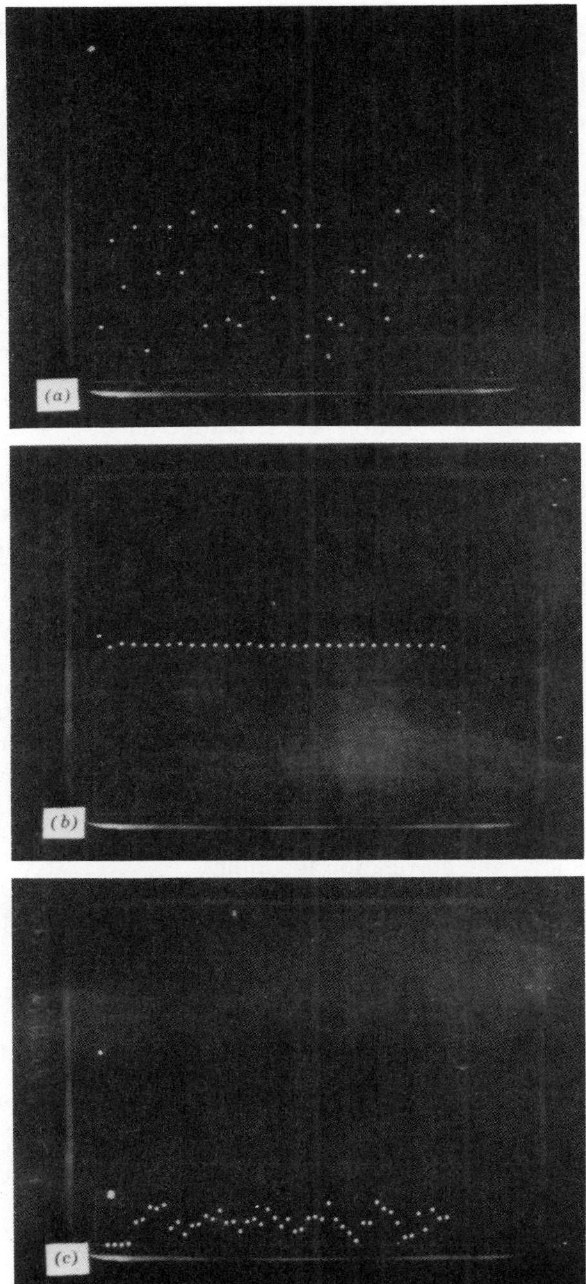

Figure 1.17 *Insect calls analysis:* (a) *interchirp intervals from katydid calls displayed as a function of the serial number of the chirp;* (b) *autocorrelation analysis based on Equation 1.3 and Figure 1.7;* (c) *autocorrelation analysis based on Figure 1.13.*

The actual correlation calculation starts at statement 418. For each C, the upper and lower boundaries (P and Q) of the time window are calculated. For each spike I, the K_1 spikes that follow are examined. If any of them arrives during the time window, 1 is added to the accumulated value of the correlation function. Otherwise, it remains unchanged.

Statements 600 to 660 produce the display of the correlation function on the scope. Figures 1.14, 1.15, and 1.16*b* show the autocorrelation functions for the three waveforms.

Figure 1.14 shows the intervals composed of only a constant period. As expected, the correlation function is periodic with the same period as the signal. In this example, the constant period $S1 = 10$ time units. Note that the period of the correlation function is also 10.

Figure 1.15 shows the interval composed of only the random component. This time the correlation function is a delta function at $C = 0$. For all other values of C, the correlation function is approximately zero.

Figure 1.16 shows a mixture of a constant period and a random period. Hence, the correlation function is the sum of the correlation functions of each component. Note the delta function $C = 0$ and the periodic component with period 10.

1.4.2. Real Data: Insect Calls

The katydid chirps have been measured on magnetic tape. Interchirp intervals have been measured and used as a raw data for correlation programs.

First the data have been read into the program based on Equation 1.3, and shown in Table 1.2. The results are shown in Figure 1.17. Figure 1.17*a* displays the measured intervals as a function of the intervals serial number. Figure 1.17*b* shows the correlation function.

Next the data have been read into the program based on the latency correlation procedure, Table 1.3. Figure 1.17*c* shows the correlation function produced by this program.

Note the following: the classical correlation function, Figure 1.17*b* shows meaningless result. The modified correlation function, Figure 1.17*c* clearly shows that a katydid interchirp intervals must be composed of two components: random and periodic. Also, one could directly read the period of the periodic component.

1.5. FOURIER ANALYSIS AND POWER SPECTRA

The most elementary periodic data is the sine wave

$$x(t) = X \sin(2\pi f t + \theta) \qquad (1.5)$$

where X = amplitude
f = basic frequency in cycles per second
θ = initial phase angle in radians
$x(t)$ = instantaneous value

The parameters X, f, and θ completely describe the sine wave. Often the period T is used:

$$T = \frac{1}{f} \tag{1.6}$$

The period is the time required for one full fluctuation or cycle of sinusoidal data.

More complex periodic data cannot be described as simply. They themselves repeat at regular intervals such that

$$x(t) = x(t + T) = x(t + 2T) = \ldots = x(t + NT) \tag{1.7}$$

These data may be treated as being composed of sinusoidal waves with different amplitudes and with frequencies f, $2f$, $3f$, . . . , Nf. By choosing the proper mixture of such waves, we could synthesize any periodic waveform with fundamental frequency f. This procedure is called a *Fourier series expansion*. Thus the periodic waveform $x(t)$ may be expanded into a series according to the formula

$$x(t) = \frac{A_0}{2} + \sum_{N=1}^{\infty} (A_n \cos N\omega t + B_n \sin N\omega t) \tag{1.8}$$

where $\omega = 2\pi/T$ is the fundamental circular frequency, and A_n and B_n are amplitudes of the sine and cosine waves at frequency $N\omega$.

One can prove that the values for A_n and B_n are

$$A_n = \frac{2}{T}\int_0^T x(t) \cos N\omega t \, dt \qquad N = 0, 1, 2, \ldots \tag{1.9}$$

$$B_n = \frac{2}{T}\int_0^T x(t) \sin N\omega t \, dt \qquad N = 1, 2, 3, \ldots \tag{1.10}$$

By combining sine and cosine waves of the same frequency into a single phase-shifted cosine, we may write Equation 1.8 as

$$x(t) = C_0 + \sum_{N=1}^{\infty} C_n \cos(N\omega t - \theta) \tag{1.11}$$

where

$$C_0 = \frac{A_0}{2} \tag{1.12}$$

$$C_n = \sqrt{A_n^2 + B_n^2} \tag{1.13}$$

$$\theta = \tan^{-1} \frac{B_n}{A_n} \tag{1.14}$$

In equation 1.11, complex periodic data $x(t)$ are composed of a static component C_0 and an infinite number of cosine waves called *harmonics*. The frequency of the Nth cosine wave is $N\omega$, the amplitude is C_n, and the phase is θ_n. Frequently the phase angles θ_n are ignored.

Substituting Equations 1.9 and 1.10 into Equation 1.13 and using Euler's formula gives

$$C_n = \int_0^T x(t)e^{-j2\pi ft}\,dt \tag{1.15}$$

Equation 1.15 is in a form that allows a natural extension of Fourier analysis to nonrepetitive waveforms. One can view such a waveform as a repetitive wave in which $T \rightarrow \infty$. For finite T, the ratio N/T is the frequency of the Nth harmonic, and the frequency separation between harmonics equals the frequency of the fundamental, $1/T$. When $T \rightarrow \infty$, the separation between harmonics approaches zero and N/T approaches the smooth frequency variable f.

Based on Equations 1.9, 1.10, and 1.13, a frequency spectrum program has been developed; see Table 1.4. This program could be used for periodic and nonperiodic waveform analysis. For periodic waveform analysis, the integration period T should be equal to the basic period of the waveform (Figure 1.18). For nonperiodic waveform analysis, T theoretically should

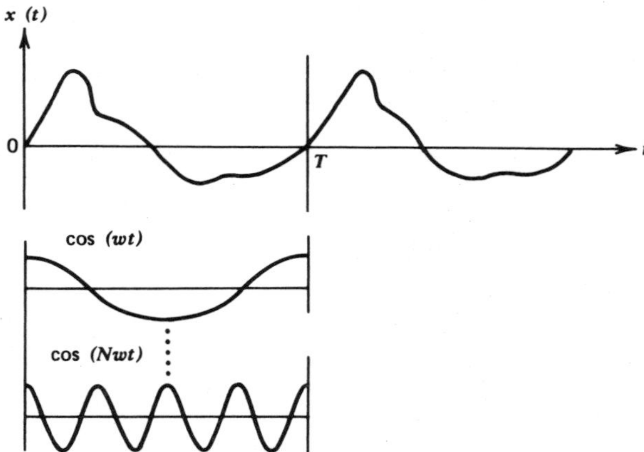

Figure 1.18 *Periodic waveform with period* T. *The Fourier integration period* T *should be equal to the basic period of the waveform.*

TABLE 1.4

```
LIST
20 REM FOURIER ANALYSIS
25 DIM D(100)
26 USE D
30 DIM X(100)
40 T=100
100 P=3.141503
110 W=2*P/T
130 REM
140 REM
145 REM SIMULATE SIGNAL
150 PRINT "ENTER AMPLITUDE,FREQUENCY,DAMPING"
151 INPUT L,C,H
152 G=C*W
155 FOR J=1 TO T
170 X(J)=COS(G*(J-1))*EXP(-H*J)
200 D=J/T
210 R=.2*X(J)+.5
215 PLOT E,F
220 DELAY
221 X(J)=L*X(J)
225 NEXT J
226 INPUT E
227 CLEAR
228 REM
229 REM
230 DIM A(11),B(11),C(11)
240 REM NUMBER OF HARMONICS Z=10
250 Z=10
300 FOR N=0 TO Z
310 A(N)=0
329 B(N)=0
330 FOR J=1 TO T
340 R=N*W*(J-1)
350 A(N)=A(N)+X(J)*COS(R)
360 B(N)=B(N)+X(J)*SIN(R)
370 NEXT J
400 A(N)=2*A(N)/T
410 B(N)=2*B(N)/T
430 C(N)=SQR(A(N)↑2+B(N)↑2)
440 NEXT N
500 REM DISPLAY THE SPECTRUM
512 FOR N=0 TO Z
520 E=N/Z
530 F=.1+C(N)
540 PLOT E,F
550 DELAY
560 NEXT N
570 STOP
```

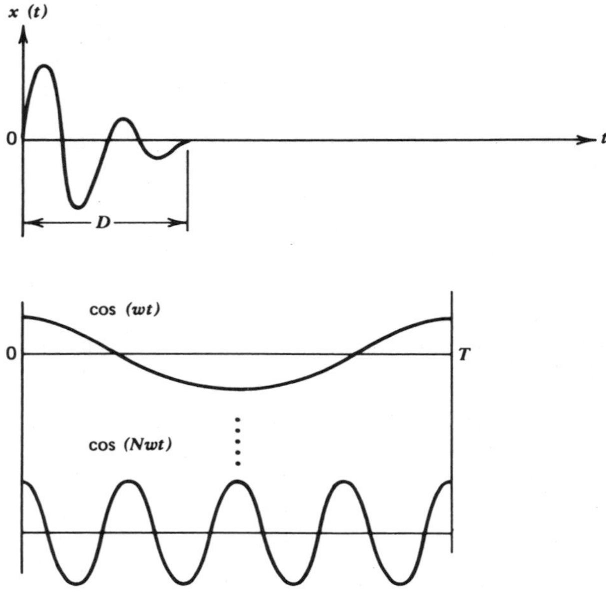

Figure 1.19 *Nonperiodic waveform. Theoretically the Fourier integration period* T *should be infinity. Usually it is enough to take* T = *10*D.

approach infinity. If the waveform is defined for $0 < t < D$ and is zero for $t > D$, then, for practical applications, it is usually enough to take $T = 10D$ (Figure 1.19).

The program in Table 1.4 divides the integration period T into 100 time steps (statement 40); hence $W = 2\pi/T = 2\pi/100$ (statement 110). The first part of the program (statements 150 to 227) is used to simulate and display different waveforms. In this example, statement 170 is used to simulate a waveform.

The actual Fourier analysis program starts at statement 230. This prograı is fixed to calculate $Z = 10$ harmonic coefficients. Statements 350 and 400 follow Equation 1.9. Statements 360 and 410 follow Equation 1.10. Statement 430 follows Equation 1.13. The rest of the program is used to display the frequency spectrum.

1.6. SOME TYPICAL SPECTRA

1.6.1. Cosine Wave

Different waveforms and their frequency spectra have been calculated by using the program in Table 1.4. The waveforms could be controlled through proper selection of the parameters in statement 151: L = amplitude of the signal; C = frequency; H = dumping coefficient for exponential part of the waveform. These parameters are used to calculate the signal (statements 170 and 221).

The cosine wave has a frequency G that is four times higher than the basic analyzing frequency W. The parameters are $L = 1$, $C = 4$, and $H = 0$. The signal is shown in Figure 1.20*a*, and its frequency spectrum is shown in Figure 1.20*b*. Note that the unit step of the abscissa is W, whereas the basic frequency of the analyzed signal is $4W$. Hence, the unit step of the abscissa is one fourth of the basic frequency of the signal. Obviously, only the basic frequency of the periodic cosine wave is found in the spectrum, and it is displayed after four unit steps. This discrete spectrum is the simplest, showing only the basic frequency G of the signal.

1.6.2. Dumped Cosine Wave

The parameters are $L = 30$, $C = 4$, and $H = 0.25$. The signal is shown in Figure 1.21*a*, and its frequency spectrum is shown in Figure 1.21*b*. Again, the unit step of the abscissa is one fourth of the basic frequency of the analyzed signal. Note that this time the spectrum is "continuous." The harmonics presented have frequencies $G/4$, $2G/4$, ... The spectrum is a maximum at frequency $4G/4 = G$. The ratio between the signal frequency and the unit frequency is G/W. In this example, $G/W = 4$, and each basic frequency is displayed with four frequency unit steps. For larger values of G/W, a more accurate frequency spectrum would be obtained, and one basic frequency range would be displayed with more points.

1.6.3. Exponential Wave

The parameters are $L = 30$, $C = 0.1$, and $H = 0.1$. The signal is shown in Figure 1.22*a*, and its frequency spectrum is shown in Figure 1.22*b*. This is another example of "continuous" frequency spectra.

1.6.4. Pulse Waveform

The pulse waveform is programmed as follows:

```
171 X (J) = 0
172 IF (J>25) GO TO 200
175 X (J) = 1
```

The waveform is shown in Figure 1.23*a*, and its frequency spectrum is shown in Figure 1.23*b*. This is another example of a continuous frequency spectrum.

Power spectra analysis is used in many areas of research. This kind of analysis also presents the basic tool in acoustic communication study. Typi-

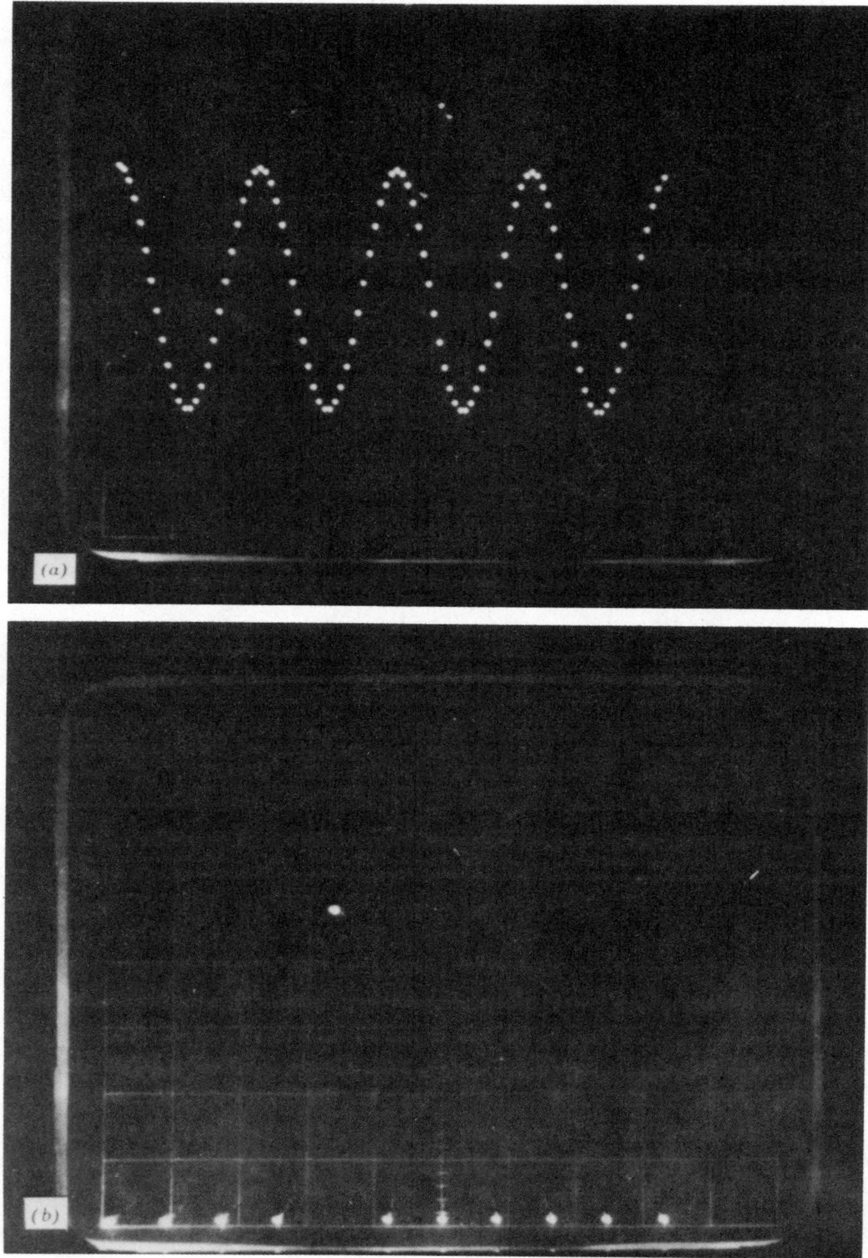

Figure 1.20 *Cosine wave analysis:* (a) *cosine wave at frequency* G = 4W, *where* W *is basic analyzing frequency;* (b) *Fourier spectra showing the frequency* G = 4W.

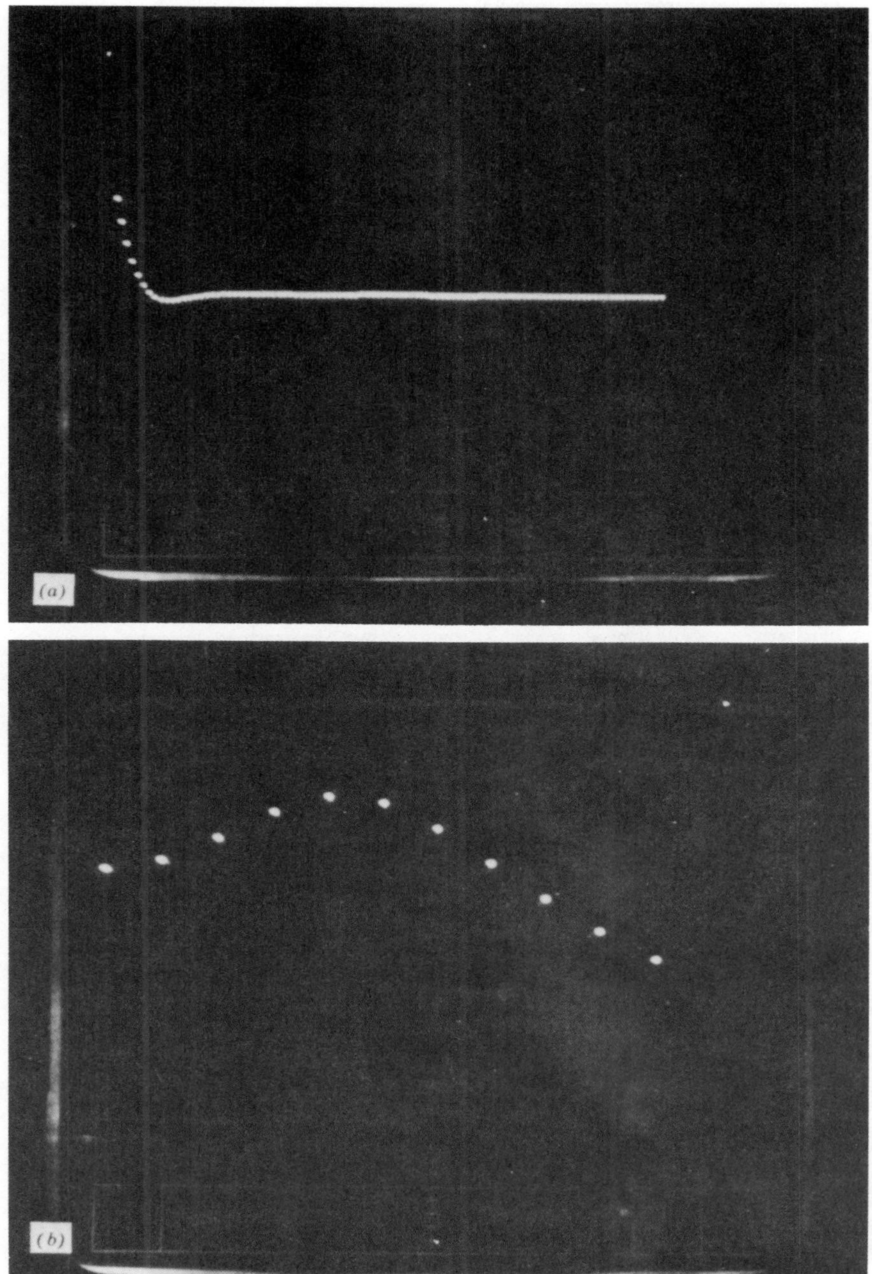

Figure 1.21 *(a) Damped cosine wave; (b) "continuous" frequency spectra.*

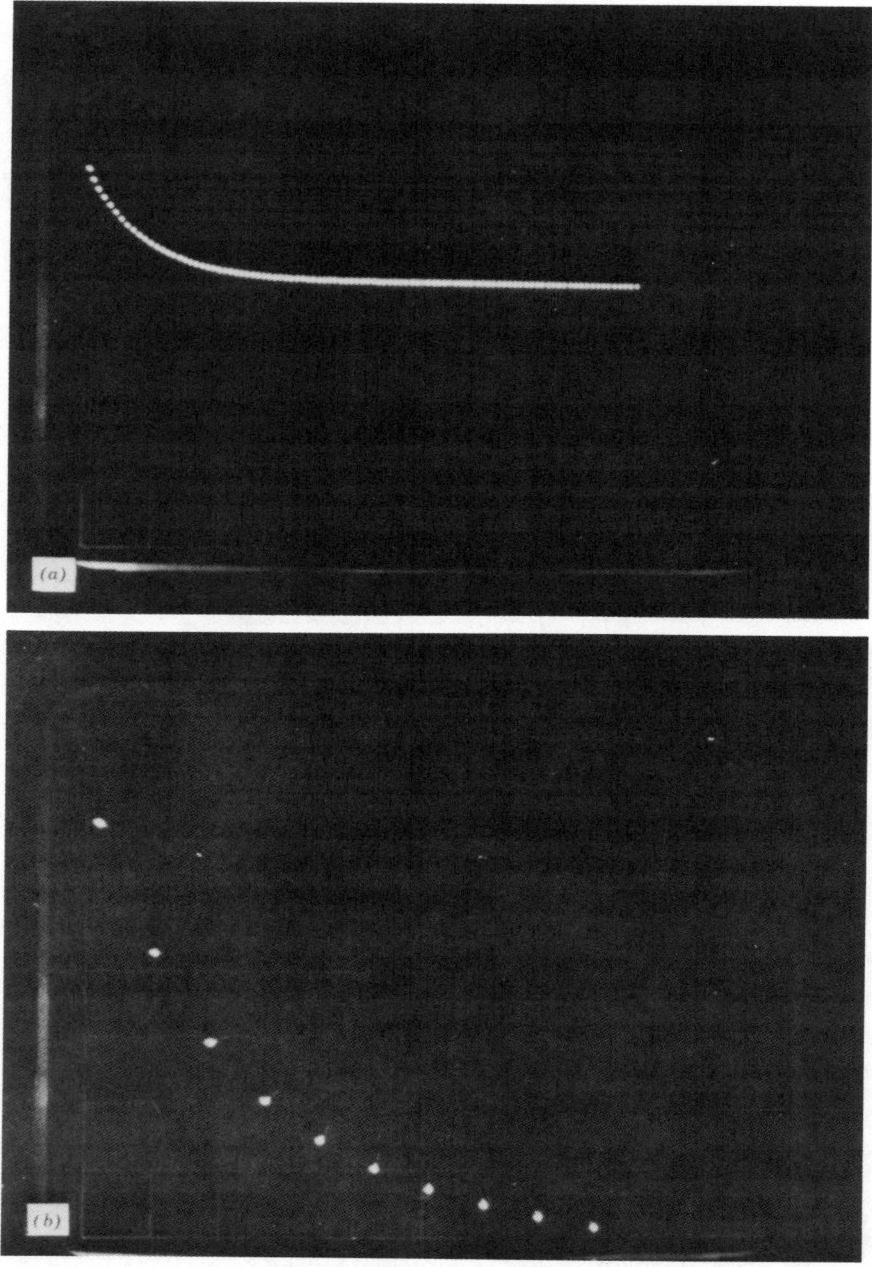

Figure 1.22 (*a*) *Exponential wave;* (*b*) *"continuous" frequency spectra.*

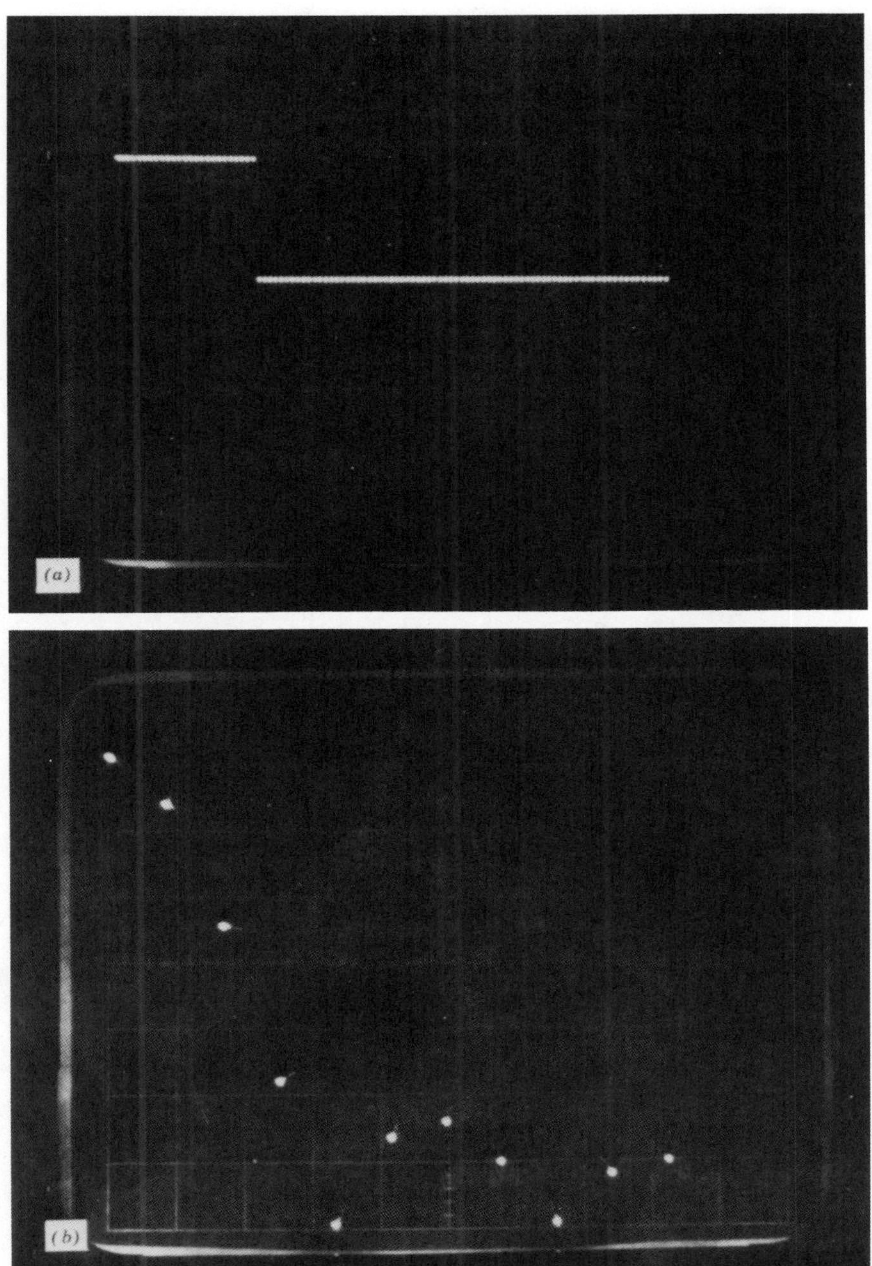

Figure 1.23 *(a) Pulse waveform. (b) "continuous" frequency spectra.*

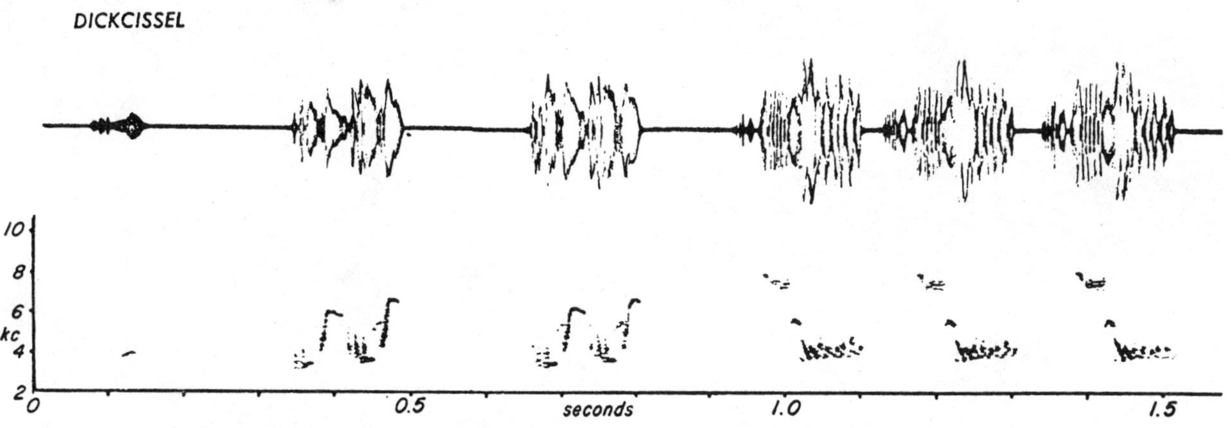

Figure 1.24 *Bird song: (a) acoustical record showing the amplitude of the song as a function of time; (b) sonogram of the same record as a function of time. (From C. H. Greenewalt:* Bird Song Acoustics and Physiology. *Smithsonian Institution Press, Washington, DC, 1968.)*

cal examples are speech analysis and bird song analysis. Special machines have been developed for spectral analysis, and one of the best known is the sonograph machine. The instrument comprises a recording and playback unit providing storage on a single-channel magnetic drum of a sound sample 2.4 ms in duration. The basic part of the instrument is a wave analyzer covering the frequency range 0–8000 Hz. The analyzer has a built-in filter with a bandwidth of 300 Hz. The center frequency of analysis changes linearly with time, 15 Hz per revolution of the recording drum. In this way the analyzer scans the waveform sample continuously, measuring the power in a given frequency window. The spectrum is then recorded on teledeltos paper, with spectral intensity roughly indicated by the density of the gray-black marking. Figure 1.24 shows an example of a sonogram produced by this instrument.

Figure 1.24*a* shows a part of the bird song in the time domain (i.e., the song waveform is a function of time). Figure 1.24*b* shows the sonogram of the same song. This display is actually three-dimensional. The abscissa is time, the ordinate is frequency, and the darkness intensity is proportional to the spectral power. Hence, the sonogram is composed of numerous power spectra, one for each 2.4-ms sample duration. The sonogram shows the variations in power spectra from one time sample to the next.

1.7. SIGNAL PROCESSING VERSUS NEURAL MAPPING

Signal processing is an established technique used in many real-time systems. Recently a new technique of mapping in neural networks has been developed (Souček and Souček[4]). When is it appropriate to use neural networks instead of signal processing?

Neurocomputing is concerned with nonprogrammed adaptive information processing systems that develop transformations in response to their environment. If we could generate a large number of examples of the function to be carried out, a neural network can use these examples as training set material. By exposing this material, the network adapts itself to eventually carry out the desired information or signal processing operation. In those instances where it is applicable, neurocomputing essentially eliminates software and algorithm bottlenecks and provides high-speed mapping (see Chapters 3, 4, and 7).

REFERENCES

1. D. Wilkinson, *Proc. Cambridge Phil. Soc.* **46**(3), 508 (1950).
2. G. Hutchinson and G. Scarrot, *Phil. Mag.* **42,** 792 (1951).

3. B. Souček, and A. D. Carlson, *Computers in Neurobiology and Behavior,* Wiley, New York, 1976.
4. B. Souček and M. Souček, *Neural and Massively Parallel Computers, The Sixth Generation,* Wiley, New York, 1988.

CHAPTER 2

Sampling, Quantizing, Servicing, and Queueing

INTRODUCTION AND SURVEY

Measurement and process control with a computer is oriented toward gathering a large amount of data. The amount of data to be collected in one experiment can be well over 10^8 data, the speed can be over 10^4 data per second. In such conditions the system designer or user must choose the proper sampling rate and quantizing step.

This chapter describes the fundamental concepts of sampling and quantizing. It explains sampling and quantizing theorems, analog-to-digital conversion techniques, and the choice of sampling and quantizing equipment.

The computer needs some time to process one datum. During this "dead time," a single-processor machine cannot accept other data, and some data coming from a real-time process will be lost. The chapter explains techniques for minimizing or avoiding dead-time losses. Basic expressions for dead-time losses are derived and explained, and concurrent systems and experiments generating data with random times of arrivals are analyzed.

A real-time system consists of a number of servers, interconnected by queues of customers or jobs to be done. The system could have a complex topology with many serial and parallel components. Measures of performance for such a system are defined with utilization factor, average number of customers, average total response time, and throughput.

2.1. SAMPLING

Most physical processes are continuous functions of time. One such process is presented in Figure 2.1. If we want to measure and analyze such a process

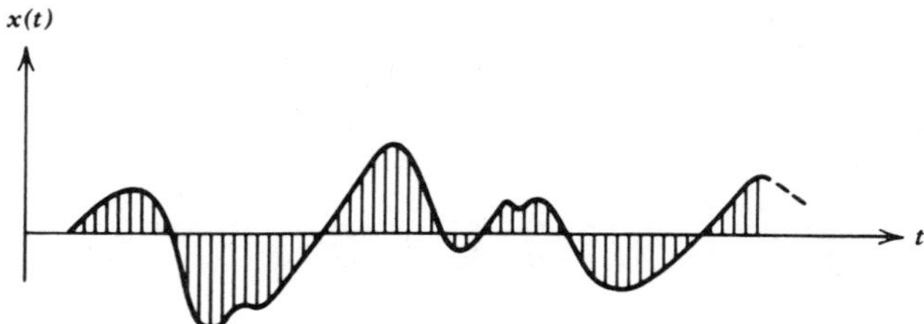

Figure 2.1 *Sampling the continuous waveform.*

with a digital machine, we must digitize the process. Digitizing consists of sampling and quantizing. *Sampling* defines the points at which the data are observed. *Quantizing* the observed data means converting the information from analog to digital form. The process of sampling is shown in Figure 2.1. It consists of measuring a continuous function only at discrete times. Such a measurement may generate serious errors if not done properly. It is important to have a sufficient number of samples per unit time so that significant high-frequency information can be properly described. On the other hand, sampling at points that are too close together will yield correlated and highly redundant data and will greatly increase the labor and cost of calculations. To reduce the number of samples, one should decrease the sampling rate to the lowest rate that will avoid errors.

The fundamental concept of sampling is the subject of the very important sampling theorem.[1,2] Any well-behaved function may be considered to be a linear combination of sinusoids of appropriate amplitudes, frequencies, and phases, composing the signal's frequency spectrum. According to the sampling theorem, if a signal $x(t)$ is sampled at times $t = \ldots, -2T, -T, 0, T, 2T, \ldots$, the frequency components of the signal greater than $fc = 1/2T$ Hz cannot be distinguished from frequencies from 0 to $1/2T$ Hz. This fact can be easily proved by elementary trigonometry.

To see why the sampling theorem is true, we need only show that

$$\cos\left[\left(\frac{\pi}{T} + \varepsilon\right) t + \rho\right] = \cos\left[\left(\frac{\pi}{T} - \varepsilon\right) t - \rho\right]$$

whenever t is a multiple of the sampling period; that is, whenever $t = kT$. The frequency fc corresponds to the circular frequency

$$\omega = 2\pi fc = 2\pi \frac{1}{2T} = \frac{\pi}{T}$$

Since $\cos x = \cos(-x)$ and has a period 2π, we have

$$\cos\left[\left(\frac{\pi}{T} + \varepsilon\right) kT + \rho\right] = \cos(k\pi + \varepsilon kT + \rho)$$

$$= \cos(-k\pi - \varepsilon kT - \rho) = \cos(2k\pi - k\pi - \varepsilon kT - \rho)$$

$$= \cos(k\pi - \varepsilon kT - \rho) = \cos\left(\left(\frac{\pi}{T} - \varepsilon\right) kT - \rho\right) \tag{2.1}$$

Thus, we see that these two sinusoids have exactly the same value whenever $t = kT$, so it is impossible to separate the two by using the sampled values.

Figure 2.2 shows two sinusoids of circular frequencies $\pi/T + \varepsilon$ and $\pi/T - \varepsilon$. It is clear that the signal with circular frequency $\pi/T + \varepsilon$ and phase $+\rho$ passes through exactly the same values at $t = kT$ as does a signal with lower circular frequency $\pi/T - \varepsilon$ and phase $-\rho$. This example shows how two sinusoids may be confused. This property is called *aliasing,* and constitutes a source of error that does not occur in analog data processing.

The sampling theorem is often paraphrased by saying that it is necessary to take more than two points per cycle of the highest significant frequency component in a signal in order to be able to recover that signal. In other words, if the frequency spectrum is given by $F(f)$, the sampling will be correct if the following condition is fulfilled:

$$F(f) = 0 \qquad f \geq fc \tag{2.2}$$

where

$$fc = \frac{1}{2T} \tag{2.3}$$

is the turnover frequency.

If condition 2.2 is not fulfilled and the spectrum contains frequencies $f > fc$, these high frequencies are aliased onto false low frequencies. Hence, when the turnover frequency fc is as shown in Figure 2.3a, a true frequency

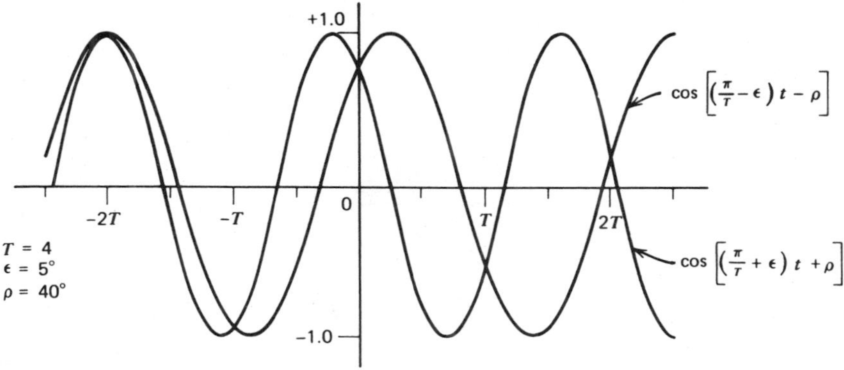

Figure 2.2 *Two sinusoids that cannot be distinguished at t = kT. (Reprinted by permission from Ref. 1).*

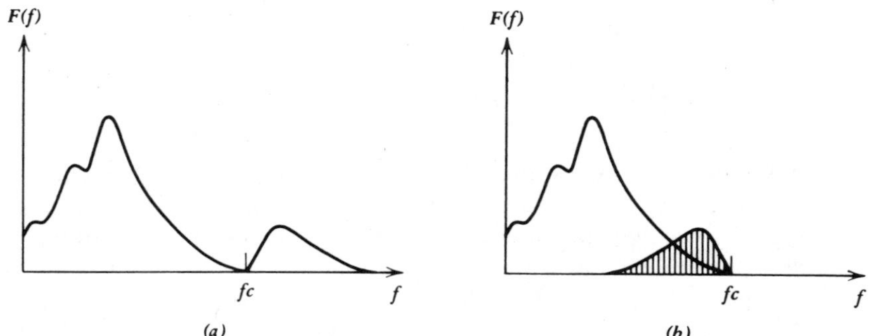

Figure 2.3 *Frequency spectrum:* (a) *true spectrum;* (b) *aliased spectrum.* (*Reprinted by permission from Ref. 1.*)

spectrum, as shown in Figure 2.3*a*, would be folded into the aliased spectrum, as illustrated in Figure 2.3*b*. Note that sampling is *not* filtering. Sampling is folding.

For any frequency f in the range $0 < f < fc$, the higher frequencies, which are aliased with f, are defined by

$$(2fc \pm f), \qquad (4fc \pm f), \; . \; . \; . \; , (2nfc \pm f) \tag{2.4}$$

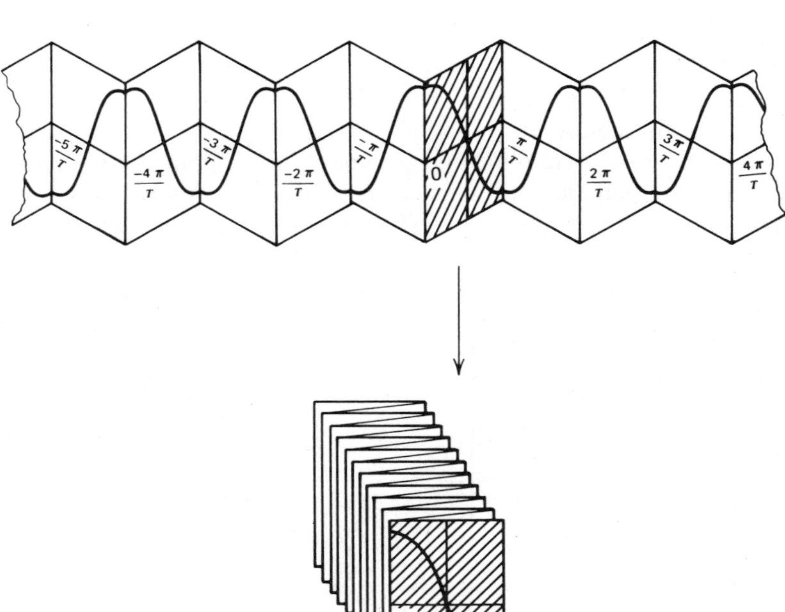

Figure 2.4 *Folding of the frequency scale* (*Ref. 1*)

To prove this fact, observe that for $t = 1/2fc$,

$$\cos 2\pi ft = \cos 2\pi(2nfc \pm f)\frac{1}{2fc} = \cos \frac{\pi f}{fc} \tag{2.5}$$

Thus, all data at frequencies $2nfc \pm f$ have the same cosine function as do data at frequency f, when data are sampled at points $1/2fc$.

The effect of sampling, therefore, is that the frequency scale is folded like an accordion with a pleat at every multiple of $1/2T$, as shown in Figure 2.4. If $fc = 100$ Hz, then data at 40 Hz would be aliased with data at frequencies of 160 Hz, 240 Hz, 360 Hz, 440 Hz, and so forth.

The important rule for sampling is as follows. If high frequencies are present in a function whose low frequencies are to be analyzed, then either a high sampling rate must be used or the function must be filtered to cut out the high frequencies before the sampling operation.

2.2. QUANTIZING

The conversion of an analog signal into digital form necessarily involves quantization (roundoff, grouping) of input data samples. The range of input of a variable x is subdivided into class intervals

$$ig - \frac{g}{2} < x < ig + \frac{g}{2} \qquad (i = 0, \pm 1, \pm 2, \ldots) \tag{2.6}$$

equal with g. The quantization operation replaces each value of x by the nearest class interval center ig. The operation of the quantizer is shown in Figure 2.5. The quantizer output x_g can be regarded as the sum of the input x and a roundoff error

$$x_g = x + n_g \tag{2.7}$$

The value n_g is called *quantization noise*. Due to the error n_g in measuring x, any value from $x - g/2$ to $x + g/2$ will produce the same output x_g.

Since the process of quantization is extremely nonlinear, it is difficult to assess precisely the effect of quantization. By restricting attention to the statistical effects of quantization, however, and working with statistical averages instead of more detailed characteristics of the signal, it is possible to obtain a satisfactorily complete analysis of quantization.

Statistical properties of the input signal can be described through the mean value $\bar{x}$, mean square $\overline{x^2}$, probability distribution $f_1(x)$, and correlation function $R_{xx}(\tau)$.

At the output of the quantizer is a new process x_g. Quantizing is correct if the statistical properties of x_g are approximately the same as those of x.

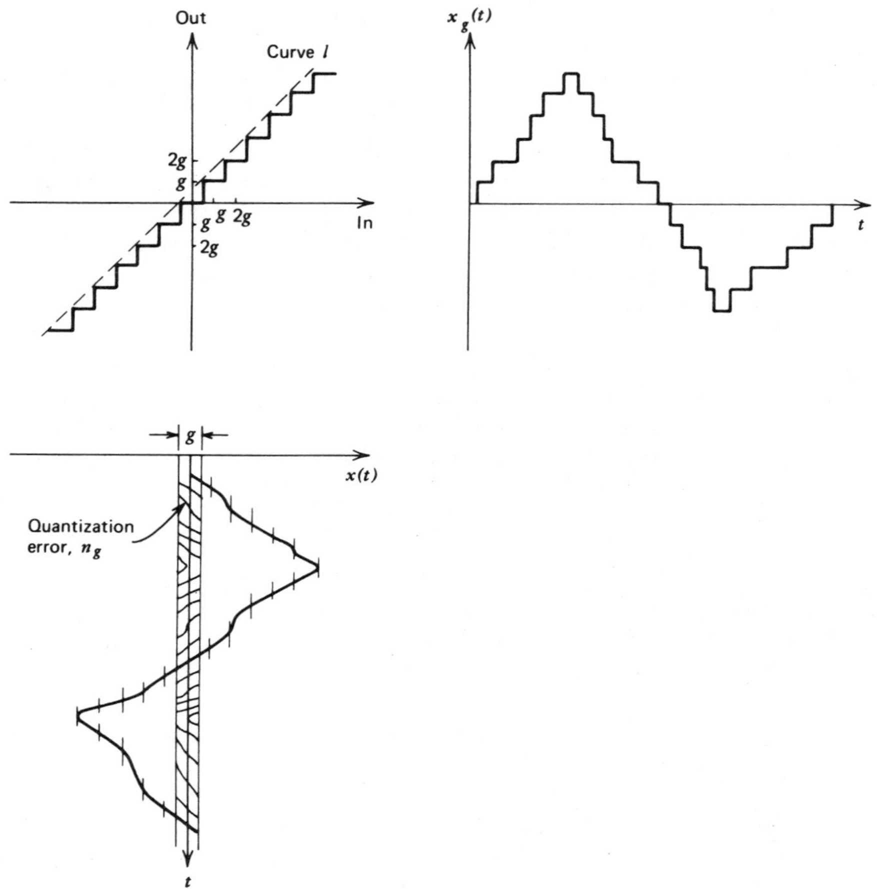

Figure 2.5 *The operation of quantizing.*

Errors introduced by quantization depend on the quantization step g. It is important to have sufficiently fine quantization steps to describe properly the fine-amplitude variations of the signal. On the other hand, fine quantization can produce highly redundant data and greatly increase the labor and cost of calculations. To optimize the measurements, one should increase the quantization step to the largest value that will avoid errors.

The fundamental concept of quantization is the subject of the very important quantizing theorem. The quantizing theorem describes the relationship between the amplitude properties of the signal and the quantization step g in the same way as the sampling theorem describes the relationship between frequency properties of the signal and the sampling period T.

The sampling theorem can be proved by elementary trigonometry, but the proof of the quantizing theorem requires more elaborate mathematics. To avoid this, we describe the quantizing theorem by analogy with the sampling theorem.

Figure 2.6*a* presents the input signal x and the sampling step T. The frequency property of the signal can be described by the frequency spectrum $F(f)$ (Figure 2.6*b*). Remember that $F(f)$ is the Fourier integral of the signal $x(t)$. To avoid errors due to aliasing, we want the sampling frequency to be higher than the highest frequency in the spectrum $F(f)$ (Equations 2.2 and 2.3).

Figure 2.6*c* presents the amplitude distribution $f(x)$ of the signal. Quantization of the function $f(x)$ in the x scale (Figure 2.6*c*) is analogous to sampling the $x(t)$ function in the t scale (Figure 2.6*a*). To make the analogy with the sampling theorem, one can treat the amplitudes as a time and make a Fourier integral of the distribution $f(x)$. Such an integral, $\rho(\alpha)$, is called a *characteristic function* of the transformation parameter α, where α corresponds to the frequency in the function $F(f)$ but has no physical meaning.

In analogy with the sampling theorem, we can now say that if the characteristic function of the signal is given by $\rho(\alpha)$, quantizing will be correct if the following condition is fulfilled:

$$\rho(\alpha) = 0 \qquad \alpha \geq \frac{1}{2g} \tag{2.8}$$

Equation 2.8 is the quantizing theorem.

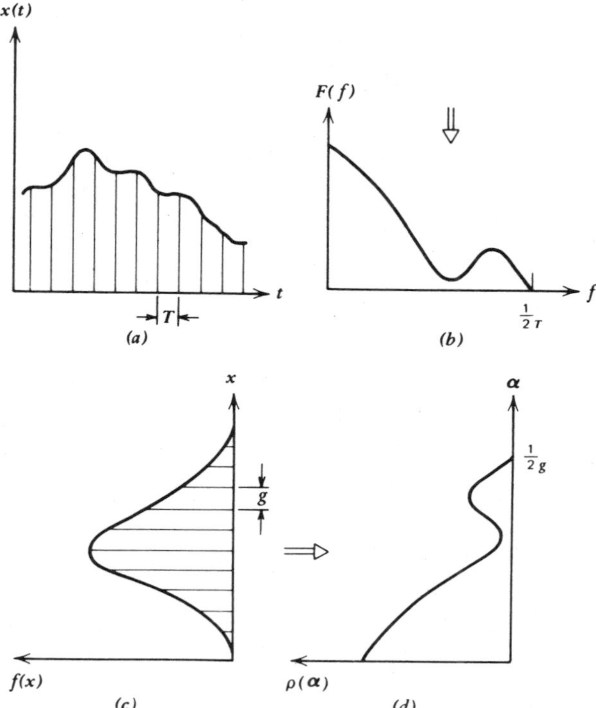

Figure 2.6 *Quantizing: (a) input signal; (b) frequency spectrum; (c) f(x)-amplitude distribution of the input signal and (d) ρ(α)-characteristic function.*

As in sampling, if $\rho(\alpha) \neq 0$ for $\alpha \geq 1/2g$, then the folding of the "α-frequency" scale will alias complementary signals in the range $\alpha \leq 1/2g$ and give erroneous results.

The sampling theorem says, in effect, that if we sample a signal at a great enough rate (that is, $1/T$ large), then the signal can be recovered. Analogously, the quantizing theorem says, in effect, that if we quantize a signal at a great enough fineness (that is, $1/g$ large), then the statistics of the signal can be recovered. The statistics of the signal can be described through the mean, mean square, and higher moments. Sheppard[1] has derived corrections

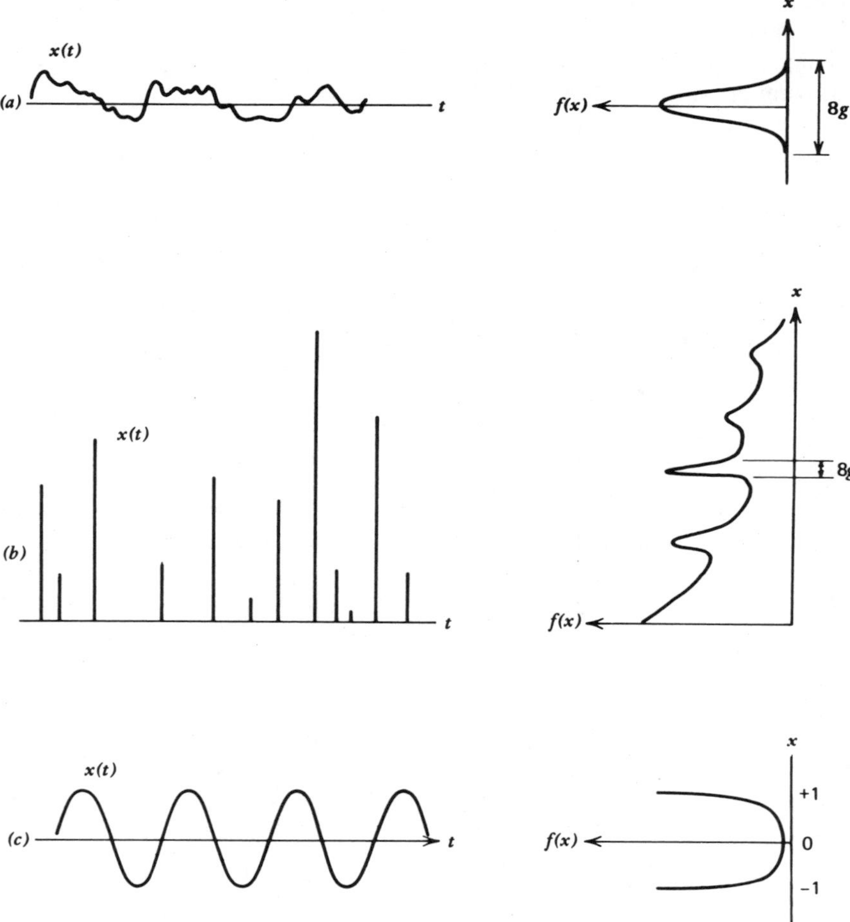

Figure 2.7 *Rule of thumb in quantization:* (a) *Gaussian distribution;* (b) *few bell-shaped peaks;* (c) *sharp peaks in the distribution.*

that can be used to calculate the mean values of the original signal x from the values of the quantized signal x_g:

$$\bar{x} = x_g$$

$$\overline{x^2} = \overline{x_g^2} - \frac{1}{12} g^2 \tag{2.9}$$

Thus, if g is chosen according to the quantization theorem, exact compensation can be made for the errors in the mean and mean square computed directly from the quantized signal.[3]

The quantizing theorem seems strange because we are not used to thinking of signals in terms of their distributions and characteristic functions. For most signals encountered in the laboratory, the following rule of thumb is an adequate substitute for the quantizing theorem: if the signal $x(t)$ has a Gaussian amplitude distribution $f(x)$, quantization will be adequate if the range of $x(t)$ is at least $8g$. In this case, the mean square error will be about 10^{-6}. The case with Gaussian distribution is shown in Figure 2.7*a*.

If the signal $x(t)$ has a distribution composed of a few bell-shaped peaks, the quantization step should be chosen so that the narrowest peak is measured in at least eight channels. This case is shown in Figure 2.7*b*.

In some cases this rule of thumb cannot be applied. For example, it cannot be applied for signals with favorite values. If the signal has favorite value x_0, where it spends much more time than at other values, it will have a sharp peak in the distribution $f(x)$ for x_0. Such a signal is the sine wave in Figure 2.7*c*. The signal varies continuously between $+1$ and -1, but spends more time at those two limiting values than at other values. Thus, the amplitude distribution has infinite peaks at ± 1, so ± 1 are extremely favorite values for the sine function. Fine quantization is necessary to measure such signals.

Fortunately, most signals encountered in practice have maxima and minima at randomly placed values so that smooth distributions result. In such cases, the rule of thumb is an adequate substitution for the quantizing theorem.

2.3. ANALOG-TO-DIGITAL CONVERSION

2.3.1. Digital-to-Analog Decoder

Digital-to-analog conversion is an operation opposite to quantization; information presented as a digital number is converted into proportional analog form (voltage, current, etc.). Digital information is presented on lines. There are as many lines as there are bits, each at one of two voltage levels (0, 1), making a binary-weighted digital word. Analog information is presented on a single line as a signal whose magnitude gives the value of the information.

Various techniques are available to convert a piece of digital information into its analog form. We shall show the basic, most frequently used technique.

Figure 2.8 represents the basic circuit of a digital-to-analog converter (DAC). The digital number X_D is expressed by n digits, $D_0, D_1, \ldots, D_{n-1}$, and is loaded into an n-stage register. The digital number can be expressed as

$$X_D = D_0 2^0 + D_1 2^1 + \cdots + D_{n-1} 2^{n-1} \tag{2.10}$$

where $D_k = 0$ or 1, $k = 0, 1, 2, n - 1$.

Each flip-flop of the register is connected through an electronic switch to a network of resistors. The values of the resistors are chosen to be 2^0R, 2^1R, $\ldots$, $2^{n-1}R$. One side of each resistor is connected through the switch to the constant reference voltage V_R. The other side is connected to an operational amplifier (op amp) summing input, which has approximately a zero voltage level.

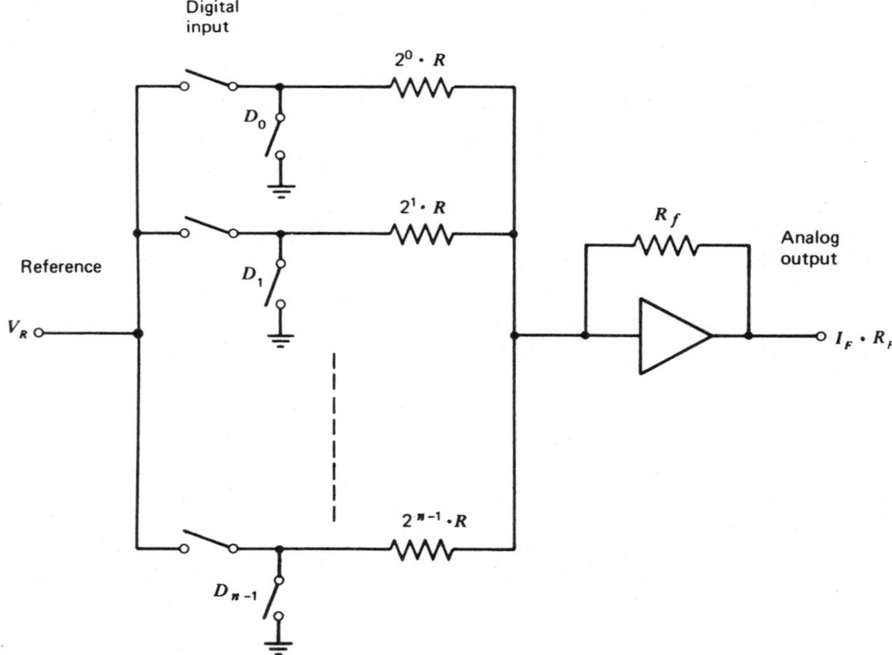

Figure 2.8 *Basic circuit of a digital-to-analog converter.*

Each bit of the decoder in state 1 acts as a current source, and the network output current is a summation of currents from each bit. The total network output current is equal to the feedback current:

$$\begin{aligned} I_F &= I_0D_0 + I_1D_1 + I_2D_2 + \cdots + I_{n-1}D_{n-1} \\ &= \frac{V_R}{R}D_0 + \frac{V_R}{2R}D_1 + \cdots + \frac{V_R}{2^{n-1}R}D_{n-1} \end{aligned} \tag{2.11}$$

Each flip-flop of the register controls its switch. If the flip-flop k is in state 0 ($D_k = 0$), the switch k connects its resistor to ground. If the flip-flop k is in state 1 ($D_k = 1$), the switch k connects its resistor to V_R and produces the current $V_R/2^kR$.

The output voltage of the op amp is I_FR_F; hence, according to Equation 2.11, it is proportional to the digital input number X_D.

The summing network branches must be composed of accurate resistances, especially for the most significant bits. Stable and accurate networks can be made with the thin-film technique.

Digital-to-analog converters are available as modules with a basic converter and, sometimes, with a buffer register to store the digital input information.

2.3.2. Successive Approximation Analog-to-Digital Converter

A method similar to that described in Section 2.3.1 can be used to convert a piece of analog information (say voltage) into its digital form. The principle is shown in Figure 2.9*a* and is based on the use of the successive approximation technique. An ADC is shown in Figure 2.9*b*.

A voltage V (approximately 9.2 V in the figure) is to be digitized to the nearest integral voltage between 0 and 16 V. The digitization is accomplished by a series of test steps. The first step tests whether V is greater than or less than 8 V (that is, the voltage range is divided in half). It is greater, so the most significant output binary digit is set equal to 1. Next the upper half of the range is itself divided in half, and a test is made to see which of these quarters contains V. In this example, V is from 8 to 12 V, so a binary 0 is entered as the next significant digit. The procedure continues through steps 3 and 4, yielding a binary 0 and 1 as the two succeeding digits. Thus, after four steps, an unknown voltage is placed in channel 9 of the 16 possible channels. In general, it takes only n steps to quantize an unknown voltage into one of 2^n channels.

The block diagram of the ADC with successive approximations is shown in Figure 2.9*b*. It uses a DAC, which reconverts the digital output X_D to a voltage αEX_D, which is compared with the analog input X_A. Assuming

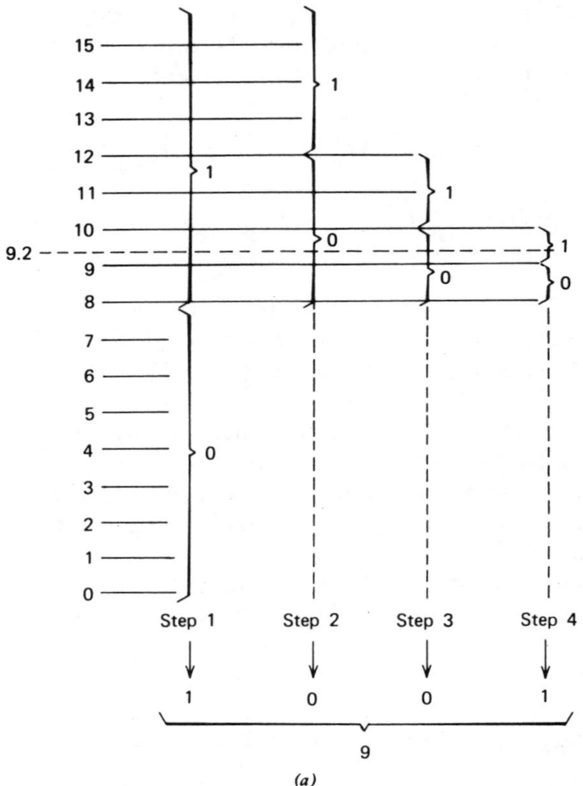

(a)

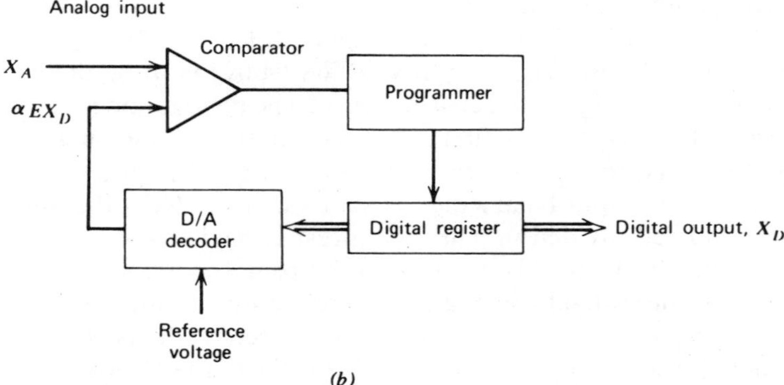

(b)

Figure 2.9 *Successive approximation analog-to-digital converter.*

$|X_A| \leq E$ and $|\alpha X_D| \leq 1$, we vary X_D during each conversion cycle until the magnitude of the analog error $e_A = \alpha E X_D - X_A$ is sufficiently small; that is,

$$X_D = \frac{X_A + e_A}{\alpha E} \qquad |e_A| < \frac{2E}{2^n}$$

This ADC requires n steps for encoding to an n-bit word. As each bit is tried, it can be used for serial output. At the end of the conversion, the whole piece of information is available in the counter register for parallel output. The main advantage of this kind of conversion is high speed, but it requires special care to achieve a constant quantization step from channel to channel.

2.3.3. Time-to-Digital Conversion

Continuous information to be quantized must not necessarily be an amplitude of the signal. Various parameters might be quantized. We now show the technique for quantization of time intervals (Figure 2.10). The time interval to be quantized is presented as a pulse controlling an AND gate. Its digital equivalent will be stored in the counter. This is done by simply opening the AND gate and counting clock pulses. The number of pulses received by the counter will be proportional to the time interval T.

Direct time digitization is simple, very accurate, and linear. The accuracy is a function of the stability of the clock frequency. To achieve this accuracy, we want the cycle time of clock pulses to be substantially shorter than the time interval T to be digitized. Therefore this kind of conversion is limited to long intervals (well over 1 μs).

2.3.4. Vernier Technique for Time-to-Digital Conversion

For long time periods, direct gating of clock pulses is possible. For shorter periods, one can convert time to amplitude and then use a standard amplitude digitization technique. Finally, there is the time expansion or vernier technique (Figure 2.11).

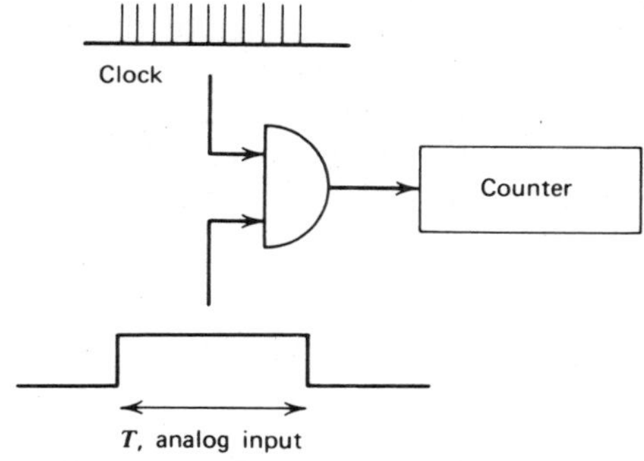

Figure 2.10 *Time-to-digital conversion.*

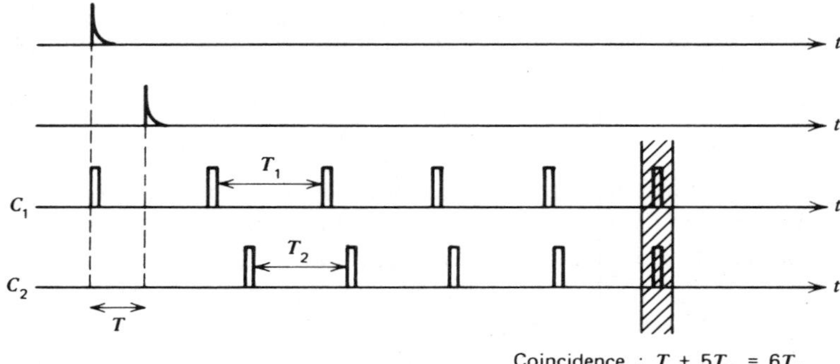

Figure 2.11 *Vernier technique for time-to-digital conversion.*

The time period T to be measured is bracketed by two pulses. The arrival of the first pulse starts clock c_1; the arrival of the second pulse starts clock c_2. The time coincidence between a pulse from c_1 and a pulse from c_2 marks the completion of the expanded time period. The proportionality constant for the expansion $T/(T_1 - T_2)$ of about 100 can be achieved. In this way a very short time interval can be expanded and then digitized without the need for very high frequency clock sources.

2.3.5. Amplitude-to-Time-to-Digital Conversion

One of the simplest and most accurate devices for implementing an analog-to-digital conversion is the amplitude-to-time-to-digital converter. The analog signal level is initially transformed to a pulse whose width in time is a function of the value of the input analog signal. The pulse width is then digitized by counting clock cycles, as shown in Figure 2.10.

The basic principle of operation of an amplitude-to-time-to-digital converter is illustrated in Figure 2.12. At the time the conversion is to begin, switch S is opened and capacitor C charges linearly with constant current I. At the same time, the counter is reset and starts counting clock pulses. The AND gate in front of the counter is controlled by the output of the comparator. When the sawtooth voltage on C equals the input voltage X_A, the comparator output changes states and inhibits clock pulses from entering the counter. The final count is the digital equivalent of the analog input voltage. Conversion speeds up to 200 channels per microsecond are used, and higher speeds are possible.

2.3.6. Correlation Employing 1-Bit Quantization

It has been shown that, for signals with an approximately Gaussian amplitude distribution, only eight levels of quantization are sufficient for most statistical operations. Experiments were carried out to investigate the effect

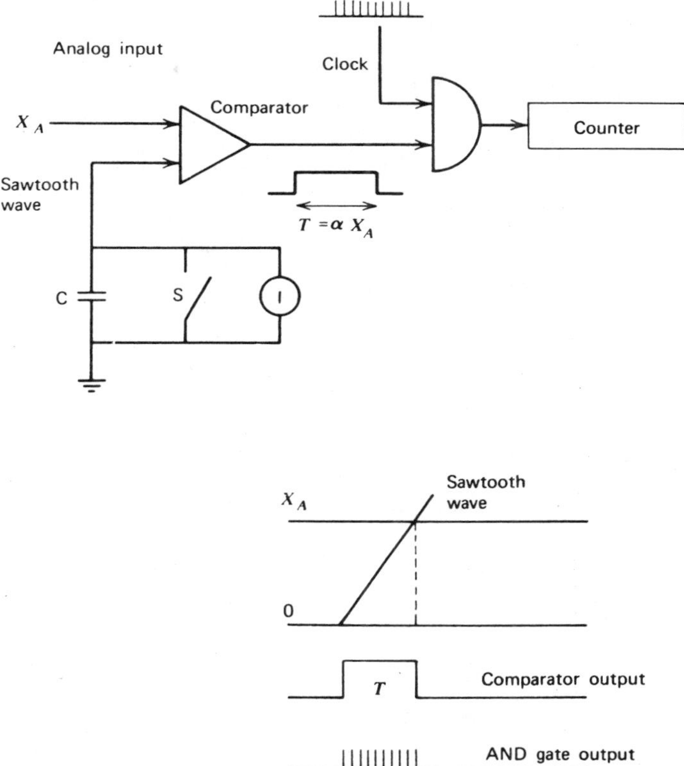

Figure 2.12 *Amplitude-to-time-to-digital conversion.*

of quantization step g on the calculation of correlation functions. Actual data from hydrodynamic tests and encephalograms were used. This test shows that autocorrelation functions using quantized data in 7, 6, . . . , 3 binary digits (bits) are practically the same. These tests were carried to the limiting case of a 1-bit signal. The signal was represented by a 1 or 0, depending on whether it had a value above or below a given level. Such a 1-bit correlator can be very useful in many applications.

Figure 2.13 shows a 1-bit correlator. Continuous signals $x(t)$ and $y(t)$ passing through the comparator attain the shape of the pulses with constant amplitude a. The sign of the pulse is the sign of the input variable. The correlation delay τ is achieved by two clocks separated by τ. The sign of the signal $x(t)$ is sampled by the first clock and stored in the flip-flop (binary variable U).

The binary variable V, which represents the sign of the signal $y(t)$, is sampled by the second clock. Multiplication is achieved through the OR gate. Coincidences $U\ V$ and $\overline{U}\ \overline{V}$ are counted into a register and represent

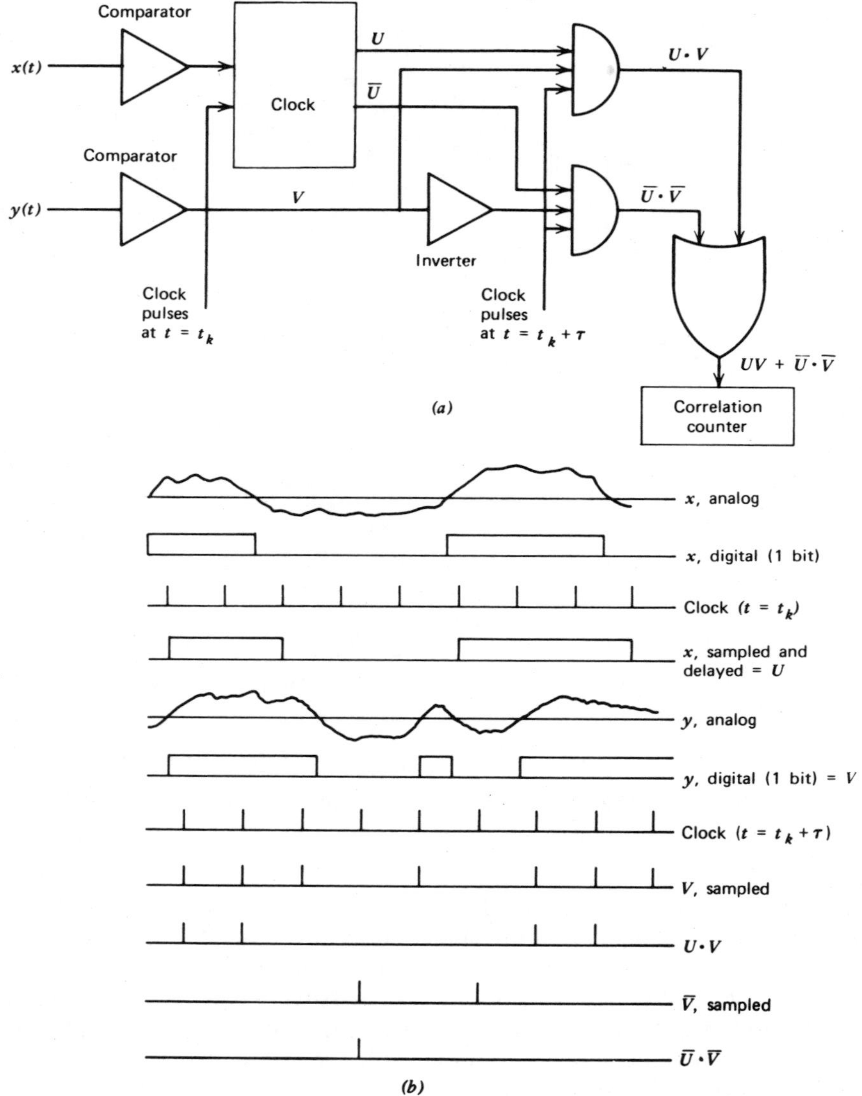

Figure 2.13 *One-bit correlator: (a) block diagram; (b) waveforms.*

the estimate of the correlation function. Such an operation can be controlled by a small computer. The computer will take care of the number of samples and the delay, and it will store the contents of the register into a core memory. In this way the correlation function can be estimated for a large range of delays.

2.4. CHOICE OF SAMPLING AND QUANTIZING EQUIPMENT

A large choice of modules is available in the domain of sampling and quantizing, DAC, and ADC. Modules differ in performance and price, and it is important to choose a module that is suitable for a given application.

The basic performance of the sampling-quantizing equipment can be described by four parameters:

- Sampling rate;
- Quantizing step;
- Integral nonlinearity; and
- Differential nonlinearity.

2.4.1. Sampling Rate

Sampling rate is given by the sampling theorem. If all frequencies of the signal are of interest, the sampling rate is defined by Equations 2.2 and 2.3. Sometimes only low frequencies of the signal are of interest for analysis. Even then the sampling rate must be high, dictated by higher frequencies in the spectrum. There is also another alternative: if the high-frequency components of the signal are of no interest, the function might be filtered to cut out high frequencies, and it can then be sampled with a lower sampling rate. Note that sampling by itself is not filtering but aliasing (Figures 2.3 and 2.4).

2.4.2. Quantizing Step

The quantizing step is determined by the quantizing theorem (equation 2.8). This theorem is difficult to use in practice, because the characteristic function of the signal is usually unknown. For most signals encountered in laboratory research, the following simple rule of thumb is an adequate substitute for the quantizing theorem. If the signal has an amplitude probability distribution composed of a few bell-shaped peaks (Figure 2.7) the quantization step should be chosen so that the narrowest peak is measured in at least eight channels. Provided that the bell-shaped peaks have an approximately Gaussian distribution, the error due to quantization will be about 10^{-6} (mean square error of the amplitude).

This rule of thumb cannot always be applied. For example, very fine quantization is needed for measuring a signal with dominant amplitude range, such as the sine wave. An opposite example is measuring the correlation function. Experiments have shown that, for many cases, the correlation functions, using quantized data in 8, 7, . . . , 3 binary digits, are practically the same. Even a 1-bit correlator can be very useful in many applications.

2.4.3. Integral Nonlinearity

The transfer function of the analog-to-digital equipment has a steplike shape (Figure 2.5). To define the linearity of conversion, we can connect all the steps by curve l. If curve 1 is a straight line, the conversion is linear; if not, it is nonlinear.

The integral nonlinearity within a given range may be defined as the relative difference between the maximum and minimum slopes of curve l.

$$\text{Integral nonlinearity} = \frac{s_{\max} - s_{\min}}{s_{\text{avg}}}$$

where the slope s is

$$s = \frac{dl}{d(\text{input})}$$

Typical figures for integral nonlinearity are

10-bit DAC, ±0.05 percent of full scale,
10-bit ADC (successive approximation), ±0.1 percent of full scale, and
10-bit ADC (amplitude-to-time-to digital), less than ±0.05 percent.

2.4.4. Differential Nonlinearity

The transfer function in Figure 2.5 shows that all the quantization steps g are of equal size. In reality, the quantization steps might vary due to the imperfect realization of the equipment. To measure this effect, we introduce differential nonlinearity.

Differential nonlinearity is defined as the maximum relative difference of the channel width, or the quantization step.

$$\text{Differential nonlinearity} = \frac{g_{\max} - g_{\min}}{g_{\text{avg}}}$$

Typical figures for differential nonlinearity are

10-bit ADC (successive approximation), more than ±1 percent, and
10-bit ADC (amplitude-to-time-to digital), less than ±0.5 percent.

Differential nonlinearity is particularly important for probability density distribution measurements, since it directly produces errors. Suppose that all amplitudes are equally probable, that all measuring channels have the same width g, and that only one channel has width 5 percent larger ($1.05g$).

This channel will then receive 5 percent more data than other channels and will produce an artificial peak in the amplitude distribution function.

Hence, only very fine ADCs should be used in probability distribution measurements. It is not enough to use the ADC with many of channels; the ADC should also have very small differential nonlinearity. Two solutions are possible: (1) the use of an amplitude-to-time-to-digital converter. Such converters have differential nonlinearities of less than ±0.5 percent. At the same time, the conversion time is long and might be 100 μs or more. (2) The use of a special successive approximation converter, with statistical averaging. A standard successive approximation converter can have a differential nonlinearity of 5 percent, and is of no use for probability distribution measurements. Statistical averaging has recently been employed to reduce differential nonlinearity substantially. The principle is that a given small-amplitude range is not measured all the time through the same quantizing channel but is moved in a random fashion and measured every time through another channel (Cottini, Gatti, and Svelto[3]). Such converters can achieve good differential linearity, and their conversion time is short, usually less than 10 μs. However, they are very complicated and expensive.

2.5. RESPONSE TIME

The *response time* of a system is the time that the system takes to react to a stimulus event from its environment. The response time must be such that the system appears to react instantaneously. What is regarded as an instantaneous reaction will depend on the process. For a system controlling the temperature in the building, response time of a minute is fast enough. Chemical and biological processes require a response time of a few milliseconds or less, while in nuclear physics, the response time should be in microseconds.

In principle, the events from environment could arrive at random times. The response time of the system should be shorter than the shortest period between two events. The situation could be improved using buffering techniques.

2.5.1. Buffering

The data are stored in some kind of storage media, one after the other, as generated by the experiment. The storage medium is called the *buffer*. Few levels of buffering can be used. The meaning and purpose of buffering can be best illustrated by a simple example, as shown in Figure 2.14. The experiment accumulates a small amount of data into a small buffer. When the small buffer is full, the data may be transferred into a large buffer. Finally, when the larger buffer is full, the data may be transferred into the final memory storage area. The simplest and most frequently used method is to have one

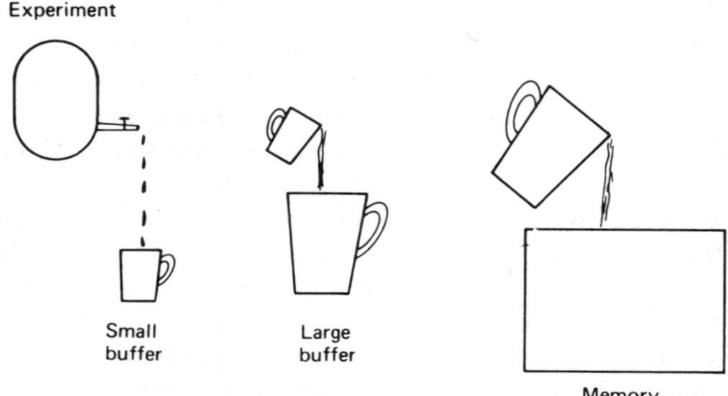

Figure 2.14 *Principle of buffering.* (*Based on Ref. 2.*)

level of buffering with only one buffer between the experiment and the final storage.

A small buffer can be a collection of hardware registers, such as a part of the interface, the simplest being just one data register. A larger buffer is usually part of the computer memory. The way the buffer is filled and emptied, as well as the buffer size, is under program control.

2.5.2. Ping-Pong Buffers

One of the most widely used buffering techniques for collecting experimental data is the ping-pong technique. This technique requires two buffers, A and B, as shown in Figure 2.15. At any time, one buffer is devoted to the experiment and the other to the data processing or outputting. In Figure 2.15*a*, buffer A belongs to the experiment, buffer B to the processing.

Two operations are going in parallel, as shown in Figure 2.15*b*. The experiment fills buffer A (interrupt transfer or cycle stealing, DMA transfer). At the same time, the computer program processes the data from buffer B. The processing of buffer B must be finished before buffer A is full. When buffer A is filled, the program switches buffers; the full buffer A will be connected to the processing, and the emptied buffer B will be connected to the experiment.

Switching buffers is simple and fast. The program keeps two addresses as the input and output buffer points. The buffers can be switched, exchanging those two addresses.

This example explains the main reasons for buffering:

1. Efficient use of computer time and memory space;
2. Continuous collection of data from experiment; and
3. Use of program interrupt and direct memory access (DMA) for inputting the data.

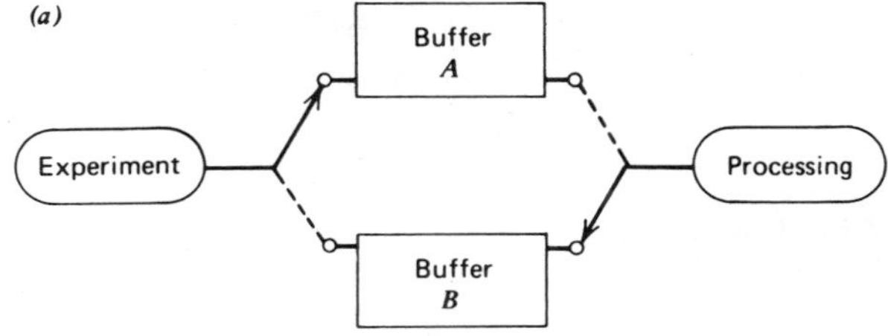

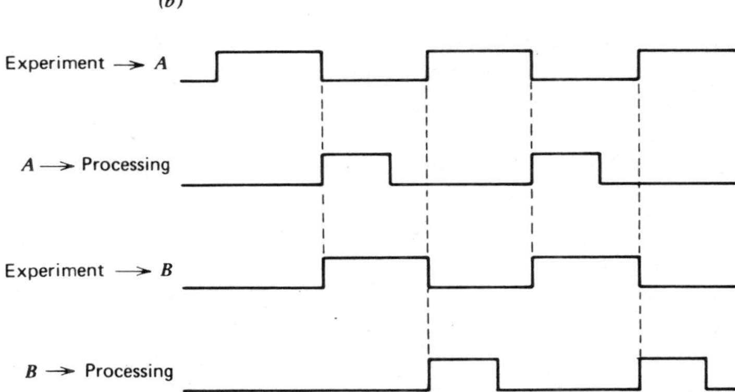

Figure 2.15 *Ping-pong buffers.* (a) *principle;* (b) *operations.*

Another reason for using buffering comes into play when dealing with random data—that is, time derandomization.

2.5.3. Derandomization

In some experiments, data are generated with random times of arrivals. In one moment, a very short time interval is between two data; in the next moment, data are separated by much longer intervals, and so on. If the computer needs a time T for processing one datum, then during this time the machine cannot accept other data. The time T is called the *dead time* of the data collecting system. Because of the dead time, some data generated by the experiment will not be accepted by the computer and will be lost. The dead-time losses can be substantially reduced by using the buffering technique.

The experiment fills the buffer with the data occurring at random. For one datum to be stored into the buffer, a short time interval τ is usually needed. Since $\tau \ll T$, there is no loss of data between the experiment and the buffer. When the buffer is full, the computer can analyze one datum after the other, spending on each datum a time T. The basic formulas for estimating dead-time losses are given in the next section.

2.6. DEAD-TIME LOSSES

For simplicity let us assume that the data collecting system is a counter. Each time an event enters the counter from experiment, the counter is blocked for dead time T (data processing). Data collecting is shown in Figure 2.16*a*. Random events that arrive at the counter input during dead time T are lost.

The situation can be markedly improved by introducing a data buffer between the counter and the experiment. Figure 2.16*b* shows a situation using the buffer with the storage space for only one datum. The first datum that comes during the dead time T is now temporarily stored in the buffer. When the dead time is finished, the system can immediately take the datum from the buffer. If more than one event comes during the dead time, all but the first will be lost. For saving those events, we need a buffer with more than one storage place.

The dead-time losses have been studied by several authors, the most careful calculations being those of Alaoughlu and Smith,[4] Blackman and Michiels,[5] and Jost.[6] They are primarily concerned with losses that occur when a counter and associated circuits have fixed dead time, and when the particles are distributed in time according to the Poisson distribution. However, in most cases the dead time is not fixed but varies widely from one input pulse to another (see Souček[7] and Souček and Prohorov[8]).

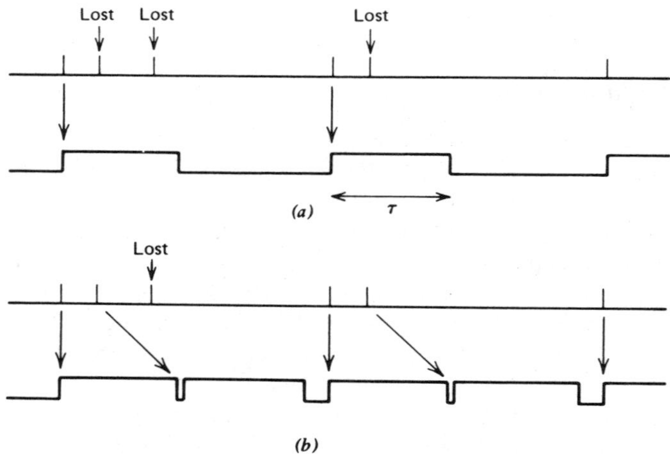

Figure 2.16 *Dead-time losses. (a) system with dead time T; (b) the same system with the one-stage buffer.*

This section derives some expressions to be used for computing losses in systems having variable dead time. Four types of systems having dead time are analyzed: (1) constant, (2) a linear function of the analyzed pulse amplitude, (3) a function of the pulse arrival moment, and (4) a function of the pulse amplitude and of the pulse arrival moment. The circuits having temporary storage systems are also studied.

2.6.1. Basic Expressions

Let us assume that the pulses to be analyzed are randomly distributed in time but at a constant average rate n. The probability of m pulses arriving in an interval T according to the Poisson distribution for random events is

$$w(m, T) = \frac{(nT)^m}{m!} \exp(-nT) \tag{2.12}$$

This distribution has the well-known properties that the average number of pulses occurring in T is nT, and its standard deviation is $(nT)^{1/2}$.

There are two possibilities of defining losses, which will be denoted by p and g. The expression for p gives the probability that losses will occur, but it is not immediately related to the magnitude of the probable loss that does occur. The expression for g gives the average number of pulses lost during one dead-time period. According to these definitions, it follows that for a constant dead time T,

$$p(T) = \sum_{m=1}^{\infty} w(m, T) = 1 - w(0, T) = 1 - \exp(-nT) \tag{2.13}$$

$$\begin{aligned} g(T) &= \sum_{m=1}^{\infty} mw(m, T) \\ &= nT \exp(-nT) \sum_{m=1}^{\infty} (nT)^{m-1}(m - 1)! = nT \end{aligned} \tag{2.14}$$

If the dead time is not constant but has a distribution $q(T)$, the probability of losses $P(T)$ and average number of pulses lost per counted pulse $G(T)$ can be obtained by averaging:

$$\begin{aligned} P(T) &= \int_T p(T)q(T)\, dT \\ &= 1 - \int_T q(T) \exp(-nT)\, dT = 1 - \psi_T(-n) \end{aligned} \tag{2.15}$$

$$G(T) = \int_T g(T)q(T)\, dT = n \int_T Tq(T)\, dT = n\alpha_{1,T} \tag{2.16}$$

where $\psi_T(-n)$ and $\alpha_{1,T}$ are the generating function and a mean value of the variable T; they are defined by the integrals in Equations 2.15 and 2.16.

Dead-time circuits can have temporary storage systems[7] that can store one pulse during the dead-time period. The stored pulse will be treated after the dead time and will not be lost. According to this, and assuming that the temporary storage system is extremely fast, we can write, for a constant dead time T,

$$p_1(T) = \sum_{m=2}^{\infty} w(m, T) = 1 - w(0, T) - w(1, T)$$

$$= 1 - \exp(-nT) - nT\exp(-nT) \tag{2.17}$$

$$g_1(T) = \sum_{m=1}^{\infty} (m - 1)w(m, T) = \sum_{m=1}^{\infty} mw(m, T) - \sum_{m=1}^{\infty} w(m, T)$$

$$= nT - [1 - w(0, T)] = nT - 1 + \exp(-nT) \tag{2.18}$$

For the dead time having distribution $q(T)$, we have

$$P_1(T) = \int_T p_1(T)q(T)\,dT$$

$$= 1 - \int_T q(T)\exp(-nT)\,dT - n\int_T Tq(T)\exp(-nT)\,dT$$

$$= 1 - \psi_T(-n) - nI_T(-n) \tag{2.19}$$

$$G_1(T) = \int_T g_1(T)q(T)\,dT$$

$$= n\int_T Tq(T)\,dT - \int_T q(T)\,dT + \int_T q(T)\exp(-nT)\,dT$$

$$= n\alpha_{1,T} - 1 + \psi_T(-n) \tag{2.20}$$

where $I_{T(-n)}$ is an integral characteristic for the distribution $q(T)$ and is defined in Equation 2.19. The obtained expressions can be applied to several systems of practical interest.

2.6.2. Dead Time as a Linear Function of Pulse Amplitude

An example of a system with dead time as a linear function of pulse amplitude is multichannel analyzers with digital memory,[7] where the dead time $T = T_m + cA$, T_m is the memory period, and cA is the amplitude-to-time conversion period. Since T is a function of the amplitude, $q(T)$ is obtained by transformation from the amplitude distribution $f(A)$

$$q(T) = f[A(T)]\left|\frac{dA(T)}{dT}\right| = \frac{1}{c}f\left(\frac{T - T_m}{c}\right) \tag{2.21}$$

On the basis of Equations 2.13 to 2.21, losses can be calculated if $f(A)$ is known. For example, the losses for the Gaussian amplitude distribution are

$$P(T) = 1 - \exp[-nT_m - nc\alpha_{1,a} + \tfrac{1}{2}(nc\sigma_a)^2]$$

$$G(T) = nT_m + nc\alpha_{1,a}$$

$$P_1(T) = 1 - [1 - nT_m - nc\alpha_{1,a} + (nc\sigma_a)^2] \times \exp[-nT_m - nc\alpha_{1,a} + \tfrac{1}{2}(nc\sigma_a)^2]$$

$$G_1(T) = nT_m + nc\alpha_{1,a} - 1 + \exp[-nT_m - nc\alpha_{1,a} + \tfrac{1}{2}(nc\sigma_a)^2]$$

If $c = 0$, the expressions for the losses in systems with fixed dead time are obtained.

2.6.3. Dead Time as a Function of Pulse Arrival Moment

An example of a system with dead time as a function of pulse arrival moment is the Hutchinson-Scarrot-type analyzers[9] with circulating memory. If the circulation period is denoted by T_0, the dead-time period may be $0 < T < T_0$, depending on the arrival moment of the pulse to be analyzed. Accordingly, the distribution $q(T) = \text{const} = 1/T_0$ does not depend on $f(A)$. From Equations 2.15 and 2.16 it follows that

$$P(T) = 1 - \frac{1}{nT_0}[1 - \exp(-nT_0)] \tag{2.22}$$

$$G(T) = \tfrac{1}{2}nT_0 \tag{2.23}$$

2.6.4. Dead Time as a Function of Pulse Amplitude and Pulse Arrival Moment

The system where dead time is a function of pulse amplitude and pulse arrival moment operates in cycles with period T_0. When a pulse to be analyzed arrives, the system retains it for a period τ, which begins at the pulse arrival moment and ends with the arrival of a new cycle. At that moment, the analysis begins and lasts for a period cA, where c is a constant of the system and A is the pulse amplitude. Accordingly, the dead time is $T = \tau + cA$. The period τ is a stochastic variable in the interval $0 < \tau < T_0$, its distribution being $\phi(\tau) = \text{const} = 1/T_0$. The period cA is a stochastic variable in the interval $0 < cA < T_0$. The distribution $q(T)$ is a function of $f(A)$ and T_0, and reads

$$q(T) = \int_A \frac{1}{T_0} f(A)\, dA = \frac{1}{T_0}\int_{(T-T_0)/c}^{T/c} f(A)\, dA \tag{2.24}$$

From Equations 2.15, 2.16 and 2.24 we then have

$$P(T) = 1 - \frac{1}{T_0} \int_T \int_{(T-T_0)/c}^{T/c} f(A) \exp(-nT)\, dA\, dT \tag{2.25}$$

$$G(T) = \frac{n}{T_0} \int_T \int_{(T-T_0)/c}^{T/c} Tf(A)\, dA\, dT \tag{2.26}$$

If all pulses have the same amplitude A, Equations 2.25 and 2.26 degenerate into

$$P(T) = 1 - \frac{1}{nT_0} \exp(ncA)[1 - \exp(-nT_0)] \tag{2.27}$$

$$G(T) = \tfrac{1}{2}nT_0 + ncA \tag{2.28}$$

For parameter $c = 0$ the expressions are identical with those for the Hutchinson-Scarrot analyzer.

2.6.5. Conclusions

The general equations 2.13 to 2.20 can also be used for the calculation of losses in other cases not considered here. For $nT < 0.3$, the probability that losses will occur (Equations 2.13, 2.15, 2.17, 2.19) is approximately the same as the average number of pulses lost during the dead time (Equations 2.14, 2.16, 2.18, 2.20). For the greater value of nT, the average number of pulses lost during the dead time is greater than the probability that losses will occur, because more than one pulse can be lost during the dead-time period. If the dead time has a distribution $q(T)$, it is sufficient, for calculating losses, to

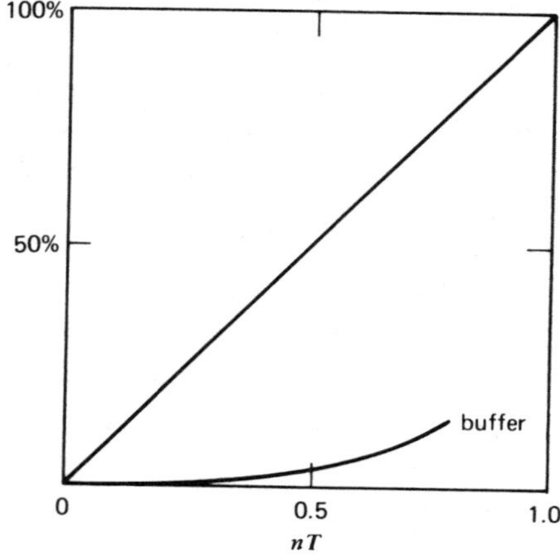

Figure 2.17 *Average number of lost pulses as a function of the input rate.*

know only the mean value, generating function, and characteristic integral of this distribution. The simple formulas obtained can be directly used for the calculating of losses in systems of practical interest (Souček[7]).

Figure 2.17 shows the average number of pulses lost during one dead-time interval, as given by Equations 2.14 (no buffering) and 2.18 (buffer with only one storage place). It is obvious that even the simplest buffer has substantially reduced dead-time losses. A buffer with more than one storage place makes losses negligible, as long as $nT < 1$. When $nT > 1$, buffering cannot reduce the losses, because on average the experiment generates the data faster than the system processes the data. In such a situation, either the input data rate should be reduced or faster data collecting and processing devices should be used.

2.7. REAL-TIME SERVICING AND QUEUEING SYSTEM

A real-time system consists of a number of servers, inter-connected by queues of customers or jobs to be done.

Servers are hardware and software modules, designated for a particular operation. A line printer is an example of a hardware server. The program that filters the signal from the noise is an example of a software server.

Queues store requests for services (customers) until the time when the servers become available. Queues can take the form of circular buffers, first-in-first-out (FIFO) buffers, or temporary memories.

Customers or jobs include input signals and transactions waiting to be processed, interprocess messages within the system, and results waiting to be written to disk or to be delivered to the instruments or process control systems.

Allworth[10] introduces several measures of performance for real-time systems, combining average customer arrival rate n and the average service time per customer, T.

Utilization factor is the product of the average arrival rate and the average service time per customer

$$\mu = nT \tag{2.29}$$

Average number of customers in the system is defined as (utilization factor/1 − utilization factor) or

$$\overline{N} = \frac{\mu}{1 - \mu} \tag{2.30}$$

The average total response time in the system $\overline{T}$, is

$$\overline{T} = \frac{T}{1 - \mu} \tag{2.31}$$

From Equation 2.31 follows: if the utilization factor μ is very small (zero), average total response time is equal to the average service time for one customer; if the utilization factor μ tends toward one, the average total response time tends toward infinity, and the system is blocked.

Servers, queues, customers, and real-time systems could have a complex topology with many serial and parallel components. The system should have a high *throughput,* defined as average number of customers completed per unit time. Analytical analysis such as one presented in Section 2.6. and by Equations 2.29, 2.30 and 2.31 is possible only for simple topologies. For more complex systems it is necessary to build a simulation model of a proposed system, see Souček and Souček.[11]

Modelling is a first step in designing the real-time system. The computer program simulates the elements and the topology of the system as well as the environment the system is connected to. The model simulates the events that occur as a result of the passing of time. While running, the program is closely monitored in order to extract the data as to the dynamic behaviour of the system being modelled. The bottlenecks should be detected and extracted from the system. Special purpose programming languages exist, to facilitate production of simulation programs. These include SIMSCRIPT, SIMULA, CSL and GPSS. Model-based reasoning and related expert systems are described in Chapter 5.

REFERENCES

1. A. Susskind, *Analog to Digital Conversion Techniques,* MIT Press, Cambridge, Mass., 1963.
2. B. Souček, *Minicomputers in Data Processing and Simulation,* Wiley, New York, 1972.
3. C. Cottini, E. Gatti, and V. Svelto, *Nuclear Instr. and Methods* **24,** 241 (1963).
4. L. Alaoughlu and N. N. Smith, *Phys. Rev.* **53,** 832, (1938).
5. M. Blackman and J. L. Michiels, *Proc. Phys. Soc.* **60,** 549, (1948).
6. R. Jost, *Helv. Phys. Acta,* **20,** 173, (1947).
7. B. Souček, Nuclear Instr. and Methods **27,** 306 (1964).
8. B. Souček and S. Prohorov, *Microprocessing and Microprogramming* **11,** 23–29 (1983).
9. G. W. Hutchinson and G. G. Scarrot, *Phil. Mag.* **42,** 292 (1951).
10. S. T. Allworth, *Introduction to Real-Time Software Design,* Springer-Verlag, New York, 1981.
11. B. Souček and M. Souček, *Neural and Massively Parallel Computers, The Sixth Generation,* Wiley, New York, 1988.

CHAPTER 3

Mapping, Adaptation, and Learning in Neural Networks

INTRODUCTION AND SURVEY

The major features of artificial neural networks are numerous processing/memory elements; several mapping structures or architectures within the same system; learning networks based on training rather than programming; and hybrid trained/programmed systems.

This chapter makes a comparative analysis of fine granularity levels suitable for achieving these features. Granularity in intelligence directly reflects into hardware, architecture, and software. A spectrum of solutions is based on granularity: field computers, neural computers, and high-order neural units.

The most widely used information processing operation in neural networks is mathematical mapping. The Kolmogorov theorem proves that two mappings are needed to classify the input data into any number of clusters. The chapter explains the back-propagation mapping network, alternating projection, stochastic network, probabilistic logic neuron, high-order neural units, and neural networks based on simulated annealing in Boolean logic. Each offers a different approach to the problems of learning and adaptation. The existence of three regimes—discrimination, fuzziness, and generalization—is explained. Learning times, number of training examples, and applications are discussed. Some of the techniques described are widely used, and others promise a major breakthrough.

3.1. INTELLIGENCE GRANULARITY

Brainlike, sixth-generation computers[1] mimic the way the brain processes information. Here are some basic facts and estimates about the human brain:

- Each neuron in the brain is an active processing unit.
- There are about 10^{11} neurons in the brain.
- A neuron can have from 1000 to 100,000 synaptic connections with other neurons.
- A system of 10^{11} units having 1000 connections per unit can be fully interconnected through a four-stage lattice structure.
- Most connections are rather short.
- There is a general symmetry of connections. If there are connections from one region to another, there are usually connections in the opposite direction.
- Neurons exchange excitatory and inhibitory signals rather than symbolic messages.
- Most neurons are either excitatory or inhibitory but not both.
- It supports the vital functions of language and thought that are not developed to such a high level in animals.

The sixth-generation project establishes the bridge between brain behavior research and computer science and engineering. In Japan the sixth generation is a national project of high priority.

New devices and systems are now entering the market. Application areas include fuzzy reasoning, neural and expert systems, intelligent information systems, instrumentation, process control, robotics, speech, image, communication, human-computer interface, and many others.

In this chapter we follow the classification of neural and massively parallel computers presented in Figure 3.1. The finest granularity is in field computers. The number of processing units is so large that it can be treated as a

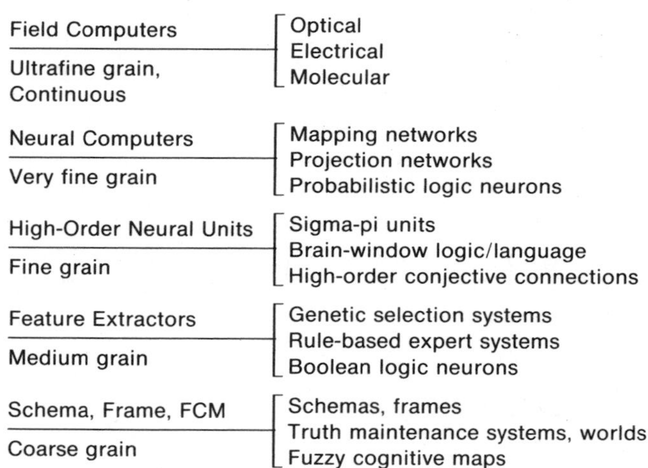

Figure 3.1 *Taxonomy tree based on intelligence granularity.*

continuous quantity. Next come neural computers, in which each processing element performs only a simple weighted sum and nonlinear transformation. To be useful, elements are connected into layers based on back-propagation learning rules. Next come high-order units, partially crafted on a priori knowledge about the problem domain. The processing element involves weighted sum, multiplication, and nonlinear transformation. The next level is feature extractors and genetic selection systems, inspired by self-organization in biological systems. In this system, selectionism could be an alternative for programming. The final level is systems of schemas, frames, bidirectional associative memories (BAMs), and fuzzy cognitive maps (FCMs). These systems settle into the solution by using a process of relaxation, without applying logical operations. Here, macroknowledge processing based on symbolic structures is merged with microknowledge processing based on connection structures.

Granularity is a major issue in sixth-generation hardware, software, and applications. Trends are shown that open new business and application areas, merging classical computers and sixth-generation technologies, as defined by Souček and Souček.[1]

3.2. FIELD COMPUTERS

The design of intelligent systems is based on massive parallelism. The ultimate level is parallelism in which the number of computational units is so large that it can be treated as a continuous quantity. It is clear that processing elements on this level of parallelism cannot be individually programmed; they must be controlled en masse. This leads to a new model of computation, based on the transformation of continuous scalar and vector fields. MacLennan[2] introduced field computers that conform to this model. The field computer can be electrical, optical, or molecular.

According to MacLennan[2], a general-purpose field computer would have field storage units for holding scalar and vector fields. Some of these units would hold fixed fields for controlling the processing. Others would hold variable fields captured from input devices or to be presented to output devices, or as intermediate fields in recursive processes.

Field transformation processes would be implemented by programmed connections between elementary field transforms. These elementary operations should permit programming any useful field transformation in a modest number of steps.

Field computers follow the cooperative-action brain theory, claiming that thoughts and perceptions are enclosed in the electromagnetic field patterns of the brain, not in the individual neurons.

Some special-purpose optical computers may be considered as belonging to the family of field computers. A general-purpose field computer is still to come.

3.3. NEURAL COMPUTERS

Neural computers are composed of numerous simple computational elements operating in parallel. The computational element sums N weighted inputs and passes the result through a nonlinearity (sigmoid function). If the result is above a built-in threshold level, the element "fires." In this way a computational element resembles the operation of a biological neuron.

Neural computers are divided into classes based on network topology, computational element characteristics, and training or learning rules. The basic features of neural computers are

- High computational rates due to the massive parallelism;
- Fault tolerance (damage to a few nodes does not significantly impair overall performance);
- Learning or training (the network adapts itself, based on the information received from the environment);
- Goal-seeking (the performance to achieve the goal is measured and used to self-organize the system; programmed rules are not necessary);
- Primitive computational elements (each element resembles one simple logical neuron and cannot do much).

Artificial neural networks are also called *parallel distributed processing* (PDP) systems. In PDP systems, the programs and data patterns are not stored. What is stored is the connection strengths between units that allow these patterns to be recreated. PDP systems could serve as a pattern associator between two sets of units. One set could serve as a visual pattern, the other as an acoustic pattern for the same object. Learning or building the knowledge structure in PDP systems involves modifying the patterns of interconnectivity. Rumelhart et al.[3,4] define the process of learning, using the notation of Figure 3.2.

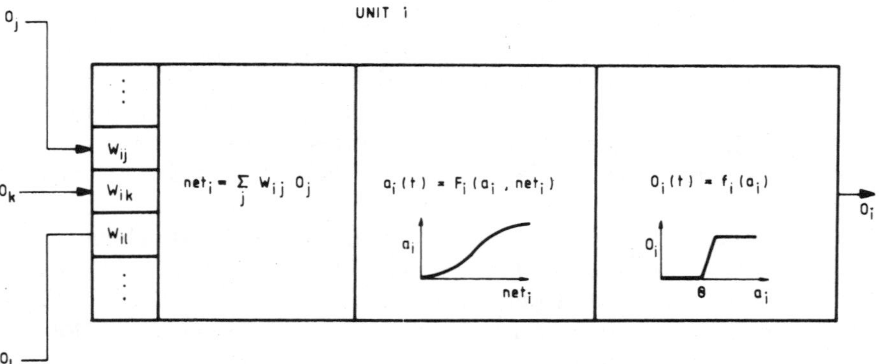

Figure 3.2 *Basic components of a parallel distributed processing system.*

Output from unit j, o_j, is connected to the input of unit i through the weight w_{ij}. The net input is usually the weighted sum of all inputs to the unit. The state of activation a_i is a function F of the old state a_i and of the net input. The useful, frequently used activation function is a sigmoid function (Figure 3.3). The output o_i is a function f of the activation state. The useful, frequently used f function is the threshold function.

Different learning rules to modify the pattern of connectivity as a function of experience have been developed. They include Hebbian learning, the Delta rule, competitive learning, the Hopfield minimum-energy rule, the generalized Delta rule, Sigma-Pi units, and the Boltzmann learning algorithm.

3.3.1. Hebbian Learning without a Teacher

$$\Delta w_{ij} = \eta a_i o_j \tag{3.1}$$

where η is the constant of proportionality representing the learning rate. A simple version of Equation 3.1 is this: where unit i and unit j are simultaneously excited, the strength of the connection between them increases in proportion to the product of their activations.

3.3.2. The Delta Rule or Widrow-Hoff Rule with a Teacher

$$\Delta w_{ij} = \eta[t_i(t) - a_i(t)]o_j(t) \tag{3.2}$$

The amount of learning is proportional to the difference between the actual activation achieved and the target activation $t_i(t)$ provided by the teacher.

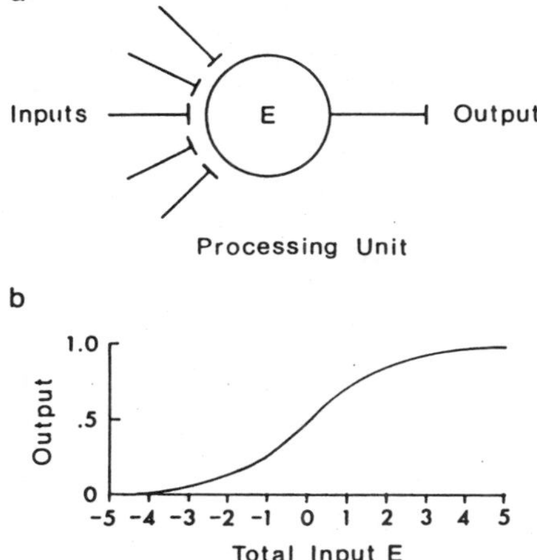

Figure 3.3 *(a) Schematic model of a processing unit receiving inputs from other processing units; (b) transformation between summed inputs and output of a processing unit.*

3.3.3. The Competitive Learning Rule without a Teacher

The competitive learning rule allows the units to compete in some way for the right to respond to a given subset of input. The competitive rules have been developed by von der Marlsburg,[5] Grossberg,[6] Fukushima,[7] Fukushima and Miyaki,[8] and Kohonen.[9] According to Rumelhart and Zipser,[10] the units in a given layer are broken into a set of nonoverlapping clusters. Each unit within a cluster inhibits every other unit within a cluster. The clusters are winner-take-all, such that the unit receiving the largest input achieves its maximum value (1) while all other units in the cluster are pushed to their minimum value (0). The fixed total amount of weight for unit j is designated $\Sigma_i w_{ij} = 1$. A unit learns by shifting weight from its inactive input lines to its active input lines:

$$\Delta w_{ij} = \begin{cases} 0 & \text{if unit } j \text{ loses on stimulus } k \\ g \dfrac{c_{ik}}{n_k} - g w_{ij} & \text{if unit } j \text{ wins on stimulus } k \end{cases} \tag{3.3}$$

where $c_{ik} = 1$ if in stimulus pattern S_k unit i in the lower layer is active and $=$ 0 otherwise; n_k is the number of active units in pattern S_k; and g is a proportionality constant.

Grossberg has developed a similar rule, of the form

$$\Delta w_{ij} = \eta a_i(t)[o_j(t) - w_{ij}] \tag{3.4}$$

3.3.4. The Hopfield Minimum-Energy Rule

Hopfield's study[11] concentrates on the units that are symmetrically connected (i.e., $w_{ij} = w_{ji}$). The units are always in one of two states: $+1$ or -1. The global "energy" of the system is defined as

$$E = -\sum_{i<j} w_{ij} s_i s_j + \sum \theta_i s_i \tag{3.5}$$

$$\Delta E_k = \sum_i w_{ki} s_i - \theta_k \tag{3.6}$$

where s_i is the state of the ith unit (-1 or 1), θ_i is a threshold, and ΔE_k is the difference between the energy of the whole system with the kth hypothesis false and its energy with the kth hypothesis true.

3.3.5. Sigma-Pi Units

The most common "additive units" form the connections through the addition $\Sigma w_{ij} a_i$. More elaborate Sigma-Pi units form the connections using both addition and multiplication. The net input is

$$\sum w_{ij} \prod a_{i_1} a_{i_2} \cdots a_{i_k}$$

where i indexes the conjuncts impinging on unit j and $a_{i_1}, a_{i_2}, \ldots, a_{i_k}$ are the k units in the conjunct. Sigma-Pi units can be used for elaborate models, including gates (weighted connections), dynamically programmable networks in which the activation value of some units determine what another network can do, and mimicking different monotonic activation and interconnection functions. Learning rules discussed so far can be modified for application on Sigma-Pi units.

3.3.6. The Boltzmann Learning Algorithm

The Boltzmann learning algorithm is designed for a machine with symmetrical connections. The binary threshold in a perceptron is deterministic, but in a Boltzmann machine it is probabilistic:

$$p_i = P(\Delta E_i) = \frac{1}{1 + e^{-\Delta E_i/T}}$$

where p_i is the probability for the ith unit to be in state 1, $P(x)$ is a sigmoidal probability function (Figure 3.3), T is a parameter analogous to temperature and measures the noise introduced into the decision; and $\Delta E_i = \Sigma\, w_{ij} s_j$ is the total input to the unit. The Boltzmann learning algorithm is closely related to maximum likelihood methods. It has been designed to solve a class of optimization problems in vision.

The learning is supervised: the input units are clamped to a particular pattern, and the network relaxes into a state of low energy in which the output units have the correct values. Due to the symmetry, the energy gradient with respect to w_{ij} depends on the behavior of only the ith and jth units. This fact helps in updating input, output, and hidden units.

3.4. THE KOLMOGOROV MAPPING NEURAL NETWORK EXISTENCE THEOREM

The most widely used information processing operation in neural networks is mathematical mapping. Given an input vector X, the network should produce an output vector $Y = \varphi(X)$. The network's basic feature is to extract and recognize essential parameters from complex high-dimensional data.

Some investigators consider the Kolmogorov theorem as a guideline to design mapping networks. According to the theorem, an input vector X can be mapped into any output function $Y = \varphi(X)$, provided elements are allowed that implement arbitrary continuous increasing functions of one input

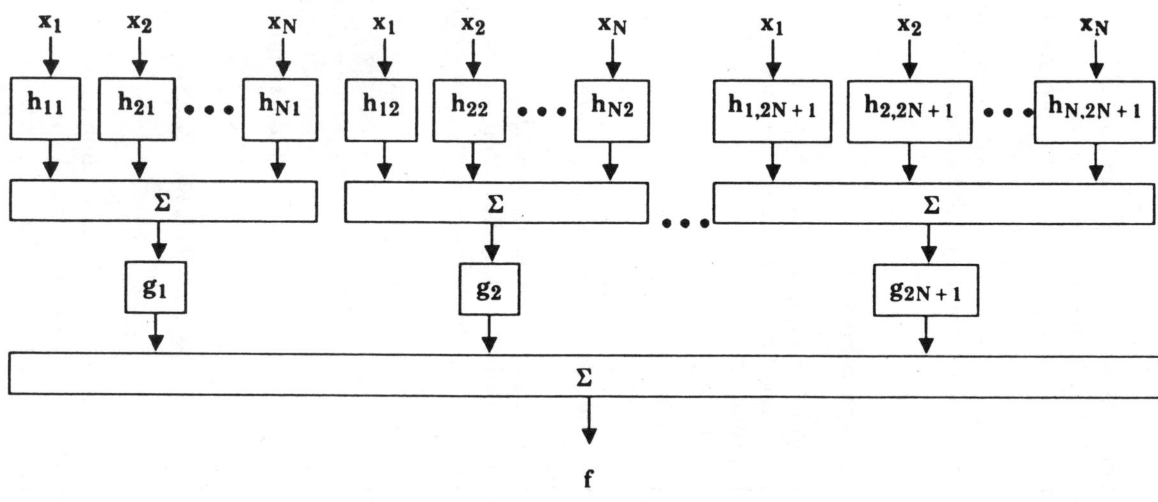

$$f(x_1, x_2, \ldots, x_N) = \Sigma^{2N+1} g_k (\Sigma^N h_{jk}(x_j))$$

Figure 3.4 *Kolmogorov representation. (See G. G. Lorentz, The 13-th problem of Hilbert. Proc. Sympos. Pure Math., Vol. 28, Amer. Math. Soc., Providence, RI, 1976, 419–430.) Adapted from Shrier, Barron, and Gilstrap.*[13] *Courtesy and copyright © 1987 by IEEE.*

variable as well as elements that simply implement the sum of several variables. In other words, no more than two mappings are needed to classify the input data into the number of clusters desired.

Two mappings can be accomplished by a three-layer neural network of input, output, and hidden units. Hecht-Nielsen[12] has formulated the Kolmogorov theorem as follows: given any continuous function

$$\varphi: I^n \to R^m \qquad Y = \varphi(X) \tag{3.7}$$

φ can be implemented exactly by a three-layer neural network having n processing elements in the first (X-input) layer, $2n + 1$ processing elements in the middle hidden layer, and m processing elements in the top (Y-output) layer. Hecht-Nielsen calls this theorem the Kolmogorov mapping neural network existence theorem. Shrier, Barron, and Gilstrap[13] give a schematic presentation of the Kolmogorov theorem; see Figure 3.4.

Kolmogorov's theorem does not indicate how weights or nonlinearities in the network should be selected nor how sensitive the output function is to variations in the weights and internal functions.

3.5. BACK-PROPAGATION NETWORK

Currently, the most popular mapping neural network is the back-propagation network of Rumelhart et al[3,4]. The back-propagation network has been shown to be capable of implementing approximations to a variety of mappings from R^n to R^m. The approximation achieved has been shown to be optimal in a certain least mean squared error sense. The back propagation is important for multilayered networks with one or more hidden layers. The question for many years was: How does a neuron deeply embedded within a network know what aspect of the outcome of an overall action was its fault? The problem was attacked in 1962 by Rosenblatt.[14] The practical solution was given by Rumelhart et al.[3,4] in 1983.

The network is composed of three types of units shown in Figure 3.5: input units; hidden units carrying an internal representation, and output units. The activation of each unit is a sigmoid function f of the weighted sum e: $o = f(e)$:

$$o_j = \frac{1}{1 + \exp(-e_j)} \qquad o_k = \frac{1}{1 + \exp(-e_k)} \tag{3.8}$$

$$e_j = \sum_i o_i w_{ji} + \theta_j \qquad e_k = \sum_j o_j w_{kj} + \theta_k \tag{3.9}$$

where θ is a threshold.

A training set of patterns is used to self-organize the network. Typically, one generates a set of sample vectors O_i. The obtained output vector O_k is

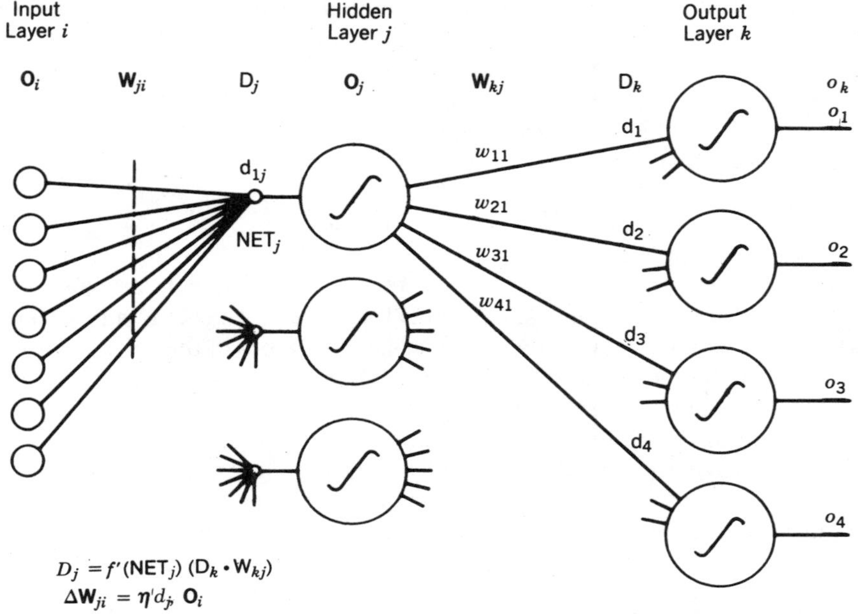

Figure 3.5 *Back-propagation algorithm. Hidden unit layer j weight changes.*

compared with the target output vector T_k provided by the teacher (Figure 3.6). Here we concentrate on one unit in layer k. The difference between vector components $t_k - o_k$ defines the error (delta) d_k. In other words, the input to the unit should be corrected by d_k to provide the target output t_k:

$$d_k = (t_k - o_k)f'(e_k) \tag{3.10}$$

Introducing Equation 3.8 for the activation function f yields the derivative and the delta, d_k:

$$f'(e_k) = \frac{df(e_k)}{de_k} = o_k(1 - o_k) \tag{3.11}$$

$$d_k = (t_k - o_k)o_k(1 - o_k) \tag{3.12}$$

This value is used to modify the weights w_{kj} on the output unit k, following the basic Hebbian law of learning. The path is reinforced in proportion to the activations on its ends:

$$\Delta W_{kj} = \eta d_k O_j \tag{3.13}$$

Weight correction starts with the output unit (Equation 3.13), and it is back-propagated toward the input.

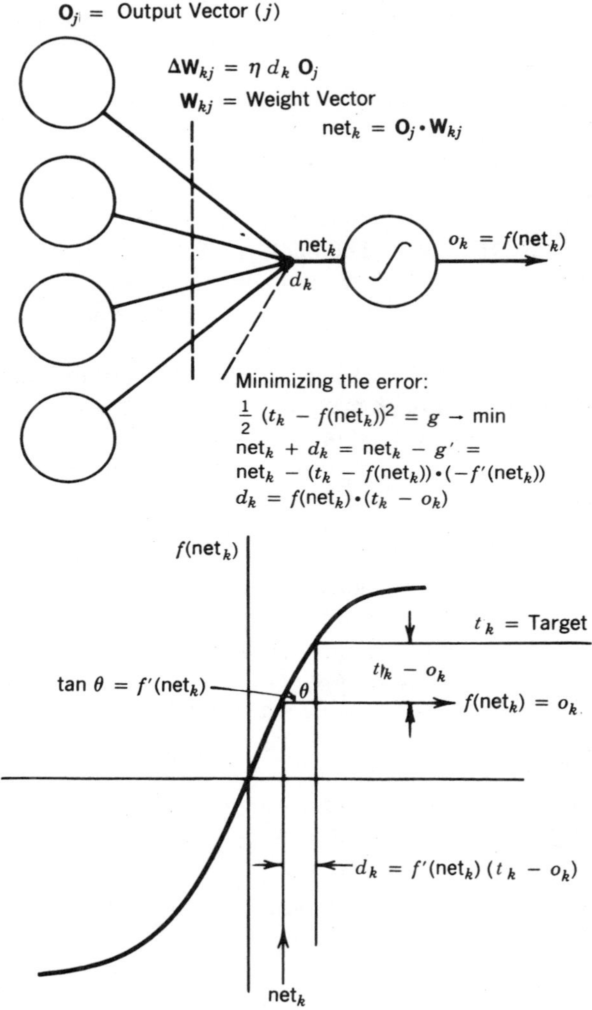

Figure 3.6 *Back-propagation algorithm. Output unit in layer k driven from units in layer j.*

The hidden layer j is shown in Figure 3.5. The error signal d_k on the right side of weight components w_{kj} back-propagates to the left side as

$$D_k W_{kj} = \sum_k d_k w_{kj} \tag{3.14}$$

In analogy to Figure 3.6, this error signal back-propagates through the units in layer j, producing the signal d_j:

$$d_j = f'(e_j) \sum_k d_k w_{kj} = o_j(1 - o_j) \sum_k d_k w_{kj} \tag{3.15}$$

This value is used to modify the weights w_{ji} on the hidden units, again following the Hebbian law:

$$\Delta W_{ji} = \eta d_j O_i \tag{3.16}$$

The operation of the network involves two phases, as shown in Figure 3.7. During the forward phase, the input is presented and propagated toward the output. During the backward phase, the errors are formed at the output and propagated toward the input. The back-propagation algorithm has been tested with different problems and generally performs well. One of the most powerful applications is NETtalk by Sejnowski and Rosenberg,[15] a letter-to-phoneme mapping systems[16].

Although artificial neural networks are inspired by research in neurobiology, there is no evidence that back propagation exists in actual brain mechanisms and that synapses can be used in the reverse direction. Back propagation must be considered only as algorithm for self-organization of artificial learning systems.

Back propagation is a time-consuming algorithm. The learning time is approximately $O(N^3)$ on a serial machine and $O(N^2)$ on a parallel machine that uses a separate processor for each connection, where N is the number of weights in the network. The number of training examples is typically $O(N)$. This means that for large N a great many training examples are needed to provide enough data to estimate the weights.

Rumelhart et al.[3,4] gave the following practical suggestions for using the back-propagation algorithm:

- Start the system with small random weights.
- Extreme values 1 or 0 are difficult to reach, so convert to binary at the values 0.9 or 0.1.
- For every recurrent network, a feedforward network with identical behavior exists.

The Back-Propagation Training Algorithm

Step 1. For all i, j, k, set all weights and thresholds to small random values.

Step 2. Put the input vector into the layer i, and specify the desired target output t_k in layer k.

Step 3. Use the sigmoid nonlinearity (Equation 3.8) to calculate outputs of layers j and k.

Step 4. Calculate the error signal $t_k - o_k$.

Step 5. Calculate d_k for the output layer and adjust the weights w_{kj}, using Equations 3.12 and 3.13.

Step 6. Working back to the hidden layer, calculate d_j and adjust the weight w_{ji}, using Equations 3.15 and 3.16.

Step 7. Repeat by going to step 2.

Figure 3.7 *Back-propagation training algorithm.*

- In most simulations the entire set of patterns was presented to the system between 1000 and 10,000 times. Investigate what would happen if only a subset of patterns were used for training the system, and watch the system generalize to remaining patterns. More theoretical and experimental research is needed in the domain of generalization.

The goal of learning is to cause the network to achieve a particular global behavior, but the learning should be implemented locally. The back-propagation algorithm with a differentiable activation function (Equation 3.8) is a step in this direction. Future research might provide other useful and necessary methods of learning.

3.6. ALTERNATING PROJECTION NEURAL NETWORK

Marks et al.[17,18] suggest a new class of neural networks called alternating projection neural networks (APNN). APNN perform by alternately projecting between two or more constraint sets, see Figure 3.8. The single point intersection between convex sets is a derived steady-state solution. For the theory of projection onto convex sets, see Stark.[19]

Criteria for desired and unique convergence are easily established. Then network can be taught from a training set by viewing each library vector only once. The network can be configured as a content addressable memory (homogeneous form) or as a classifier (layered form). The number of patterns that can be stored in the network is approximately the number of input and hidden neurons. If the output neurons can take on only one of two states, then the trained layered APNN can be easily configured to converge in one iteration. More generally, the APNN converges exponentially. Convergence can be improved by using sigmoid-type nonlinearities, network relaxation, and/or increasing the number of neurons in the hidden layer. The manner in which the network generalizes can be directly evaluated.

The neurons in the homogeneous APNN can be clamped to a preassigned value and provide the network stimulus, or they can float according to the stimulus of other neurons. The status of a neuron as clamped or floating may change from application to application. The APNN in this form acts as a content addressable memory. After being trained with several library vectors, the APNN can generally reconstruct any library vector by clamping a subset of the neurons to the values equal to the elements of that vector. The states of the remaining floating neurons will then converge to the unknown vector elements.

The input neurons of the layered APNN provide the network's stimulus. The use of neurons in the hidden layer increases storage capacity, convergence rate, and classification diversity. The states of the output layer provide the classification index.

The l neurons are divided into two sets: one in which the states are known (clamped neurons) and the reminder in which the states are unknown (floating neurons). Let p be the number of clamped neurons and $s_k(m)$ the state of the kth neuron at time m. The iteration state equation is

$$S(m + 1) = \boldsymbol{\eta} \boldsymbol{T} S(m)$$

where the interconnect matrix $\boldsymbol{T}$ is the orthogonal projector onto the n dimensional subspace T formed by the closure of the library vectors, and $\boldsymbol{\eta}$ is the orthogonal projector onto the $m - n$ dimensional linear variety η formed by the set of all l tuplets with their first p elements equal to the elements of the library vectors. It is easy to proof that

$$\lim_{m \to \infty} \| S(m) - F \| = 0$$

where F is some library vector. The basic idea of an alternating projection neural network is shown in Figure 3.8.

Marks et al.[17,18] compare the APNN with mapping neural networks in the following way:

1. As their name suggests, APNNs perform by alternately projecting between two or more constraint sets. Criteria can be established for proper iterative convergence. This is in contrast, for example, to the conventional technique of forming an energy metric for the neural networks, establishing a lower energy bound, and showing that the energy reduces each iteration. Such procedures generally do not address the accuracy of the final solution. To ensure that such networks arrive at the desired globally minimum energy, computationally lengthly procedures, such as simulated annealing, are used. For synchronous networks, steady-state oscillation can occur between two states of the same energy. The accuracy of the steady-state solution of APNNs, on the other hand, can be straightforwardly ensured for both synchronous and asynchronous networks.
2. Many homogeneous neural networks do not scale well; i.e., the storage capacity less than doubles when the number of neurons is doubled. Marks shows that, in layered form, the number of stored patterns in an APNN is roughly equal to the number of input and hidden neurons.
3. The speed of backward error propagation learning can be painfully slow. Layered APNN on the other hand, can be trained on only one pass through the data. If the network memory does not saturate, new data can easily be learned without repeating previous data. Neither is the effectiveness of recall of previous data diminished. Marks shows that in certain important applications, the APNN will recall in one iteration. Generally, the cost of this performance is more hidden neurons. Hence, we are trading computational time for architectural real estate.

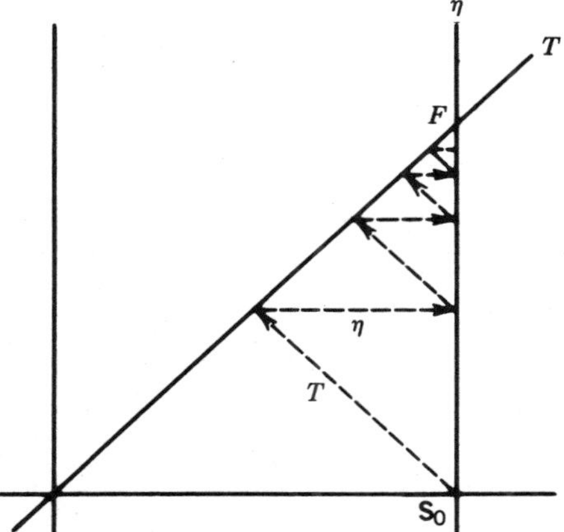

Figure 3.8 *Alternating projection neural network. (Adapted by permission from Marks et al.*[17,18])

4. The manner in which the layered APNN generalizes to data for which it was not trained can be found analytically in a straightforward fashion.

Research on APNN is in progress.

3.7. STOCHASTIC COMPUTING

Stochastic computing uses the probability of a binary variable to encode an analog or digital value. The sequence of bits with a probability P of being on is used to represent the real number P. Stochastic computing was investigated in the late 1960s by Gaines,[20] Poppelbaum and Afuso,[21] and Ribeiro.[22] However, the speed and cost limitations of using conventional digital circuit elements in a random mode restricted practical applications.

Stochastic processors are intrinsically more powerful computing devices than are deterministic automata. Uncertain networks can perform computations that are beyond deterministic networks. Stochastic operands can be added by an OR gate and multiplied by an AND gate. Neural networks require a massive amount of multiplications and additions. It appears that neural networks are good candidates for implementing stochastic processing.

Nguyen and Holt[23] performed numerical experiments on stochastic multiplication as a basis for neural hardware. A simple stochastic multiplier is presented in Figure 3.9. Its operation is as follows: An operand is represented by the sequence of samples. Each sample X of the operand sequence, from 0 to 1, is first converted into an unweighted binary-valued representation. The sample is compared with noise N, uniformly distributed between 0

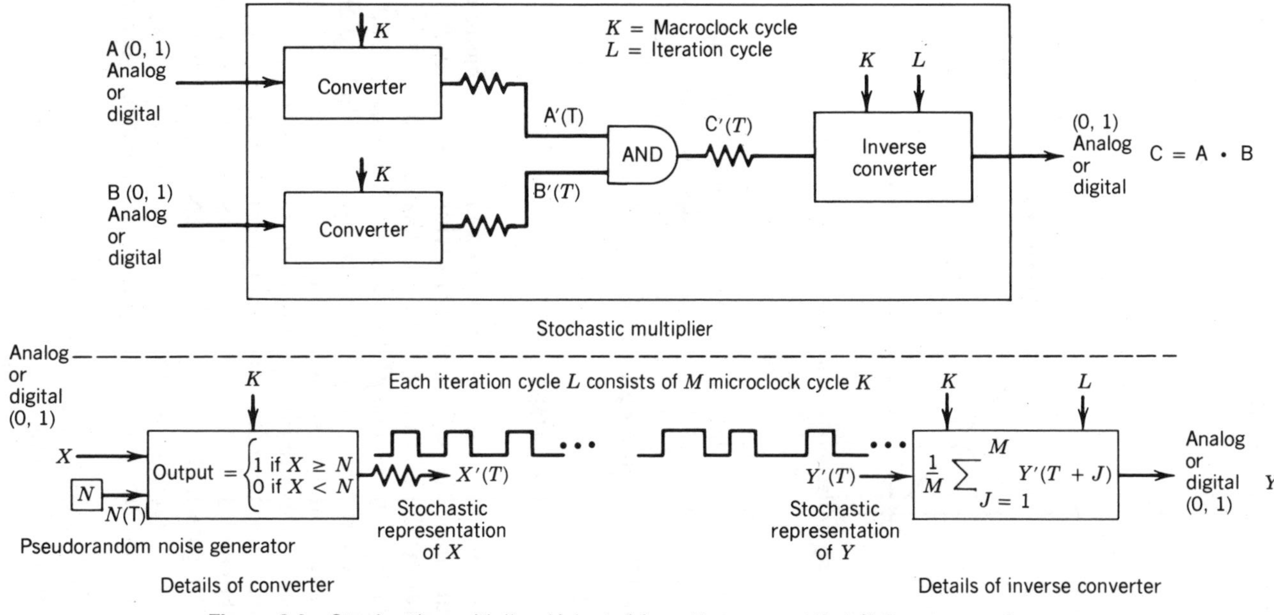

Figure 3.9 *Stochastic multiplier.* (*Adapted from Nguyen and Holt.*[23] *Courtesy and copyright © 1987 by IEEE.*)

and 1. If $X \geq N$, X is represented by a stochastic value $X' = 1$. If $X < N$, X is represented by a stochastic value $X' = 0$. In this way the binary variable X represents the probability of the input sample X being 1.

For two sequences or operands A and B, we use the laws of probability:

$$P(A = 1) = A'$$
$$P(B = 1) = B'$$
$$P((A = 1) \text{ AND } (B = 1)) = A' \cdot B'$$
$$P((A = 1) \text{ OR } (B = 1)) = A' + B'$$

Hence, multiplication can be performed by an AND gate and addition by an OR gate, provided that sequences A and B are exclusive.

To recover the result of the stochastic multiplication of two sample sequences, the output of the AND gate is time-averaged.

The conversion step requires a random noise source. Nguyen and Holt used a pseudorandom noise generator based on a shift register with linear feedback. The shift register of R bits generates $2^R - 1$ pseudorandom numbers. In other words, all integers from 1 to $2^R - 1$ will be generated exactly once before the sequence repeats itself. If these numbers are scaled into the range between 0 and 1, they approximate random noise with a uniform distribution.

The multiplication can be extended to cover bipolar operands from -1 to $+1$. A bipolar system is shown in Figure 3.10. Experiments with stochastic systems lead to the following conclusions:

1. Stochastic multiplication performs well in this application domain. The accuracy is equivalent to digital processing with a 10-bit parallel multiplier.
2. A stochastic multiplier requires up to four AND gates, whereas an equivalent digital multiplier requires thousands of gates.
3. Stochastic processing requires no more than four signals to be routed between elements. Digital processing routes the full word in parallel between elements.
4. Stochastic processing involves binary signals that are immune to noise and distortion.

The drawbacks of stochastic processing are

1. Increased computation time;
2. Conversion of signals between analog (or digital) representation and stochastic representation; and
3. Totally uncoded representation, which means that, without randomness, n binary events are needed for a precision of one part in n.

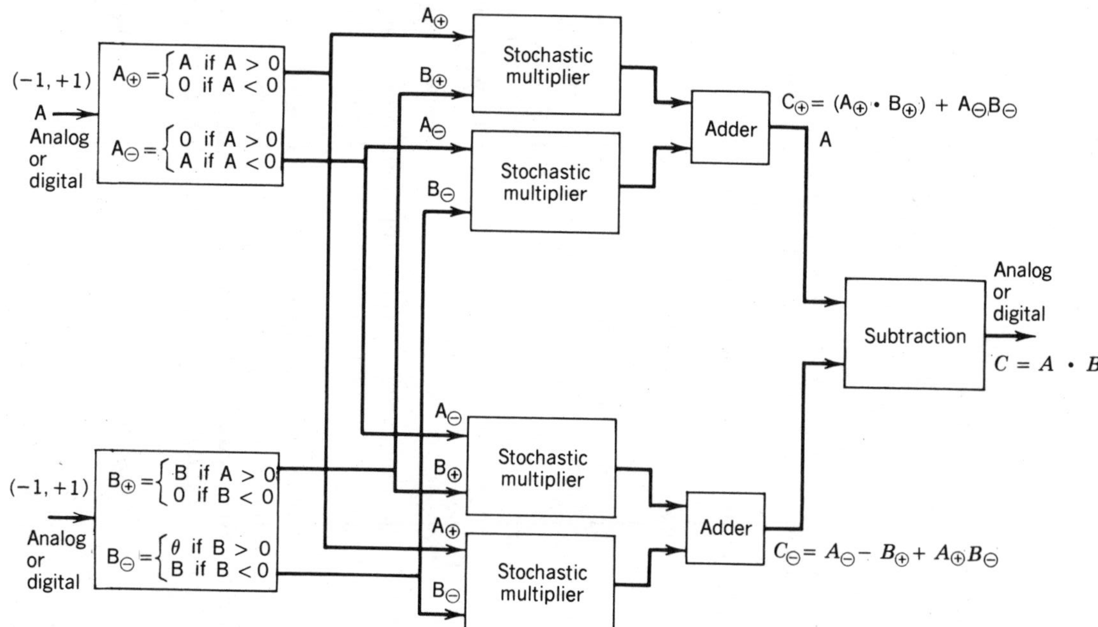

Figure 3.10 *Bipolar stochastic multiplier. (Adapted from Nguyen and Holt.[23] Courtesy and copyright © 1987 by IEEE.)*

Stochastic processing has been proposed by Marks[24] for neural associative memory. This research might lead to a compact architecture for associative networks.

3.8. PROBABILISTIC LOGIC NEURON BASED ON RAM

A random-access memory (RAM) model of the neuron was first proposed by Aleksander,[25] and extended by Kan and Aleksander[26] and by Milligan and Gurney.[27] In most neural nets, training is accomplished by altering weights, resulting in a search through weight space. In RAM networks there are no weights. The contents of the memory and sets of state transitions are modified instead. The RAM unit responds with a randomly generated output on inputs on which it has not been trained. For this reason the unit is called a *probabilistic logic neuron* (PLN).

The generic form of a PLN neuron consists of

1. A set of input lines,
2. A RAM accessed by being given an "address" that is the binary values on the input lines,
3. An output line that returns a binary value,
4. One or more (or none) internal states, which indicate the status of the PLN neuron,
5. One or more control lines, which signify the operation needed to perform (e.g., read or write operation), and
6. The "hardware" to perform the operations.

The PLN neuron used in the multilayer associative network is more complex than the primitive form. First, it has an internal state. The value of the state decides what should be written into the memory of a node during training. Second, unlike the primitive form that stores only binary values, the PLN used in the multilayered associative network has an initial value of "undefined" before training. This value means that the correct answer must be guessed. This value also enhances the performance and the generalization of the network.

According to Kan and Aleksander,[26] a pattern on the input nodes of the network with feedback represents a network state of the network. From one network state, every node determines its next state completely by the contents of its memory. The operation of the network is assumed to be synchronous. A network state has only one exit, and the network states form a set of "confluents" of states (see Figure 3.11). Starting from one state, the network will eventually reach a cycle of states (or one state).

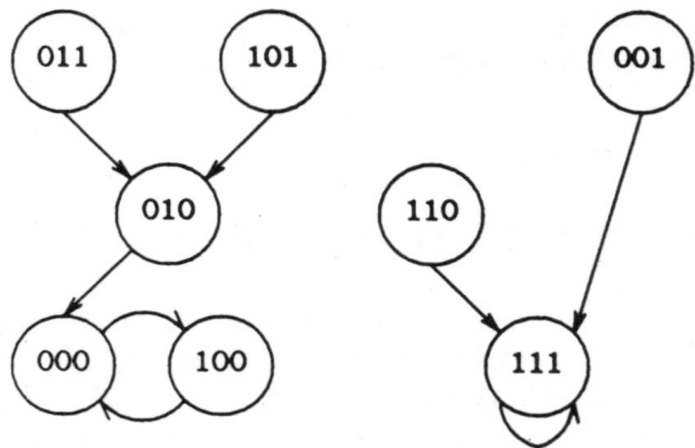

(111) is an invariant state. (000) and (100) are cyclic states. (010) is a transient state, and (001), (011) (110) and (101) are precursor states.

Figure 3.11 *Probabilistic logic neuron: state diagram for three nodes. (Adapted from Kan and Aleksander.[26] Courtesy and copyright © 1987 by IEEE.)*

The set of all possible network states is called the *state space* of the network. There are four kinds of network states:

1. Precursor states, which have no predecessor states;
2. Transient states, which have both successor and predecessor states and are traversed once only;
3. Cyclic states, which are traversed repeatedly once the network enters into any of the states in the cycle; and
4. Invariant states, which are cycles containing only one state.

The network will not change its state once it reaches an invariant state.

The multilayered associative network solves the problem by filling the memory of the nodes with a special value of "undefined" before training. When an addressed location has this value, a random binary value is put on the output of the node. A different value may appear even if the same location is addressed next time. Unless no nodes address locations with the value of "undefined," a state does not have a fixed next state. Therefore the structures of the state space keep changing. The learning algorithms change trained states to invariant states by writing binary values into the appropriate memory locations. When a pattern is given to the input terminals of an address module, each node of the address module writes a binary value into the addressed location if the addressed location has an undefined value. The value to be written is determined by the state of the node.

After the write operation, the state of the node will also change its value. The state of a node has one of three possible values, namely, 1, 0, and undefined. This value indicates which binary value gives the largest differ-

Train pattern	Addressed Location	Created Pat.(Name)	States after learning
101000	uuuuuu	101101 (P1)	010010
101011	uuuuuu	010010 (P2)	uuuuuu
101101	0u11uu	011100 (P3)	100011
101110	1u00uu	100011 (P4)	u1uu00

(*a*) Creation of four internal patterns

	P1	P2	P3
P2	6		
P3	3	3	
P4	3	3	6

(*b*) Hamming distances of the created patterns

Figure 3.12 *An example of the interval pattern creation algorithm. (Adapted from Kan and Aleksander.[26] Courtesy and copyright © 1987 by IEEE.)*

ence from the binary values in the memory of the node. It eliminates counting the number of binary values in the RAM for every learning phase. If the state of a node has a value of 1 or 0, the value of the state will be written into the addressed location and the state of the node changes its value to undefined. If a state has a value of undefined, a random binary value is written into the addressed location and the state of the node takes a value complement to the random value. The states of all nodes have the value of undefined before training. If the addressed location has a binary value, that value will not be changed. The state of the node changes its value to undefined if both the value of the state and the value of the addressed location are the same. Otherwise, the value of the state is the complementary value to that of the addressed location. Figure 3.12 gives an example of how the internal patterns are created in an address module of six nodes, and each node has three input lines. The input patterns all differ in 2 bits. The example shows that the patterns created all have Hamming differences greater than that of the input patterns.

In the system of Kan and Aleksander,[26] training does not involve error propagation but relies instead on the faster method of local adjustment based on Hamming distance amplification. Much work has to be done to fully understand probabilistic logic neuron networks.

3.9. HIGH-ORDER NEURAL UNITS

A neural network is a special-purpose mapping system. The construction of a complex mapping can be split into two steps: (1) crafting the network in advance by embodying prior knowledge about the problem domain; (2) adaptation and learning through communication with the environment.

If crafting is not present, adaptation and learning might be difficult or impossible. After crafting, adaptation and learning can be very efficient within their designated environment. Crafted layers can be used for preprocessing and postprocessing, with the adaptive layers between them.

A priori knowledge could also be built into the individual neural nodes. This leads to higher-order units. Giles and Maxwell[28] define the order by the equation

$$y_i(x) = S\left[w_0(i) + \sum_j w_1(i,j)x(j) + \sum_j \sum_k w_2(i,j,k)x(j)x(k) + \cdots\right] \tag{3.17}$$

A unit that includes terms up to and including degree k will be called a *kth-order unit*. The order of the network should be matched to the order of the problem. A single layer of kth-order units will solve a kth-order problem (as defined by Minsky and Papert[29]).

Note: First-order units are based on addition. Higher-order units use both addition and multiplication.

Why higher-order units? The basic idea is as follows. Neural networks of practical interest must have nonlinear discrimination functions. This can be achieved through a cascade of slabs containing the first-order threshold logic units. However, training in cascades is very difficult, because there is no simple way to provide the hidden units with a training signal. Multislab learning rules, such as back propagation, may require thousands of iterations to converge. Also the system might converge to a local, rather than a global, minimum.

These problems can be overcome by using a single slab of high-order units instead of many slabs of first-order units. Since there are no hidden units to be trained, the extremely fast and reliable single-slab learning rules can be used. Furthermore, the number of units is reduced.

The best representative of high-order units is a Sigma-Pi unit. Other examples include high-order conjunctive connections, associative memories, and high-order extension of the Boltzmann machine.

Using all possible combinations of inputs to build the high-order unit is clearly unfeasible. Giles and Maxwell[28] discussed two ways to minimize the network.

1. Match the order of the network to the order of the problem. As an example, Giles and Maxwell[28] consider the network that should learn the Exclusive-OR problem:

$x(1)$	$x(2)$	$t(x)$
1	1	1
1	−1	−1
−1	1	−1
−1	−1	1

For this second-order problem, consider a second-order unit of the form

$$y(x) = \operatorname{sgn}[w_1(1)x(1) + w_1(2)x(2) + w_2x(1)x(2)] \tag{3.18}$$

with learning rules

$$w'_1(i) = w_1(i) + [t(x) - y(x)]x(i) \tag{3.19}$$

$$w'_2(i) = w_2 + [t(x) - y(x)]x(1)x(2) \tag{3.20}$$

Here $t(x)$ is the correct output for input $x = (x_1, x_2)$. Since there is no correlation between x_1 or x_2 and the desired output $t(x)$, the $w_1(i)$ terms average to zero in the learning process. However, since $x(1)x(2)$ is perfectly correlated with $t(x)$, w_2 converges in one iteration to the solution $w_2 > 0$.

2. Implement invariances. Giles and Maxwell[28] consider the problem of distinguishing between a shifted and rotated T and C. If the T and C are represented within a 3×3 square, one must simultaneously inspect three squares to discriminate between these letters:

```
x x x    x x x
  x      x
  x      x x x
```

Thus the *TC* problem is a third-order problem, requiring a simple third-order unit with short-range (3×3 windows). The unit has the form

$$y(x) = \operatorname{sgn}\left[\sum_{d_{j_1}} \sum_{d_{j_2}} w_3(i, d_{j_1}, d_{j_2}) \sum_j x(j)x(j + d_{j_1})x(j + d_{j_2})\right] \tag{3.21}$$

with weight update rule

$$\begin{aligned} w_3(i, d_{j_1}, d_{j_2}) = {} & w_3(i, d_{j_1}, d_{j_2}) \\ & + \left[t(i) - y(i) + \sum x^s(j)x^s(j + d_{j_1})x^3(j + d_{j_2})\right] \end{aligned} \tag{3.22}$$

where $d_j = j - k$ is the relative coordinate between two point patterns, limited to the 3×3 window. The training procedure converges to a correct set of weights in less than 10 iterations. Note that learning rules with hidden units usually take thousands of iterations to converge.

Giles and Maxwell[28] suggest that a general-purpose learning network might be constructed from specialized modules designed for specific types of tasks and combined with more general networks to handle new and unusual situations.

Although the high-order computational unit is more sophisticated than the first-order unit, it still mimics the operation of a single neuron. How much the unit can do is an open question.

3.10. LEARNING NETWORKS OF NEURONS WITH BOOLEAN LOGIC

Learning and self-organization are not limited only to fine granularity. They could also be applied to networks composed of medium to large grains. An experiment in this direction has been reported by Patarnello and Carnevali.[30] They address the general problem of training a network of Boolean operators (gates) on a set of examples of an operation (addition between two binary operands each of L bits, which gives a result of the same length). Nevertheless, the approach is completely general and permits, in principle, the treatment of any function that maps a string of binary digits into another string. For training, the system is provided with examples of input values together with the corresponding correct results. During the training procedure, the system organizes its connections to minimize, on these examples, the discrepancy between the correct results and those obtained by the network.

Patarnello and Carnevali[30] specify the network by N_G gates and their connections. Each gate has two inputs and an arbitrary number of outputs and realizes one of the 16 possible Boolean functions of two variables. This defines an array Λ_i ($i = 1, \ldots, N_G$) with integer values between 1 and 16 that specifies which of these operations is implemented by the ith gate. The connections are described in terms of two incidence matrices, X^l_{ij} and X^r_{ij}, whose elements are zero except when gate j takes its left (right) input from the output of gate i; then $X^l_{ij} = 1$ ($X^r_{ij} = 1$). The index i can refer either to the output of another gate or to one of the $N_I = 2L$ input bits. The N_I input bits are coded with the negative numbers $-N_I + 1$ to 0. Thus, index j runs from 1 to N_G, the total number of gates, and index i runs from $-N_I + 1$ to N_G. The properties of the matrices X depend on the constraints imposed on the system: in the experiments, a gate can take input either from the input bits or from one of the preceding gates (that is, feedback is not allowed in the circuit). This implies that $X^{(l,r)}_{ij} = 0$ when $i \geq j$. The output bits could in principle be connected to any gate in the network. However, to simplify programming, the output bits are connected to the last L gates of the circuit. The optimization is performed as a Monte Carlo procedure toward zero temperature (simulated annealing[31]), where the energy or "cost function" E

of the system is the difference between the correct result of the operation and the one obtained from the circuit, averaged over the number of examples N_E shown to the system (which are chosen randomly at the beginning and kept fixed during the annealing):

$$E\{\Lambda, X\} \equiv \sum_{l=1}^{L} E_l \equiv \sum_{l=1}^{L} \frac{1}{N_E} \sum_{k=1}^{N_E} (E_{lk} - A_{lk})^2 \tag{3.23}$$

Here E_{lk} is the exact result for the lth bit in the kth example, and A_{lk} is the output for the same bit and example as calculated by the circuit. Therefore, A_{lk} is a function of $\{\Lambda, X\}$. Thus, E is the average number of wrong bits for the examples used in the training and for the network described by $\{\Lambda, X\}$. For a random network, for example, one picked at high temperatures in the annealing procedure, $E_l \sim 1/2$.

The search for the optimal circuit is done over the possible choices for Λ and X. At the beginning of the annealing procedure, Λ is chosen randomly and kept fixed during the annealing procedure. Given this restriction, the "partition function" for the problem is

$$Z = \sum_{(X)} \exp \left| - \frac{E\{X, \Lambda\}}{T} \right| \tag{3.24}$$

A step of the optimization procedure simply consists of changing an input connection of a gate, calculating the resulting energy change ΔE, and accepting the move with probability $\exp[-\Delta E/T]$, where T is the temperature, a parameter that is slowly decreased to zero according to some suitable "annealing schedule."

In principle, evaluating the system is straightforward: given the optimal circuit obtained after the learning procedure, one checks its correctness over the exhaustive set of the operations—specifically all possible additions of two L-bit integers, of which there are $N_0 = 2^L 2^L$. This can be afforded for the set of experiments described here, for which $L = 8$ and $N_0 = 65{,}536$. Thus, another figure of merit is introduced:

$$P \equiv \sum_{l=1}^{L} P_l = \sum_{l=1}^{L} \frac{1}{N_0} \sum_{k=1}^{N_0} (E_{lk} - A_{lk})^2 \tag{3.25}$$

This quantity is defined in the same way as E, but the average is taken over all possible operations, rather than just over the examples used in the training. P is only used after the training procedure as an evaluation tool. Roughly speaking, E and P are all that are needed to understand the behavior of the network: low values of E mean that it is at least capable of "memorizing" the examples shown to it during the training. If P is small as well, then the system was able to generalize properly since it was able to calculate the

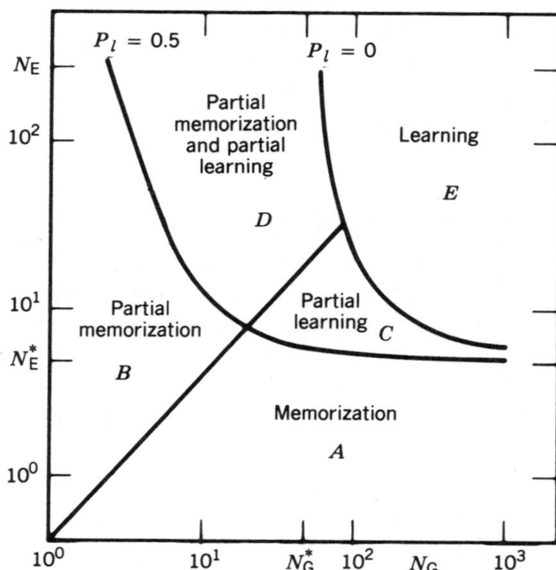

Figure 3.13 *Phase diagram illustrating the different regimes in the plane (N_G, N_E). In region A ($E_l = 0$, $P_l = \frac{1}{2}$), the system only stores the examples. In region B ($E_l > 0$, $P_l = \frac{1}{2}$), memorization is limited by the capacity of the system. In region C ($E_l = 0$, $\frac{1}{2} > P_l > 0$), the system is large enough to store all patterns, and generalization starts to take place. Both memorization and learning are partially achieved in region D ($\frac{1}{2} > P_l$, $E_l > 0$). In region E ($E = P = 0$), the system has been able to fully generalize and is completely error-free. (Adapted from Patarnello and Carnevali.[30])*

correct result for operations it was never exposed to. Therefore, one expects the existence of two regimes (discrimination and generalization), between which possibly a state of "confusion" takes place, as shown in Figure 3.13.

Patarnello and Carnevali[30] forsee many directions for further investigation. For example, relaxing the constraint of quenching for the gate types Λ would probably result in better gate utilization, namely fewer gates needed for a given problem. The application of this approach to more complex problems than binary addition is promising. Moreover, although the main motivations for this work are not related to biology, learning processes in the model show a rich behavior, which could provide some interesting hints. The model opens an interesting approach for pattern recognition and for intelligent system design.

REFERENCES

1. B. Souček and M. Souček, *Neural and Massively Parallel Computers: The Sixth Generation,* Wiley, New York, 1988.

2. B. J. MacLennan, Technology-independent design of neuro-computers: the universal field computer. *Proc. IEEE First Int. Conf. on Neural Networks,* San Diego, June 21–24, 1987, Vol. III, 39–49.
3. D. E. Rumelhart and J. L. McClelland, *Parallel Distributed Processing: Explorations in the Microstructure of Cognition,* Volume 1, MIT Press, Cambridge, MA, 1986.
4. D. E. Rumelhart, G. E. Hinton, and J. L. McClelland, A general framework for parallel distributed processing. In Rumelhart and McClelland (eds.), *Parallel Distributed Processing,* MIT Press, Cambridge, MA, 1986, 45–76.
5. C. von der Marlsburg, Self-organizing of orientation sensitive cells in the striated cortex. *Kybernetic* **14,** 85–100 (1973).
6. S. Grossberg, Adaptive pattern classification and universal recording. *Biol. Cybernet.* **23,** 121–134 (1976).
7. K. Fukushima, Cognitron: A self-organizing multilayered neural network. *Biol. Cybernet.* **20,** 121–136 (1975).
8. K. Fukushima and S. Miyaki, Neocognitron: a new algorithm for pattern recognition tolerant of deformations and shift in position. *Pattern Recognition* **15**(6), 455–469 (1982).
9. T. Kohonen. Clustering, taxonomy and topological maps of patterns. In Lang (ed.), *Pattern Recognition,* IEEE Computer Society Press, Silver Spring, MD, 1982.
10. D. E. Rumelhart and D. Zipser, Feature discovery by competitive learning. In Rumelhart and McClelland (eds.), *Parallel Distributed Processing,* MIT Press, Cambridge, MA, 1986, 151–193.
11. J. J. Hopfield, Neural networks and physical systems with collective computational abilities. *Proc. Nat. Acad. Sci. U.S.A.* **79,** 2554–2558 (1982).
12. R. Hecht-Nielsen, Kolmogorov's mapping neural network existence theorem. *Proc. IEEE First Int. Conf. on Neural Networks,* San Diego, June 21–24, 1987, Vol. III, 11–14.
13. S. Schrier, R. L. Barron, and L. O. Gilstrap, Polynomial and neural networks: analogies and engineering applications. *Proc. IEEE First Int. Conf. on Neural Networks,* San Diego, June 21–24, 1987, Vol. III, 431–439.
14. F. Rosenblatt, *Principles of Neurodynamics,* Spartan, New York, 1962.
15. T. J. Sejnowski and C. R. Rosenberg, Parallel networks that learn to pronounce English text. *Complex Syst.* **1,** 145–168 (1987).
16. J. L. McClelland and D. E. Rumelhart, *Parallel Distributed Processing,* Volume 2, MIT Press, Cambridge, MA, 1986.
17. R. J. Marks II, L. E. Atlas, S. Oh, and J. A. Ritcey, The performance of convex set projection based neural networks. In Anderson (ed.), *Neural Information Processing Systems,* American Institute of Physics, New York, 1988, 534–543.
18. R. J. Marks II, S. Oh, L. E. Atlas, and J. A. Ritcey, Homogeneous and layered alternating projection neural networks. *Proc. SPIE Int. Symp. on Optimal Engineering and Industrial Sensing for Advanced Manufacturing Technology,* Dearborn, MI, June 1988.
19. H. Stark, *Image Recovery,* Academic Press, New York, 1987.
20. B. R. Gaines, *A Stochastic Analog Computer.* Standard Telecommunication Laboratories Internal Memorandum, 1–10 (1965).

21. W. J. Poppelbaum and C. Afuso, *Noise Computer*. Quarterly Technical Reports, University of Illinois, April 1965–January 1966.

22. S. Ribeiro, Random pulse machine. *IEEE Trans. Computers,* **EC-16,** 261–276 (1967).

23. D. Nguyen and F. Holt, Stochastic processing in a neural network application. *Proc. IEEE First Int. Conf. on Neural Networks,* San Diego 1987, Vol. III, 281–291.

24. R. Marks II, Class of continuous level associative memory neural nets. *Appl. Optics* **26**(10), 2005–2010 (1987).

25. I. Aleksander, *Microcircuit Learning Computers,* Mills and Boon, London, 1971.

26. W. Kan and I. Aleksander, A probabilistic logic neuron network for associative learning. *Proc. IEEE First Int. Conf. on Neural Networks,* San Diego, 1987, Vol. II, 541–548.

27. D. K. Milligan and K. N. Gurney, RAM-unit learning networks. *Proc. IEEE First Int. Conf. on Neural Networks,* San Diego 1987, Vol. II, 557–566.

28. C. L. Giles and T. Maxwell, Learning, invariance and generalization in high-order neural networks. *Appl. Optics* **26**(23), 4972–4976 (1987).

29. M. L. Minski and S. Papert, *Perceptrons,* MIT Press, Cambridge, MA, 1969.

30. S. Patarnello and P. Carnevali, Learning networks of neurons with Boolean logic. *Europhys. Lett.* **4**(4), 503–508 (1987).

31. S. Kirkpatrik, C. D. Gelatt, and M. P. Vecchi, *Science* **220,** 671 (1983).

CHAPTER 4

Neural Networks in Real-Time Applications

INTRODUCTION AND SURVEY

Real-time sensory functions, process control, and motor control are the most meaningful tasks for neural computing. A neural network can be successfully trained to recognize the features in a signal, speech, or image. By observing samples, neural networks are fully capable of discovering hidden information in industrial process control. As a result, the network can learn the data and develop a control law with minimal assistance from specialists. Thus, conventional analytical work and model building are avoided or minimized.

This chapter presents selected real-time applications of neural networks. Signal processing covers sonar, electrocardiograms (EKG), noise cancelation, speech recognition, and the phonetic typewriter. Image analysis is described on the examples of manufacturing inspection, pattern recognition, reading handprinted characters, adaptive resonance theory, and categorization based on multiple neural networks. Process control applications include web winding, tank filling, pole balancing based on a graded learning network, and robot manipulator control.

In most cases no initial data collection, extensive system analysis, or model construction is needed. The networks are able to achieve near-optimal performance without a priori knowledge about the structure of the signals to be classified or processes to be controlled.

4.1. GORMAN-SEJNOWSKI SONAR SIGNAL PROCESSING

This section is based on the work of Gorman and Sejnowski,[1,2] who applied neural networks to a sonar target classification problem. Networks were trained to classify sonar returns from an undersea metal cylinder and a cylindrically shaped rock of comparable size.

The networks used were feedforward with two or three layers of processing units with continuous-valued outputs. The output of the ith unit was obtained by calculating the activation level E_i:

$$E_i = \sum_j w_{ij} p_j + b_i \tag{4.1}$$

where w_{ij} is the weight from the jth to the ith unit, p_j is the output of unit j, and b_i is the bias of the ith unit. A sigmoidal transformation was then applied to the activation level to obtain the ith unit's state or output p_i:

$$p_i = \mathrm{P}(E_i) = \frac{1}{1 + e^{-\beta E_i}} \tag{4.2}$$

where β is a constant that determined the slope of the sigmoid at $E_i = 0$ ($\beta = 1.0$ for these experiments). The input layer was made up of 60 units, each unit being clamped to an amplitude value of the signal to be classified. The number of output units was arbitrarily set at two. The states of the output units determined the class of the signal: (1,0) represented a return from the metal cylinder, and (0,1) represented a return from the rock. Experiments were conducted using networks with two layers and networks with a hidden layer. A schematic of the three-layered architecture is shown in Figure 4.1.

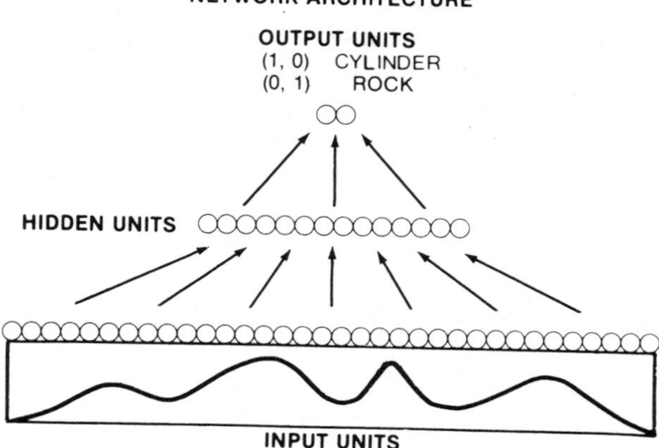

Figure 4.1 *Schematic diagram of the network. The bottom layer has 60 processing units with their states "clamped" to the amplitude of the preprocessed sonar signal, shown in analog form below the units. The two output units at the top represent the two sonar targets to be identified. The layer of hidden units between the input and output layers allows the network to extract high-order signal features. The connections between the layers of units are represented by arrows. (Reprinted by permission from Gorman and Sejnowski.[1] Copyright © 1988 by Pergamon Press.)*

The back-propagation learning algorithm (Rumelhart, Hinton, and Williams[3]) was used to train the network. The networks were simulated on a Ridge 32 computer (comparable to a VAX 780 FPA in computational power), using a simulator written in the C programming language developed at The Johns Hopkins University.

The data used for the network experiments were sonar returns collected from a metal cylinder and a cylindrically shaped rock positioned on a sandy ocean floor.

Gorman and Sejnowski[1] selected a set of 208 returns (111 cylinder returns and 97 rock returns) from a total set of 1200 returns on the basis of the strength of the specular return (4.0 to 15.0 dB SNR). An average of five returns was selected from each aspect angle. Figure 4.2 shows a sample return from the rock and the cylinder. The temporal signal was filtered, and spectral information was extracted and used to represent the signal on the input layer.

The preprocessing used to obtain the spectral envelope is indicated schematically in Figure 4.3, where a set of sampling apertures (Figure 4.3*a*) is superimposed over the two-dimensional display of a short-term Fourier transform spectrogram of the sonar return. As shown in Figures 4.3*b*,*c*, the spectral envelope $P_{t_0,v_0}(\eta)$ was obtained by integrating over each aperture. The spectral envelope was composed of 60 spectral samples, normalized to take values between 0.0 and 1.0.

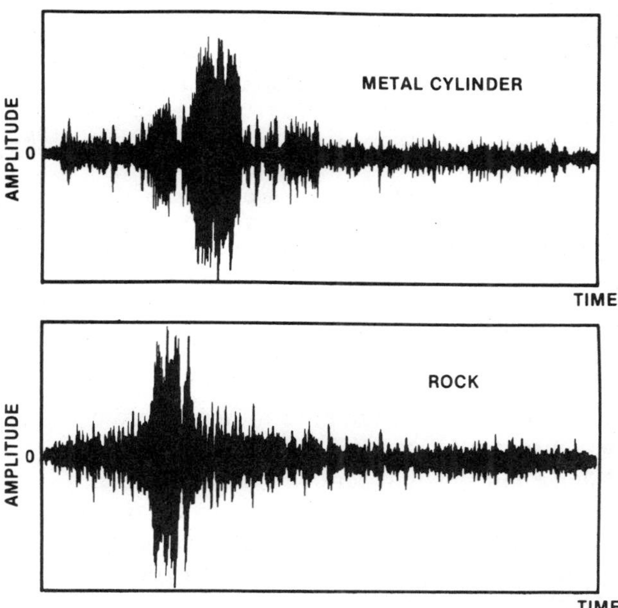

Figure 4.2 *Amplitude displays of a typical return from the cylinder and the rock as a function of time. (Reprinted by permission from Gorman and Sejnowski.[1] Copyright © 1988 by Pergamon Press.)*

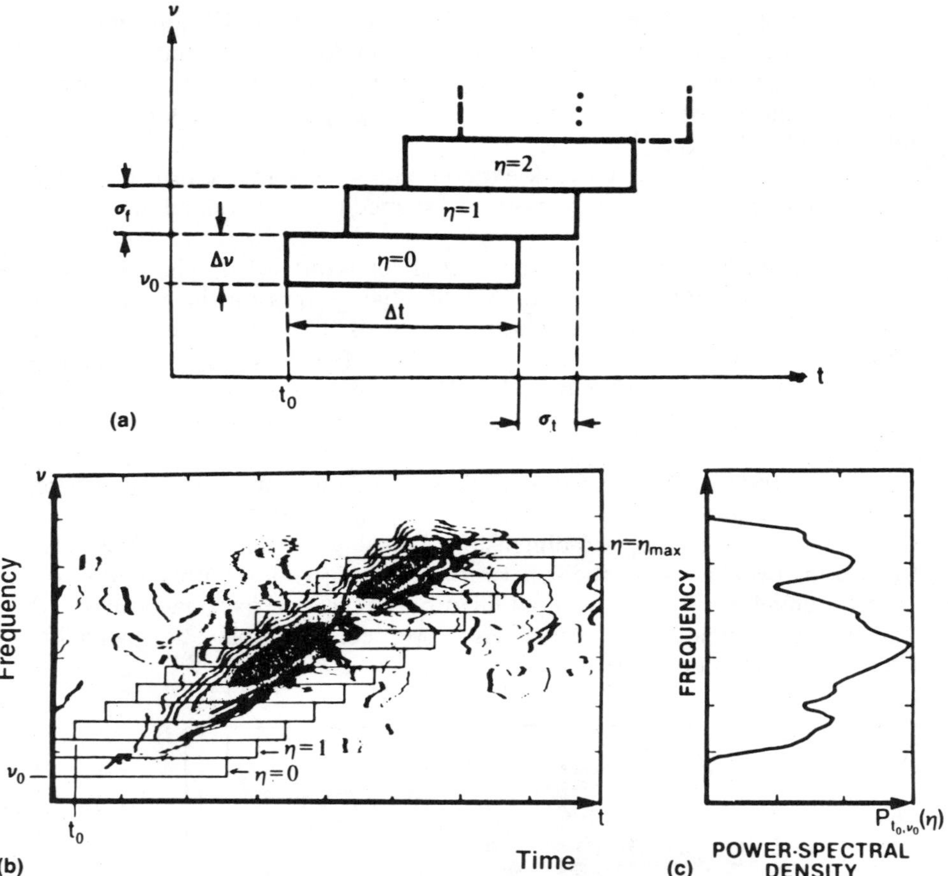

Figure 4.3 *The preprocessing of the sonar signal produces a sampled spectral envelope normalized to vary from 0.0 to 1.0 for input to the network. (a) The set of sampling apertures offset temporarily to correspond to the slope of the FM chirp. (b) Sampling apertures superimposed over the two-dimensional display of the short-term Fourier transform. (c) The spectral envelope obtained by integrating over each sampling aperture. (Reprinted by permission from Gorman and Sejnowski.[1] Copyright © 1988 by Pergamon Press.)*

The number of hidden units required to accurately classify the returns was determined empirically.

The aspect-angle independent series conducted using randomly selected training sets consisted of 130 trials for each network with a given number of hidden units. The overall performance of each network was taken to be the average over a set of 13 values obtained from experiments with different training sets. These 13 values were in turn averages over 10 trials differing in initial conditions. Figure 4.4 shows the overall average learning curves for three of the networks trained on randomly selected returns.

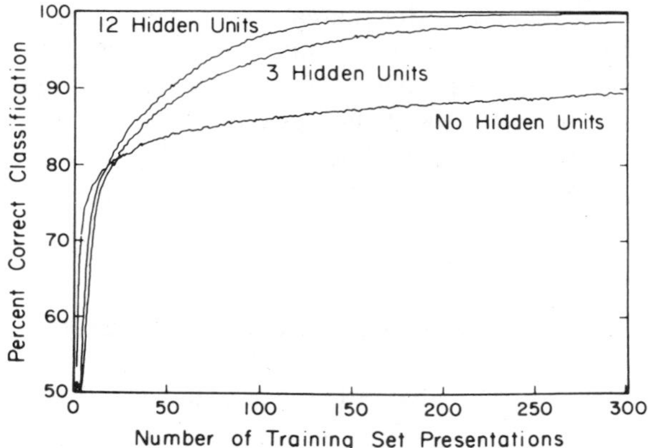

Figure 4.4 *Network learning curves for the aspect-angle independent series of experiments using randomly chosen training sets. Each curve represents an average of 130 learning trials for a network with the specified number of hidden units. (Reprinted by permission from Gorman and Sejnowski.[1] Copyright © 1988 by Pergamon Press.)*

Figure 4.5 shows the pattern of weights of a network with three hidden units trained to classify returns from the rock and cylinder. Each hidden unit is represented in the figure by a labeled gray region. The area of the rectangles within these regions is proportional to the absolute value of the weights on connections to other units in the network. White and black rectangles represent positive and negative weights, respectively. The lower set of 60 rectangles represents weights on the connections from input units. The two upper rectangles in the center represent weights to the output units, and the single rectangle in the upper left represents the weight from the true unit or bias to the hidden unit.

According to Gorman and Sejnowski,[1] network classifiers should provide a viable alternative to existing machine-based techniques. The performance

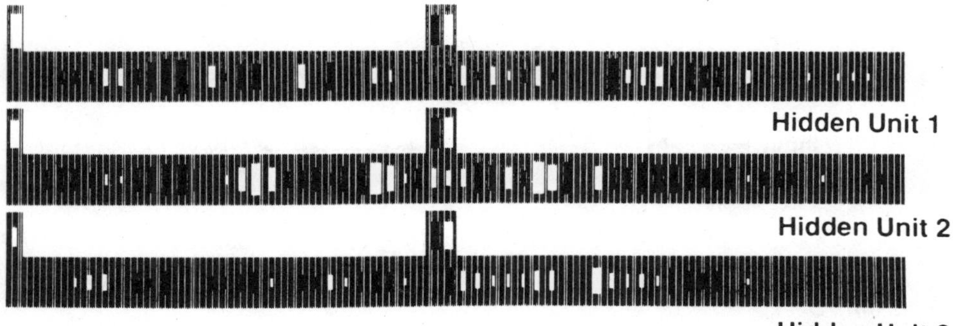

Figure 4.5 *The weight pattern for a trained network with three hidden units. (Reprinted by permission from Gorman and Sejnowski.[1] Copyright © 1988 by Pergamon Press.)*

of the network classifiers is better than a nearest-neighbor classifier and less expensive in terms of storage and computation. In addition, the networks are able to achieve near-optimal performance without requiring a priori knowledge or assumptions about the underlying statistical structure of the signals to be classified. Finally, and perhaps most importantly, the network's performance and classification strategy appear to be comparable to those of humans.

4.2. WIDROW-WINTER ADAPTIVE NOISE CANCELER

An adaptive linear neuron called Adaline was developed by Widrow.[4] The output of Adaline is compared with a desired response, the difference or

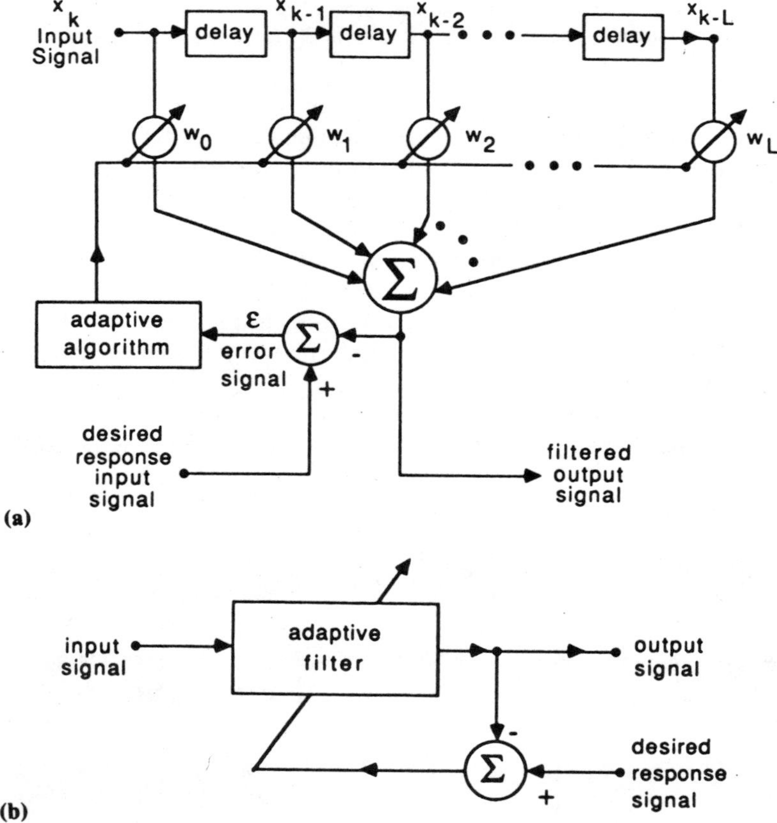

Figure 4.6 *Adaptive digital filter: (a) details of a tapped-delay-line digital filter; (b) symbolic representation of an adaptive filter. (Reprinted by permission from Widrow and Winter.[7] Copyright © 1988 by IEEE.)*

error is used to adjust the weights, and the Widrow-Hoff least mean square algorithm[5] is used to minimize the error. Ridgway[6] combines several Adalines into a system called Madalines (many Adalines). Widrow and Winter[7] use adaptive neurons as a part of an adaptive filter and noise canceler.

An adaptive digital filter is shown in Figure 4.6. The sampled input signal is applied to a string of delay boxes, each delaying the signal by one sampling period. An adaptive linear combiner produces an output that is a linear combination of the current and past input signal samples. The desired response is supplied during training. The weights are usually adjusted so that the output signal provides the best least square match over time to the desired response.

Figure 4.7 shows an adaptive filter used for noise canceling. Figure 4.7*a* shows the classical approach; the optimal filter passes a signal s without distortion while stopping the noise n_0. Figure 4.7*b* shows the adaptive noise canceling principle. This approach is viable only when an additional reference input is available containing noise n_1, which is correlated with the original corrupting noise n_0. The adaptive filter filters the noise n_1 and subtracts the result from the primary input $s + n_0$. For this adaptive filter, the noisy input $s + n_0$ acts as the desired response. The "system output" acts as

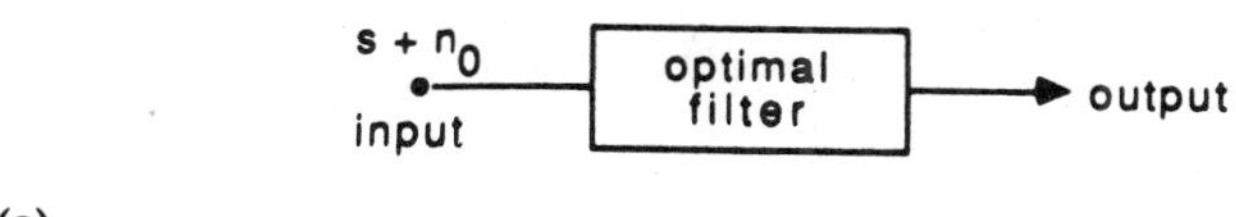

(a)

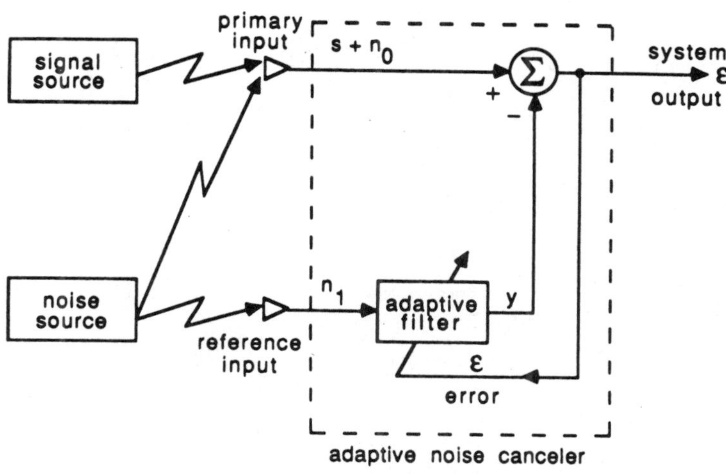

(b)

Figure 4.7 *Separation of signal and noise: (a) classical approach; (b) adaptive noise canceling approach. (Reprinted by permission from Widrow and Winter.[7] Copyright © 1988 by IEEE.)*

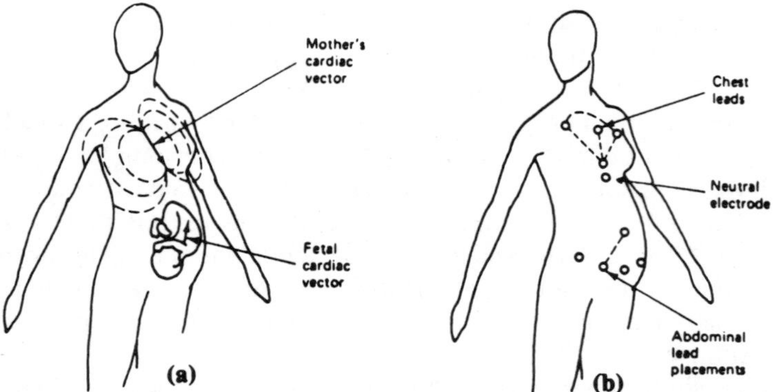

Figure 4.8 *Canceling maternal heartbeat in fetal electrocardiography:* (*a*) *cardiac electric field vector of mother and fetus;* (*b*) *placement of leads.* (*Reprinted by permission from Widrow and Winter.*[7] *Copyright © 1988 by IEEE.*)

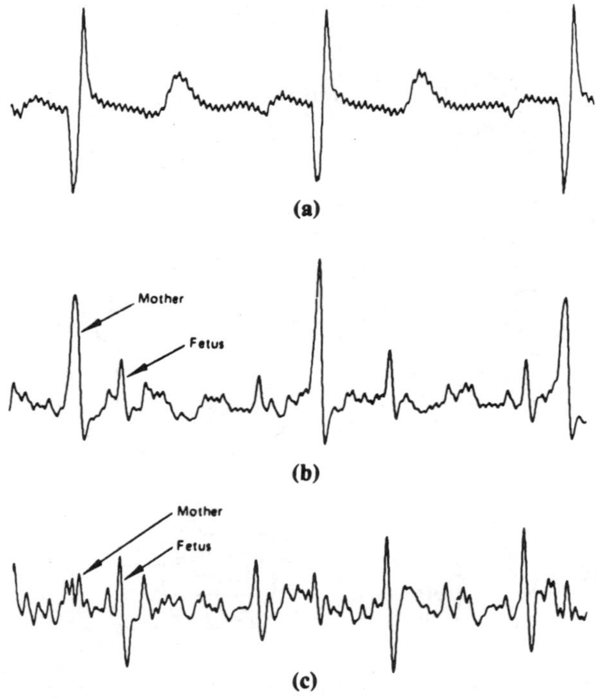

Figure 4.9 *Result of fetal EKG experiment* (*bandwith 3–35 Hz, sampling rate 256 Hz*): (*a*) *reference input* (*chest lead*); (*b*) *primary input* (*abdominal lead*); (*c*) *noise canceler output.* (*Reprinted by permission from Widrow and Winter.*[7] *Copyright © 1988 by IEEE.*)

the error for the adaptive filter. Adaptive noise canceling generally performs much better than the classical filtering approach because the noise is subtracted out rather than filtered out.

Widrow and Winter use adaptive noise canceling in EKG experiments. The system is used to cancel the interference from the mother's heart when attempting to record clear fetal electrocardiograms. Figure 4.8 shows the locations of the fetal and maternal hearts and the placement of the input leads. The abdominal leads provide the primary input containing fetal EKG and interfering maternal EKG. The chest leads provide the reference input or noise, which contains pure interference (the maternal EKG). Figure 4.9 shows the results. The maternal EKG was adaptively filtered and subtracted from the abdominal signal, leaving the fetal EKG.

4.3. EKG PROCESSING ON AN ANZA NEUROCOMPUTER

In conventional approaches to the gathering and processing of EKG signals, noise must be removed from the signal before the signal can be used. Sophisticated filtering techniques are currently used to remove unwanted information from the data. This filtering operates on frequency information found in the data, rejecting high frequencies thought to be unrelated to a valid EKG signal. Even though an EKG signal appears to be relatively low frequency, those portions of the signal with rapidly changing values contain high-frequency components that can be affected by filtering. If the filter frequency is set high enough to minimize distortion of the EKG signal, high-frequency noise is also allowed through the filter. If portions of the EKG signal are relatively weak with respect to the noise, human observers may have trouble identifying them when the EKG signal is displayed on a CRT.

A neural network has been successfully trained to recognize the features in a normal EKG signal. A short overview of the network, based on ANZA manuals, follows. A powerful learning method was used in conjunction with the ANZA and ANZA Plus products to learn those portions of an EKG signal that repeat periodically. During the learning process, the neural network reinforced features that appeared periodically while suppressing random noise. The network was eventually able to reproduce the features learned at its output.

New data were then presented to the trained network, and the learned features were identified and reproduced at the network output. Since minimal learning of noise signals had occurred, minimal noise was reproduced at the output. The resulting EKG signal showed no high-frequency distortion. The trained network was also able to identify a valid EKG signal even when it was buried in the noise and not seen by human observers. The neural network provided results that were superior to conventional approaches in use today.

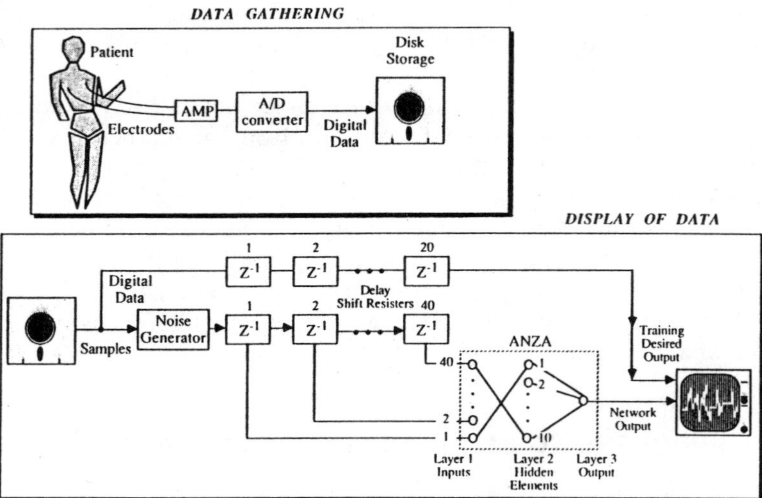

Figure 4.10 *EKG processing on ANZA neurocomputer. (Courtesy and copyright © 1988 by Hecht-Nielsen Neurocomputer Corporation.)*

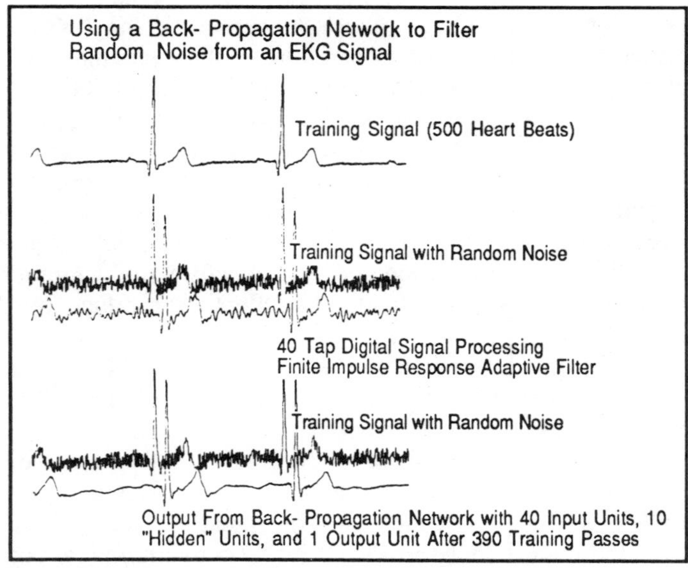

Figure 4.11 *EKG processing. Training and output signals. (Courtesy and copyright © 1988 by Hecht-Nielsen Neurocomputer Corporation.)*

There is no need to develop a conventional algorithmic program for signal processing. The network learns from exposure to the data. A neural network can learn to identify features even when the data are noisy.

The network was configured with 40 input processing elements (PEs), 10 PEs in the hidden layer, and 1 output PE, as shown in Figure 4.10. The network was trained by running the original EKG signal in parallel with 10 or 20 different noisy variations of the same signal with varying levels of noise. Within 400 training passes, the network was delivering a clean signal when presented with a very noisy input. The results are presented in Figure 4.11.

A back-propagation network can be used in place of a digital signal processing (DSP) filter, and the EKG application demonstrated the advantages of a neural network in continuous signal processing. Unlike the DSP filter, which has fixed bandwidth over the entire cycle of a repetitive signal such as an EKG, the neural network displays a selective response. In effect, the network "knows" the general shape of EKG signals and adapts its bandwidth over time to fit that shape. This makes it capable of filtering out low-level high-frequency noise in the EKG without suppressing the (also high-frequency) QRS signal, which is an important indicator of the strength of the heart.

4.4. SPEECH RECOGNITION

Voice recognition systems (VRS) must sample or learn a word in the way that humans speak it. These devices have important applications, especially in "hands-free" environments, which include various dispatching services, counting, manipulating, operation of machines by voice, and product and parcel routing. Particular applications involve baggage routing, reservations

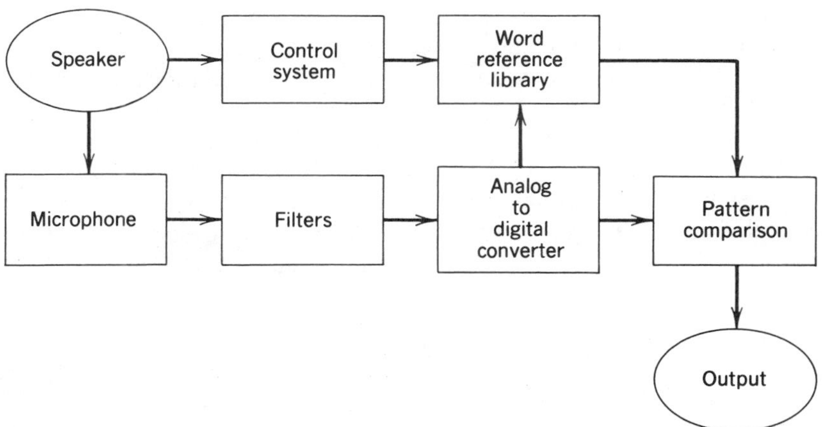

Figure 4.12 *Typical voice recognition system.*

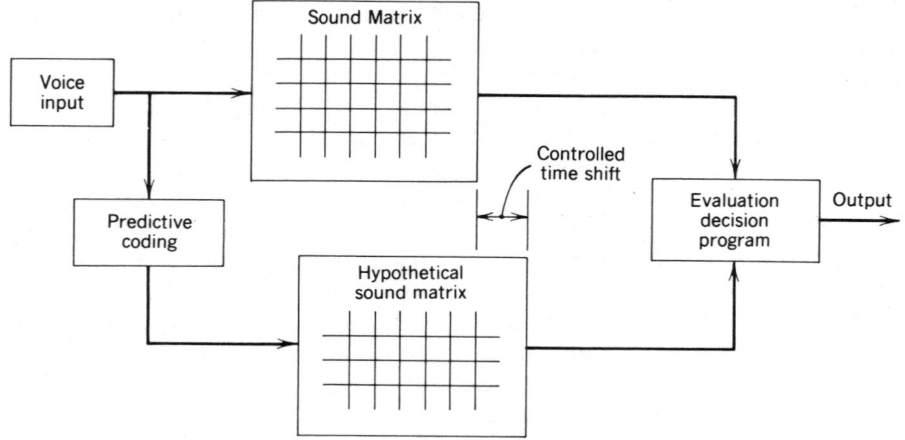

Figure 4.13 *Dynamic programming in voice recognition system.*

systems, inventory control, automated query systems, inspection and grading of produce, microscope-telescope-based data entry, and aids for handicapped people.

The simplest speaker-dependent VRS samples each word up to 100 times per second. During this teach mode, the VRS digitizes this information and stores it as a series of matrices in memory. Later, when a word is spoken into the system, the VRS compares the new speech input matrix with the matrices stored in memory. When a match is obtained, the computer responds with the preprogrammed routine to fit that matrix. A typical VRS is shown in Figure 4.12. Such a system has a limited vocabulary. For a larger vocabulary, more memory is needed and the response time increases.

A more efficient way of developing VRS is dynamic programming. The principle is outlined in Figure 4.13. It utilizes a shifting comparison of the actual sound input matrix and a predicted match matrix. Thus, a sort of floating sample-matching device eliminates defined memory point storage.

More advanced systems convert the time waveform into the frequency domain, where the parameters are given about 100 times per second. Usually the fast Fourier transform (FFT) on the speech signal sampled at 10 kHz is used to produce frames consisting of 128 frequency points. These frames become the input pattern for the neural network, as described by Prager, Harrison, and Fallside,[8] Rumelhart and McClelland,[9] and Kohonen.[10]

4.5. KOHONEN PHONETIC TYPEWRITER

The Kohonen[10] phonetic typewritter is a neural speech recognition system that recognizes phonetic units, called *phonemes,* from a continuous speech signal. The acoustic preprocessor of the Kohonen[10] system consists of

1. A noise-canceling microphone;
2. A preamplifier with a switched-capacitor, 5.3-kHz low-pass filter;
3. A 12-bit ADC with 13.02-kHz sampling rate;
4. A 256-point computed every 9.83 ms using a 256-point Hamming window;
5. Logarithmization and filtering of spectral powers by a fourth-order elliptic low-pass filter;
6. Grouping of spectral channels into a 15-component real-pattern vector;
7. Subtraction of the average from all components; and
8. Normalization of the resulting vector into constant length.

Operations 3 through 8 are computed by the signal processor chip TMS 32010 (this design is four years old: much faster processors are now available).

The instantaneous spectral power values on the channels formed from the FFT can be regarded as a 15-dimensional real vector in a Euclidean space. We might think that the spectra of the different phonemes of speech occupy different regions of this space so that they could be detected by some kind of multidimensional discrimination method.

Imagine now that a fixed number of discrete neurons is in parallel, looking at the speech spectrum or the set of input signals. Imagine that each neuron has a template, a reference spectrum with respect to which the degree of matching with the input spectrum can be defined. Imagine further that the different neurons compete, the neuron with the highest matching score being regarded as the "winner." The input spectrum would then be assigned to the winner in the same way that an arbitrary vector is assigned to the closest reference vector.

Figure 4.14 outlines the principle of operation of the Kohonen network. It uses an association matrix connecting two pools of units: input units (frequency frame vector) and output units (phonemes). Each node in one layer is connected to all the nodes of the opposite layer through adaptive synapses.

On top of the association matrix is a "Mexican hat" feedback matrix. Each neuron is connected to its neighbors laterally. The coupling coefficients of the feedback connections are not adaptive. The strengths of the lateral connections as a function of distance have a form like a Mexican hat. Hence, an active neuron inhibits its neighbors in the negative parts of the hat. Various neurons of the network become sensitized to spectra of different phonemes. The input spectra are clustered around phonemes, and the process finds these clusters. The maps can be calibrated by using spectra of known phonemes. If a new or unknown spectrum is presented at the inputs,

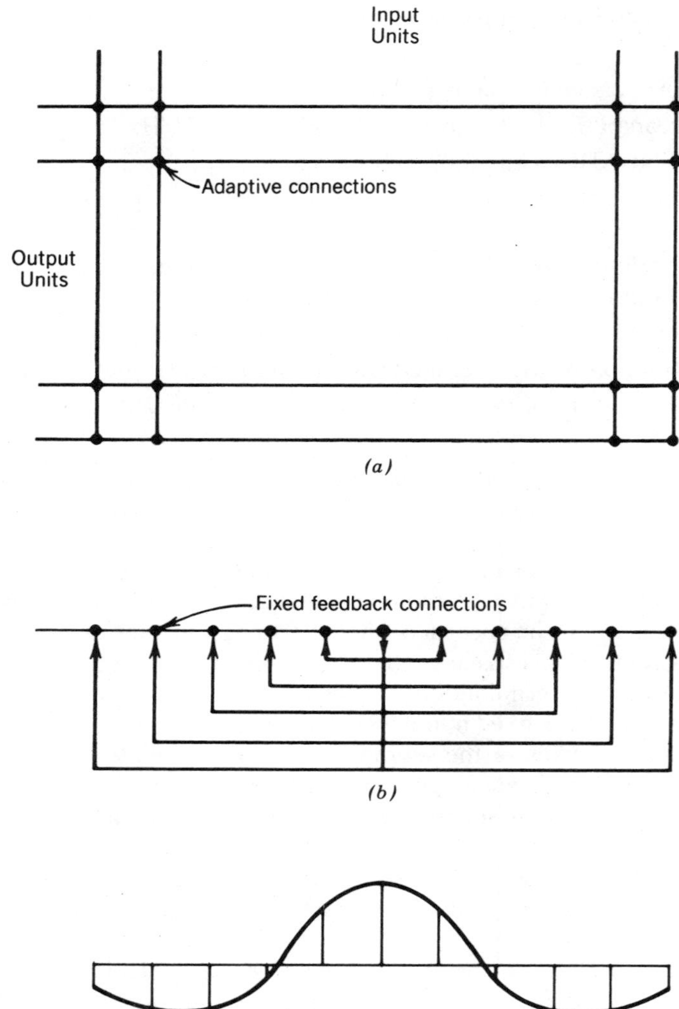

Figure 4.14 *Kohonen phonetic typewriter:* (a) *association matrix;* (b) *feedback matrix;* (c) *"Mexican hat"—the strengths of lateral connections in feedback matrix as a function of distance.*

the neuron with the closest transmittance vector gives the response, and classification occurs.

The "Mexican hat" as a function of distance or as a function of time has been observed in experiments with real neural and behavioral structures. Souček and Carlson[11] observed a similar function for a communication system based on light flashes in fireflies (*Photinus macdermotti*). In biological structures the function performs time (or distance) clustering and discrimination.

Kohonen's[10] phonetic typewritter includes postprocessing of phonemes in symbolic form. The phonemes are influenced by neighboring phonemes. There may be many hundreds of different *frames* or *contexts* of neighboring phonemes in which a particular phoneme may occur. Kohonen[10] has developed a context-sensitive grammar, the rules of which are derived from real experiments. By combining neural and symbolic processing, he achieved isolated-word recognition from a 1000-word vocabulary with an accuracy of 96 to 98 percent.

4.6. IMAGE ANALYSIS AND VISUAL RECOGNITION

Visual recognition[12] has been defined as the addition of some form of computer intelligence and decision making to digitized visual information received in a machine sensor. The combined information is then utilized to control robotic movement or conveyor speed, or to perform production inspection.

A typical visual recognition system is shown in Figure 4.15. The system could be broken down into the following components:

- Light source;
- Image sensor (camera, etc.);
- Image digitizer;
- Pattern recognition computer;
- Custom software;
- System control computer; and
- Input control unit.

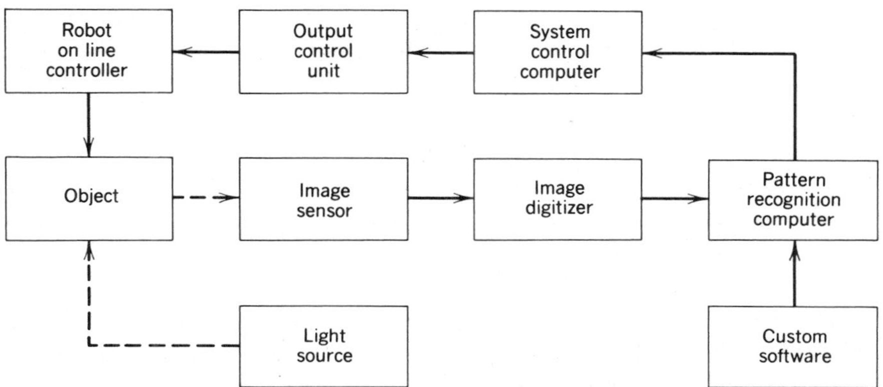

Figure 4.15 *Typical machine-vision system.*

Visual recognition is composed of several steps:

1. The image sensor surveys an object. Through the scanning process the object's image is broken down into pixels.
2. The computer determines the object's highlights according to the pixels (curved outline of a bottle, or the concavity of a tea cup).
3. Shape, size, outline, edge, and dimensionality are considered.
4. Object characteristics are compared and correlated to image characteristics previously entered into the system's memory.
5. An algorithmic rule-based expert system or an adaptive neural network is used.

Applications of visual recognition include

- Checking package labels;
- Object acquisition by robot arms;
- Guidance of seam welders;
- Printed circuit board inspection;
- Electronic component inspection;
- Electronic component identification;
- Inspection of integrated circuit masks;
- Screening of x-ray images;
- Checking castings;
- Real terrain analysis;
- Landing site selection;
- Remote planetary landing;
- Blood cell sorting;
- Interpretation of maps;
- Recognition of faces using a TV camera;
- Processing of images from satellites to identify specific features;
- Cell screening and identification of cells; and
- Industrial inspection and quality control.

4.7. REBER-LYMAN ROTATION AND SCALE-INVARIANT PATTERN RECOGNITION EXPERIMENTS

Brousil and Smith[13] suggested the use of a preprocessing unit for classification problems dealing with pattern translation, rotation, and dilation. A property filter, based upon two successive Fourier transforms (FTs) was developed for generalizing the recognition of translated, rotated, and scaled classes of two-dimensional images. Weiman and Chaikin[14] describe a logarithmic spiral grid for picture digitization.

Reber and Lyman[15] propose the following pattern transformations: (1) polar transform, (2) log/polar transform, and (3) one-dimensional discrete FT. The polar transform converts rotation and scale changes of a pattern to translations along either the angular or radial axes. The log/polar transform produces a logarithmic coordinate mapping of the radial axis of the polar transform. Therefore, translations along the log/radial axis, resulting from scale changes to a pattern, appear more linear. The magnitude of the one-dimensional discrete FT will remove the translation associated with the angular axis, or the radial or log/radial axis, of the polar or log/polar transforms.

Reber and Lyman[15] performed a set of experiments on the TRW MARK III ANS processor. Mapping functions were defined for implementing the polar, log, and one-dimensional discrete FT.

The ANS experimental design consists of seven slabs or parallel computational structures as shown in Figure 4.16.

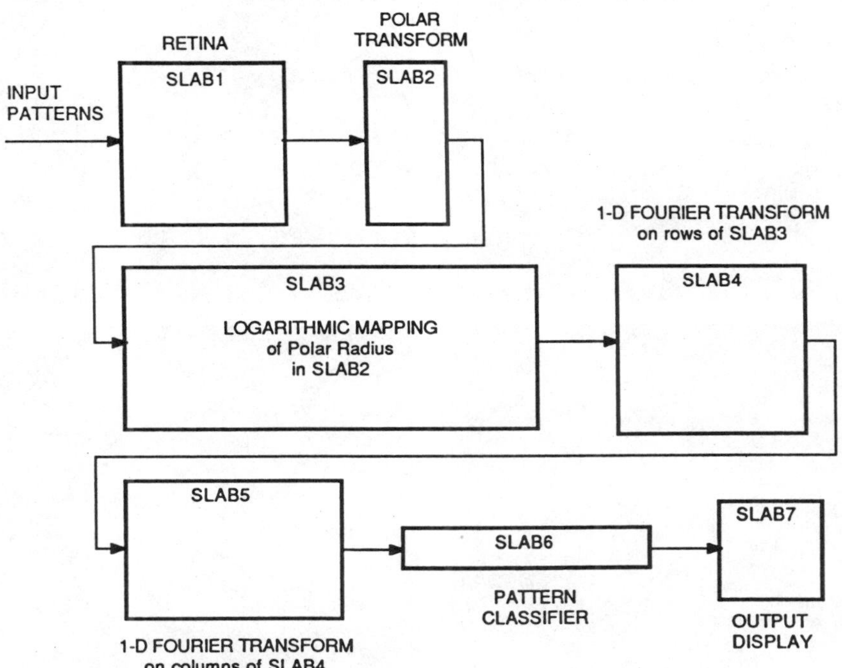

Figure 4.16 *Schematic diagram of the proposed ANS experimental design. (Reprinted by permission from Reber and Lyman.[15] Copyright © 1987 by IEEE.)*

Slab 1	Input pattern display	32 × 32 PEs
Slab 2	Polar transform	28 × 14
Slab 3	Log/polar transform	28 × 79
Slab 4	One-dimensional FT on log/polar rows	28 × 40
Slab 5	One-dimensional FT on slab 3 FT columns	15 × 40
Slab 6	Classifier	1 × 36
Slab 7	Output display	7 × 5

The entire experimental design required 5419 PEs and 238.266 PE interconnections.

Figure 4.17 illustrates the recognition of the letter *E* at 2× in any of the four 90° orientations. Note the invariance of the generalized representation in slab 5 for the different orientations. Throughout the simulations, the invariance indicated by slab 5 was much stronger for rotation than for scale. The training set consisted of a single instance of character *E* at 4× and 0° rotations. The results indicate the stability of the ANS design to produce a representation in slab 5 that is generalized for both scale and rotation variations to the input pattern.

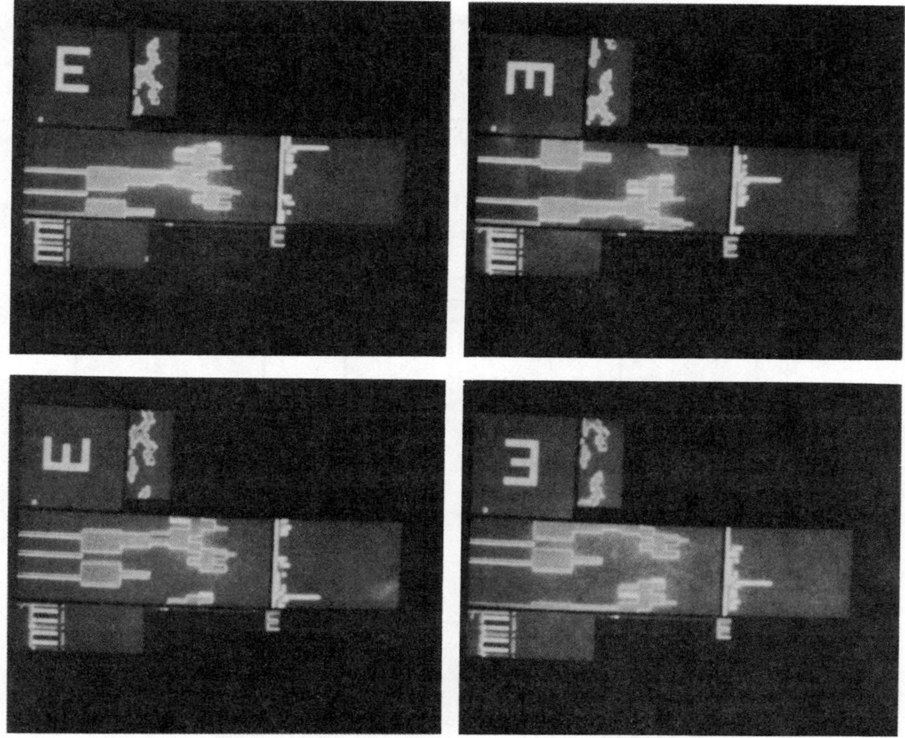

Figure 4.17 *Rotation- and scale-invariant classification of E. (Reprinted by permission from Reber and Lyman.[15] Copyright © 1987 by IEEE.)*

4.8. LIGHTWARE-ANZA MANUFACTURING INSPECTION

Neural network capabilities are used to analyze images and to identify specific features or characteristics within those images. The "smart camera" system produces two-dimensional FTs, which are sampled to produce a "signature" of the original image. A short overview of the system based on Lightware-ANZA manuals follows. The back-propagation network on a host PC/AT is used to classify the signatures and their images as required by the problem being solved. Examples of uses for this system include checking orientation of labels on bottles, inspecting assembled products, or measuring particle sizes on a conveyer belt.

Fourier image analysis reduces the time and expense required for installing a real-time automated inspection system on the factory floor. Objects do not need to be precisely fixed in the field of view because the Fourier analysis is shift-tolerant. Objects may wobble, rotate, or be scaled in the field of view, and these changes are conveniently represented in the Fourier features. The smart camera manages the timing for high-speed asynchronous image acquisition, providing interfaces for a position sensor, strobe light, and charge-coupled device (CCD) video camera. Real-time statistical process control (SPC) information, utilizing a universal "goodness-of-fit" metric, is available for on-screen display or transfer to factory computer integrated manufacturing (CIM) computers via standard RS-232.

The smart camera provides a new technique for analyzing images in real time. Applications include high-speed food, beverage, packing, and pharmaceutical inspection, verification, and sorting. The smart camera is inexpensive and easy to integrate into turnkey factory inspection systems. The essential performance advantages for lightware laser technology include:

- Fast processing speed;
- Global characterization of video images;
- Universal image analysis and massive data compaction for all applications: two-dimensional Fourier feature extraction;
- Low cost;
- Flexibility and "teach by show" ease of use; and
- Factory rugged.

Artificial neural systems offer high performance and simplicity of setup and training, even for difficult multiclass recognition and sorting applications. The system can perform complex discrimination analysis even when input signature patterns are noisy, incomplete, topologically distorted, or comprise classes with highly non-Gaussian data distributions. A customized "back-propagation" network has demonstrated less than 0.1 percent classification error for large population trials. Typically the operation of the network is completely transparent to the end-user, and a "teach-by-show"

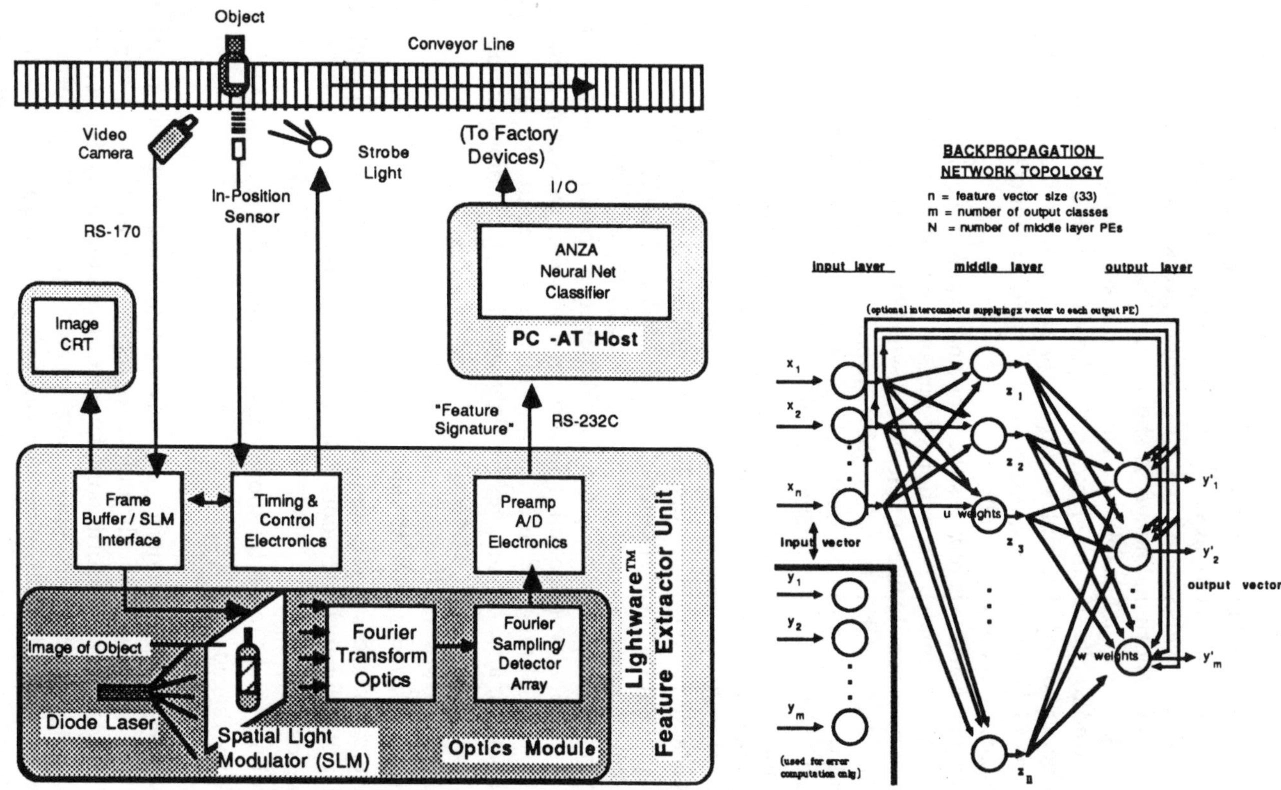

Figure 4.18 *Smart camera for manufacturing inspection.* (*Courtesy and copyright © 1988 by Global Holonetics Corporation.*)

training procedure may be used. Training is accomplished by simply passing sets of objects to be classified before the video camera. The neural version of the Smart Camera Host Pak software (which controls the ANZA coprocessor) includes a unique network status display of particular interest to systems integrators and original equipment manufacturer (OEM) customers. A Lightware-ANZA system is shown in Figure 4.18.

4.9. READING HANDPRINTED NUMBERS

Conventional approaches to machine reading of handprinted numbers usually involve the development of an algorithm to recognize the characters and the variations to be expected. Several methods are used, but in general they depend on either a direct or a statistical representation of the numbers to be read. The success of the method and the variability allowed in the numbers depend entirely on the algorithm developed. The more sophistication the designers put in the algorithm, the greater the ability of the finished application to read variations of numbers.

With neural networks, the work of developing an algorithm is eliminated. In one implementation, 1600 samples of handwritten numbers were taken from many people by using a digitizer tablet attached to the ANZA host PC/AT. The samples were used to train a network to recognize numeric characters through repeated exposure to the sample data.

Once trained, the network successfully recognized numbers handprinted on the tablet, even if printed by people whose samples were not included in the training set. It was able to recognize numbers printed as a series of broken lines, and to identify embedded characters (e.g., an 8 inside a 0). In another test, the number 7 was written with a series of very small 0 characters and successfully detected. The resulting recognition capability exceeded the performance of the algorithmic approaches.

Uses for this capability include

- Reading amounts and/or account numbers from credit card charge slips and bank checks;
- Reading zip codes from letters; and
- Reading income tax return data or other numeric form data.

4.10. NESTOR LEARNING SYSTEM FOR PATTERN RECOGNITION

The Nestor learning system (NLS) and its component restricted Coulomb energy (RCE) neural software systems are designed for applications in pattern recognition. A short overview of these systems, based on Nestor manuals, follows.

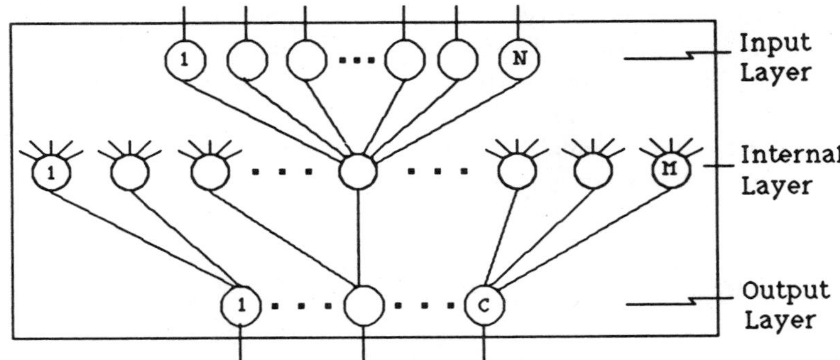

Figure 4.19 *Restricted Coulomb energy (RCE) neural networks. (Courtesy and copyright © 1988 by Nestor Inc.)*

The architecture of the RCE network specifies three processing layers: an input layer, an internal layer, and an output layer (see Figure 4.19). Each node in the input layer registers the value of a feature describing an input event. If the application is character recognition, these features might be counts of the number of line segments at various angles of orientation. If the application is signal processing, the features might be the power in a signal at various frequency bandwidths. If the application is emulating the judgment of a mortgage underwriter, the features would represent financial ratios derived from the mortgage application.

Each cell in the output layer corresponds to a pattern category. The network assigns an input to a category if the output cell for that category "fires" in response to the input. If an input causes only one output cell to become active, the decision of the network is said to be "unambiguous" for that category. If multiple output cells are active, the network nonetheless offers a set of likely categorizations. Cells in the middle or internal layer of the network construct the mapping that ensures that the output cell for the correct category fires in response to a given input pattern.

The essence of the network function can be seen by regarding a pattern category as a collection of points in the N-dimensional feature space defined by the N cells of the input layer. A pattern of activity among the cells of the input layer corresponds to the location of a point in this feature space. All examples of a pattern category define a set of points in this feature space that can be characterized as a region (or a set of regions) having some arbitrary shape (see Figure 4.20).

Just as a category of patterns defines a region (or regions) in the feature space of the system, a cell in the internal layer of the RCE network is associated with a set of points in the feature space. The geography of this set of points is defined by the transfer function of the internal cell. As an illustration, consider an RCE network with only two cells in the input layer. (In

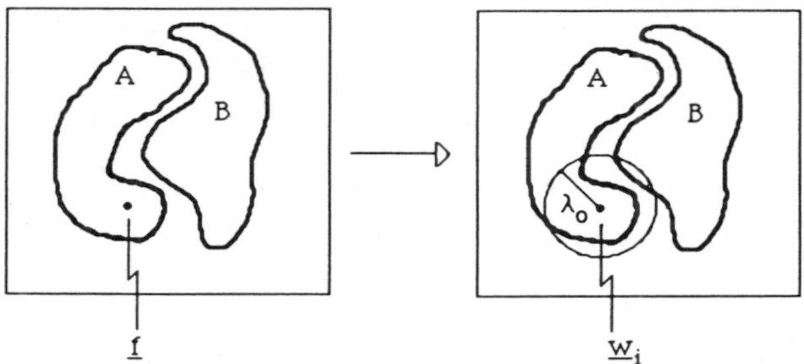

Figure 4.20 *Feature space representation of cell commitment in internal layer. (Courtesy and copyright © 1988 by Nestor Inc.)*

practice, a user defines as many input cells as he needs to represent his input feature vector to the system.)

The transfer function can be thought of as defining a disk-shaped region centered at the feature space point $\mathbf{W}_i$ (the vector of weights coupling the ith internal cell to the input layer), with a radius l around the point $\mathbf{W}_i$ (see Figure 4.21). Any point (feature vector) falling within this region makes this internal cell active. Each PE in the internal layer sends its signal, via a unit strength connection, to only one cell in the output layer. The response properties of the output layer are such that, if any of the internal elements to which a given output cell is connected are firing, the output cell will fire.

Learning involves two distinct mechanisms at work in the network. The first is cell commitment. Cells are "committed" to the internal layer as well as to the output layer, though less frequently. When cells are committed, they are "wired up" according to the RCE network paradigm. Each cell in the internal layer is connected to the outputs of each of the cells in the input layer. Each cell in the internal layer projects its output to only one cell in the output layer. The second learning mechanism is modification of the thresholds associated with cells in the internal layer. Thus, each internal PE has its own weight vector $\mathbf{W}_i$ and threshold l_i and their values are changed under separate modification procedures.

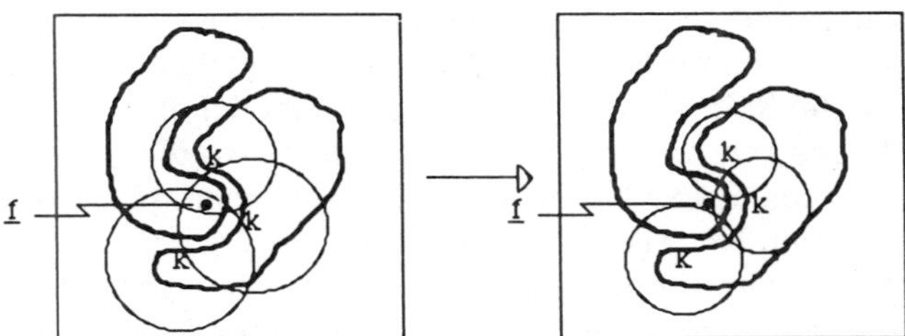

Figure 4.21 *Threshold reduction for active internal layer cells associated with kth output cell. After modification, f is no longer covered by any internal cell disk for kth output cell. (Courtesy and copyright © 1988 by Nestor Inc.)*

Both the commitment of cells and the adjustment of internal cell thresholds are controlled by training signals that move from the output layer back into the system. If an output cell (representing a given category of patterns) is off (0) but should be on (1), an error signal of +1 is generated for that output cell. If an output cell is on (1) that should be off (0), an error signal of −1 travels from that cell back into the internal layer.

An error signal of +1 traveling from the kth output layer cell into the system causes a new internal PE to be committed. Its output is connected to the kth cell in the output layer, and its vector of connections $\mathbf{W}_i$ to the input layer assumes the value of the current feature vector of the input layer ($W_{ij} - f_j, j = 1, \ldots, N$). The threshold of the cell is set at some positive value l_0. In the feature space of the system, this adds a new disk-shaped region that covers some portion of the class territory for this input's category.

If an error signal of −1 is sent from the kth output unit back into the system, then the system responds by reducing the threshold values (l_i) of all the active internal units that are connected to the kth output cell. This has the effect of reducing the sizes of their disk-shaped regions so that they no longer cover the input pattern (see Figure 4.21).

We can easily see how this network meets some of the important pattern recognition requirements discussed earlier. First, it can learn to distinguish pattern categories even when they are defined by complex relationships among the features characterizing the patterns. From seeing training samples, the system builds up a set of disks that covers the territories for the two hypothetical pattern classes A and B. Each disk corresponds to the "win region" of an internal unit, and each disk is "owned" by a pattern category because of its unique connection to one output cell. The size of the disk is related to the threshold of the corresponding internal unit. If the disk is too large, that internal unit will fire in response to an example of the wrong category. The resultant −1 training signal will reduce the disk to prevent it from firing for that pattern (or patterns like it) again.

This process of committing disks and reducing their sizes allows the system to develop separating mappings even for nonlinearly separable pattern categories. In principle, an arbitrary degree of nonlinearity can be achieved.

An important property of the RCE network is that it can store an arbitrarily large number of memories without degrading system performance. It can do this because the RCE network is related to a model of neural information storage that likens the memory of the system to a collection of negative electrostatic charges at fixed sites in the feature space. Clamping a feature vector onto the input layer is analogous to introducing a positive test charge into this system. From the laws of physics, we know that the charge will move under the influence of the electrostatic field until it comes to rest at a site with negative charge. In the RCE network, the memory represented by this site is the one recalled in response to the input. The analogy with electrostatics makes it readily apparent that one can store an arbitrarily large number of memories in the system (in principle, up to the number of sites available in the space). No sites other than those explicitly stored are ever introduced. In fully interconnected models, storage of memories beyond the maximum allowed often creates spurious, undesired memories that block correct recall for a given input. For details see Reilly et al.[16,17]

4.11. CARPENTER-GROSSBERG ADAPTIVE RESONANCE THEORY

An adaptive resonance theory (ART) network classifies input patterns into categories. It is based on competitive learning without the teacher. Ideally, the sequence of patterns is presented to the ART network, and a neuron that represents a category becomes active.

According to Carpenter and Grossberg,[18] the learning system is a compromise between *plasticity* and *stability*. The system must be plastic, or adaptive, in order to respond to new inputs and to form new categories. On the other hand, the system must remain stable in response to irrelevant events or noise.

The ART network connects two layers of neurons, F_1 and F_2, as shown in Figure 4.22. These two layers present two short-term memories (STM). STM F_1 is the feature-detecting layer: it accepts the input pattern (e.g., letters of the alphabet). STM F_2 is the category layer: each neuron in F_2 represents a different category. For instance, each neuron might represent a different letter.

Within the STM F_2 layer, lateral connections between neurons enable the competition, in which the winner takes all. In other words, only the most active neuron remains active; all other neurons become inactive.

The STM F_1 and STM F_2 layers are interconnected by a bidirectional matrix, which represents the long-term memory (LTM). Each neuron of one layer is connected to all the neurons of the other layer. Bottom-up connections carry the basic information from the input and serve to select the category. Top-down connections carry a *template* or set of critical features in the category, and represent *attentional priming*.

According to Stork,[19] any neuron in F_1 might be receiving two activities—one due to the bottom-up input, the other due to the top-down priming. During recall and categorization, the bottom-up and top-down information lead to a *resonance* in neural activity, with the critical features in F_1 being reinforced and thus having the greatest activity. Such a resonance is used in BAMs. However, ART has two parts that make it different from other neural learning networks: attentional gain control and reset wave (see Figure 4.22).

Attentional gain control prevents purely top-down signals alone from leading to F_1 activity. So long as the input is present, the gain is high. If there is no stimulus input and just F_2 is active, then the gain is low and only little activity can arise in F_1.

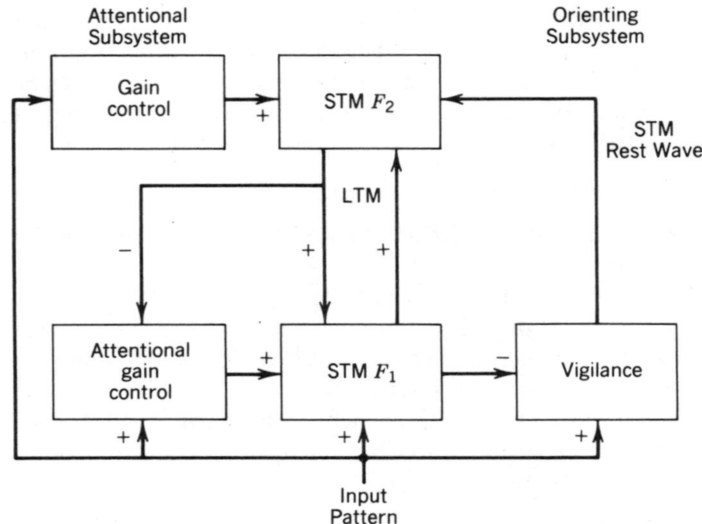

Figure 4.22 *ART 1 system: Two successive stages, F_1 and F_2, of the attentional subsystem encode patterns of activation in short-term memory (STM). Bottom-up and top-down pathways between F_1 and F_2 contain adaptive long-term memory (LTM) traces that multiply the signals in these pathways. The remainder of the circuit modulates these STM and LTM processes. Modulation by gain control enables F_1 to distinguish between bottom-up input patterns and top-down priming, or expectation patterns, and to match these bottom-up and top-down patterns by the two-third rule. Gain control signals also enable F_2 to react supraliminally to signals from F_1 while an input pattern is on. The orienting subsystem generates a reset wave to F_2 when sufficiently large mismatches between bottom-up and top-down patterns occur at F_1. This reset wave selectively and enduringly inhibits previously active F_2 cells until the input is shut off. (Adapted from Carpenter and Grossberg.[18])*

There are three inputs to F_1 neurons: bottom-up stimulus input, top-down prime, and gain control. According to Carpenter and Grossberg's two-thirds rule, at least two out of three inputs must be active for the F_1 neuron to become active.

The *reset wave* is generated by the orienting subsystem shown in Figure 4.22. The wave is generated only when sufficiently large mismatches between bottom-up and top-down patterns occur at F_1. This reset wave selectively and enduringly inhibits previously active F_2 cells until the input is shut off. Hence, the orienting subsystem acts as a novelty detector and controls the fineness or coarseness of the categories.

The input pattern presents an excitation, the F_1 pattern an inhibition, to the orienting subsystem. Under normal circumstances, inhibition overpowers excitation, and the orienting system remains inactive.

Consider a new stimulus input pattern that shares only a few features with a previously encoded pattern. This pattern could be encoded by a previous category neuron in F_2 or by a new category neuron in F_2. The ART network has a *vigilance* parameter that tells how large a mismatch is tolerated between two patterns. High vigilance forces the system to search for new categories in response to small differences between input and expectation. Lower vigilance implies coarser grouping. If there is a severe mismatch at F_1 between the top-down template and the stimulus input pattern, the activity in F_1 decreases. Thus F_1 cannot inhibit the orienting system very much. The stimulus input pattern makes the orienting system active. A strong reset wave is sent to F_2 that enduringly shuts off activity in any F_2 neuron that might be active. The network now hunts for another active neuron in F_2. This neuron presents a new category for the input pattern.

Carpenter and Grossberg[18] performed numerous experiments with ART, which quickly learned to stable classify input patterns. In one experiment, 50 analog input patterns were grouped into 34 categories. In another experiment, the same 50 input patterns were quickly classified into 20 coarser categories after a single learning trial, using a smaller setting of the vigilance parameter.

4.12. PROCESS CONTROL APPLICATIONS

One of the most promising application areas for neural networks is industrial process control. Expert systems have proven to be effective tools for mimicking an expert's problem-solving techniques when the expert can explicitly state the necessary rules, but they have failed to capture the "soft" knowledge that experts cannot put into words. Neural nets, however, are fully capable of discovering this hidden information by observing samples of an expert's behavior during a problem-solving task. As independent systems, or working together with conventional expert systems, neural networks can reduce development and maintenance costs for process control applications by automatically learning rules and by providing graceful degradation through inherent redundancy.

As an example, AI WARE uses a Rumelhart network to solve the problem of transferring a web product (such as paper or plastic film) from one roll to another (see Figure 4.23). A human operator controls the speed of the roll motors to maintain constant tension and linear speed; this is difficult, due to the changing radius of each roll. The AI-NET system observes the reactions of the operator in different situations and "learns" how to control the system. This form of application typifies how neural nets can learn by example the rules necessary to control dynamically changing systems.

Filling multidiameter tanks has been a difficult problem to solve with conventional engineering approaches, because it is not well understood how to build control systems that work reliably over all possible system states. Neural nets automatically generalize over the range of samples presented.

Figure 4.24 depicts a tank-filling system controlled by a human operator while the AI-NET system observes the operator's actions. Given a constant

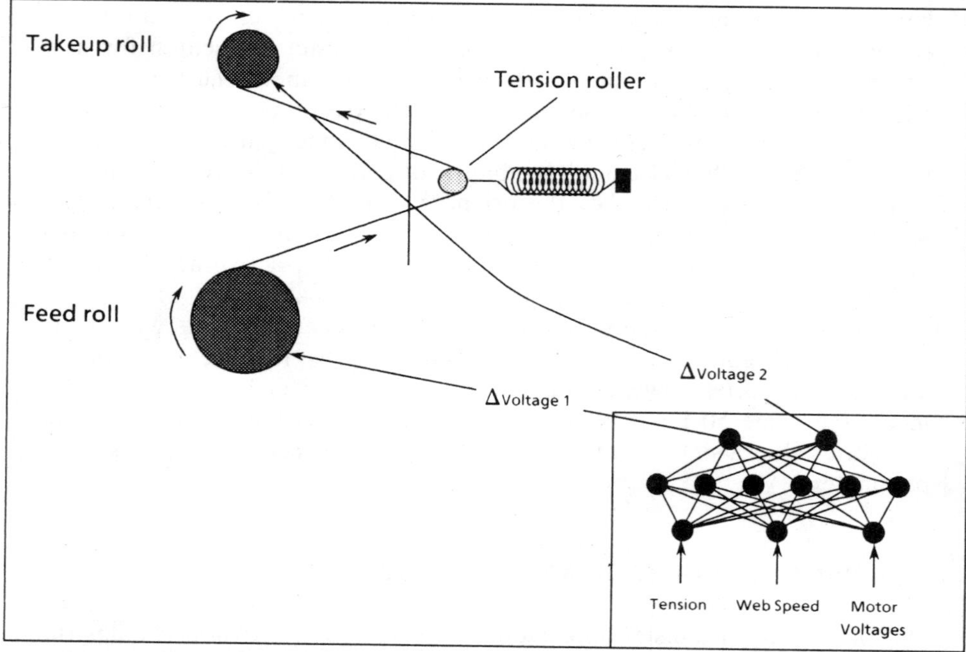

Figure 4.23 *Web winding controlled by AI-NET. (Courtesy and copyright © 1988 by AI WARE Inc.)*

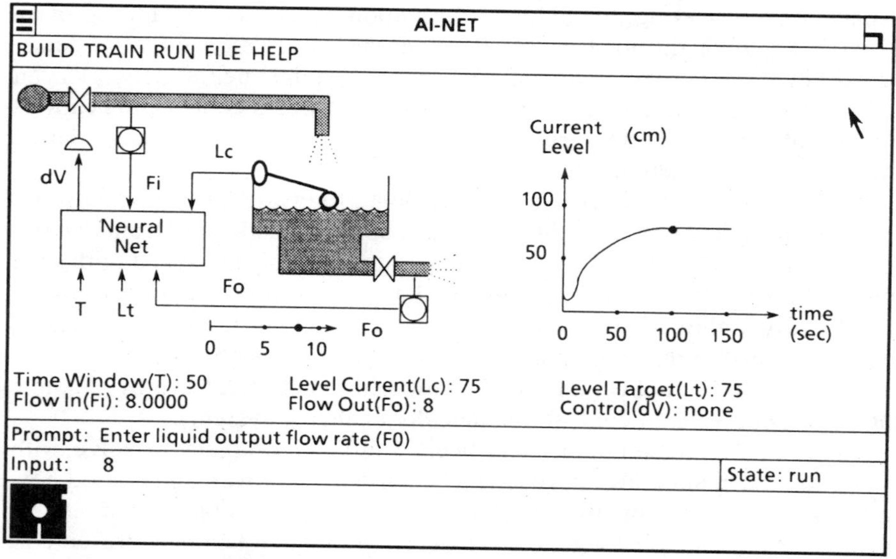

Figure 4.24 *Tank filling controlled by AI-NET. (Courtesy and copyright © 1988 by AI WARE Inc.)*

output flow (Fo), the operator's objective is to open and close the input valve (dV) such that the current tank level (Lc) changes to the target tank level (Lt) in a specified time (T). AI-NET learns how to control the input valve with only a few representative samples of the operator's actions in various system states.

In conventional approaches to process control, a significant amount of time and money is spent developing a control law that describes how a process works and how it can be controlled. Usually, that control law is implemented in a simulation of the process. After the simulation, the control law is refined and readied implementation with the real process. This procedure is an "analytical bottleneck" in system design.

If a neural network has direct access to data describing the process, it can learn the data and develop a control law with minimal assistance from specialists. A simulation model can be used to help refine the control law, and the resulting time to develop and validate the control law is significantly less than with conventional approaches.

4.13. POLE BALANCING

Pole balancing is a complex control task based on *delayed reinforcement:* a failure signal used for performance evaluation is available only after a sequence of actions has been taken. In delayed reinforcement situations it is difficult to identify which actions produce results and which do not.

A two-dimensional pole and wheeled-cart system is shown in Figure 4.25*a*. The cart can travel along a track. The state at time t of this dynamic system is specified by four real-valued variables:

x_t: the horizontal position of the cart relative to the track;
$\dot{x}_t$: the horizontal velocity of the cart;
θ_t: the angle between the pole and vertical, clockwise being positive; and
$\dot{\theta}_t$: the angular velocity of the pole.

The goal is to produce a sequence of forces F_t upon the cart's center of mass such that the pole is balanced for as long as possible and the cart does not hit the end of the track. An external reinforcement signal r_t, which signals a failure, is defined as follows:

$$r_t = \begin{cases} 0 & \text{if } -0.21(\text{radius}) < \theta_t < 0.21(\text{radius}) \text{ or } -2.4 < x_t < 2.4, \\ -1 & \text{otherwise} \end{cases}$$

In other words, the pole must stay within the prespecified angle, and the cart must stay within the prespecified distance from the center of the track.

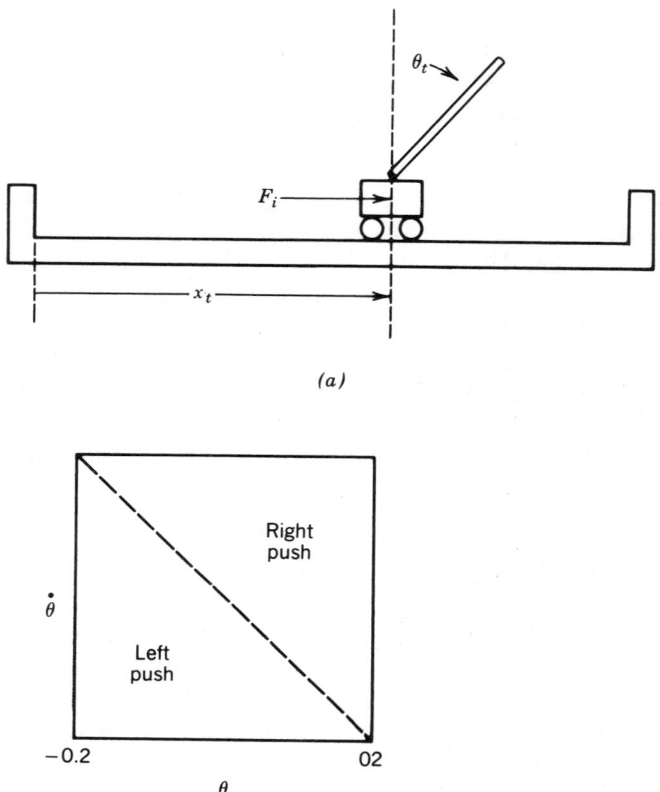

Figure 4.25 *(a) Pole balancing; (b) desired function for pole-balancing solution. (Adapted by permission from Anderson[20].)*

Anderson[20] simulated pole balancing on a digital computer. The dynamics of the cart-pole system are given by the following equations of motion:

$$\ddot{\theta}_t = \frac{g \sin \theta_t + \cos \theta_t \left[\dfrac{-F_t - m_p l \dot{\theta}_t^2 \sin \theta_t + \mu_c \operatorname{sgn}(\dot{x}_t)}{m_c + m_p} \right] - \dfrac{\mu_p \dot{\theta}_t}{m_p l}}{l \left[\dfrac{4}{3} - \dfrac{m_p \cos^2 \theta_t}{m_c + m_p} \right]} \tag{4.3}$$

$$\ddot{x}_t = \frac{F_t + m_p l [\dot{\theta}_t^2 \sin \theta_t - \ddot{\theta}_t \cos \theta_t] - \mu_c \operatorname{sgn}(\dot{x}_t)}{m_c + m_p} \tag{4.4}$$

where

$m_c = 1.0$ kg = mass of the cart;
$m_p = 0.1$ kg = mass of the pole;

l = 0.5 m = distance from center of mass of pole to the pivot;
μ_c = 0.0005 = coefficient of friction of cart on track;
μ_p = 0.000002 = coefficient of friction of the pivot; and
g = -9.8 m/s^2 = acceleration due to gravity.

A simulation time step τ = 0.02 s is used. The system is described by the following difference equations:

$$x(t+1) = x(t) + \tau \dot{x}(t) \rightarrow x_1(t) \tag{4.5}$$

$$\dot{x}(t+1) = x(t) + \tau \ddot{x}(t) \rightarrow x_2(t) \tag{4.6}$$

$$\theta(t+1) = \theta(t) + \tau \dot{\theta}(t) \rightarrow x_3(t) \tag{4.7}$$

$$\dot{\theta}(t+1) = \dot{\theta}(t) + \tau \ddot{\theta}(t) \rightarrow x_4(t) \tag{4.8}$$

Figure 4.25*b* shows the desired action function for generating a push on the cart. States in the upper right region require a push to the right, and states in the lower left require a left push. The magnitude of the force is constant; only the sign can be changed, resulting in a simple *bang-bang* controller.

The knowledge of the desired function was not used during learning. The learning network must learn the desired action function. A back-propagation two-layer network with hidden units was analyzed, as well as a reinforcement network of Barto, Sutton, and Anderson.[21] The input vector consists of components $x_1(t)$, $x_2(t)$, $x_3(t)$, and $x_4(t)$, which are scaled versions of the state variables from Equations 4.5 to 4.8. An additional input $x_0(t) = 0.5$ provides a threshold.

The network generates a binary-valued output $a(t)$ that is used to generate the force F_t:

$$F_t = \begin{cases} 10 \text{ nT} & \text{if } a(t) = 1 \\ -10 \text{ nT} & \text{if } a(t) = 0 \end{cases} \tag{4.9}$$

The simulation time step τ = 0.02 s corresponds to a state sampling and force-applying rate of 50 Hz.

Anderson[20] divided experiments into trials and runs. Each trial starts from the cart-pole system state chosen at random and ends with the appearance of the failure signal. A series of trials constitutes a run, with the first trial of a run starting with weights initialized to random values between -0.1 and 0.1.

A two-layer network with five hidden units and 35 weights was used in the experiments. The learning curve is shown in Figure 4.26. The curve shows the number of steps per trial versus the number of trials. Clearly the performance improves with experience. The trial length is 2000 steps initially, and after 30,000 trials more than 15,000 steps occur per trial. In other words,

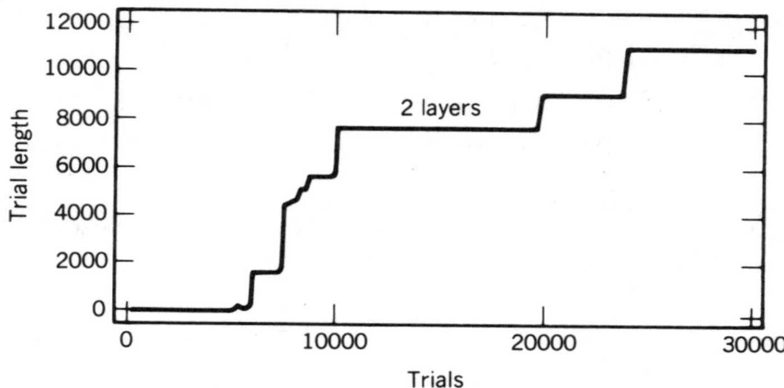

Figure 4.26 *Balancing time versus trials for two-layer system. (Reprinted by permission from Anderson[20].)*

with $\tau = 0.02$ s, the controller balanced the pole for 9 min. A simulated one-layer network was able to balance the pole only for 30 steps per trial. The pole-balancing task has potential applications in related control domains.

4.14. PROCESS CONTROL BASED ON ANZA AND GRADED LEARNING NETWORK†

A graded learning network (GLN) is a real-time, closed-loop adaptive control system that learns how to perform a control operation, without programming, through trial and error. No initial data collection, extensive systems analysis, or model construction are needed. As a demonstration, GLN has been trained to balance a broom on end by using a stepper mechanism. The neural network is implemented on the ANZA, a neurocomputing coprocessor that uses an IBM-compatible host for input-output (I/O) processing. A short overview of GLN, based on GLN-ANZA manuals, follows.

The neural network has no knowledge of the physics of falling brooms. Instead, the network learns to balance the broom in the center of a track by using information about a point on the broom. This information is relayed every 130 ms, and a performance grade occurs every 15 s. This demonstrates the ability of a neural network to solve difficult process control problems without having detailed knowledge of the process. See Figure 4.27.

Along with this position information, the network receives a delayed speed and an even more delayed acceleration, all of which are derived from the position data by the host computer rather than by the stepper mechanism. These delays are important data characteristics that must be learned by the network. They permit the network to function without receiving any

† Section 4.14 is adapted from GLN-ANZA manuals. Courtesy and copyright © 1988 by Hecht-Nielsen Neurocomputer Corporation.

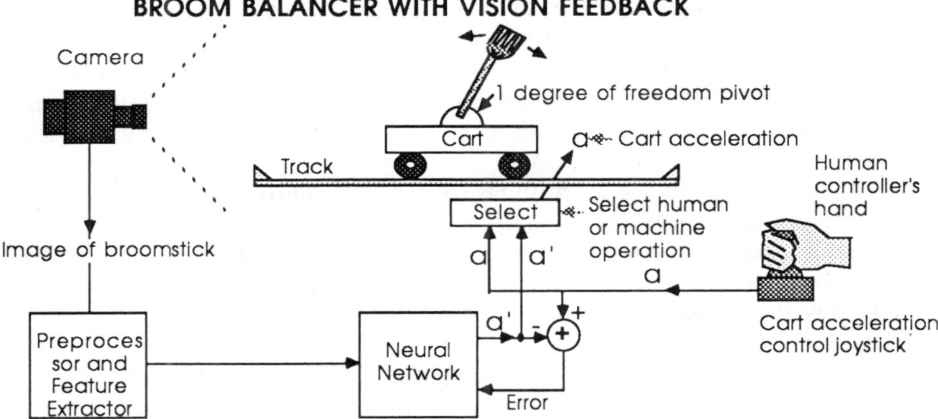

Figure 4.27 *Broom balanced with vision feedback. (Courtesy and copyright © 1988 Hecht-Nielsen Neurocomputer Corporation.)*

positioning, velocity, or acceleration information from the stepper mechanism, which moves the base of the broom.

During training, the neural network tries to balance the broom for 15 s. At the conclusion of each trial, it receives a performance grade derived from a simple algorithm in the host computer. The neural network uses this grade to try to improve its performance during the next trial. The network learns to quickly bring the broom to the center of the track and balance it there with virtually no angular motion. In addition, the network can compensate for changes in the system (including physical shocks, such as a person tapping on the broom) during operation.

As illustrated by the broom-balancing demonstration, the GLN has several advantages for process control and automation. First, since it learns independently through trial and error, rather than requiring extensive systems analysis and programming, the GLN can deliver accurate control solutions based on the actual performance of the system rather than on a model that may not be an accurate approximation of the system's dynamics.

Second, because the GLN learns from the actual performance of the system, it deals easily with nonlinearities and other aberrations in the system it is controlling. This permits the use of less expensive components without loss of control accuracy.

Third, the graded learning approach permits the use of visual feedback, eliminating the need for expensive and, all too often, fragile position, velocity, and acceleration sensors in applications using stepper mechanisms. Other equally simple feedback mechanisms may be used.

Fourth, the GLN systems can adapt to changing conditions, permitting the design of systems that will automatically compensate for wear, damage, and environmental changes.

The GLN learns a task through trial and error. A detailed description of the task is not needed; only the success or failure of several trials is used to judge task performance. Success or failure can be measured in different ways. In the broom balancer demonstration, it is derived quite simply from the orientation of the broom during a 15-s trial, as measured by a video camera.

Contrast this with the algorithmic computing approach, which requires the designer to describe the behavior of the entire system, and then devise a computer program to control it. The self-programming capability of the GLN will enable engineers to develop systems faster, and, in some cases, may make possible applications that would have been too complex for traditional techniques.

When combined with simulation techniques to speed up the training process, this ability could have a near-revolutionary impact on the design of control systems. For instance, a process optimization system might be developed primarily by exposing the controlling network to repeated simulations of the process. In many cases, historical data from operation records may already exist and be sufficient for training.

The GLN deals easily with nonlinearities and other aberrations in the mechanism it controls because neural networks are dynamic, self-organizing systems. They learn the behavior of the entire system during training, including typical aberrations. This capability can yield significant cost saving because it eliminates the need for expensive high-accuracy components in positioning and control systems. In addition, the developer of a GLN control system does not need to predict system aberrations because the network will learn to control aberrations automatically.

The GLN can use visual feedback to control a system. In the broom balancer, the GLN receives no positioning information from the stepper. Instead, it watches the broom through a video camera (which is fairly nonlinear as well) and uses the broom position, delayed speed, and delayed acceleration as feedback to develop its control strategy. Again, this enables the use of less expensive components. There are many applications, such as steel production, where heavy-duty robots would be very useful in process control. Progress in these areas has been stalled by industry's inability to develop position sensors that are highly accurate and able to withstand the heat and vibration of the robot's environment. Visual feedback eliminates this problem.

Other types of feedback can also be used. In a chemical processing system, the feedback might be derived from the purity percentage of the desired output, or perhaps from a combination of this parameter with another, such as the lack of dangerous by-products, safety concerns, etc. In many cases, it may be possible to derive the "success signal" from easily developed algorithms.

Since the GLN is able to continue learning during operation, it can update its control response during operation to automatically compensate for equipment wear, damage, or changes in the environment. This substantially cuts down on maintenance costs.

For example, in the broom balancer, the incoming data that the network used for learning had a significant noise component, which introduced an element of uncertainty, especially in the acceleration data. A comparison of trials using noise-free simulated data versus trials using noisy, real-world data showed that the network used the acceleration data far less in the noisy environment than in the noise-free environment. In effect, it automatically adapted to the noise by deemphasizing the data most affected.

4.15. INTELLIGENT ROBOTS

No matter how much mechanical and electrical hardware is built up around a conventional robot, it is still only a sophisticated machine tool. The major step forward is achieved now by the introduction of sophisticated real-time software and neural networks. Standardized real-time software with the following capabilities are now available: fast response to real-world events, priority-driven multitasking, reentrant programming languages, extremely fast response to interrupts, support for special I/O devices, and for special I/O programming.

Real-time operating systems provide important functions needed in reprogrammable systems. Real-time kernels provide minimal functions needed in embedded applications.

Standardization is a major issue. Development of proprietary software requires large investments and produces systems that are incompatible with the rest of the world. Designers are therefore using well-established software tools and systems, such as DEC's VAXELN operating system, Intel's DEM modular Systems Operations, and Lynx Unix-compatible real-time operating system.

Neural networks open the road toward learning robots. The robot learns from what is happening rather than from what it has been told to expect. A new class of *neural robots* requires self-adapting sensing feedback systems and hand-eye coordination. The first neural robots consisted of a stereocamera, a machine-vision system, and an industrial robot arm. The operation of a neural robot is similar to neural process control, pole-balancing, and graded learning networks (see Sections 4.12 to 4.14). Conventional robots cannot correct for process variations or for part preparation errors. To compensate for such variations or error, robots must include real-time sensor feedback and the features of adaptation and learning. These features might result in a widespread use of neural robots in automated manufacturing laboratories and services. Hybrid neural, expert, and concurrent robot systems promise the best characteristics (see Sections 9.5 and 9.10).

4.16. MIYAMOTO-KAWATO-SETOYAMA-SUZUKI ROBOTIC MANIPULATOR

The neural robotic manipulator is based on a hierarchical arrangement of the transcortical loop and the inverse dynamics model for a learning trajectory. Although neither strict modeling of the manipulator nor precise parameter estimation were required, the control performance by the neural network model improved gradually during 30 min of learning. Once the neural network model learned to control some movement, it could control quite different and faster movements. That is, the neural network model is able to generalize learned movements.

This section is based on Miyamoto et al.[22]

The neural network model[23,24] for the control and learning of voluntary movement is shown in Figure 4.28. The model is considered as an identifier of an unknown nonlinear system. It approximates the output $z(t)$ of the unknown nonlinear system by monitoring both the input $u(t)$ and $z(t)$. The

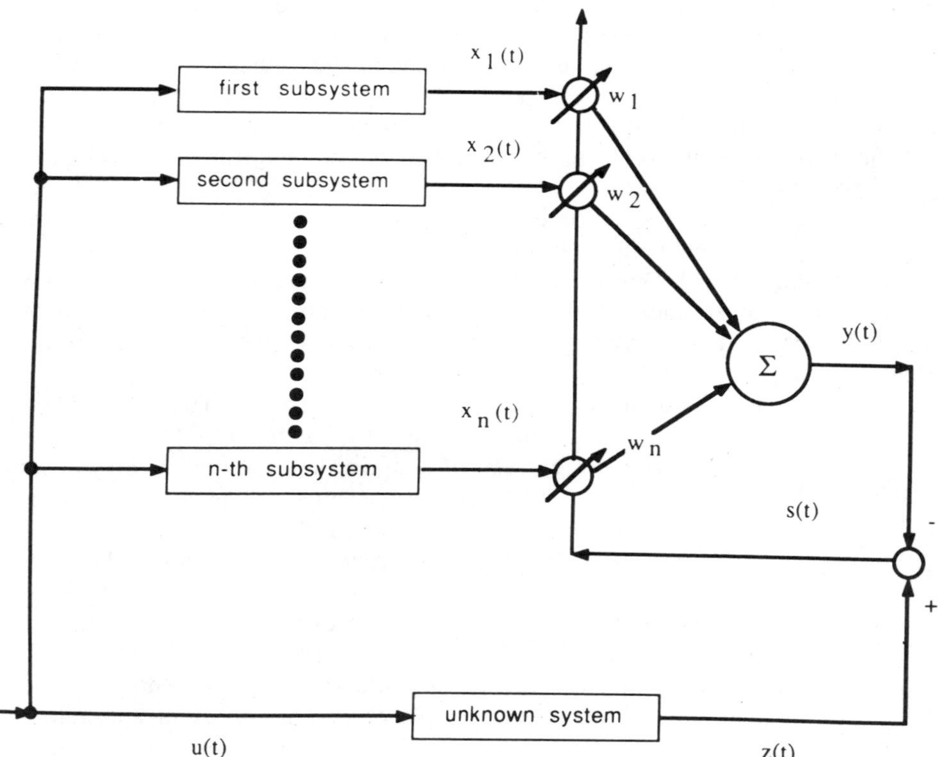

Figure 4.28 *A neural identifier of an unknown nonlinear system comprises many nonlinear subsystems and a neuron with heterosynaptic plasticity. (Reprinted by permission from Miyamoto, Kawato, Setoyama, and Suzuki.[22] Copyright © 1988 by Pergamon Press.)*

input $u(t)$ is also fed to n subsystems and is nonlinearly transformed into n different inputs $x_k(t)$ ($k = 1, \ldots, n$) to the neuron with plasticity. Let w_k denote a synaptic weight of the kth input. The output signal of the neuron $y(t)$ is the sum of n postsynaptic potentials: $y(t) = W^T X(t)$.

The second synaptic input to the neuron is an error signal, and is given as an error $s(t)$ between the output of $y(t)$ and $z(t)$: $s(t) = z(t) - y(t)$. The weight w_k changes when the conjunction of $x_k(t)$ and $s(t)$ occurs:

$$\tau\, dW(t)\, dt = X(t)s(t) = X(t)z(t) - X(t)^T W(t)$$
$$X = (x_1, x_2, \ldots, x_n)^T \quad W = (w_1, w_2, \ldots, w_n)^T \tag{4.10}$$

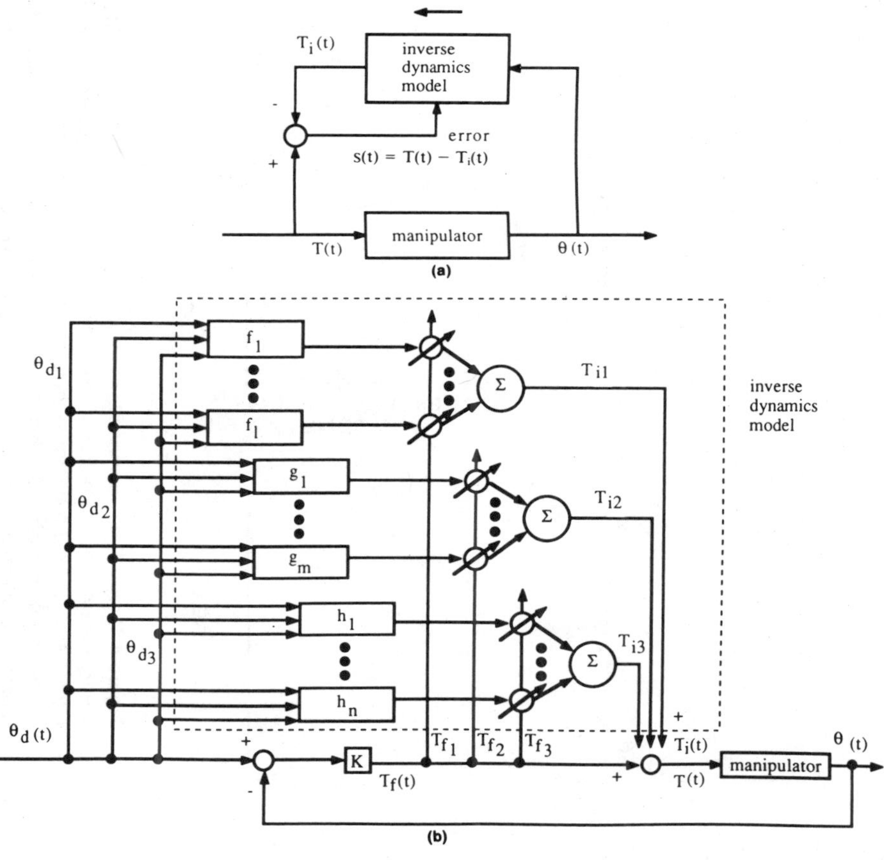

Figure 4.29 *Learning schemes of the inverse dynamics model of the controlled system: (a) The simplest learning method. The arrow shows the direction of signal flow in the inverse dynamics model. (b) The feedback-error-learning scheme and internal structure of the inverse dynamics model for a three-degree-of-freedom robotic manipulator. (Reprinted by permission from Miyamoto, Kawato, Setoyama, and Suzuki.[22] Copyright © 1988 by Pergamon Press.)*

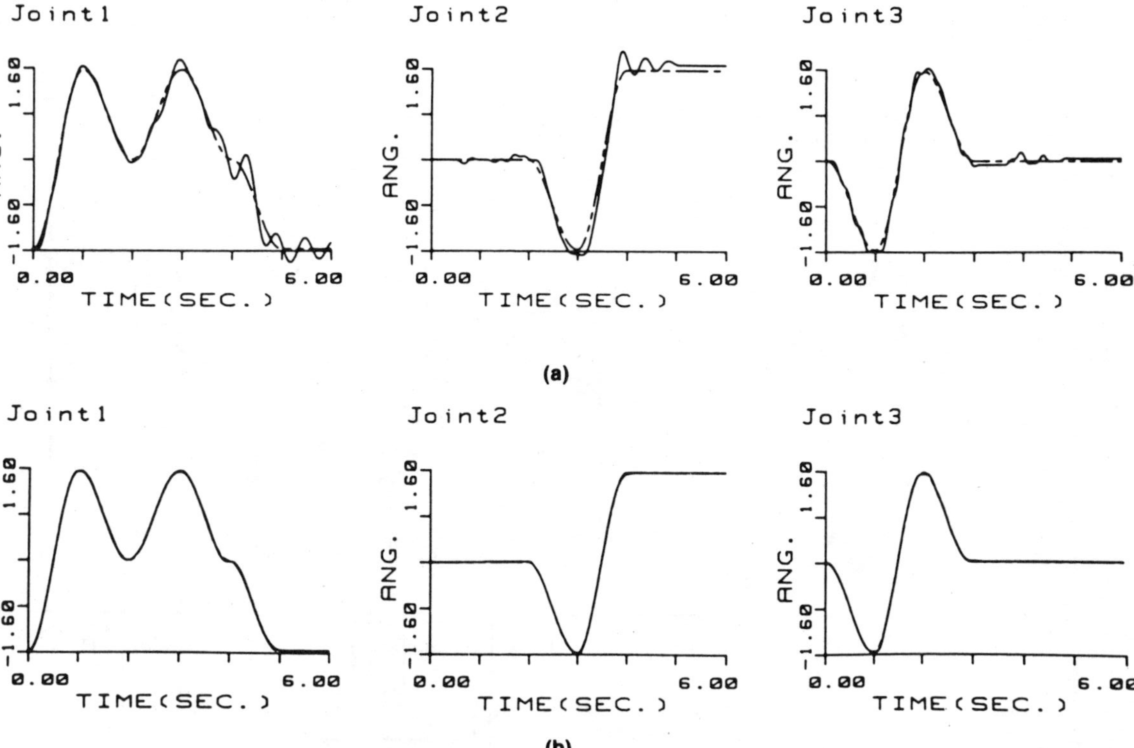

Figure 4.30 (*a*) *Time courses of the three joint angles during 6 s of a single repetition of the training movement pattern before learning. Desired trajectories are shown by chain curves and realized trajectories by solid curves. The unit of the ordinate is radians.* (*b*) *Same as* (*a*), *but after 30 min of learning. (Reprinted by permission from Miyamoto, Kawato, Setoyama, and Suzuki.*[22] *Copyright © 1988 by Pergamon Press.)*

Here, τ is a time constant of change of the synaptic weight. The simplest block diagram for acquiring the inverse dynamics model of a controlled object by the heterosynaptic learning rule is shown in Figure 4.29*a*. As shown in Figure 4.29*b*, the manipulator receives the torque input $T(t)$ and outputs the resulting trajectory $\theta(t)$. The inverse dynamics model is set in the input-output direction opposite to that of the manipulator, as shown by the arrow. That is, it receives the trajectory as an input and outputs the torque $T_i(t)$. The error signal $s(t)$ is given as the difference between the real torque and the estimated torque: $s(t) = T(t) - T_i(t)$.

Figure 4.29*b* shows the detailed structure of the inverse dynamics model; the block diagram illustrates the arrangement of the inverse dynamics model, the controlled object (manipulator), and the feedback loop. This neural network was applied to learning trajectory control of an industrial robotic manipulator (Kawasaki-Unimate PUMA 260).

In the first experiment the learning time constants τ of all the synaptic weights were set to 1000 s. A desired trajectory lasting for 6 s, which is shown by chain curves in Figure 4.30*a*, was given 300 times to the control system. Figure 4.30 compares control performance of this test movement before (*a*) and after (*b*) 30 min of learning.

The model was adaptable to a sudden change in dynamics of the manipulator. The multilayer neural network does not require any a priori knowledge about interactions. All we need to do is to feed the neural network model necessary information (desired trajectory, desired force, desired impedance, feedback motor command) and let it learn by examples. The present model can be easily implemented in a PDP machine, since both the nonlinear transformations in subsystems and the synaptic modifications are essentially parallel.

REFERENCES

1. R. P. Gorman and T. J. Sejnowski, Analysis of hidden units in a layered network trained to classify sonar targets. *Neural Networks* **1,** 75–89 (1988).
2. R. P. Gorman and T. J. Sejnowski, Learned classification of sonar targets using a massively-parallel network. *IEEE Trans. Acoustic Speech Signal Processing* (submitted)
3. D. E. Rumelhart, G. E. Hinton, and R. J. Williams, Learning internal representations by error propagation. In Rumelhart and McClelland (eds.), *Parallel Distributed Processing,* MIT Press, Cambridge, MA, 1986, 318–362.
4. B. Widrow, Generalization and information storage in networks of Adaline "Neurons." In Yovitz, Jacobi, and Golstein (eds.), *Self-Organizing Systems 1962,* Spartan Books, Washington, DC, 1962, 435–461
5. B. Widrow and S. D. Stearns, *Adaptive Signal Processing,* Prentice-Hall, Englewood Cliffs, NJ, 1985.
6. W. C. Ridgway III, An adaptive logic system with generalizing properties. PhD. thesis, Stanford Electronics Labs. Rep. 1956-1, Stanford University, 1962.

7. B. Widrow and R. Winter, Neural nets for adaptive filtering and adaptive pattern recognition. *Computer* 25–39, March (1988).
8. R. W. Prager, T. D. Harrison, and F. Fallside, Boltzmann machines for speech recognition. *Computer Speech and Language* **1,** 3–27 (1986).
9. D. E. Rumelhart and J. L. McClelland (eds.), *Parallel Distributed Processing,* MIT Press, Cambridge, MA, 1986.
10. T. Kohonen, The neural phonetic typewriter. *Computer* 11–22, March (1988).
11. B. Souček and A. D. Carlson, Flash pattern recognition in fireflies. *J. Theor. Biol.* **55,** 339 (1975).
12. D. Marr, *Vision,* W. H. Freeman, New York, 1982.
13. J. K. Brousil and D. R. Smith, A threshold logic network for shape invariance. *IEEE Trans. Computers* **EC-16,** 818–828 (1967).
14. C. Weiman and G. Chaikin, Logarithmic spiral grids for image processing and display. *Computer Graphics and Image Processing* **11,** 197–226 (1979).
15. W. L. Reber and J. Lyman, An artificial neuron system design for rotation and scale invariant pattern recognition. *Proc. IEEE First Int. Conf. on Neural Networks,* San Diego, CA, 1987, Vol. IV, 277–283.
16. D. L. Reilly, L. N. Cooper, and C. Elbaum, A neural model category learning. *Biol. Cybern.* **45,** 35–41 (1982).
17. D. L. Reilly, C. Scofield, C. Elbaum, and L. N. Cooper, Learning system architectures composed of multiple learning modules. *Proc. First IEEE Int. Conf. on Neural Networks,* San Diego, 1987.
18. G. A. Carpenter and S. Grossberg, The ART of adaptive pattern recognition by a self-organizing neural network. *Computer,* 77–88, March (1988).
19. D. Stork, A very brief introduction to the operation of an adaptive resonance network. *Synapse Connection* **2**(8) 1–7 (1988).
20. C. W. Anderson, Learning and problem solving with multilayer connectionist systems. Ph.D. Thesis, Department of Computer and Information Science, University of Massachusetts, 1986.
21. A G. Barto, R. S. Sutton, and C. W. Anderson, Neuronlike elements that can solve difficult learning control problems. *IEEE Trans. Systems, Man and Cybernet.* **13,** 835–846 (1983).
22. H. Miyamoto, M. Kawato, T. Setoyama, and R. Suzuki, Feedback-error-learning neural network for trajectory control of a robotic manipulator. *Neural Networks* **1,** 251–265 (1988).
23. M. Kawato, Adaptive and learning in control of voluntary movement by the central neurons system. *Advanced Robotics* **2.**
24. M. Kawato, Y. Uno, M. Isobe, and R. Suzuki, A hierarchical neural network model for voluntary movement with application to robotics. *IEEE Control Systems Mag.* **8,** 8–16 (1988).

CHAPTER 5

Knowledge Chaining in Real-Time Applications

INTRODUCTION AND SURVEY

This chapter deals with coarse-grain intelligent processes: artificial genetic selection and forward-backward chaining of knowledge. These processes coexist with neural networks in many real-time systems.

Selectionism as an alternative to programming and connectionism is described. Selectionism can arrive at complex intelligent structures.

Rule-based representation of knowledge is described, including forward and backward chaining of knowledge, knowledge frames, knowledge world, truth maintenance systems, schemas, fuzzy cognitive maps, and expert systems.

Examples of expert systems in engineering are presented, including automatic fault diagnosis, factory cell simulation, and knowledge-based robot and process control. Expert systems and neural networks let robots and control systems think, learn, adapt, and interact with their environment. A new generation of intelligent real-time systems is born, based on a mixture of fine and coarse intelligence granularity.

5.1. FEATURE EXTRACTORS AND GENETIC SELECTION SYSTEMS

There are several ways to design intelligent units and networks:

- Using a priori knowledge of the problem domain to weed out the terms that have a small likelihood of being useful;
- Using genetic mutation and crossover algorithms introduced by Holland[1] to design goal-directed selection systems;

- Creating specialized modules for specific types of tasks, with limited adaptation;
- Mixing specialized modules with more general adaptive networks to handle new and unusual situations; and
- Mixing adaptive and programmed modules.

In general, the best way to simplify the design is to introduce modular, hierarchical structures, in which different modules are only loosely coupled. This corresponds to the feature extraction theory and group selection theory of the brain, described by Edelman and Mountcastle.[2] There should be a variety of modules, capable of certain predefined operations inherited from the designer (natural, born with) and able to learn a slightly more difficult set of tasks (nurtured). The problem of nature versus nurture was analyzed by Bergman and Kerszberg,[3] who concluded that

1. Machines with random structures (nonperiodic (NP) arrays) do not perform well. Random start leads nowhere.
2. Machines with identical links between all submodules (totally periodic (P) arrays) never manage. Their architecture is too limited.
3. Machines that are partially, layerwise periodic (LP arrays) are by far the best. Neither too complicated, like the NP machines, nor too simple, like P's, they are the best learners, because they have the structural features adapted to the problem to begin with.

According to Bergman and Kerszberg,[3] the question of whether intelligent behavior can be generated efficiently by using a proper balance of nature versus nurture remains open. Biological reality seems to be located somewhere between these two extremes. A good illustration is provided by Marler,[4] who studied song learning in birds: initially, almost random singing patterns fall slowly into the characteristic species song or into some modification thereof, depending on the auditory environment of the young bird.

It is expected that the theories of feature extraction, group selection, genetic mutation/recombination, and goal-directed systems will inspire the design of new classes of algorithms and computers. In particular, self-organization through selection might prove a powerful alternative to explicit programming in some applications (see Souček and Souček[5]).

Self-organization in biological systems is described by Nicolis and Prigogine.[6] Selectionism is a special form of self-organization. The effect is not to create a new structure but to have one structure that is already present in the starting population to be dominant. Steels[7] has identified a few examples where selectionist processes could be an alternative for programming:

- Recognition: To recognize a word, we almost need to know which word we are looking for. Elements of recognition ignite the process of domination. This process, after a while, will feed back to the elements that caused it to happen in the first place.

- Context: Context is needed to understand the text, but the text provides information on what the context is. Hence, we start with an initial population of many possible contexts. Specific words in the text enforce the domination of a particular context, and, conversely, the context enforces the words in the text.
- Goal selection: All potentially executable goals form the initial population. Initial success in execution of the goal will further enforce the goal, the more resources and supports from the environment will go toward it.
- Rule learning: The process starts with a diverse set of rules. When rules are successful, they gain in strength; otherwise they become weaker.

Steels[7] places selectionism above connectionism and symbolic structures. Connectionist models are still too weak to cope with complex representations. Symbolic structures (expert systems) are too rigid in real-world applications where there are always uncertainties and deviations.

Selectionism can arrive at complex structures. Being an open system in a feedback loop with the environment, the selection system provides for uncertainties and deviations.

5.2. RULE-BASED REPRESENTATION OF KNOWLEDGE

A set of programmed rules that could perform at, or near, the level of a human expert in a specific domain is called an *expert system*. Expert systems are being developed to diagnose diseases, locate mineral deposits, configure complex computer hardware, assist managers with complex planning and scheduling tasks, and aid mechanics in troubleshooting. Only recently the expert systems and related hardware have become fast enough for applications in real-time signal processing, process control, and robotics. Newly developed associative memories and processors present the hardware base for high-speed expert systems (see Souček and Souček[5]). Also, concurrent processors, described in Part II, open the door toward real-time expert systems.

Expert systems can usually be viewed as composed of two modules, as shown in Figure 5.1: a knowledge base and an inference machine. This structure nicely reflects the two main tasks of knowledge engineering: representing and storing large amounts of problem-domain knowledge in the computer, and actively using the problem-domain knowledge for solving problems and answering user queries.

The knowledge base contains facts, relations between facts, and possible methods for solving problems in the domain of application. The inference machine implements algorithms that solve problems and answer user queries

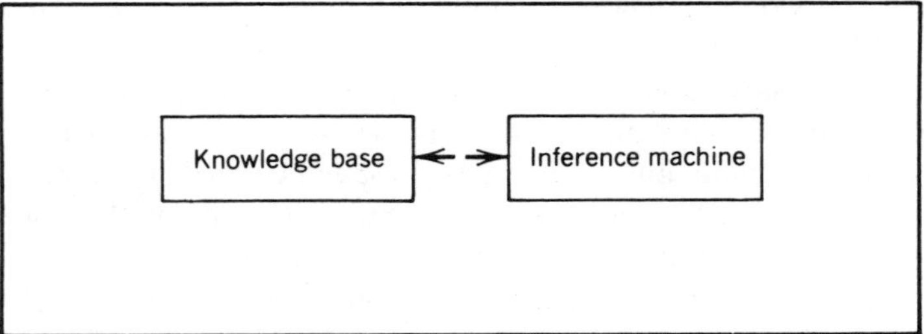

Figure 5.1 *Structure of expert systems.*

by either simply retrieving facts from the knowledge base or by inferring new facts from facts explicitly stored in the knowledge base. Inferring new facts involves the use of general relations or principles, which can also be stored in the knowledge base.

A production system[8–11] is defined by a set of rules, or productions, which form the production memory (PM), together with a data base of assertions called the working memory (WM). Each production consists of a conjunction of pattern elements, called the left-hand side (LHS) of the rule, along with a set of actions called the right-hand side (RHS). The RHS specifies information to be added to (asserted) or removed from WM when the LHS successfully matches against the contents of WM. In operation, the production system repeatedly executes the following cycle of operations:

1. Match: For each rule, it determines whether the LHS matches the current environment of WM. All matching instances of the rules are collected in the conflict set of rules.
2. Select: It chooses exactly one of the matching rules according to some predefined criterion.
3. Act: It adds to or deletes from WM all assertions specified in the RHS of the selected rule, or it performs some operation.

During the selection phase of production system execution, a typical interpreter provides conflict-resolution strategies based on how recent the matched data in WM are and on syntactic discrimination. Rules matching data elements that were more recently inserted in WM are preferred, with ties decided in favor of rules that are more specific (i.e., have more constants) than others.

In general, rules are of the "if-then" form, but they can have different interpretations. Some examples:

If precondition P, *then* conclusion C.

If situation S, *then* action A.

If conditions C_1 and C_2 hold, *then* condition C does not hold.

A more concise notation is often used: $C \rightarrow A$. The meaning of this depends on interpretation; that is, "if condition C, then action A."

Basically an expert system could operate in two ways:

1. Data-driven forward-chaining mode: At every computational cycle, the LHS of the set of rules are examined to determine which rules are satisfied by the data pattern in the storage.
2. Goal-driven backward-chaining mode: At every computational cycle, the RHS of the set of rules are examined to see if a desired goal can be found.

Programming of an expert system can be done in a high-level language. Artificial intelligence (AI) programmers commonly use LISP or PROLOG. LISP consists of operators that facilitate the creation of programs that manipulate lists. Commercial LISP machines have been developed, such as the Symbolics 3600 series. Lists are the fundamental data structures in LISP, and their implementation must allow for rapid access and compact storage. They are achieved through a stack-oriented architecture. Most LISP instructions are executed in one machine cycle. The architecture also provides for incremental compilation so that each new function can be compiled independently of the rest of the program of which it is a part.

PROLOG contains constructs that make it easy to write programs that manipulate logical expressions. The execution of a PROLOG-based program can be speeded up by exploiting various kinds of parallelism. AND parallelism refers to the simultaneous execution of logically ANDed clauses. OR parallelism refers to the concurrent search for alternative solution paths. The best-known PROLOG machine is a PIM multicomputer under development at ICOT in Japan, as a part of the Japanese fifth-generation computing project.

We use the simple "animal-game" to explain the operation of the expert system. Figure 5.2 illustrates a semantic net of the animal hierarchy. The top level represents specific animals (species). The middle level defines broad classes such as mammals, birds, and fish. The bottom level list the characteristic features: gives milk, eats meat, etc. The expert system generates the results by using production rules. Some of the rules used for the animal-game are listed in Figure 5.3.

Figure 5.4 shows the trace of the goal-driven backward-chaining operation: identifying a tiger.

5.3. KNOWLEDGE FRAMES

A *frame* is a way of representing knowledge about the objects and events common to a situation. Originally frames were introduced by Minski[13] to semantically direct the reasoning of scene analysis systems. Modern frame-

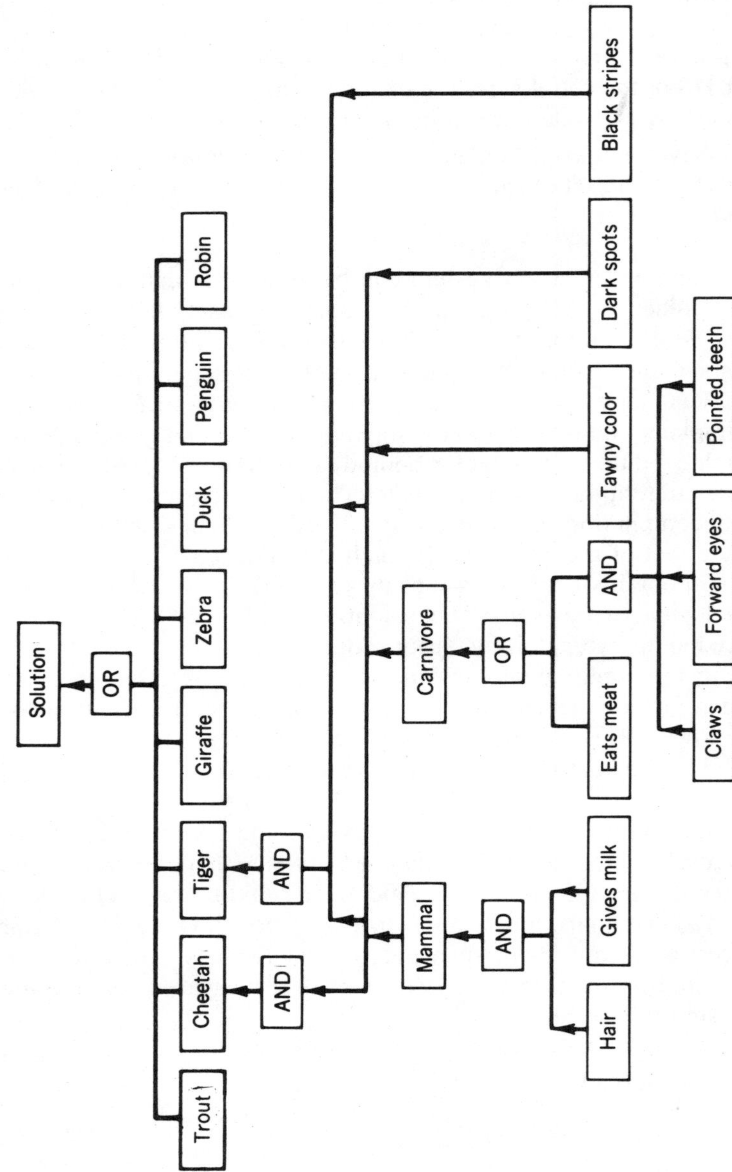

Figure 5.2 *Semantic net of the animal hierarchy. (Adapted from Lewis and Lynch[12].)*

1. IF has-hair AND gives-milk THEN is mammal
2. IF eats-meat THEN is-carnivore
3. IF has-pointed-teeth AND has-claws AND has-forward-eyes THEN is-carnivore
4. IF is-mammal AND is-carnivore AND has-tawny-color AND has-dark-spots THEN is-cheetah
5. IF is-mammal AND is-carnivore AND has-tawny-color AND has-black-stripes THEN is-tiger

Figure 5.3 *Some of the "animal-game" rules. (Adapted from Lewis and Lynch[12].)*

based systems focus on structural representation of knowledge as well as on reasoning. The frame-based representation language developed by a knowledge engineering environment (KEE) provides constructs for describing objects and classes of objects in an application domain. In the example presented by Fikes and Kehler,[14] one frame might represent a truck and another frame a whole class of trucks (see Figure 5.5). Constructs are available in a frame language for organizing frames that represent classes into taxonomies. These constructs allow a knowledge-base designer to describe a class as a specialization of other more generic classes. Thus, trucks can be described as vehicles plus a set of properties that distinguish a truck from other kinds of vehicles.

The objects of a frame are stored in *slots*. *Own slots* are used to describe attributes of the object or class represented by the frame. *Member slots* can occur in frames that represent classes and are used to describe attributes of

Attempting to deduce "is-mammal"
  Using Rule 1
  Is this true: animal "has-hair"? YES
  Is this true: animal "gives-milk"? YES
  Rule 1 deduces animal "is-mammal"
Attempting to deduce "is-carnivore"
  Using Rule 2
  Is this true: animal "eats-meat"? YES
  Rule 2 deduces animal "is-carnivore"
Attempting to deduce "is-cheetah"
  Using Rule 4
  Is this true: animal has "tawny-color"? YES
  Is this true: animal has "dark-spots"? NO
  Rule 4 failed to deduce "is-cheetah"
Attempting to deduce "is-tiger"
  Using Rule 5
  Is this true: animal has "black-stripes"? YES
  Rule 5 deduces "is-tiger"

Figure 5.4 *The trace of the process: identify a tiger. (Adapted from Lewis and Lynch[12].)*

```
---------------------------------------------------------

Frame: TRUCKS in knowledge base TRANSPORTATION
   Superclasses: VEHICLES
   Subclasses: BIG.NON.RED.TRUCKS, HUGE.GREY.TRUCKS
   MemberOf: CLASSES.OF.PHYSICAL.OBJECTS

---------------------------------------------------------
          .
          .
          .
MemberSlot: HEIGHT from PHYSICAL.OBJECTS
   ValueClass: INTEGER
   Cardinality.Min: 1
   Cardinality.Max: 1
   Units: INCHES
   Comment: "Height in inches."
   Values: Unknown

MemberSlot: LENGTH from PHYSICAL.OBJECTS
   ValueClass: NUMBER
   Cardinality.Min: 1
   Cardinality.Max: 1
   Units: METERS
   Comment: "Length in meters"
   Values: Unknown
          .
          .
          .
OwnSlot: LONGEST from CLASS.OF.PHYSICAL.OBJECTS
   ValueClass: TRUCKS
   Cardinality.Min: 1
   Cardinality.Max: 1
   Comment: "The longest known truck"
   Values: Unknown

OwnSlot: TALLEST from CLASS.OF.PHYSICAL.OBJECTS
   ValueClass: TRUCKS
   Cardinality.Min: 1
   Cardinality.Max: 1
   Comment: "The tallest known truck"
   Values: Unknown
          .
          .
          .

---------------------------------------------------------
```

Figure 5.5 *The frame describing class TRUCKS as a subclass of class VEHICLES and as a member of class CLASSES.OF.PHYSICAL.OBJECTS. Member slots in the TRUCKS frame, like LENGTH and HEIGHT, provide a prototype description of each class member. Own slots like LONGEST and TALLEST describe attributes of the class as a whole. From Fikes and Kehler.[14] (Copyright © 1985 by ACM.)*

each member of the class rather than of the class itself. For example, a frame representing the TRUCKS class might have own slots for LONGEST and HEAVIEST and member slots for LENGTH and WEIGHT. Member slots allow class frames to play a role in knowledge bases similar to that of schemas in relational data bases.

The frame facility supplies an expressively powerful language for describing the objects being reasoned about by the rules and automatically performs a useful set of inferences on those descriptions. It provides a means of organizing and indexing modular collections of production rules according to their intended usage.

The prototype descriptions included in class definitions specify criteria for class membership. A classification algorithm could use a taxonomy to first determine that a given object is a vehicle as opposed to a machine or an instrument. That it is a truck as opposed to an auto or boat, etc.

Doyle,[15] London,[16] and de Kleer et al.[17] recognized that the facilities for recording dependencies, dependency-directed backtracking, and "currently believing" particular assumptions could be incorporated into an expert system. These facilities are called a *truth maintenance system* (*TMS*).

KEE has introduced an extension, called a *world,* to both frames and TMS. According to Filman,[18] a world represents a set of related facts: for example, a situation, a simulation check point, a belief set, or a hypothetical state of a problem solver. A world is characterized by a set of assumptions. The TMS remembers the assumptions on which each deduced fact is based. A world sees a deduced fact if and only if the world's assumptions are a superset of the assumptions that support that deduction.

A major advantage of this kind of facility is that it makes the organizational and expressive power of object-oriented programming available to domain experts who are not programmers. In this way, knowledge system technology becomes directly available to a broad class of users. Thanks to advances in software and in hardware engineering, the time to develop major large-scale expert system has been reduced from several man-years (in the 1970s) to several man-months (in the late 1980s).

Faught[19] lists examples of typical engineering applications: fault diagnosis, factory cell simulation, and system configuration.

5.4. SCHEMA, FRAME, BAM, AND FCM

The part of the data base or the chunk of knowledge necessary to carry reasoning, language, memory, and perception for a specialized domain is called the *schema* of the domain. Schema has been discussed by authors in psychology and in AI.

The first problem with schema is knowing what information is relevant to the task at hand. The second problem is the composition of necessary pieces of information into one chunk. The question is: Is intelligent behavior decomposable at all? If intelligence is not decomposable, it is not incrementally achievable.

Schemata are data base structures for representing the generic concepts underlying objects, situations, actions, or events. They represent the model of the outside world stored in the memory (hypotheses). We can define understanding as a locking procedure between the hypotheses and the sensory data stream. The process of understanding selects the internal model that best fits the incoming information. This phenomenon is termed *adaptation*. The system settles into the solution by using a process of relaxation without applying logical operations.

According to Rumelhart et al,[20] sensory input comes into the system and activates a set of units. These units are interconnected and form a sort of constraint satisfaction network. The inputs determine the starting state of the system and the exact shape of the landscape. The system than moves toward one of the goodness maxima (landscape minima). When the system reaches one of these states, there is little tendency to migrate toward another state.

Rumelhart et al.[20] take the example of the schema for a room, composed of description units such as sofa, stove, sink, bookshelf, refrigerator, television, and so on. The descriptions are arranged in a matrix (Figure 5.6). The coefficients indicate the strength of connection between descriptors. For example, we expect the refrigerator and oven to be found together (kitchen), or the bookshelf and television to be found together (living room). Positive coefficients in the matrix represent connection; negative coefficients represent inhibition (pieces do not match together).

The notation +1, −1 is also used to describe an input vector. Hence, input vectors for the kitchen and for the living room have the form:

$$\text{kitchen (sofa, stove, sink, book, refrigerator, television)} = (-1,1,1,-1,1,-1)$$

$$\text{living room (sofa, stove, sink, book refrigerator, television)} = (1,-1,-1,1,-1,1)$$

This approach offers an interpretation of the schema in terms of the emergent properties of simple PDP networks, similar to artificial neural networks and, particularly, to bidirectional associative memories (BAMs). In both cases, the network settles toward the minimum in the landscape, or, in other words, it operates on the principle of minimum energy.

Hopfield[21] showed that if the weights in the matrix are symmetrical and the units are updated one at a time, the iterative retrieval process can be viewed as a form of gradient descent in an energy function.

In a BAM, several vectors are superimposed in the same matrix. The question comes in the form of a distorted or partially specified vector.

	Sofa	Stove	Sink	Book	Refrig.	Telev.
Sofa	0	−1	−1	1	−1	1
Stove	−1	0	1	−1	1	−1
Sink	−1	1	0	−1	1	−1
Book	1	−1	−1	0	−1	1
Refrig.	−1	1	1	−1	0	−1
Telev.	1	−1	−1	1	−1	0

Figure 5.6 *Matrix representation of schema.*

Through an iterative retrieval process, the best match is found in the matrix memory. The iterative BAM process is described by Kosko.[22,23] Kosko[24] also uses the matrix to store if-then rules of an expert system in the form of connection strengths. The systems are called *fuzzy cognitive maps* (FCM).

In this way macroknowledge processing based on symbolic structures is merged with microknowledge processing based on connection structures. This fact opens new avenues in software and in hardware design. A variety of novel and hybrid systems are under development. An example of a hybrid system is SAMPAN, developed by Chun and Mimo.[25] SAMPAN combines marker passing with connectionist spreading activation for schema selection. A network was constructed to represent five different schemas: restaurant, theater, subway, shopping, and sport.

The network currently contains 70 concept templates and 4830 links. The templates encode concepts that may be shared by several schemata. An example of the concept template is a person sitting on a chair. For experimentation, new stories were constructed and fed to the network. An example of a sentence from the story is: John sat down in the restaurant. SAMPAN correctly matches concepts it knows about in the stories and generates the appropriate expectations.

SAMPAN sends each concept in the story to all 70 nodes in the network and relaxes the network for one cycle. During relaxation, pattern matching and marker merging was performed. Figure 5.7 is a screen printout showing the state of the SAMPAN network processing one simple new story. Each row represents the network activation at a particular cycle (one sentence of the story). Each column represents a node in the network. The darkness of the shading is proportional to the activation level in a node. As a result, the network formed coalitions of concepts in each cycle as it processed the story.

Hybrid systems such as SAMPAN open new possibilities in knowledge acquisition. According to Feigenbaum,[26] knowledge acquisition is a long-standing problem of AI. Is it possible to acquire the knowledge automatically, or at least semiautomatically? Could a computer transfer the knowl-

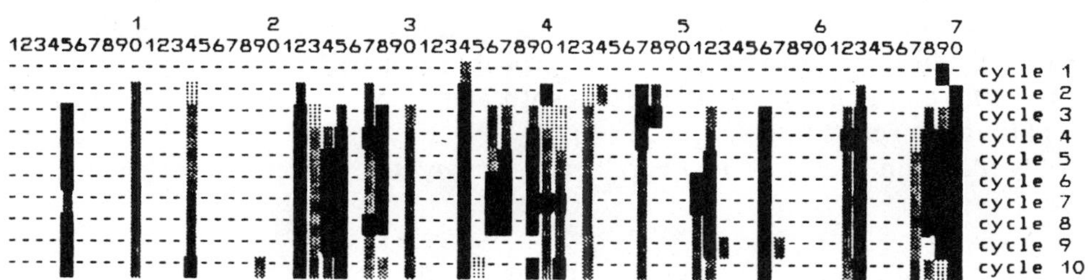

Figure 5.7 *SAMPAN: The activation level of the 70 nodes in the example network. (Following Chun and Mimo[25]. Courtesy and copyright © 1987 by IEEE.)*

edge from human practitioners, their texts, or their data to the symbolic data structures that constitute the knowledge representation in the machine? Learning in hybrid systems is a promising new tool for knowledge acquisition.

With this class of tools, it seems possible to build a "knowledge refinery" as envisaged by Mickie.[27] The product to be refined is codified human knowledge. Improvement can be brought about by a machine-based technique known as knowledge refining. Refining is the improvement in knowledge representation when back-translated from an advice program. One of the first experiments in knowledge refining was Bratko's[28] set of six chess rules (king and rook against king). Many researchers and students using expert systems found that these systems are better sources of knowledge than the textbooks are.

Knowledge refining might be the basis of a new industry, with schema, frame, BAM, and FCM being the first set of tools.

5.5. LEARNING IN RULE-BASED SYSTEMS

Rule-based machine learning has been investigated by Winston,[29] Michalski, Carbonell, and Mitchell,[30] and Forsyth and Rada.[31] One of the most successful methods is empirical learning (EL). According to Gams and Petkovšek,[32] EL can be regarded as a knowledge acquisition tool for expert systems. Its advantages over classical knowledge acquisition methods are that it gives an explanation (a) during classification of a new example and (b) of the entire problem domain. This ability is obtained by tracing the classification rules and by constructing the knowledge base.

The problem of EL is to find an optimal classification rule. Pruning of the rule set is used to find a global optimum according to the given (usually error estimate) function.

A set of learning examples $L = (x,c)$ consists of pairs (x,c), where x is a vector denoting properties of the object in a measurement space X, and c represents the index of the class of example x. Components of vectors x are called *attributes* or *variables*. The values of attributes can be numerical or categorical.

A classification or a decision rule $d(x)$ is a mapping that maps every x from X into some c from C or into the probability distribution $(p_1, p_2, \ldots, p_J)$, where p_i is a real number between 0 and 1. A classification rule $d(x)$ splits the space X into subspaces $X_1, X_2, \ldots, X_J$ such that for every X_i only a certain subset of $d(x)$ is relevant. The syntax of a classification rule $d(x)$ is

```
    <d> : : = <Rule>|<Rule> and <d> ;
classication rule
 <Rule> : : = <Class> if <Cpx>       ; rule
```

```
  <Cpx> : : = <Sel> |<Sel>  and <Cpx>; complex
  <Sel> : : = ε   | Atr <op><Values>   ;
selector
<Values>: : = Val| Val  or <Values>  ; values
 <Class>: : = 1|2|3 ...|J              ; class
 <op>    : : = < |=| >                 ;
operators
```

Atr corresponds to the name of an attribute, and Val is a categorical or a numerical value.

An example of EL is GINESYS (generic inductive expert system shell), developed by Gams and Petkovšek.[32] The top-level syntax of GINESYS is

```
repeat
  initialize Rule ;
  generate Rule ;
  add Rule to  d(x) ;
  L = L -  examples covered by Rule  (learning
  examples )
until satisfiable (d(x))
```

In this general view, GINESYS represents a prototype of a unifying algorithm for EL covering many other systems. In a slightly more specific description, we obtain the following algorithm:

```
repeat
  generalize Rule ;
  repeat
    specialize Rule
  until stop (Rule) ;
  postprocess (Rule) ;
  add Rule to d(x) ;
  L=L - examples covered by Rule
until satisfiable (d(x))
```

The main difference between other EL systems and GINESYS is in "confirmation rules." The basic idea of confirmation rules is to use several sources of information for classification. That seems to be common practice in everyday life. For example, when we try to predict the weather, we look at the official weather report, but we also look at the sky and ask our neighbors. The implementation of this idea in GINESYS is that instead of using only one rule for classification, several rules confirm or confront the first one.

In general, EL achieved good results in practical testing in several real-world domains, practically approaching or even outperforming domain experts and statistical methods.

Self-learning is a difficult task in both neural networks and rule-based expert systems. Fine granularity in neural networks and coarse granularity in expert systems have their advantages and limitations. For many applications, a mixture of these techniques provides the best solution. It is also conjectured that the human mind may use symbolic representations as well as connectionist networks.

5.6. REAL-TIME KNOWLEDGE SYSTEMS AND LANING–INTELLICORP RECOMMENDATIONS†

Knowledge system applications in on-line, real-time environments, such as automated factories and continuous and batch process plants, typically involve reasoning on large complex systems. A two-stage development approach, which includes an on-line phase, is recommended. First create and test an off-line prototype of the system being modelled and analyzed, and then integrate and scale up the prototype into the on-line environment. If the eventual goal is to build a closed-loop system, such as an automated machine controller, it is recommended that the second stage include the development of an intermediate open-loop system, with the knowledge system acting in the capacity of an operator's assistant.

Not surprisingly, at each stage different issues arise which are addressed by different aspects of AI technology. In the first stage the knowledge system developer's efforts focus on understanding how best to represent the system of interest in order to build a computational model which can be reasoned over and analyzed by other components of the application. At this point the developer is concerned principally with how easily and rapidly scale models of the system being analyzed can be prototyped; the issues of real-time performance and on-line integration are secondary.

While the model developed in the first stage serves as the basis for the on-line real-time application, new issues emerge as the application is moved from the off-line to the on-line environment. The developer must now deal with the following issues of real-time performance and on-line integration:

1. Human–machine interfaces;
2. Machine–machine interfaces and configurations;
3. Data transfer rates;
4. The impact of "garbage collection" on real-time performance;
5. Hardware configurations for industrial environments;
6. Reasoning speed; and,
7. Concurrence of data with the reasoning process.

Laning[33] discusses the preceding issues in the following way.

† This section adapted from D. B. Laning, *Moving Knowledge Systems Into Real-Time, On-Line Environments: A Look at the Issues*. Intellicorp Report, 1986.

5.6.1. Human–Machine Interfaces

The major payoff of a well designed interface in an on-line environment is reduced operator fatigue and error, and improved system performance. The higher process speeds, closer tolerances, more complex dynamics, and integration and interaction with other systems of people and machines make it imperative that applications developed for use by process and factory operators provide them with clear and understandable information. With such facilities as the ActiveImages graphics workbench, KEE provides an extremely powerful set of tools and options for defining and customizing human-machine interfaces that are highly usable and consistent with the principles of good systems engineering.

5.6.2. Machine–Machine Interfaces

A practical approach to introducing knowledge systems into on-line real-time environments involves using symbolically oriented machines in conjunction with numerically oriented machines, such as a process control systems. Numerically intensive and data acquisition processes are performed on the conventional machine, while reasoning-intensive processes are performed on the symbolically oriented machine. The development of the necessary dedicated machine-machine interfaces commonly requires some custom software development, and the specific approach will depend on the data communication needs of the particular application. Reading and writing of data into and out of KEE knowledge bases is relatively straightforward, as is the implementation of the hardware communication link through a network, RS232 port or dedicated bus. Most of the effort involved in developing the interface is embodied in writing the software to create a format understandable by both machines for the transmission, reception, storage, and access of data.

5.6.3. Data Transfer Rates

Tests performed at IntelliCorp indicate that a significant portion of the time spent transferring data from an external, conventional machine to a KEE-based application running on a symbolic processor is devoted to moving the data from machine to machine, and not in entering it in the knowledge base itself. Two tests were run using a Symbolics 3640 LISP machine with 4 Megabytes of RAM and 52 blocks of virtual page space netted to a VAX 11/750 on a quiet ethernet connection. In the first test 0.626 seconds were required to read 4000 integer data points from a file already in the Symbolics to a KEE knowledge base. In the second test 9.87 seconds transpired in the two step process of reading the same data in from the VAX over the ethernet and then putting it into the KEE knowledge base.

5.6.4. Garbage Collection

The periodic need to reclaim memory cells when running LISP-based applications, (i.e., "garbage collection,") becomes an important issue once data has entered a knowledge system. If the required response time for control actions is much larger than the time required to do background garbage collection and knowledge system analysis there should be no problems with real-time control. However, certain strategies may be taken to minimize the impact of this basic LISP machine operation, including: using a machine with continual background garbage collection capabilities; designing the application to reduce the use of memory-hungry functions such as window creation; compiling the code; and, off-loading low level computational processes to conventional machines where appropriate.

5.6.5. Hardware Configurations for Industrial Environments

Equipment incorporated into an industrial environment must be ruggedized and highly reliable. In general, computer systems used to directly control an industrial process should have a mean-time-between-failure much larger than the process being controlled. From this standpoint, a prudent strategy for the integration of a LISP-based processor into the industrial environment would be to use a LISP machine as a high-level process analysis executive linked to a dedicated conventional computer (such as an IBM mainframe, a VAX super-mini or a process control system such as a Honeywell TDC 3000), which in turn is linked directly to the process.

5.6.6. Reasoning Speed

There are actually two issues to consider when using rule-based reasoning within a knowledge system: predictability and speed. Closed-loop systems often include processes which require that an action be taken within a specific period of time. The number of possible combinations of a large rule set may make it unsuitable for operation within specific time constants. Attempts to control the amount of time consumed by any particular rule chain, perhaps by the use of meta-rules, may produce unpredictable behavior. Therefore, rule-based reasoning may not be an appropriate strategy for certain closed-loop control systems, regardless of their performance or implementation language.

Also, for those applications where it is possible to use simple, rule-based formulations it is probably the case that straightforward algorithms, implemented using active values or object-oriented programming, would be computationally more efficient. The KEE system's hybrid architecture enables the developer to explore alternative reasoning approaches—rules, object-oriented programming, active values, and truth maintenance systems—in order to determine which is best-suited to the constraints imposed by the particular real-time environment.

In summary, recommendations when implementing reasoning systems are:

1. Use the approach—rules, algorithms, active values, and so on—best-suited to solving the problem;
2. Organize the system into modules in order to expedite the understanding, validation, and performance of time-critical components;
3. Experiment with different encodings to optimize speed.

5.6.7. Data Concurrence

In general, during backward chaining, changes reported by a data acquisition system must be queued until reasoning halts. However, in many real-time situations the application involves event consequence analysis for system control, an application area that is more likely to use forward chaining or object-oriented programming, both of which allow changes to be more freely mixed with execution. Finally, in addition to rule-based backward and forward chaining, it is possible to perform totally asynchronous reasoning where needed through the use of active values.

5.7. A CONTROL SYSTEM SIMULATOR†

According to Nielsen[34] an automated factory can be thought of as containing a coordinated set of computer-controlled devices. Examples of such devices are:

- Production machines—devices for manufacturing products (e.g., lathes, drill presses, and grinders);
- Assembly machines—devices that assemble products from components (e.g., robots and specialized equipment); and
- Material-handling equipment—devices that transport components and products from point to point in the factory (e.g., robots, conveyors, and moving carts).

The control of such devices is often distributed throughout the factory. Attached to each device is a controller, either general purpose or specialized, depending on the device. Groups of machines or machining centers and their controllers can then be clustered into cells, with cell computers used to sequence the work of the machines and to direct their controllers. Similarly,

† This section adapted from N. R. Nielsen, "The Impact of Using AI-Based Techniques in a Control System Simulator," *Proceedings of the Conference on AI and Simulation: Simulation Series,* **18**(3) San Diego, July 1987.

cells can be clustered into areas under the control of area computers, and the area computers can be connected to a top-level or factory-wide computer. Processors on the same or different levels are linked with various types of networks or communications mechanisms.

As products are manufactured or assembled in the factory, various messages (transactions) flow through the control network, triggering various processing actions and further information flows. For example, messages are sent from controllers signalling the completion of processing on a workpiece; other messages are sent to obtain the control programs for the next part to be produced or assembled. Routing information must be sent to material-handling controllers; status reports and alarms must be sent to supervisory processors.

The issues to be addressed by the simulation model are the design of a control system for a particular factory environment and the evaluation of that system's performance as these issues relate to both the processors (controllers) and the network interconnecting them. Specifically, the simulator investigates:

1. The number of levels that the control hierarchy should contain between the factory level computer at the top of the hierarchy and the machine controller at the bottom
2. The power of the processor/controller at each node in the hierarchy;
3. The level at which various types of data should be stored (and whether those data should be stored redundantly at multiple locations);
4. The level at which various types of control processing should be performed; and
5. The bandwith and priority mechanism that should be associated with each communication link.

5.8. COMPUTER INTEGRATED MANUFACTURING (CIM)

There is a view of CIM which seems to consist of simply replacing the acronym CAD/CAM with the more fashionable one of CIM and adding the notion of increased application integration. Often, this perspective is accompanied by the assumption that automating the creation and distribution of numerical control data sets for operating machine tools is the fundamental goal of CIM.

According to Lindsay[35] adherence to this narrow view of CIM would grossly miss the mark in an environment such as that found at Northrop or any other major aerospace manufacturer. The majority of production activity at the Northrop Aircraft Division consists of other than material removal operations. In a division which employs approximately 15,000 people, less than 200 perform the NC programming function. Therefore, more than

14,000 individuals are busy doing something else to deliver Northrop's product. This is not to suggest that effective CAD/CAM applications directed toward NC generation are not necessary. Instead this indicates the need for a much broader view of CIM, that may include these applications, but which embraces the other functions within the manufacturing enterprise as well.

Another view of CIM recognizes that "islands of automation" have been created in many enterprises and that these can be categorized into four groups. These groups are listed below along with typical islands of automation found in these groups, following Appleton.[36]

1. CAD/CAM
    - Group technology
    - Computer-aided engineering
    - Computer-aided design
    - Computer-aided manufacturing
2. Manufacturing planning and control
    - Inventory control
    - Shop loading
    - Capacity planning
    - Master scheduling
    - Purchasing
3. Factory automation
    - Computer-aided manufacturing
    - Robotics
    - NC/DNC/CNC
    - Flexible manufacturing systems
    - Automated materials handling systems
    - Automated test equipment
    - Process controllers
4. General business management
    - General and cost accounting
    - Marketing
    - Order entry
    - Decision support
    - Labor collection
    - Payroll

From this perspective CIM involves the integration of the islands of automation within these groups and the integration between the groups themselves.

It should be remembered that many activities which create and use data within an enterprise may not have reached an island of automation and are, figuratively speaking, still in the water fighting off the sharks. A complete view of CIM includes all usage of data within the enterprise.

CIM has two major technical components, other than the underlying technologies of a physical communication structure and transaction management. The first component is the management of all enterprise information within a single logical but distributed database shared by all functions which have reason to create and/or use such data. This database management system (DBMS) must provide the various functions of the enterprise with multiple concurrent views of enterprise information from a single source. This component is the backbone of CIM. If implemented, such a DBMS would achieve CIM regardless of whether the data was created or used manually or automatically. The second component encompasses the various computer applications which automate or assist in the creation, analysis, transformation and use of enterprise data.

5.9. MODEL-BASED REASONING†

According to Nardi and Simons[37] the heart of model-based reasoning is the development of an *explicit model* of the system of interest. Many knowledge based systems "compile away" knowledge in heuristic rules instead of explicitly building a model of the problem. Although this may be appropriate for some applications, for others it means the development of a less powerful system which can solve fewer problems, as illustrated in Koton.[38] Koton built two versions of a problem solver to reason about the behavior of bacterial operons (a problem in molecular biology). The first program used only "large-grained compiled knowledge" in the form of rules. The second program provided an explicit model of the problem including a detailed description of each object and its control mechanisms. The second program was able to solve more difficult problems than the first. Koton noted that "[The first program] cannot discover the mechanism by which [the gene's behavior] occurs, because the particular combination of mutations does not correctly match any of its heuristics". The model-based program, on the other hand, "should be able to solve any problem that is derivable from the model of the domain."

In industrial applications, Nardi and Simons[37] believe that model-based reasoning will give leverage to developers by (1) providing a system capable of generating more solutions to a problem, and (2) providing a cost-effective means of integrating the efforts of many individuals working on different parts of a complex problem. Because an explicit model is the point of departure for performing different kinds of analyses over a single domain, knowl-

† Sections 5.9, 5.10, and 5.11 are adapted from B. A. Nardi and R. K. Simons, *Model-Based Reasoning and AI Problem Solving,* Workshop on High Level Tools for Knowledge-Based Systems, Columbus, Ohio, October 1986.

edge about the domain is *accessible*. The importance of the accessibility of knowledge cannot be over-emphasized.

Model-based reasoning gives project team members a shared reference point for their individual efforts. Working with a model, team members make the same assumptions about the problem domain. A shared model is an effective means of communicating information among group members. Duplication of effort is avoided as the central model is developed collectively and then used by all.

Model-based reasoning casts a model in terms of structured objects representing discrete entities, object behaviors and relations between objects. Because discrete objects are the conceptual basis for the model, they are easy to represent graphically (since it is easy to draw a picture of an object and to understand what that picture means). Graphics themselves provide new perspectives on a problem. Model-based reasoning is thus valuable in generating *multiple views of the same knowledge*. This aids problem solving as a different view of the same knowledge often yields new insights into a problem, leading to new solutions.

Knowledge contained in a model is more easily modified because of its accessibility. As understanding of the problem evolves, the model can be changed because structure and behavior are embodied in discrete objects, easy to conceptualize. As a system grows and matures, it typically becomes more complex. Model-based reasoning helps to manage that complexity via a system that is easy to view and manipulate. This flexibility makes a model-based program a suitable tool for the kinds of complex problems of ten tackled with knowledge based systems.

5.10. THE FACTORY MODEL

According to Nardi and Simons[37] the factory model is the basis for a simulation of factory operations. Items of different types move from one machine to another until they have finished processing. Machines must be set up to process an item whose type is different than the last item processed. The factory model contains:

1. Structured objects (''units'' in the KEE system) described in terms of membership in a class hierarchy and in terms of the attributes of each object.
2. Behaviors for the objects implemented using rules, methods and active values.
3. Relations among objects (e.g., upstream and downstream).

Model objects and their relations are represented graphically and can be viewed, created and connected to one another through a SimKit graphic interface called the model editor. A ''library'' of model objects is created in which each type of object is represented by a class. A bitmap picture of the object is part of the library and is used to graphically represent the object in the Model Editor. Each of the objects is automatically created as an instantiation of the class object defined in the library (i.e., as an instance unit in the knowledge base). Both a visual representation of the model and its representation as objects with attributes in a knowledge base are automatically performed through simple interactions with the model editor.

The use of the model editor promotes a "specification by reformulation" approach in which it is not necessary to specify ahead of time exactly what the model will look like. As it becomes visible, the model can be critiqued and improved. It is also extremely easy to build, extend, and modify models with such an interactive graphic interface. The model editor is useful for anyone building a model, but in particular it broadens access to knowledge based system tools to those who are domain experts, but not necessarily proficient in knowledge engineering. An expert can directly participate in the process of model-building and task solution without much additional training. The "knowledge acquisition bottleneck" is thus alleviated to some degree by a tool such as the model editor.

As the simulation model is run with varying parameters, the user needs to watch for changes in variables such as inventory levels, lateness of parts, and machine utilization.

5.11. THE FACTORY MODEL APPLICATION

Nardi and Simons[37] give the following suggestions.

5.11.1. Adaptive Scheduling

Adaptive scheduling is a scheme in which each machine dynamically makes its own scheduling decisions with full knowledge of the operations in all parts of the factory. The decisions are made "on the fly" in order to respond to the very latest conditions, such as a machine failure. This is in contrast to conventional scheduling methods which generate a complete schedule for a day (or some unit of time) and then attempt to reschedule everything when interruptions occur.

The way that adaptive scheduling compares with other scheduling methods can be partially tested with the Factory Model. (Field testing is also critical.) We wrote several scheduling algorithms and are testing them with the use of Gantt charts, as described below. Using a model-based reasoning approach facilitated writing the scheduling algorithms as the work was done across project sites. Having the model as a continual point of shared reference proved valuable in coordinating this work. It also provided the basis for developing the custom graphics that are the basis of the testing work.

5.11.2. Graphics

Because the underpinnings of the factory model are discrete objects, it was not difficult (with the aid of the KEE system's KEE Pictures graphics facility) to create some helpful graphics tools. The Gantt chart, for example, has been useful in developing and testing new scheduling algorithms. The Gantt chart shows each object as it moves through the factory, how long it took to process, its setup time and its due date. A schedule is generated using a method (such as shortest-processing-time) and is displayed on the Gantt chart. The schedule may be displayed dynamically as the schedule is actually being run, or displayed in full after the run is complete. The unit underlying an object can be seen by middle clicking on the object. The path of a particular object through the factory can be seen by left clicking on the graphical object which causes the object to be highlighted.

Testing scheduling algorithms is accomplished by displaying Gantt charts for different schedules and comparing them. Testing itself actually becomes an interesting analytical activity with the right graphical interface. Instead of poring over output, the user can watch the schedule as it is created, and view the objects in an arresting visual way which yields insights into what is happening in the schedule.

5.11.3. Alarms Management

The second problem to be solved with the model is alarms management. In a highly automated, integrated factory with several thousand parts and resources such as equipment, workers, tools, and computers, the amount of data collected when in operation will be exorbitant. Alarm conditions include machine malfunction, (or "downtimes") part unavailability and item lateness. It is not enough to collect data points; complete detection of alarm conditions often requires analysis with respect to time. For example, the detection of increased variance of a drill's boring size indicates that the drill bit requires replacement. Tools to help factory engineers schedule preventative maintenance of tools and machines are likely to be very cost-effective.

The factory model project first focused on signalling alarms for machine downtimes and item lateness. Machine downtimes are introduced at random into the schedule. The scheduler generates a schedule based on due dates of items. As simulated machine failures occur, the time for the introduction or completion of an item to be processed on a machine (an "operation") may be delayed. This delay in the operation signals an alarm condition. Because of system dependencies, subsequent operations may be late, and each operation is marked with information about the cause of the alarm condition. The Gantt charts again proved useful in recognition of alarm states. When an alarm occurs, the item operation which caused the alarm flashes. Machine downtimes can also be introduced in a nonrandom fashion wherein the user specifies when and for how long a particular machine will be unavailable.

This enables users to run precise what-if scenarios in order to analyze various scheduling algorithms.

The choice for this implementation of alarms allows for the expansion of the definition of alarms. It will be easy to extend the model to allow for delays in transport times as potential alarm conditions since such delays inevitably result in the delay of part operations. It is also possible to further delineate alarms. Tolerance bands can be used to determine that an alarm triggered from a part five minutes late is low priority, while an alarm triggered from a part two hours late is of high priority.

5.11.4. Data Entry Editor

In general, present tools for model-based reasoning support the creation of objects and relations in the model (e.g., machines, queues, downstream relations). In other words, constructing the basic model itself is fairly well-supported. However, *using* the model could be made easier. For example, entering data such as general model parameters, options for data display or the creation or selection of items such as batches, lots or orders, is left to the user. A data entry editor, in the general shape of a "form" to be filled out, would be very helpful here.

5.11.5. Multi-User Knowledge Systems

Because model-based reasoning lends itself to solving many problems emanating from a single central model, it is inevitable that project teams of many individuals will work with the knowledge bases that comprise a model. Sophisticated tools for building knowledge systems are only a few years old at most, and have not yet been refined to handle multiple users with ease.

One difficulty is that when more than one developer must make changes to a knowledge base, version problems may result. This is especially true for multisite project teams who do not share a file server and are not in daily personal communication. A facility for comparing and merging knowledge bases would be useful. This facility might generate a lot of changes and then step the user through each change, updating appropriate files as needed.

Another problem is that when knowledge bases get large and must be updated at several sites, much time is spent making small, simple changes, because the entire knowledge base must be saved. An incremental save capability would be helpful. This would dovetail with the compare/merge facility suggested above.

5.12. EXPERT SYSTEMS IN ENGINEERING

Typical engineering applications of expert systems are automatic fault diagnosis, factory cell simulation, and knowledge-based robot and process control. These expert systems follow the concept of model-based reasoning. The model contains an explicit description of a domain, objects, relationships between objects, and a taxonomy of the object classes.

Faught[19] describes two engineering applications of expert systems, based on software development systems KEE: automatic fault diagnosis and factory cell simulation. Automatic fault diagnosis was developed at the NASA Johnson Space Center for the space station; see Figure 5.8.

The expert system simulates the behavior of the CS-1 device, an electrochemical CO_2 subsystem for removing CO_2 from cabin air. It allows the user to interactively identify the cause of a fault (by graphically choosing the component on the schematic to fail) and to diagnose the fault.

The system is composed of frames (units) to represent each of the components and classes of components in the CS-1 device; graphics objects to represent (1) the graphic images of the device components, (2) various gauges that instrument the device, and (3) images that control the execution of the diagnostic system; and two sets of rules for diagnosing faults.

Each component in the CS-1 device is represented by a unit or frame data structure and is connected to other components by slots or attributes in the frames. The frame representation reduced the number of rules in the system by eliminating the requirement for rules expressing the relationship between objects.

The upper right-hand gauges represent temperature, pressure, and voltage values; the lower left-hand images indicate values for flags to control the diagnostic system.

The processing strategy (which mimics the expert's strategy) at each rule level is a standard backward-chaining process; hypotheses are tested in sequence. A unique characteristic of the expert's strategy was the subdivision of the problem into two levels. The expert first determined the subsystem in which the fault occurred. He then identified the faulty component within that subsystem. The diagnostic expert system decomposed the problem according to this strategy: One set of rules determined which subsystem was faulty according to heuristics that examined the pattern of voltages on the multiple cells removing the CO_2. The second set of rules, within the context of the subsystem, determined which component was faulty by examining gauge measurements along the flow of gases in the subsystem. These two sets of rules were invoked separately—the first set by a top-level command to start the diagnosis, the second set by the first set's successful conclusion.

Factory cell simulation is shown in Figure 5.9. It uses the KEE system to simulate a factory sheet metal fabrication cell to perform studies on part routing, capacity evaluation, and scheduling decisions. The simulation was needed to answer several questions:

1. How can setup times be reduced and throughput increased? In particular, what is the impact of having a workstation choose from the three

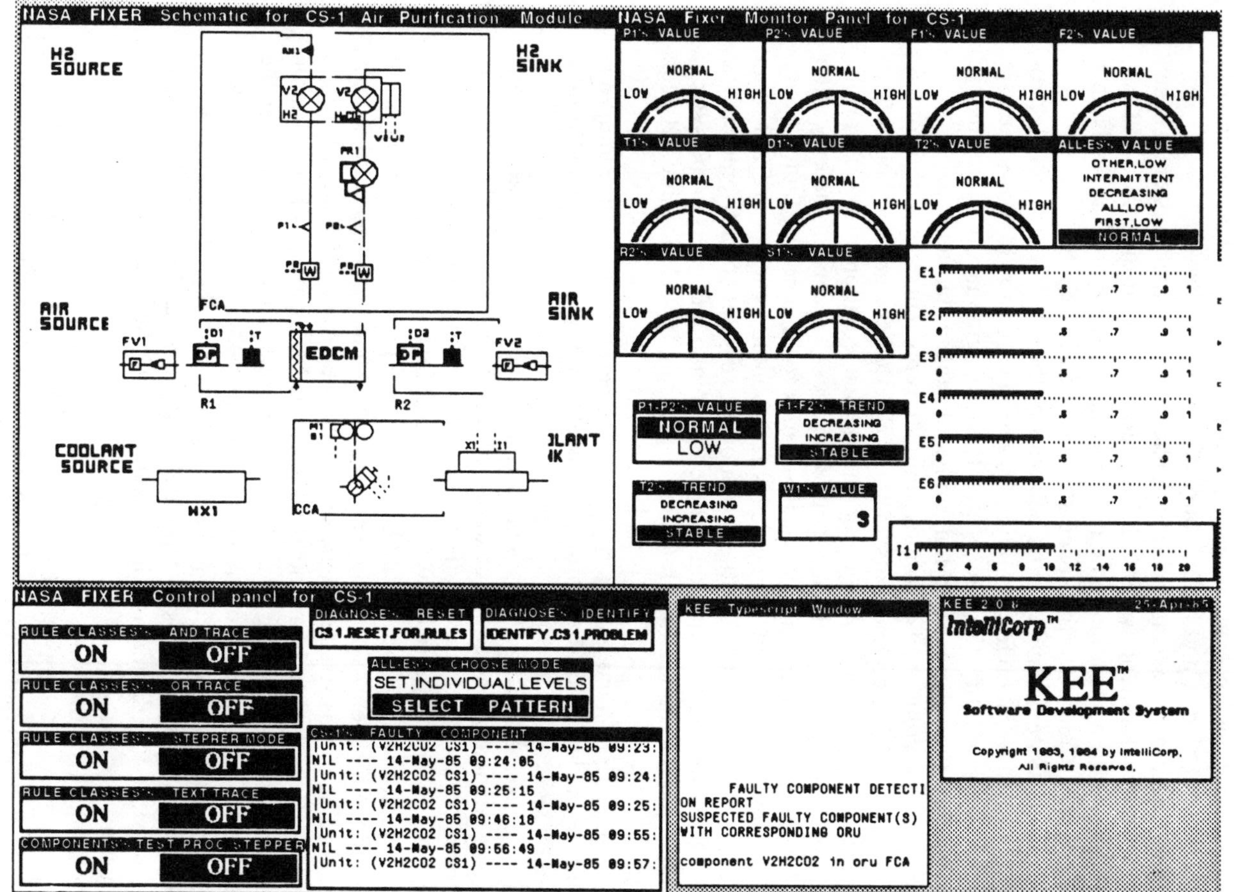

Figure 5.8 *The NASA diagnostic system for the space station subsystem uses multiple sets of rules provided by NASA experts. From Faught.*[19] *(Courtesy and copyright © 1986 by IEEE.)*

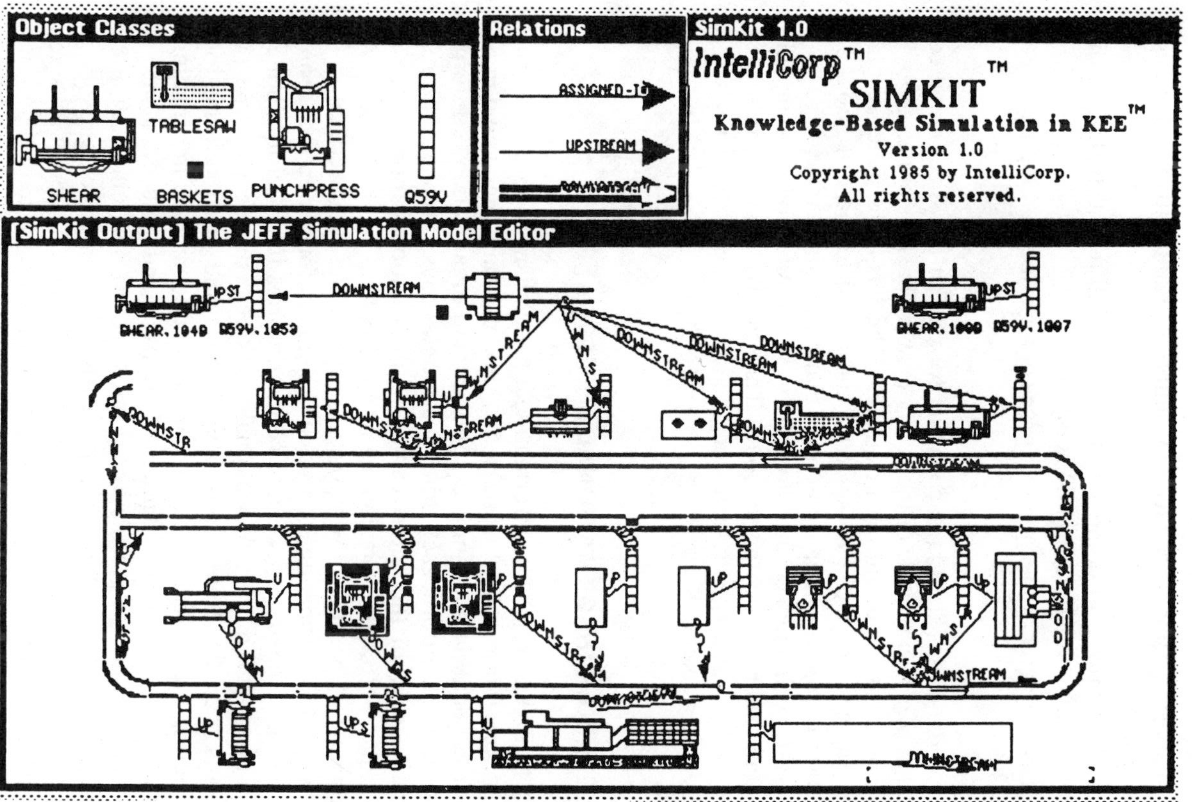

Figure 5.9 *The Northrop sheet metal factory simulation aids planners in determining the effect of part thickness and setup times on plant throughput. (From Faught[19]. Courtesy and copyright © 1986 by IEEE.)*

or four waiting jobs to reduce setup as opposed to selecting the first one that arrived (FIFO—first in–first out)?

2. How can setup time be reduced by simply working with a single thickness of metal in any day?
3. What is the impact of doing a rush job with a different thickness, thus requiring substantial additional setup time?
4. What is the actual time spent in process for a job, as opposed to the ideal?

Figure 5.9 illustrates the graphic display for part of the sheet metal cell. The central area is a schematic of the cell floor, with baskets of parts moving along the conveyors and waiting in queues. The left-hand panel displays classes of machines that can be selected and added to the cell floor. The images at the top represent gauges on simulation parameters.

Expert systems in engineering allow the user without programming skills to modify and experiment with the model. They provide visibility into structure, parameters, strategies, behavior, and data collected for analysis through graphic depictions.

5.13. ŽELEZNIKAR INFORMATIONAL LOGIC

According to Železnikar,[39,40,41] informational parallelism is one of the most complex notions that mankind was able to think of, comprehend, and implement. Informational parallelism is a structure and organization of informational processes that inform each other in a spontaneous, circular, recurrent, unforeseeable way. In this interweaving of informational forms and processes, complex information is coming into existence.

The principle of parallel informational program can be described in the following way. An informational program is simply information that spontaneously informs, embeds, arises, and counterinforms in an informationally circular manner, within an informational machine. An informational program informs (i.e., generates and changes itself and other informational programs during their execution) and is influenced in such an informational way by other informational programs. It is used and embedded into an informational machine for production of information. This information can be, for instance, intelligent, specialized creativity, expert, problem solving, dedicated informational functions, and so forth. Evidently, there is an essential difference between a computer program and an informative program. The former is algorithmic, mathematical, procedural, and informationally static, whereas the latter is informational, intelligent, and informationally dynamic.

The logic, which in its main part deals with informational parallelism, is being developed up to the form of an informational axiomatic system. In this regard, the system is not a usual axiomatic approach of pure mathematical doctrines, but, above all, it incorporates informational principles. This logical theory represents a generative axiomatic system, the intention of which is to preserve semantically the nature of the redefined notion of information.

The new formalism introduces several symbols for operators, along with those already known, and a new semantics. The axiomatic basis of informational logic is still in the phase of development and formal construction. Some operators of general parallel informing are informing in parallel; possible informing in parallel; necessary informing in parallel; noninforming in parallel; informational carrying off; informational bringing; blocking to carry off; blocking to bring; sending and informing; receiving and informing; nonsending and noninforming; nonreceiving and noninforming; causing of informational appearance; noncausing of informational appearance; coming into existence; noncoming into existence; causing informational end; coming to end; noncausing informational end; noncoming to end; choosing among informational alternatives; choosing and informing; being informationally impressed or memorized; recalling, disintegrating, and informing; informing similarly; interrupting; breaking down; enriching; and cyclical parallel informing. The Železnikar[39,40,41] theory of parallel processing within informational logic can be the basis for conception, design, and application of future parallel computing systems. In this context, the development of informational philosophy and adequate axiomatization and formalization of informational concepts could be the way to new intelligent systems.

5.14. FROM FINE TO COARSE INTELLIGENCE GRANULARITY

Kolmogorov's theorem is considered a guide to the design of mapping networks. As the theorem suggests, three layers (two mappings) are needed to classify the input data into the number of clusters desired. The hidden layer is specified through the back-propagation training algorithm.

Back propagation is a time-consuming algorithm. It is good to create a prototype mapping network for a given task. Once the weights are established, the network can be transferred into the fixed-chip structure.

Higher-order neural units simplify the network. However, it is necessary to use some a priori knowledge to choose the optimal structure of the unit. In this way, a general-purpose learning network might be constructed from specialized modules.

Self-organization through selection might prove a powerful alternative to connectionism in neural networks and to programming in symbolic systems. As opposed to connectionist models, selectionism can arrive at complex structures. As opposed to symbolic expert systems, the selection system is not rigid but it provides for uncertainties and deviations.

Schemas and frames are treated similarly to BAMs and FCMs. In this way, symbolic processing is merged with connection adaptation.

The system settles into the solution by using a process of relaxation.

Hecht-Nielsen[42] distinguishes neural and programmed computing in the following way: neurocomputing and programmed computing are fundamentally different approaches to information processing. Neurocomputing is based upon transformations, whereas programmed computing is based upon algorithms and procedures. What is being discovered is that these two types of information processing are conceptually incompatible. In other words, it is becoming clear that it may often be impossible to satisfactorily describe the operation of a transformation in terms of an algorithm, and vice versa. This fact is often disquieting to people who think exclusively in procedural terms, since it means that neurocomputing may provide solutions to important information processing problems without allowing us to discover the fundamental ideas used in the solution (at least in terms of present-day information processing concepts).

A fascinating thought is that neuroscience may run into this same problem in the future. Specifically, the thought is that an accurate understanding of the mechanics of the individual neurons and their interactions may be achieved, but that this will reveal virtually nothing about how brains process information. The resolution of both of these difficulties may require an intellectual revolution in information processing as profound as that in physics brought about by the Copenhagen interpretation of quantum mechanics. Because of the potential development and implementation cost and time savings, 10 years from now neurocomputing may become the information processing paradigm of choice in every application where it can be used.

Kohonen[43] favors the following definition of neural computers: artificial neural networks are massively parallel interconnected networks of simple (usually adaptive) elements and their hierarchical organizations that are intended to interact with the objects of the real world in the same way as the biological neurons systems do. In other words, artificial sensory functions and automatic motor control are then the most meaningful tasks for neural computing. Because neural networks are meant to interact with the real world, their operation must be related to the interaction with natural objects. Whatever the prospects for this "new AI," understanding the operation of the brain is already a challenge that alone would motivate this endeavor.

According to Widrow and Winter,[44] generalization in neural networks is a key issue. Merely learning the training patterns can be accomplished by storing these patterns and desired responses in a look-up table. Generalization means that the network is insensitive to the pattern size, as well as to translation and rotation. Also, the network should extract the dominant features from a limited number of samples and recognize these features in patterns not used for training.

Different approaches to generalization are possible: back propagation, alternating projection, stochastic computing, scrambling/descrambling, probabilistic logic neuron, high-order units, Boolean logic neuron, and others. A combination of these approaches may be needed to produce the required generalization.

Souček and Souček[5] emphasize the role of computer models of brain and behavior as the basis for fine- and medium-grain intelligent system design. Brain and behavior models provide processes and models that are more powerful than the simple neuron model. These processes can be emulated by adaptive, selective, and concurrent networks. The features found in brain behavior models include brain window logic, language based on adaptive receive and send windows, "Zeitgeber" curves that control innate release mechanisms, stimulus-response nonlinear functions and belts, context switching between these belts, event-train logic, frequency and time coding, all-or-none information transmission, and many more.

Minski[13] and Arbib[45] focus on the role of frames and schemas. *Schemas* are program units especially suited for a system that has continuing perception of, and interaction with, its environment. Schemas provide the coarse-grain level of neural computing, whose design is motivated by the style of the brain. The sixth generation is configured as a network of specialized subsystems, some of which are configured as arrays of (possibly adaptive) neuronlike components.

Computer researchers are now discovering how to construct neural and massively parallel computers and systems. Programming is here to stay. However, for many applications, programming has powerful competitors: adaptation, learning and training, self-organization, genetic selection, and relaxation. A mixture of programming and of these techniques leads to a wide spectrum of granularity in hardware and in software: field computers, neural processors, high-level neural elements, feature extractors, genetic systems, schemas, frames, BAMs, and FCMs. The systems are implemented as virtual processors, RISC, associative memories and processors, hypercubes, arrays, programmable connection machines, and concurrent systems. In this way, the sixth generation, with a variety of new devices, computers, and systems, opens new business and application areas.

REFERENCES

1. J. H. Holland, *Adaption in Natural and Artificial Systems: An Introductory Analysis with Applications to Biology and Artificial Intelligence,* University of Michigan Press, Ann Arbor, 1975.
2. G. M. Edelman and V. B. Mountcastle, *The Mindful Brain,* MIT Press, Cambridge, MA, 1978.
3. A. Bergman and M. Kerszberg, Breeding intelligent automata. *Proc. IEEE First Int. Conf. on Neural Networks,* San Diego, June 21–24, 1987, Vol. II, 63–70.
4. P. Marler, Song learning: innate species differences in the learing process. In Marler and Terrace (eds.), *The Biology of Learning,* Springer-Verlag, Berlin, 1984.

5. B. Souček and M. Souček, *Neural and Massively Parallel Computers: The Sixth Generation,* Wiley, New York, 1988.
6. G. Nicolis and I. Prigogine, *Self-Organization in Nonequilibrium Systems,* Wiley-Interscience, New York, 1985.
7. L. Steels, Self-organization through selection. *Proc. IEEE First Int. Conf. on Neural Networks,* San Diego, June 21–24, 1987, Vol. II, 55–62.
8. I. Bratko, Expert systems and PROLOG. In Summer (ed.), *Supercomputer Systems Technology,* Series 10, No. 6, Pergamon Infotech, London, 1982, 188–209.
9. A. Newell, Production systems models of control structures. In Chase (ed.), *Visual Information Processing,* Academic Press, New York, 1973.
10. M. Rychener, Production systems as programming language for artificial intelligence research. Ph.D. thesis, Carnegie-Mellon University, 1976.
11. J. McDermott, R1: The formative years. *AI Mag.* **2,** 21–29 (1981).
12. J. W. Lewis and F. S. Lynch, GETREE: A knowledge managment tool. In *Proceedings of Trends and Applications. Automatic Intelligent Behavior, Applications and Frontiers,* IEEE, New York, 1983.
13. M. Minski, A framework for representing knowledge. In Winston (ed.), *The Psychology of Computer Vision,* McGraw-Hill, New York, 1975, 211–277.
14. R. Fikes and T. Kehler, The role of frame-based representation in reasoning. *Comm. ACM* **28**(9), 904–920 (1985).
15. J. Doyle, A truth maintenance system. *AI* **12**(3), 231–272 (1979).
16. P. London, Dependency networks as representations for modelling in general problem solver. Tech. Rep. 698, Dept. of Computer Science, University of Maryland, College Park, 1978.
17. J. de Kleer, J. Doyle, G. L. Steele, and G. J. Sussman, Explicit control of reasoning. In Winston and Brown (eds.), *Artificial Intelligence: An MIT Perspective,* MIT Press, Cambridge, MA, 1979, 93–116.
18. R. E. Filman, Reasoning with worlds and truth maintenance in a knowledge-based programming environment. *Comm. ACM* **21**(4), 382–401 (1988).
19. W. S. Faught, Applications of AI in engineering. *Computer* 17–27, July (1986).
20. D. E. Rumelhart, P. Smolensky, J. L. McClelland, and G. E. Hinton, Schemata and sequential thought processes in PDP models. In McClelland and Rumelhart (eds.), *Parallel Distributed Processing,* MIT Press, Cambridge, MA, 1986, Vol. 2, 7–57.
21. J. J. Hopfield, Neural networks and physical systems with emergent collective computational abilities. *Proc. Natl. Acad. Sci. USA* **79,** 2554–2558 (1982).
22. B. Kosko, Constructing an associative memory. *Byte* **12**(10), 137–144 (1987).
23. B. Kosko, Adaptive bidirectional associative memories. *Applied Optics* **26**(23), 4947–4960 (1987).
24. B. Kosko, Fuzzy knowledge combination. *Int. Intell. Syst.* **1,** 293–320 (1986).
25. H. W. Chun and A. Mimo, A massively parallel model of schema selection. *Proc. IEEE First Int. Conf. on Neural Networks,* San Diego, June 21–24, 1987, Vol. II, 379–386.

26. E. A. Feigenbaum, Knowledge engineering: the applied side. In Mickie and Hayes (eds.), *Intelligent Systems,* Halsted Press, New York, 1983.
27. D. Mickie, A prototype knowledge refinery. In Mickie and Hayes (eds.), *Intelligent Systems,* Halsted Press, New York, 1983.
28. I. Bratko, Proving correctness of strategies in the AL1 assertional language. *Information Processing Lett.* **7,** 223–230, 1983.
29. H. P. Winston, *Artificial Intelligence,* Addison-Wesley, Reading, MA, 1984.
30. R. S. Michalski, J. G. Carbonell, and T. M. Mitchell (eds.), *Machine Learning: An Artificial Intelligence Approach,* Tioga, Palo Alto, CA, 1983.
31. R. Forsyth and R. Rada, *Machine Learning Applications in Expert Systems and Information retrieval,* Ellis Horwood Series, 1986.
32. M. Gams and M. Petkovšek, Learning from examples in the presence of noise. Semes Journees Internationales Les Systemes Experts et Leurs Applications, 2, 609, Avignon, 1988.
33. D. B. Laning, *Moving Knowledge Systems Into Real-Time On-Line Environments: A Look at the Issues.* Intellicorp Report 1986.
34. N. R. Nielsen, "The Impact of Using AI-Based Techniques in a Control System Simulator," *Proc Conf. on AI and Simulation, Simulation Series,* **18**(3), San Diego, July 1987.
35. K. J. Lindsay, *Expert Systems in the CIM Environment,* Manufacturing Technology International, Sterling Publications, Ltd., 1987.
36. D. S. Appleton, "Integration Technology," *CIM Technology,* Spring 1986.
37. B. A. Nardi and R. K. Simons, *Model-Based Reasoning and AI Problem Solving,* Workshop on High Level Tools for Knowledge Based Systems, Columbus, Ohio, Oct. 1986.
38. P. A. Koton, "Empirical and Model-Based Reasoning in Expert Systems," *Proc. Ninth Int. Joint Conf. on Artificial Intelligence,* 297–299 Los Angeles, 1985.
39. A. P. Železnikar, Principles of information. *Cybernetica* **31** 99–122 (1988).
40. A. P. Železnikar, Informational logic I. *Informatica* **12**(3), 26–38 (1988).
41. A. P. Železnikar, Informational logic II. *Informatica* **12**(4), 3–20 (1988).
42. R. Hecht-Nielsen, Neurocomputer applications. *Proc. Nat. Computer Conf.* 1987, American Federation of Information Processing Societies, 1987, 239–244.
43. T. Kohonen, *Self-Organization and Associative Memory,* 2nd ed., Springer-Verlag, 1987.
44. B. Widrow and R. Winter, Neural nets for adaptive filtering and adaptive pattern recognitions. *Computers* 25–39, March (1988).
45. M. A. Arbib, *The Metaphorical Brain: An Introduction to Schemas and Brain Theory,* 2nd ed., Wiley-Interscience, New York, 1988.

PART II

Intelligent Systems

Computers in Instrumentation and Process Control
High-Speed Neural Chips and Systems
Concurrent Chips and Languages
Concurrent System Design and Applications
Transputer-Based Computing Surface, Clusters, and Hyperclusters
Markets and Trends

CHAPTER 6

Computers in Instrumentation and Process Control

INTRODUCTION AND SURVEY

The introduction of integrated circuits and tens of thousands of small computers known as minicomputers and microprocessors is rapidly changing the profile of laboratory research and of measurement and control techniques. The cost of microprocessors and minicomputers, from several hundred to several thousand dollars, is now comparable with the cost of typical laboratory instruments. As a result, minicomputers and microprocessors are becoming standard laboratory tools.

Direct connection of the minicomputer into the measuring chain results in a new, highly sophisticated kind of experiment, with significantly increased accuracy and a large volume of data.

This chapter gives an overview of laboratory minicomputers and microprocessors. Interfacing the minicomputer to experiment and to the process control systems is explained. Programmed input-output transfer of data is described. Interrupt mode of operation and high-speed direct memory access are shown.

Recently, catheters have been implanted in a human body. Under the control of the stored program microprocessor, such a system processes the biological signals. For example, a surgically inserted catheter can monitor the flow rate and the blood pressure in the various chambers of the heart. The attached microprocessor immediately analyzes the data.

The chapter starts with an overall description of a computerized laboratory system. It then concentrates on basic principals, which will help one to choose, design, and operate computerized sensors, instruments, robots, and control systems.

Real-time system consists of a number of processes, exchanging information through channels. Items of information that are of interest for a number of processes in the system are placed into pools. Interdependent activities between processes, channels and pools must be synchronized, monitored, and scheduled, in colaboration with real-time operating system.

6.1. MINICOMPUTERS AND MICROCOMPUTERS

The cost of microprocessors and minicomputers runs from several hundred to several thousand dollars, which is comparable with the cost of typical laboratory instruments, such as a display scope or a counter. As a result, minicomputers and microprocessors have found their way into scientific and industrial laboratories. Each year thousands of those machines enter the area of experiment and process control and system simulation.

The main merits of microprocessor and minicomputer application in scientific or industrial laboratory are

- Money and manpower saving;
- Speedup of experiment or production time;
- Highly improved quality of results;
- Highly increased volume of data;
- New kinds of experiments, which are feasible only through computer-controlled instrumentation; and
- New kinds of production processes, which are feasible only through computer control of the process.

Early process control computers needed highly skilled professionals for program development in assembly language and to design electrical interfaces between machines and instruments. Modern minicomputers and microprocessors have come much closer to the end-uses. Many of those machines could be programmed by the end-user in easy-to-learn high-level language. The most frequently used languages are C, OCCAM, real-time FORTRAN, real-time BASIC, and PL/M. Also, interface design has moved from the level of digital circuit design to the level of plug-in interfacing cards.

Figure 6.1 is a simplified block diagram of a typical minicomputer or microcomputer (Souček[1], Korn[2]): memory, major registers, and data ways between part of the machine.

Memory is composed of many locations or words. Each location has a unique address and can store one piece of information. This information can be data, but it can also be an instruction to tell the computer what to do.

The *accumulator* (ACC) is prime register of the computer. It is used to keep the data and results during arithmetic or logical operations. It is also

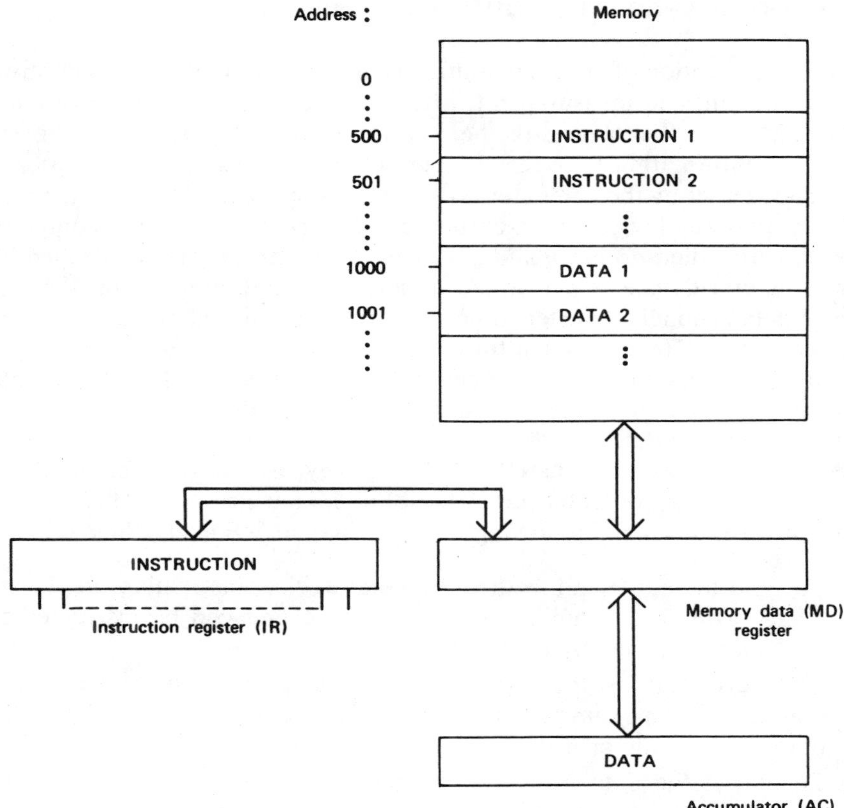

Figure 6.1 *Simplified block diagram of a small computer.*

used as the end point for I/O transfer of data between the computer and peripheral world.

The *memory data* (MD) register is used for reading the data out of the memory or for writing the data into memory.

The *Instruction register* (IR) is used to keep the operation code of the instruction currently being performed by the computer. The IR decodes the operation code of the instruction and initiates the steps necessary to execute the instruction.

During the computer operation, instructions are read from the memory and routed to the IR to tell the computer what to do. The data are routed to the ACC. The results are formed in the ACC, then routed to different memory locations. During I/O transfer, data are routed on one side between the ACC and the peripheral devices and on the other side between the ACC and the memory.

6.2. PROGRAMMED INPUT-OUTPUT TRANSFER

A major application of small computers is in the domain of process control, data collection, and measurement. The computer must be capable of communicating with the devices of the measuring and control chains. The exchange of information between the peripheral device and the computer is controlled either by the computer program or by specially designed elements of the peripheral device. Input-output transfers controlled by the computer program are called *programmed data transfers*. The transfer controlled by the peripheral device is performed without program intervention through special data channels that steal time slices from the central processor whenever necessary. Hence, such a transfer is called the *cycle stealing transfer*. In some machines, this transfer is called by other names, such as data break, data channel, and direct memory access (DMA). In this section we discuss only programmed data transfers.

A programmed data transfer is performed by the I/O transfer (IOT) instruction. A small computer has at least one IOT instruction. This instruction can be used for the following tasks (Weitzman[3], Finkel[4], Souček[5]):

- To send the command to the peripheral device, instructing the device what to do. For example, a magnetic tape unit can be instructed to backspace the tape by one record.
- To receive and test the information describing the status of the peripheral device. An example is a test to determine if a magnetic tape transport is rewinding or if it is ready for recording.
- To output the data from the computer to the peripheral device. An example is the output of X and Y data to be used as coordinates of the point to be displayed on the CRT.
- To input the data from the peripheral device to the computer. An example is the input of the digitized data from the measured process.

These tasks can be performed in one of three ways: unconditional transfer, conditional transfer, and program interrupt.

6.2.1. Unconditional Transfer

Unconditional transfer is used only for processes whose timing is fixed and known. The peripheral device must be ready for communication. The program for unconditional transfer is simple and straightforward, as shown schematically in Figure 6.2. The IOT instruction is inserted in the program between other instructions at the place where the transfer is needed.

6.2.2. Conditional Transfer

Conditional transfer is used often. It is performed under program control, but only if the peripheral device is ready for communication. The computer

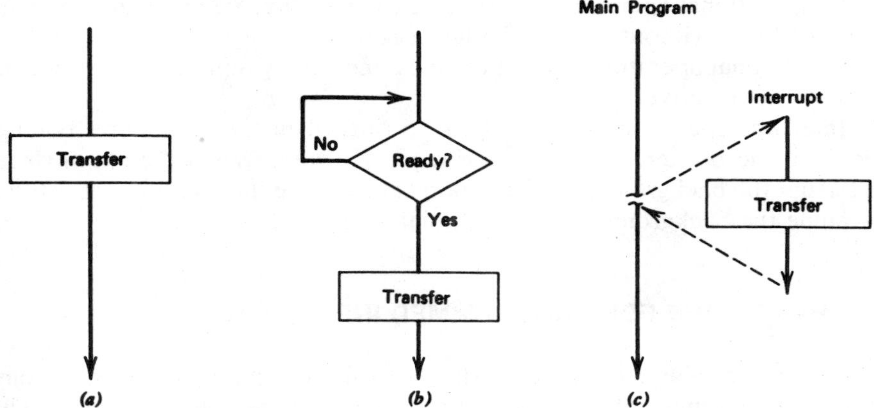

Figure 6.2 *Programmed input-output transfer:* (*a*) *unconditional;* (*b*) *conditional;* (*c*) *program interrupt.*

program is shown schematically in Figure 6.2. Two IOT instructions are usually used to perform the transfer. The first instruction is used to bring into the computer the information describing the status of the peripheral device. The program then tests the status and makes the decision. If the device is not ready, the program can perform the loop and check the status repeatedly. When the device becomes ready, the program executes the second IOT instruction, which performs the desired action. The main advantage of the conditional transfer is that it allows synchronization between the computer operation and the peripheral device operation. The main disadvantage is the waste of computer time if one has to wait for the device to become ready.

6.2.3. Program Interrupt

Program interrupt transfer makes more efficient use of the computer time possible. The transfer will be performed under the program control, but the computer does not have to check repeatedly if the device is ready for transfer. The computer program can perform a calculation that is independent of the transfer. Let us call this program the background job. When the peripheral device is ready, it will interrupt the computer and cause it to leave its background program for a moment and to perform a special interrupt subroutine for transfer. This operation is shown schematically in Figure 6.2. The IOT command is part of the interrupt subroutine. When this subroutine is completed, the control is returned to the background program.

6.2.4. Simple Example

Let us compare the unconditional, conditional, and program interrupt transfer in the following way. One member of the family is "programmed" to watch over the milk and to take it off the stove when cooked.

Unconditional operation: go in the kitchen at, say, 8:25 and take the milk off the stove, without caring whether it is cooked.

Conditional operation: look at the milk once every minute. When cooked, take it off the stove.

Interrupt operation: set the alarm to ring when the milk starts boiling. Perform the background job of writing homework. When the alarm rings, interrupt the background job for a moment and take the milk from the stove. Resume the background job at the point of interruption.

6.3. PARTY LINE FOR PROGRAMMED INPUT-OUTPUT

Normally, peripheral devices are slower than the computer. Hence, a computer can communicate, if necessary, with several peripheral devices. The I/O lines of a computer form a bus to which all the peripheral devices are connected.

Figure 6.3 shows the computer bus with peripheral devices. This mode of operation is called the *party line operation*. The I/O lines from the computer are bused to all devices on the party line, so the devices appear as a single device to the computer. Each peripheral device must have its own controller. The controller must have a device selection address so that the computer can call a specific device for transfer.

The controller must

- Decode the device selection code received from the computer and respond only if the code is identical with its address;
- Decode the command code received from the computer and initiate operations;

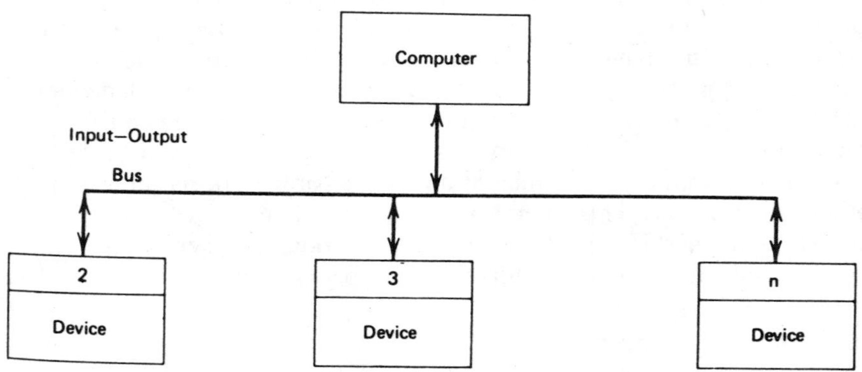

Figure 6.3 *Party line input-output transfer. A single computer controls a number of measuring and control points.*

- Send the computer the information describing the status of the peripheral device; and
- Perform the gating for data transfer between the computer and the device.

6.3.1. IOT Instruction

The computer communicates with the controller through the IOT instruction. An example of the IOT instruction is shown in Figure 6.4. The instruction has three parts: operation code, device selection address, and command code.

Operation Code. In the example, 4 bits are used for operation code and 1 out of 16 possible combinations of those bits is the code of the IOT instruction. These bits are loaded in the computer instruction register. The specific action for the I/O instruction is initiated.

Device Selection Address. In the example, 8 bits are used for the device selection address. Hence, this computer can identify up to 256 different devices. The decoding is performed in the peripheral device.

Command Code. In the example, 4 bits are used for the command code. Hence, this computer can send up to 16 different commands to the peripheral device. The decoding is performed in the peripheral device.

Figure 6.5 shows the information flow that affects a programmed data transfer with the peripheral device. The IOT instruction, like any other instruction of the program, is read from the main memory into the MD buffer register. The operation code (first 4 bits) is transferred in the IR. The instruction decoder activates the IOT timing generator. As a result, the computer enter the I/O state.

6.3.2. I/O State and Timing Signals

The I/O state is characteristic of the I/O instruction. During the I/O state, the computer generates timing signals, which are used to perform the opera-

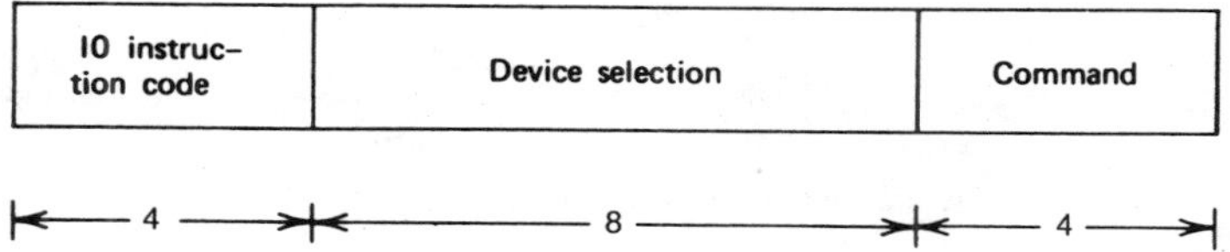

Figure 6.4 *Instruction format for input-output transfer. Sixteen-bit computer word is presented. A similar structure is also in machines with 8 or 32 bits.*

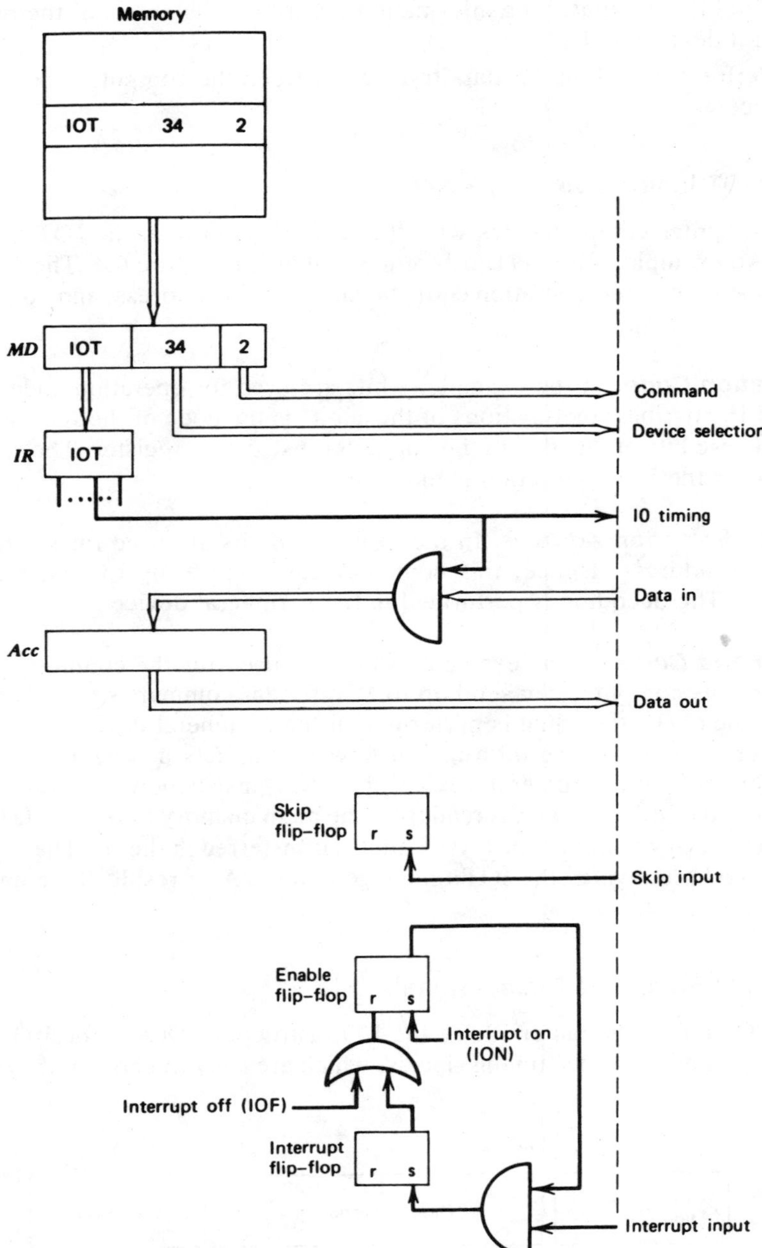

Figure 6.5 *Parts of the small computer involved in the programmed input-output transfer.*

tions needed for communication with the peripheral device, for strobing the data lines, and for gating the command lines.

6.3.3. Device Selection Lines

The device selection bits of the I/O instruction sit in the MD register. Using those bits, the I/O instruction selects the peripheral device. These bits are transmitted over the party line bus to all peripheral devices. The device selection code presents the key to the peripheral device. Each peripheral device has its specific lock, called the *device selector*. The device selection code will match with only one device selector; hence, only one device will be coupled for communication with the computer. In the example, 8 bits are used for device selection; hence, eight device selection lines go out of the computer.

6.3.4. Command Lines

The command code of the I/O instruction sits in the MD register. Using those bits, the I/O instruction tells the selected peripheral device what to do.

The command lines are connected to all peripheral devices. However, the device address code will couple one device to the bus. Hence, the command will be received only by the peripheral device selected by the device selection part of the I/O instruction. In the example, 4 bits are used for command code; hence, four command lines go out of the computer.

6.3.5. Data Lines

Data transfer takes place between the peripheral device and the ACC. Sixteen input and 16 output lines present the data way. Data lines are connected to all peripheral devices. Each peripheral device has gating logic for data lines. Only the device selected by the device selection part of the I/O instruction will open the gates for data lines.

The output lines are provided with driving amplifiers. These lines present the contents of the ACC throughout the operation. The selected peripheral device should strobe these lines into its data buffer register.

The input lines bring the data from the peripheral device. These lines are gated inside the computer so that they do not disturb the contents of the accumulator. Only during the execution of an IOT instruction will the computer strobe the input lines into the ACC.

6.3.5. Skip Line

The computer has one skip input. The computer senses the flag of the peripheral device through this input. The flag is a 1-bit register (flip-flop) in the peripheral device. If the device is ready for communication, it will set its flag. If the device is not ready, it will keep its flag reset.

If the flag shows that the device is ready, the computer may issue an I/O instruction and it can perform the transfer. On the other hand, if the flag shows that the device is not ready, the computer will have to delay the IOT. The flags of all peripheral devices are connected to the same skip line. Each device has a gating logic between the flag and the skip line, controlled by the device selector.

The computer examines the flag by issuing an I/O command with the address of the device. The selected device connects its flag to the skip line. The states of the flag will be copied through the skip line into the skip flip-flop in the computer. The computer is wired so that each I/O instruction checks the skip flip-flop. If the skip flip-flop is in state 0 after the I/O instruction is performed the program counter will point to the next instruction in the program. If the skip flip-flop is in state 1, after the I/O instruction is performed the program counter will be incremented by 2 and the next instruction will be skipped. In this way the program can be split in two branches: the first branch if the device is busy, and the second one if the device is ready for transfer.

6.3.6. Interrupt Line

The computer has one interrupt line. The computer receives requests from peripheral devices through this line. Upon receiving a request, the computer stops the background program and performs the interrupt routine for the peripheral device. The interrupt line is connected directly without gating to the flags of the peripheral devices. As a result, if any of the peripheral devices requests the interrupt service, the computer will receive the request.

A simiplified interrupt logic is composed of the input gate, enable flip-flop, and interrupt flip-flop (Figure 6.5). The input gate is controlled by the enable flip-flop, and is closed if the flip-flop is not set. The enable flip-flop is under program control. The computer has the instruction interrupt on (ION), which will set the enable flip-flop. Another instruction, interrupt off (IOF), will reset the enable flip-flop. Hence, by program control it is possible to disconnect (disable) or to connect (enable) the interrupt line from the computer. (IOF and ION belong to the class of I/O instructions with a special code.)

If the programmer wants to use the interrupt feature, the ION instruction must be issued. The input gate will be open and will wait for a signal on the interrupt line.

The signal on the interrupt line will set the interrupt flip-flop. Each computer instruction examines the interrupt flip-flop. When the interrupt flip-flop is set, the following takes place:

- The computer will complete the current instruction of the program.
- The contents of the program counter will be automatically deposited in a specific memory location, for example in address 0.
- The specific address, say 1, will be set in the program counter.

The two characteristic interrupt addresses are fixed for a given computer. In our example we use addresses 0 and 1.

The features described here can be used to transfer program control from the background program to the specific interrupt routine whenever the device sets the request. Upon the execution of the interrupt routine, the background job is resumed.

6.4. EXAMPLE OF PROGRAMMED INPUT-OUTPUT TRANSFER

Here we show a simple example of data transfer between the computer and the peripheral device. The computer collects the data from measuring points. Each measuring point is treated as an independent peripheral device. A selection address must be assigned to each device. Figure 6.6 shows one

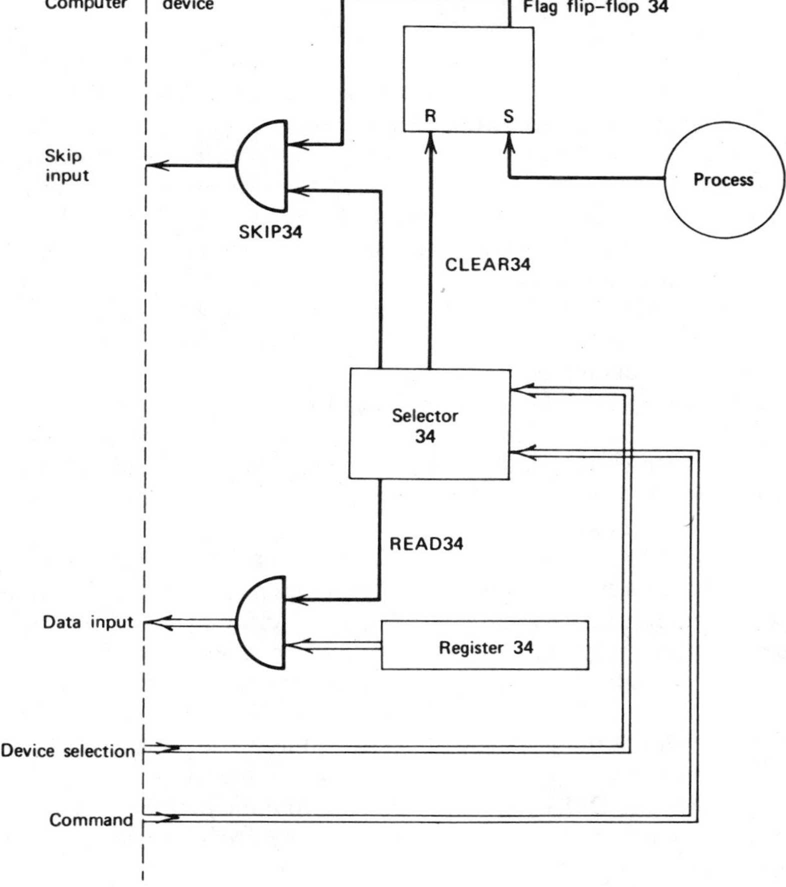

Figure 6.6 *Interface components for programmed, conditional transfer.*

of the measuring points, for which the designer has decided to use selection address 34. The interface is composed of flag flip-flop, selector, and data register.

Flag flip-flop will notify the computer when the process has generated new data. The computer examines the flag by issuing a skip instruction, which connects the flag flip-flop to the skip input. If the computer finds out that the flag is set, the computer will start service routine for this device. As a first step, the computer will issue instruction to clear this flag.

Selector presents the specific lock, in this example the lock with selection address 34. The computer will use the code 34 to distinguish this peripheral device from other devices.

Data register is a one-word storage device into which the measured data is stored. The computer will issue a read instruction to open the gates and transfer the datum over party lines into the ACC.

6.5. DIRECT MEMORY ACCESS

Direct memory access allows I/O transfer without program intervention. The transfer is performed through special channels that steal time slices from the central processor whenever necessary. During each stolen time slice, one transfer is performed. This kind of transfer is also known by other names, such as data channel, data break, and cycle stealing transfer.

The computer logic performing the DMA is basically independent of the logic involved in the programmed transfer. The main point is that the DMA does not perform the transfer with the ACC. Rather the transfer is performed via the MD register directly with the computer memory. Since program execution is not involved in the DMA transfer, the computer working registers are not disturbed.

Each basic step of DMA is under the control of the peripheral device that sets the request for transfer. For inputting the data in the computer, the device sets the request when the data are prepared; for outputting the data from the computer, the device sets the requests when it needs the data and is ready to receive them.

Having the DMA facility, the computer can perform in parallel two jobs that might be entirely independent: (1) programmed job (2) DMA transfer.

The computer examines the DMA requests during the execution of every instruction of the programmed job. If the DMA request is received, the next time slice is given to the DMA transfer. The programmed job is delayed for this time slice.

Figure 6.7 shows the principle of cycle stealing. The upper line shows the time slices during which the computer performs the programmed job. The arrows indicate the DMA requests received from the peripheral device. The lower line presents the time slices stolen from the programmed job and given for execution of the DMA transfer.

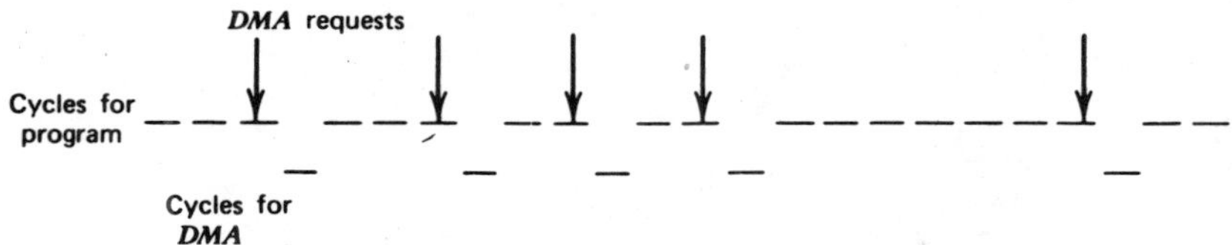

Figure 6.7 *Principle of cycle stealing for direct memory access.*

The DMA transfer is particularly useful for devices with high speed and a large amount of data in block form. An example is the high-speed magnetic tape system or high-speed disk memories.

6.6. INSTRUMENT AND CONTROL SYSTEM COMPONENTS

6.6.1 Typical System

Computer-oriented measurement and control systems could be divided into two families: data acquisition systems and direct digital process control systems (Katz[6], Jović[7]). In both cases, the transducers take a physical parameter such as amplitude, interval, temperature, strain, or position and convert it to voltage or current. All further signal processing is then done by electronic circuits. The signal first passes through analog shaping and filtering. Its signal is then coverted to digital form and fed to the computer for digital processing. Computer-produced results are then used as feedback controls or for display. If control elements and display units are analog devices, digital computer output must pass through the DACs producing analog driving signals.

A complete representative data acquisition, conversion, and data processing system is illustrated in Figure 6.8. The system is composed of different units connected to the computer party line bus. The party line bus of the computer is divided into three subbuses: device selection and command bus, data-in bus, and data-out bus.

The device selection and command bus is used by the computer to select one device at a time for communication and to specify the operations performed by the selected device (such as read, write, input, output, reset). The data-in bus carries the data from the selected peripheral device data register into the computer. The data-out bus carries the data from the computer into the selected peripheral device data register.

Each device interface is composed of device data register and I/O gates, device selector and command decoder, and flag flip-flop. Flag flip-flops are connected to the computer skip and interrupt inputs. The flag flip-flop of a device informs the computer if the device is busy or ready for communication.

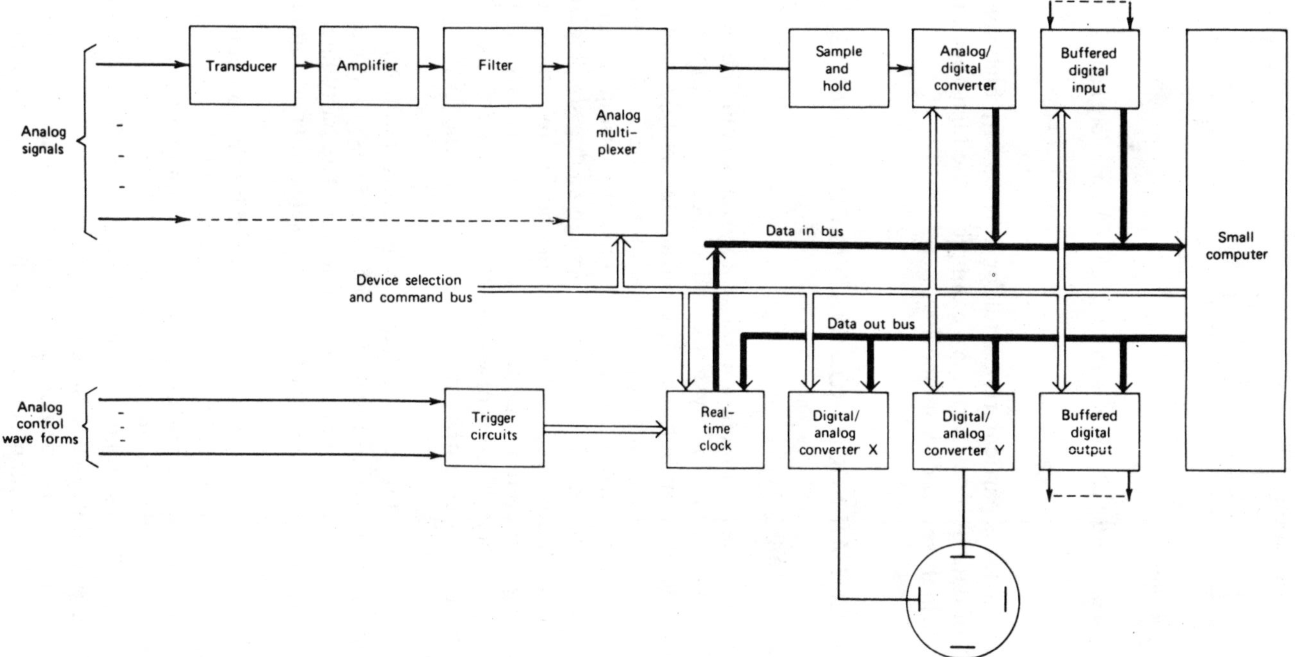

Figure 6.8 *Typical data acquisition, conversion, and data processing system.*

The system in Figure 6.8 is composed of a transducer, amplifier, filter, analog multiplexer, sample-and-hold circuit, ADC, DAC, CRT display, real-time clock, trigger circuit, buffered digital input, and buffered digital output.

6.6.2. Amplifiers and Filters

The first part of the data acquisition and processing system is concerned with extracting the signal to be measured. The initial signal processing is done with an amplifier and possibly a filter. The amplifier performs one or more of the following functions: boost the amplitude of the signal, buffer the signal, convert a signal current into a voltage, separate the differential signal from common noise. For most analog multiplexers, sample-and-holds, and ADCs, the desired voltage level at the amplifier output is 5 to 10 V full scale.

Following the amplifiers in the system is a filter, if necessary. Filters are usually used for two reasons: (1) reduce noise and improve SNR and (2) limit signal bandwidth and avoid high-frequency signal components if those components are not needed. In this way, the signal could be sampled at a moderate sampling rate, and the data processing is less expensive.

6.6.3. Analog Multiplexers and Sample-and-Hold Circuits

Analog multiplexers are used for time sharing of ADCs between analog channels. An analog multiplexer has many analog inputs but only one output. The multiplexer comprises analog switches, each switch connecting one analog input to the common output. The switches can be addressed by a digital input code through the computer bus. Only one input is connected to the output at any one time. Usually the input channels are sequentially connected to the output of the multiplexer.

The output of the analog multiplexer goes into a sample-and-hold circuit, which samples the output of the multiplexer at a specified time and then holds the voltage level at its output until the ADC performs its conversion operation.

6.6.4. Buffered Digital Input and Output

In some cases, the peripheral unit is a digital device. In such circumstances, the data are already in a digital form, and direct communication with the computer is possible. To eliminate the need for interface design, many laboratory systems provide a buffered digital input unit and a buffered digital output unit (Figure 6.8). Interface components, such as device selector, flag flip-flop, data registers, and gates, are already built into the unit. Digital input or output lines are directly available to the user.

If the user has an instrument that generates digital data, the output lines of the instrument could be directly connected to the digital input lines. If the user has a control or display device that operates on digital data, the digital output lines could be directly connected to the input lines of such a device.

6.7. REAL-TIME CLOCK

6.7.1. Programmable Clock

Computer-oriented experiment and control systems could be divided into three classes: (1) event-driven systems, (2) computer-driven systems, and (3) clock-driven systems.

Event-driven systems are typical in the data acquisition area. The events, in the form of external stimuli, are usually physical or biological processes that must be responded to in a time-critical manner. The design of a real-time system is predicted upon being able to respond to events not only at a rapid rate but also in terms of servicing these events under peak load conditions.

Computer-driven systems are typical in the process or experiment control area. The computer program is the actual master of the system. The program determines both the timing of operations and the scheduling. The computer program also determines the sampling rates and the data display rates. This mode of operation is usually used for relatively slow processes, because it is difficult to achieve precise timing using computer programs. It is especially difficult to estimate the time needed to execute a part of the program written in a high-level language.

Clock-driven systems are found in all real-time applications. A special unit, call the *real-time clock*, is actual master of the timing and scheduling operations. The real-time clock is an oscillator that produces pulses at a constant rate. The clock pulse rate is under program control. Usually the computer program can control the clock rate from 10 MHz to 100 Hz.

The real-time clock is usually connected to the computer interrupt input. Interrupt requests produced by the clock could force the computer to perform different operations with precise timing. Typical clock-driven operations are sampling or display at precise rate, switching from one task, or experimental mode, to another task at precise time intervals, and digitizing the time intervals, such as interspike intervals, by counting the number of clock pulses between two spikes.

6.7.2. Parts of the Real-Time Clock

Figure 6.9 shows the basic parts of the real-time clock: oscillator, clock counter, buffer-preset register, and overflow flag. Typical interactions between the computer and the clock are timing mode and digitizing mode.

Timing Mode. The computer program determines the pulse rate of the oscillator and presets the count into the clock count register. The program then connects the oscillator to the clock counter. The computer now switches its attention to the background program, which might be an entirely independent operation. Simultaneously, the clock counter is incremented by the oscillator. Eventually, the clock counter will produce an overflow, and it will

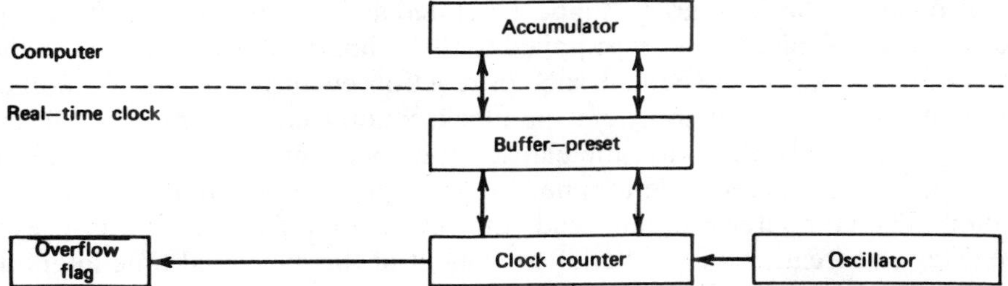

Figure 6.9 *Basic components of the real-time clock.*

set the overflow flag. The overflow flag is used to interrupt the computer. In this way, the computer is switched from one task to another at a precise time, as dictated by the real-time clock.

The buffer-preset register is usually set through the ACC to the negative (two's complement) value of the number of counts desired before overflow. Note that the computer programmer has not only determined the rate of counting but also the number of counts before overflow, thus allowing him two dimensions in selecting the time intervals between overflow.

Digitizing Mode. Digitizing mode is useful for determining the total elapsed time between some initial event (e.g., a stimulus) and subsequent events that might be caused by the initial event (e.g., muscle reaction).

The real-time clock is connected to a set of trigger circuits or control inputs (known also as a *Schmitt trigger;* Figures 6.8 and 6.10). The Schmitt trigger firing is governed by setting the threshold control. Each time the input waveform crosses the preset threshold voltage, the Schmitt trigger fires, causing a pulse to be generated. The Schmitt trigger is a 1-bit ADC: if the input waveform is more positive than the threshold, the Schmitt trigger produces the output equal to logical 1; if the input waveform is less positive than the threshold, the Schmitt trigger produces the output equal to logical 0. The positive pulse produced by the Schmitt trigger is used to start or stop the real-time clock.

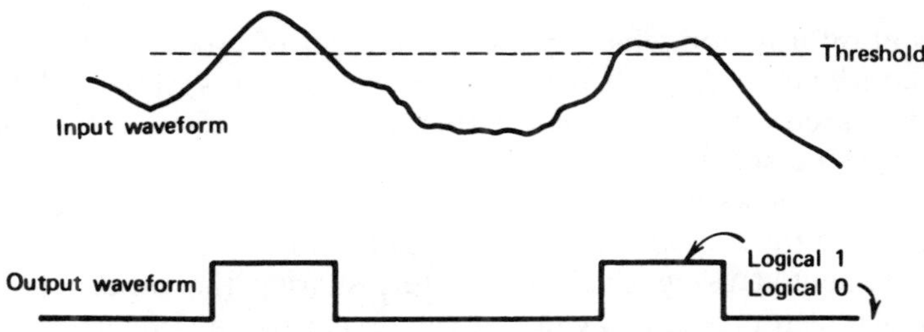

Figure 6.10 *Schmitt tigger, input, and corresponding output waveforms.*

A poststimulus histogram can be generated as follows. First, a stimulus is issued to the subject. It is also applied to the Schmitt trigger, and it starts the real-time clock. A subsequent subject reaction event is applied to another Schmitt trigger, and it transfers the clock counter content into the buffer-preset register. In this way, the elapsed time between the stimulus and the subsequent event can be determined, and it is proportional to the saved time count. The computer program reads the saved count from the buffer-preset register and treats it as the digital equivalent of the measured time interval.

All units shown in Figure 6.8 are available as modules or as plug-in cards. Also, many turnkey computer-oriented laboratory systems are available. New miniature low-cost microprocessors are finding their way into the laboratory as integral parts of the new instruments, or as process control and data acquisition systems.

6.8. PROCESSES, CHANNELS, AND POOLS

A real-time system can be seen as one that carries out a set of activities. The combination of programs and hardware pieces which together implement one activity is called a *process*. Typically a real-time system involves several processes which are mutually dependent and the system operation includes the interaction between processes. The interaction between processes will reflect the interaction of the devices they control. The action of one device may start or stop the activity of the other. Also one device is looking at the status of the other and of the whole system, and behaves accordingly.

Communication between processes is performed through *channels*. A channel provides the medium for items of information to be passed between one process and another. The information is best designed as a fixed-format message. It usually contains identification or name of the sending or receiving process, data items, and/or pointers to the data. A widely used form of channel implementation is the first-in-first-out (FIFO) queue. Messages are placed on the tail of the queue by the sending process and removed from the head of the queue by the receiving process. An alternative channel mechanism is a circular buffer. The transmitting process uses and moves the loading pointer, while the receiving process uses and moves the unloading pointer.

Items of information which interest a number of processes in the system are placed into a *pool*. Pools usually take the form of system tables, shared files, and shared data areas. Data structures model items in the controlled system or in the software system itself.

Figure 6.11 shows a real-time system consisting of five processes, communicating via three channels and two pools. Early real-time systems have been implemented using single computer, sharing the processor and the memory between processes. Current trends is toward concurrent systems, with processes being distributed between a number of small inexpensive

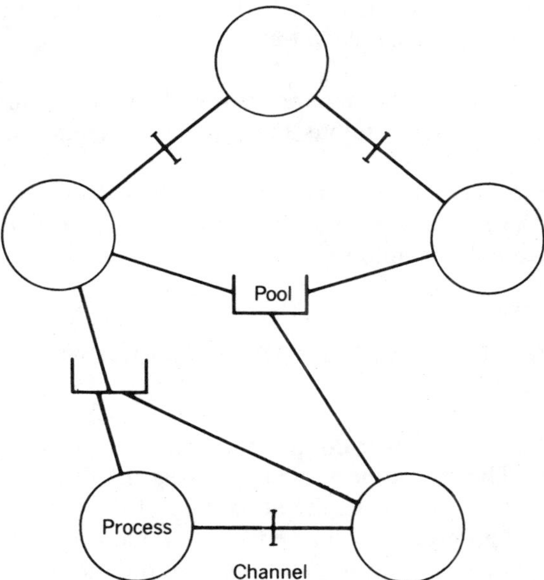

Figure 6.11 *Processes, channels, and pools.*

processors, with enough memory for software modules. A concurrent system is flexible, reliable, and uses modular hardware and software. It could be easily expanded or modified, (see Chapters 8, 9, and 10).

6.9. SYNCHRONIZATION

Interdependent activities must be synchronized which involves the ability of one process to triger or inhibit its own action or that of other processes. Synchronization is based upon communication of a piece of information between processes, that a particular event has occurred. Typical synchronization features include commands STOP, or GO, or WAIT (for an event), or SIGNAL (event exists).

Dijkstra[8] has introduced the concept of synchronization semaphore in the following way:

- *Semaphore* is nonnegative integer manipulated by three procedures: initialize, wait, and signal.
- *Initialize* (*semaphore, value*) sets the value of the semaphore to *value*.
- *Signal* (*semaphore*) increments the value of the semaphore by one. It is issued by the significant event in the system.
- *Wait* (*semaphore*) decreases the value of the semaphore by one, but

only if the result in nonnegative. It is issued by the dependent process that must wait for the significant event to occur.

At any time, the value of the semaphore is equal to its initial value plus the number of signal operations, minus the number of completed wait operations.

If the semaphore has the value zero at the time the process executes the wait operation, the process must wait until significant process executes a signal operation in the semaphore.

6.10. REAL-TIME OPERATING SYSTEMS, MONITORS, AND SCHEDULERS

The collection of programs that control the computing system is called the *operating system*. The operating system controls the devices that make up the system's hardware, optimizes the utilization of the hardware resources, and provides utility programs such as editors and file-organization facilities.

An operating system handles job management functions, system management functions, and data management functions.

Job management functions include executive functions of job and I/O control, scheduling and system resource management.

System management functions include error diagnostics, system and program maintenance and compiler interfaces.

Data management functions deal with file functions, I/O support facilities, retrieving and displaying selected portion of the file.

Collection of routines controlling the operation of channels and pools in a real-time system is called a *monitor*. When a process wishes to read or write to a channel or pool, it asks the relevant monitor to do the reading or writing for it.

Part of the system doing time and event scheduling is called real-time *scheduler*. The scheduler can initialize a task in three different ways:

- At a specified time of day;
- After a specified delay; and
- Upon occurrence of an external event.

A scheduler is designed to sense when the external event interrupt has occurred, and signals that such an event has occurred by recording significant information about the event. At the completion of the program statement being executed, the scheduler checks to determine whether a task has been scheduled by time or external event. If such is the case and if that task

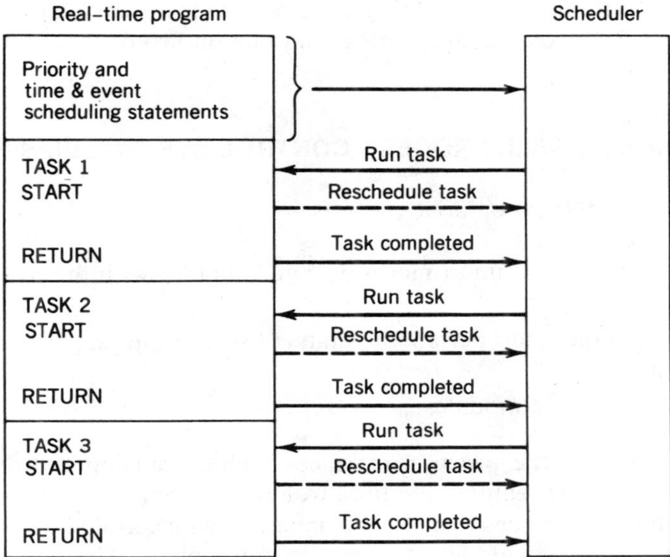

Figure 6.12 *Time and event scheduling. The scheduler examines task timing and priorities.*

is a higher priority than the task currently being executed, the latter task will be suspended and the just scheduled task will begin execution, as shown in Figure 6.12.

In a single processor system, scheduling and rescheduling is a time consuming operation. In a concurrent system rescheduling is usually not necessary. Processes and tasks are running on several processors, exchanging data and synchronization messages through channels and pools.

Standardization is a dominant trend in real-time software and real-time operating systems. Several systems are widely used in instrumentation, process control, and robotics. These include VAXELN, Modular System Operation and Lynx OS.

DEC's VAXELN operating system is intended for real-time applications such as servo motors and embedded controllers in the robots, unit-control level, and area-control level. One of its key features is its ability to treat the physical memory of any real-time VAX or Micro VAX computer as if it were a high-speed disk.

Intel's Modular Systems Operation supports 80286, 80386, 80287, and 80387 micro processors. It can function as a nucleus, a file system, a bootstrop and application loader, and a system debugger.

Lynx OS is a fully UNIX-compatible real-time operating system, for 80286 and 80386. Based on a real-time, multitasking, multiuser kernel, LynxOS interfaces with a number of networking schemas commonly found in factory environments, including Ethernet, Transmission Control Protocol/Internet Protocol, Manufacturing Automation Protocol, and X.25.

6.11. TYPICAL SMALL PROCESS CONTROL SYSTEM: DIPS 85†

The system hardware comprises:

- Central processing unit (micro- or minicomputer with the related modules),
- Standard computer peripheral units (disks, printers, CRT terminals etc.), and
- Process interface modules.

The wide range of the process interfaces includes analog and digital I/O modules with all the features required from monitoring and controlling systems, as well as interfaces to make it compatible with certain types of similar equipment that might already be installed at a plant. The use of CMOS integrated circuits guarantees a high degree of reliability and high noise immunity.

The main systems of the DIPS family are:

- DIPS 85-1 microcomputer remote station for a small number of I/O signals,
- DIPS 85-2 microcomputer station for a larger number of I/O signals,
- DIPS 85/300 (/210), a small control center, and
- DIPS 85/230 (340), (/240), a larger control center.

The system software comprises:

- An executive program,
- Application programs, and
- A data base.

The software performs data acquisition and processing, and conveys process control information to the operator. The programs are written in macro assembly language, or C.

Both the hardware and software are composed of modules, which is an optimal solution allowing gradual build-up and supplementation of the system. Alongside with the hardware and software the vendor provides customers with the following services:

† Sections 6.11 and 6.12 are adapted from Sistemi za Energetiko manuals.

- Propose solutions to the customer's technical problems,
- Give advise in the customer's specific applications,
- Educate the personnel,
- Provide maintenance of the system, and
- Cooperate in the further development of the application programs, and in the upgrading of the system.

For the automation of a plant the following functions are available:

- Local process control,
- Optical and audible indication of process status and alarms,
- Absolute chronology,
- Regulation,
- Backup protection,
- Sequential control,
- Data acquisition and processing,
- Telemonitoring of plants and subsystems,
- Control of a complex process with limited functions,
- Front-end processing to interface the computer centre to a more complex process system, and
- Connection of the system to a computer or other telecommunication network.

Typical applications include:

Energy

- Production, transmission, and distribution of electrical energy (hydroelectric, thermal, nuclear power stations; transformer and distribution stations from 10 to 400 kV; dispatching centres)
- Oil refineries, oil/gas fields, oil, and gas pipelines
- Waterworks and heat distribution networks

Industry

- Automation of production
- Control of energy consumption
- Supervisory control of steam boilers and furnaces
- Automation of chemical processes
- Provisions of industry
- Mining

Traffic

- Roads
- Railways

Tourism and Hotel Industry

- Control of energy consumption

Buildings, Airports, and so on

- Safeguarding
- Monitoring

DIPS 85 can be used for local monitoring and control in functions of the following type:

- Optical and audible indications of signaling,
- Measurement of analog variables and their display on request,
- Exact-time keeping,
- Pulse counting with local display,
- Measurement of the mains frequency 50 Hz with display,
- Local control from the control panel,
- Control of simple technological and production processes, and
- Connection to other systems of the type DIPS 85.

This microcomputer teleprocessing system is designed for local and remote monitoring and control of a wide variety of applications. In addition to data acquisition it performs the following functions:

- Communication with the control center,
- Process control and monitoring, and
- Display of processed data.

When used for remote control the system is connected to the central station or computing system via a communication channel. The basic units of the hardware (microcomputer) and software (executive program) are the same be the station used as a remote or central station, but the rest varies according to the specific needs.

Standard capacity of the system DIPS 85 can accommodate up to 248 I/O addresses of the following type:

8 one-bit or 4 two-bit status inputs

8 one-bit or 4 two-bit momentary outputs

32 single-ended or 16 differential analog inputs
1 analog output (set-point)
8 pulse inputs
8 one-bit continuous outputs

Transmission priorities:

At least 4 levels of priorities (assigned according to the importance of the data)

Self-testing and diagnostics of:

communication module
power supply
other basic units, (e.g. memory module and system buses)

Communication:

transmission rates of 50, 100, 200, 300, 600, 1200, and 2400 bauds
half-duplex transmission
duplex transmission
checking for transmission errors
the communication follows the CCITT V23, V24, V26, V27, and V29 standards

Momentary relay outputs:

Adjustable duration of the output pulse (from 20 ms onward)
Output contact rating

60 V	0.5 A	10 VA
60 V	1 A	30 VA
110 V	10 A	100 VA

Digital set-point outputs:

BCD- or binary-coded relay outputs (contact rating the same as for the momentary relay outputs)

Analog outputs:

0 — 5 mA or ±2.5 mA	R ≤ 2 k ohm
0 — 10 mA or ±5 mA	R ≤ 2 k ohm

0 — 20 mA	$R \leq$ 1 k ohm
0 — 3 V or ± 1.5 V	$R \geq$ 10 k ohm
0 — 10 V or ± 5 V	$R \geq$ 10 k ohm

Accuracy 0.4%.

Analog inputs:

0 — 5 mA or ± 2.5 mA	$R \leq$ 1 k ohm
0 — 10 mA or ± 5 mA	$R \leq$ 500 ohm
0 — 20 mA	$R \leq$ 250 ohm
4 — 20 mA	$R \leq$ 250 ohm
0 — 3 V or ± 1.5 V	$R \geq$ 1 M ohm
0 — 10 V or ± 5 V	$R \geq$ 1 M ohm

Accuracy 0.6% or 0.25%.

Digital coded inputs:

BCD inputs
Binary inputs

Status inputs:

Relays or optocouplers
Input voltages of 24 V, 48 V, 60 V, and 110 V
Minimum signal duration of 25 ms

Pulse inputs:

relays or optocouplers
input voltages of 24 V, 48 V, 60 V, and 110 V
minimum pulse duration of 10 ms
maximum pulse frequency of 20 Hz

Reliability:

Mean time between failures (MTBF) $\geq$ 15 000 hours
Mean time to repair (MTTR) $\geq$ 2 hours

Rate of undetected transmission errors (channel error rate 10^{-4}):

cyclic transmission 10^{-6}
spontaneous transmission 10^{-10}
transmission of commands 10^{-14}

DIPS 85 is a VAX-based system produced by Sistemi za Energetiko.

6.12. TYPICAL SMALL PROCESS CONTROL SOFTWARE: NIVO

The software system NIVO is designed for remote and local monitoring of a variety of processes (e.g., in energetics, pipeline systems, industries). The software includes:

- Operating system for real time processing
- The user's program package containing modules for:
  - Communication with remote stations and/or a local station,
  - Sorting and analysis of process data (status; alarms; measurement of analog, digital and pulse signals; command),
  - Generating and displaying historical event data, alarms and errors in the process or the control system via CRT terminals and printers,
  - Displaying the statuses of the process and telecontrol network on the screen,
  - Process monitoring and control via the CRT terminal,
  - Generating reports (hourly, daily, monthly), and their display (periodically or on the operator's request),
  - Changing the process and system parameters, and allowing the extension of the system,
  - Start and restart of the system,
  - Synchronization of time,
  - Real-time diagnostics, and
  - Application programs.
- Data base with:
  - Process variables and system status,
  - Instructions for processing and displaying the parameters of the process variables,
  - CRT displays, and
  - Reports.

The basic functions of the software system are to control and data acquisition from local and remote terminal units (RTU), display of all process parameters, indicate alarm conditions, and automatic process control (optional).

All these functions are performed in real time, in order to ensure fast response to changes in the process under control.

The multiprogramming technique used in the software system enables the real-time operation. Its main program modules are (see Figure 6.13):

- Executive program which supervises and controls the operation of all the programs in the software system,
- Communication program for exchanging data with the remote stations,

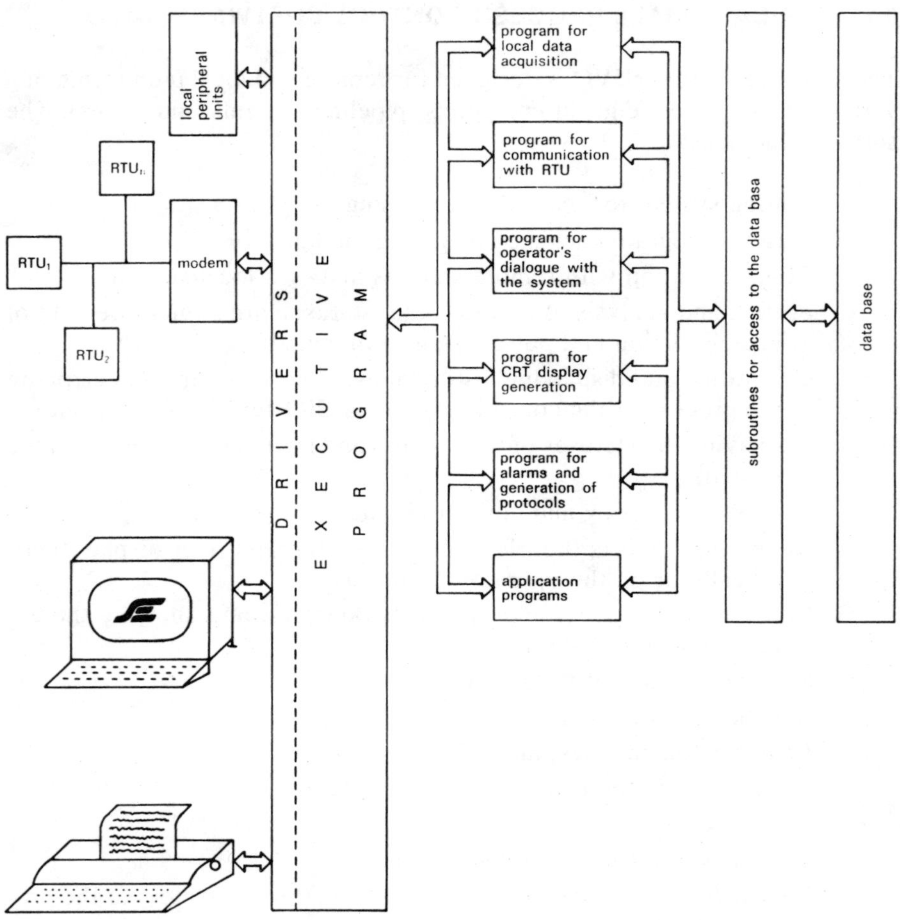

Figure 6.13 *Process control software NIVO. Adapted from Sistemi za Energetiko.*

- Program for local data acquisition,
- Program for operator's interaction with the system,
- Program for CRT display generation,
- Program for the generation of alarms, messages and protocols,
- Program library for access to the data base,
- Data base, and
- Application programs (optional).

Depending on the application, the data base and the application programs vary. The system programs, however, are changed only upon special request.

6.12.1 Executive Program

The core of the whole programming system is a small executive program that provides synchronized performance of all the software modules in the system. It is a central manager of the computer resources, which it allocates to the users (i.e., programs) according to their level of priority. Through efficient handling of the I/O devices and a powerful set of system directives it ensures real time execution and high degree of software modularity.

6.12.2 Data Collection and Real-time Control

These functions are performed by a set of programs performing the following tasks: exchange of information with the local and remote stations, verification of data, initial data processing, and entering of data to the data base. All relevant data are passed on to a program with the task of informing and alarming the operator.

Communication between the operating center and the remote stations functions by the transmission-on-demand method using asynchronous serial communication channels. The flow of data is optimized, (i.e., the remote stations transmit only data indicating a change in the process under control). The same data can be transmitted in different types of data blocks, which allows the fastest possible up-dating of the data base at the operating center. The data transmission network can be of any configuration.

6.12.3 Dialogue between the Operator and the System

The operator communicates with the system via standard black and white (VT100 compatible), or color CRT terminal. He uses only a few of the keys in a standard keyboard, each having a specific meaning. The bottom line of the screen tells the operator which functions he is allowed to initiate, continue or execute at a certain moment, as well as the related keys.

The operator can intervene with the process, or change the parameters of the data base via interactive points in the CRT display. With a simple choice of an interactive point the operator can request:

- Displays in a graphic or tabular form,
- Display of changes in the process parameters (e.g., critical limits of the measurements),
- Execution of telecommands (digital or analog),
- Printout of the CRT displays on the printer, and
- Printout protocols on the printer.

6.12.4 Programs for CRT Displays Generation

All the CRT displays are composed of three main sections:

- Fixed section,
- Interactive points for the operator's intervention, and
- Changing section (dynamic process data).

The displays are encoded by macroinstructions which are simple and easy to use. The code for display generation is passed on to a program which is a kind of interpreter converting organised collections of data into CRT displays.

6.12.5 Data Base

The data base is structured hierarchial consisting of data at the system, station and point levels. Each item of data is described by parameters such as name, momentary value, coefficient, areas of normal and alarm values, allowed processing of data, logical connection of the data to the process, and so on. Some of these parameters are fixed, while others can be altered by the process or the operator. In order for the nature and location of a malfunction to be immediately specified, all the diagnostic data generated by the DIPS remote stations are transmitted also to the operating centre. Efficient access to the data base is provided through a special reentrant program library.

6.12.6 Application Programs

Several types of application programs can be added to the preceding program modules. They make the whole telecontrol system more powerful and economic (e.g., in automatic regulation). NIVO is a VAX-oriented system produced by Sistemi za Energetiko.

6.13. HP COMPUTERS FOR REAL-TIME AND FOR NETWORKING†

6.13.1 Versatile Design for Real-Time Uses

HP 1000 computers are open, modular machines that are designed for real-time multiprogramming, multi-user applications in manufacturing, communications, research, and other fields that require real-time response. A choice of four processors and a wide variety of interfaces and software equips HP 1000 computers to solve many different applications, taking advantage of these HP 1000 real-time performance features.

Fast, Efficient Handling of I/O. External sensors, measurement instruments, and other I/O devices connect to HP 1000 systems via I/O interfaces

† Section 6.13 is adapted from Hewlett-Packard manuals.

and an I/O system with multilevel, vectored hardware interrupt that expedites I/O. Each I/O channel has its own interrupt priority level, from which interrupts directly initiate service programs. Direct memory access controlled under a distributed intelligence I/O design speeds data transfers to and from memory with minimal involvement of the CPU.

Fast Processing of Data. HP 1000 systems can process data at base instruction rates to 1.3 MIPS and floating point processing speeds to 820 KWIPS-B1D. This minimizes the time needed to process input data, evaluate results, and initiate real-time action.

Clocked Operations Timing is provided by time base generator interrupts that maintain a real-time clock.

Large Main Memory Capacity. Up to 32 megabytes of main memory can be provided to keep most critical programs resident and ready to execute quickly, avoiding the delays inherent in moving programs to and from disk.

A Powerful Real-Time Operating System. The RTE-A system supports memory-based or disk-based real-time multiprogramming operation with easy, efficient interprocess communication, and priority-based scheduling of programs in response to event interrupt, time-of-day, or program or user request. RTE-A manages sharable memory-resident data arrays up to 2 megabytes and virtual data arrays up to 128 megabytes in main memory and on disc. With its VC+ extension, RTE-A supports execution of programs as large as 7.75 megabytes.

6.13.2 IEEE-488 Interface Bus

Hewlett-Packard developed the company's HP-IB industry standard interface, also known as IEEE-488 or GP-IB, in the early 1970s to provide a standard bus for instrumentation and peripherals. Since then, this interface has grown to become the standard way to communicate with instruments throughout the measurement automation community.

All active interface circuitry is contained within the various HP-IB devices, and the interconnecting cable (containing 16 signal lines) is entirely passive. The cable's role is limited to that of interconnecting all devices in parallel so that any one device may transfer data to one or more other participating devices (See Figure 6.14).

Every participating device (instrument, controller, accessory module) must be able to perform at least one of the roles of talker, listener, or controller. A talker can transmit data to other devices via the bus, and a listener can receive data from other devices via the bus. Some devices can perform both roles (e.g., a programmable instrument can listen to receive its control instructions and talk to send its measurement results). A minimum

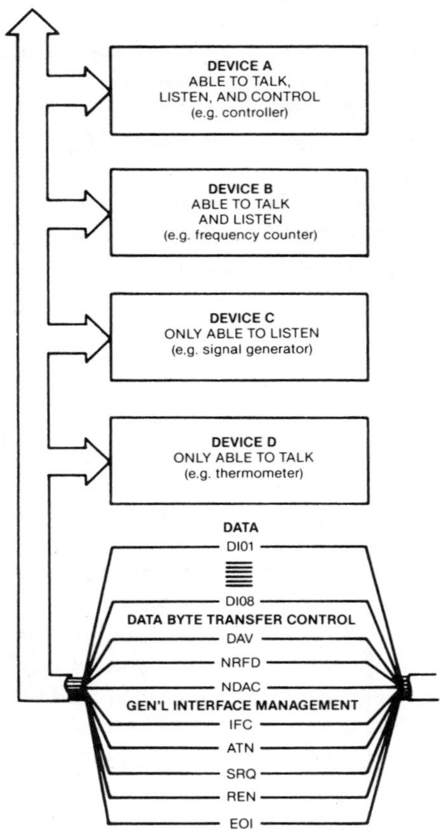

Interface connections and bus structure.

Figure 6.14 *Interface connection and bus structure. Adapted from Hewlett-Packard Corporation manuals.*

HP-IB system consists of one talker and one listener, without a controller. In this configuration, data transfer is limited to direct transfer between one device manually set to "talk only" and one or more devices manually set to "listen only" (e.g., a measuring instrument talking to a printer for semiautomatic data logging). A controller manages the operation of the bus system primarily by designating which devices are to send and receive data, and it may also command specific actions within other devices.

The full flexibility and power of the HP-IB become more apparent, however, when one device that can serve as controller/talker/listener (e.g., calculator or computer) is interconnected with other devices that may be either talkers or listeners, or both (e.g., frequency synthesizers, counters, power meters, relay actuators, displays, printers), depending on the application.

An HP-IB *controller* participates in the measurement by being programmed to schedule measurement tasks, set up individual devices so that they can perform these tasks, monitor the progress of the measurement as it proceeds, and interpret the results of the measurement. HP offers controllers that can be programmed in high-level languages such as Basic, Fortran, HPL, and Pascal.

The HP-IB has a party-line structure wherein all devices on the bus are connected in parallel. The 16 signal lines within the passive interconnecting HP-IB cable are grouped into three clusters according to their functions:

1. Data bus (8 signal lines),
2. Data byte transfer control bus (3 signal lines), and
3. General interface management bus (5 signal lines).

The data bus consists of eight signal lines that carry data in bit-parallel, byte-serial format across the interface. These signal lines carry addresses, program data, measurement data, universal commands and status bytes to and from devices interconnected in a system. Identification of the type of data present on the DIO signal lines is indicated by the ATN (attention) signal. When the ATN signal is true (asserted), either addresses or universal commands are present on the data bus and all connected devices are required to monitor the DIO lines. When the ATN message is false, device-dependent data (e.g., programming data) is carried between devices previously addressed to talk and listen.

Transfer of each byte on the data bus is accomplished via a set of three signal lines: DAV (data valid), NRFD (not ready for data), and NDAC (not data accepted). These signals operate in an interlocked handshake mode. Two signal lines, NRFD and NDAC, are each connected in a logical AND (wired OR) to all devices connected to the interface. The DAV signal is sent by the talker and received by potential listeners whereas the NRFD and NDAC signals are sent by potential listeners and received by the talker.

The general interface management lines manage the bus to effect an orderly flow of messages. The IFC (interface clear) message places the interface system in a known quiescent state. SRQ (service request) is used by a device to indicate the need for attention or service and to request an interruption of the current sequence of events. REN (remote enable) is used to select between two alternate sources of device program data. EOI (end or identify) is used to indicate the end of a multiple byte transfer sequence or, in conjunction with ATN, to execute a polling sequence.

It is not possible in this limited space to go into detail on each signal line's role. But you should note that every HP-IB device need not be able to respond to all the lines. As a practical and cost-effective matter, each HP-IB device usually responds only to those lines that are pertinent to its typical function on the bus.

6.13.3 Information Network For Computer Integrated Manufacturing

Networking provides instant information exchange among all manufacturing functions, including planning and control, financial systems, production processes, production engineering and product design. Computer integrated manufacturing (CIM) is the key to gaining the competitive edge by improving quality, productivity, and flexibility.

Networking also solves the problem of making terminal connections to a wide range of systems and applications. By keeping terminal transactions separate from system-to-system communication, the network allows many terminal types to access a variety of computers throughout the site.

Modular approach makes it easy to implement a network step by step. Each module is designed to help solve a particular networking problem in the wiring system, departmental subnets, data centers and plantwide integration.

Hewlett-Packard's Advance Net is a communications strategy and network architecture designed to provide a broad range of networking alternatives. Advance Net is a modular, scalable network that improves communication and productivity. To increase productivity, Advance Net links engineering workstations through a high-speed local area network (LAN) so engineers can move large design files quickly. Workstations are connected to larger computers by using industry standard protocols.

While the network improves communications, it also lowers costs by allowing everyone to share expensive peripherals, thus minimizing the cost per user.

Using Advance Net, engineers can share transparent access to files, data bases and sophisticated peripherals like printers, plotters, and disks.

In the HP-UX environment, a user on any engineering workstation can access resources on any other network station. A workstation can also act as a dedicated peripheral server for heavy use.

Advance Net is based on industry standards. It provides multivendor communications by supporting industry and de facto standards important to the engineering community, including 802.3 and Ethernet, Transmission Control Protocol and Internet Protocol (TCP/IP), ARPA, Berkeley, and NFS networking services.

In addition, Advance Net supports other protocols commonly used in mainframe computer centers, such as SNA and HYPER channel, providing easy access to these essential resources. Additional services provide such capabilities as file and peripheral sharing and the ability to develop customized network protocols. The Advance Net architecture connects the many systems in multivendor computing environment. To allow these systems to communicate, two things are required:

- Common wiring-HP recommends IEEE 802.3; Ethernet is also supported.

- Common software protocols—each communicating system must use the same protocol, either ARPA Services, Berkeley Services or HP's Network Services.
- ARPA Services—Developed by the U.S. government to allow its many computing installations to communicate, this protocol has become a de facto standard throughout the computing industry. Features include network file transfer, electronic mail, interactive access, and remote execution of commands and programs.
- Berkeley Services—Developed by the University of California at Berkeley, these services have also become a de facto industry standard. Features include network file transfer, electronic mail, interactive access, and remote execution of commands and programs.
- Network Services—Hewlett-Packard's Network Services allow network file transfer and remote file access to/from other HP systems. HP's Network Services are implemented on almost all HP workstations and computers. HP also offers Network Services for DEC VAX computers.

AdvanceNet is composed of a variety of solution modules designed to address specific problems. The modules for engineering include: engineering work group, engineering computer center, site computer center, company-wide access, and site wire.

6.13.4 Engineering Work Groups

The most effective and productive way to connect a group of workstations is with a local area network (LAN). HP's LANs provide engineers the ability to work together as members of a team. They can share disks, printers, plotters, and other peripherals. They can share computing resources and applications programs. And most importantly, they can share data and information.

HP offers two different local area networks for engineering work groups. One, the Ethernet/IEEE 802.3 local area network, is for engineers using workstations running HP-UX*. The other, the shared resource manager (SRM) LAN, is for engineers using either BASIC or Pascal environments. The two networks can be connected through a workstation running HP-UX SRM Access Utilities.

The LAN for HP-UX workstation is presented in Figure 6.15. It is appropriate if you:

- Are using HP-UX or a UNIX-based operating system and,
- Need high bandwidth communications (10 Mbits per second),
- Need handy access to other computers/servers in the company,
- Require fast file transfer, or
- Require interactive access.

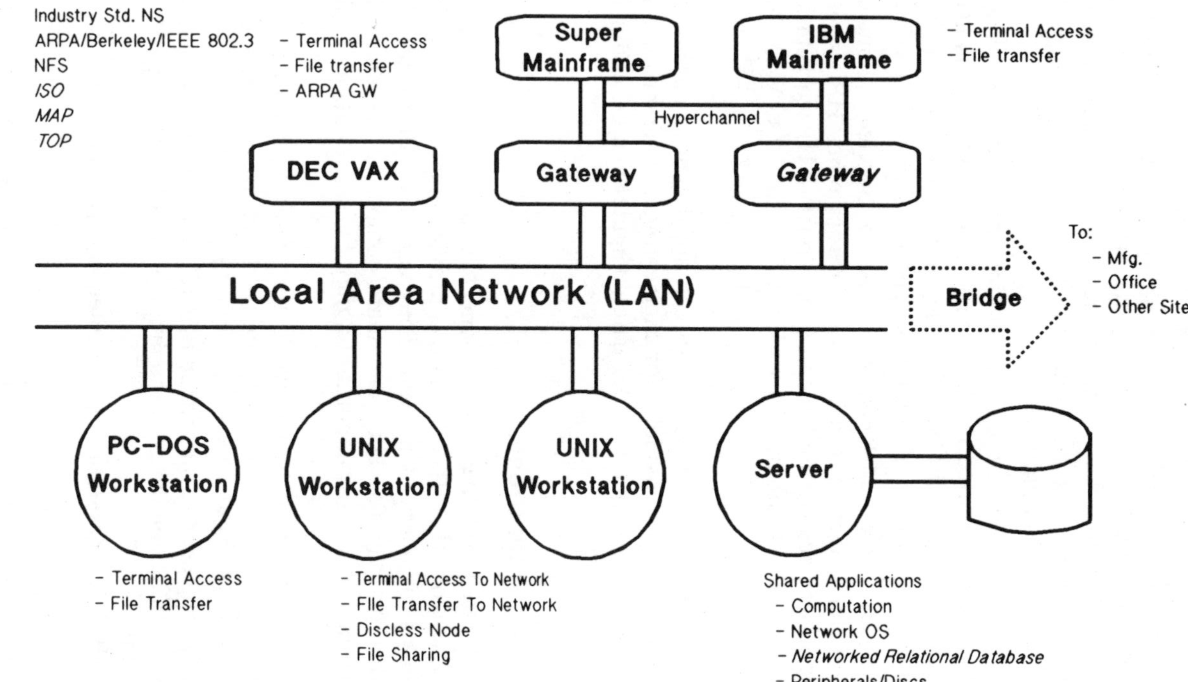

Figure 6.15 *Model networking environment. (Adapted from Hewlett-Packard Corporation manuals.)*

HP's local area network for workstations running HP-UX provides the de facto-standard U.S. Department of Defense ARPA Services and Berkeley Services. ARPA Services are available on several operating systems including the UNIX operating system, PC-DOS, and VMS. Berkeley Services are available only on the UNIX system and UNIX-based systems. The implementation of both ARPA and Berkeley Services provide compatibility with as many other vendors workstations as possible. Multi-vendor compatibility is also increased by the fact that these services are provided on both an Ethernet and IEEE 802.3 LAN.

Also included in the LAN for HP-UX workstations is HP's Network Services. Network Services (NS) can coexist with both ARPA Services and Berkeley Services, offering a method of copying files to and from other computers on the LAN. For Hewlett-Packard computers, NS also offers remote file access, allowing use of a file located on another computer as if it were on a local disk.

The SRM Network is appropriate when you:

- Are using Basic- or Pascal-based workstations and,
- Need high bandwidth communications,
- Want diskless workstations,
- Want to share information among Basic/Pascal workstations or with HP-UX computers or the HP Vectra PC,
- Need centralized, shared peripherals,
- Want to access data while it is being collected, or
- Want to connect to other networks/systems (like LANs, IBM, DEC).

6.13.5 Engineering Computer Center

Connecting computers in the engineering computer center to each other and to other computers within the facility can significantly improve productivity. The connection will allow engineers easy access to the computer center's peripherals, compute power and applications. This module assumes that the computers in your engineering computer center are minicomputers or superminis running either a proprietary or UNIX-based operating system. Examples of an engineering computing system are HP 9000 Series 800 computers and DEC VAX computers (see Figure 6.16).

ARPA and Berkeley Services are appropriate when you:

- Want multivendor communication,
- Have a network contained in a single building,
- Require industry-standard networking/operating system,
- Need fast file transfer, or
- Require interactive access.

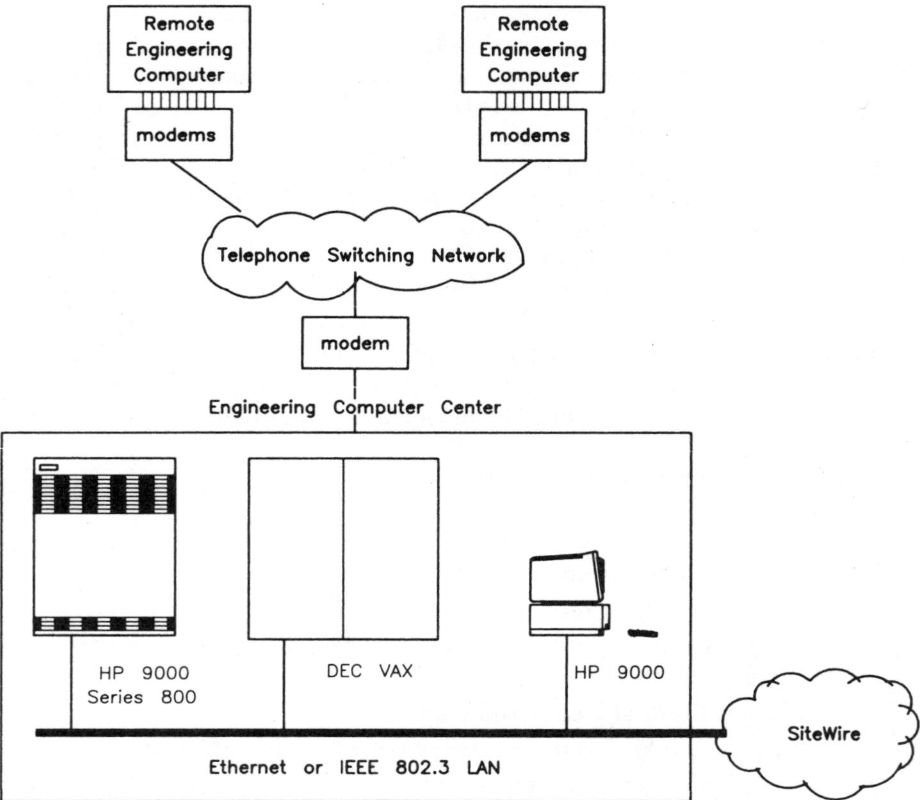

Figure 6.16 *Asynchronous connections of engineering computer centers. (Adapted from Hewlett-Packard Corporation manuals.)*

HP Network Services are appropriate when you:

- Want communication with other HP systems,
- Want to communicate with DEC VAX computers running VMS,
- Have a network contained in a single building, or
- Require fast file transfer.

6.13.6 Site Computer Center Access

Connecting computers in a site computer center to each engineer's workstation significantly improves productivity. The connection will allow engineers to easily access the mainframe computer center's data bases, peripherals, compute power and applications programs, while maintaining the flexibility of a workstation environment.

SNA Gateway connection is appropriate when you:

- Want to connect to an IBM SNA network,
- Want interactive access to IBM mainframes,
- Want HP-to-IBM file transfer capability, or
- Want to connect workstations on a LAN to an IBM SNA network.

HP's SNA gateway offers interactive access to IBM and IBM-compatible mainframes. This gateway emulates an IBM cluster controller and can support multiple terminals and workstations emulating IBM 3278 display stations. The SNA gateway also offers efficient file transfer capabilities and IBM 3287 printer emulation.

The SNA gateway interface hardware and emulation software is installed in an HP 9000 Series 300 workstation. The gateway connects to an IBM 3705 or 3725 Communications Controller via a modem or modem eliminator. Line speeds to 19.2 k baud are supported with greater line speeds planned. Workstations can access the gateway over an Ethernet or IEEE 802.3 LAN. Terminals access the gateway through asynchronous ports.

6.13.7 Company-wide Access

The company-wide access module addresses a need to expand your engineering network to connect computers at different sites together, allowing engineers at different sites within the company to more easily work together. When they have company wide access engineers can share computing resources, data, data bases, reports, and application programs. Company-wide access allows engineers to take advantage of existing computing facilities throughout the company.

HP offers three primary methods of connecting computers at different sites:

- Asynchronous Communications,
- X.25 Public Packet Switching, and
- X.25 Private Packet Switching.

Asynchronous company-wide connections are appropriate when you (see Figure 6.16):

- Require a low cost solution,
- Have low file transfer traffic,
- Have portable, frequently moved computers,
- Require short interactive communications,

- Do not require high-speed transfer,
- Require access to multiple systems, or
- Require an interim while X.25 is being installed.

The HP-UX operating system provides the standard cu (connect user) and uucp (UNIX® system-to-UNIX system copy) services. These services can be used with either dial-up or leased lines to connect engineers using UNIX-based operating systems. cu provides interactive access by allowing a workstation to function as a terminal to log into the remote system. uucp provides file sharing by allowing transfer of files to remote computers.

X.25 is appropriate if you:

- Need to connect to sites throughout the world,
- Have many dispersed sites with relatively low volume communications, or
- Want to try an X.25 network with a minimal capital investment.

6.13.8 Site Wire

An engineering network makes it easy for members of different departments and different teams within a department to work together. Once they are on the engineering network, these employees can share computing resources, data, data bases, reports, application programs, and peripherals.

The engineering network must maximize use of new workstation technology while protecting the investment in minicomputers or mainframes. The network must be modular and flexible to grow or change with project requirements. Multivendor connectivity is necessary to protect the investment and ensure that engineers have access to all available resources, no matter where they are located. To achieve all this connectivity, the engineering network must be based on a comprehensive wiring foundation. And this foundation must be based on industry standards.

The predominant network of choice for engineering is an Ethernet/IEEE 802.3 baseband LAN. HP offers two media for implementation of this Carrier-Sense Multiple Access with Collision Detection (CSMA/CD) 10 Mips baseband system:

- ThinLAN—a small cable (IEEE Type 10 Base 2) for connecting systems in close proximity, providing inexpensive, easy-to-install cabling.
- ThickLAN—a larger, backbone-type cable (IEEE Type 10 Base 5) capable of forming an information pipeline throughout a facility.

ThinLAN and ThickLAN are baseband cabling, providing a single information channel, excellent data services, and inexpensive cabling capable of spanning moderate distances. If an application requires multiple information channels, data/audio/video services, and longer distances, you will want to consider a multiple-channel broadband network.

6.14. MICRO VAX AND MICRO PDP-11†

6.14.1 Hardware And Operating System

The MicroVAX and the MicroPDP-11 supermicrosystems are based on different, but related, architectures. Although there are many architectural similarities between the VAX and PDP-11 system designs, there are some differences as well. Both share such characteristics as use of physical-address space, some virtual-address space, memory management, general registers, addressing modes, interrupts, and instruction sets. The designs differ in the size and type of these characteristics.

- The MicroVAX II can accommodate over 30 concurrent, active users depending on the configuration and application.
- The MicroVAX I can accommodate up to four concurrent, active users depending on the application.
- The MicroPDP-11/83 can accommodate over 30 concurrent, active users depending on the configuration and application.
- The MicroPDP-11/73 can accommodate up to 12 concurrent, active users depending on the application.
- The MicroPDP-11/23 can accommodate up to four concurrent, active users depending on the application.

VAX laboratory hardware is shown in Figure 6.17

Coordination and management of the VAX system's resources are the central responsibilities of the VMS operating system. An operating system is the group of programs that controls computing operations. The operating system is loaded into memory when the system is initialized, and remains there until the system is powered down. It performs both automatically and manually, and provides users with a consistent operating environment. This simply means that VAX/VMS system's resources are always used in the most efficient manner possible.

VMS Core software products include (see Figure 6.18):

- The VMS operating system and
- VMS core services

    Core subsystems

† Section 6.14 is adapted from Digital Equipment Corporation manuals.

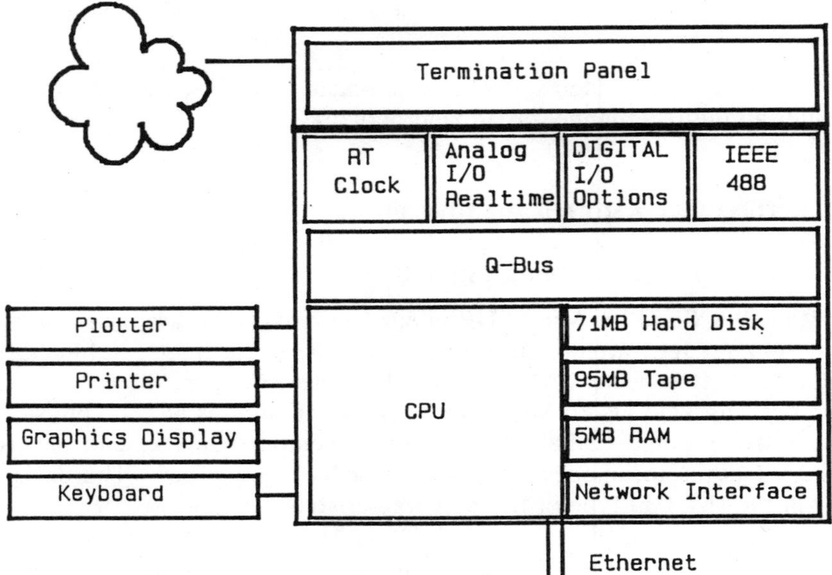

Figure 6.17 *VAX laboratory hardware.*

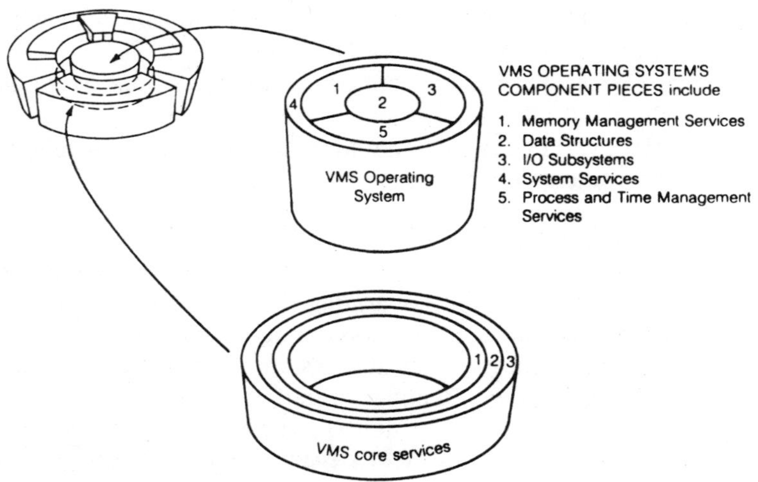

VMS CORE SERVICES include

1. Core Subsystems, which include
   - The Digital Command Language (DCL)
   - VMS Record Management Services (RMS)
   - VMS Runtime Library (RTL)
2. VMS Program Development Utilities, which include
   - VMS Text Processing Utilities
   - VMS Program Development Utilities
3. VMS Utilities, which include
   - System Management Utilities
   - System User Utilities

Figure 6.18 *VMS core software products. (Adapted from Digital Equipment Corporation manuals.)*

Core program development utilities
VMS system management utilities

The operating system itself is divided into five components (see Figure 6.19): these include

- Memory management facilities.
- Data structures.
- The I/O subsystem.
- Process and time management services.
- System services.

Applications can be developed and run across the entire line of VAX processors within limits of existing program size and available memory. User-mode applications developed with VMS will run on MicroVMS without modification. Virtual memory management allows the writing of programs that are larger than physical memory and lets any number of jobs share memory. VAX laboratory software is shown in Figure 6.20

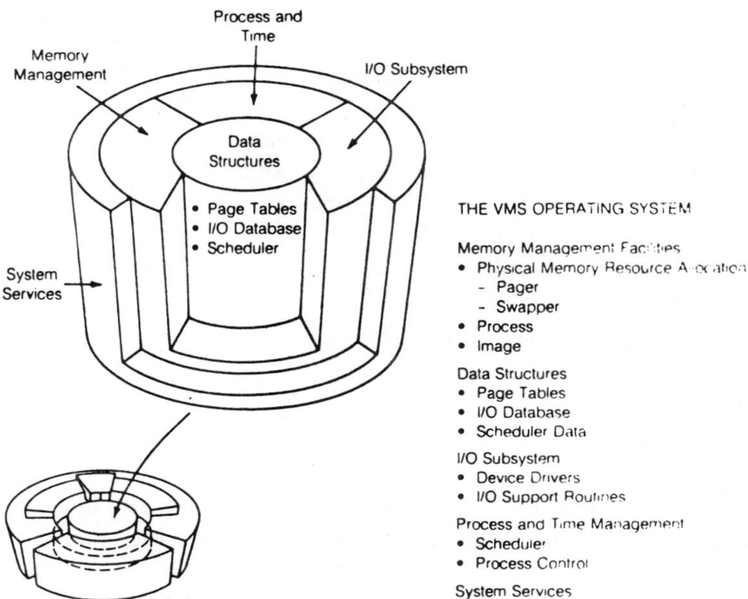

Figure 6.19 *The VMS operating system. (Adapted from Digital Equipment Corporation manuals.)*

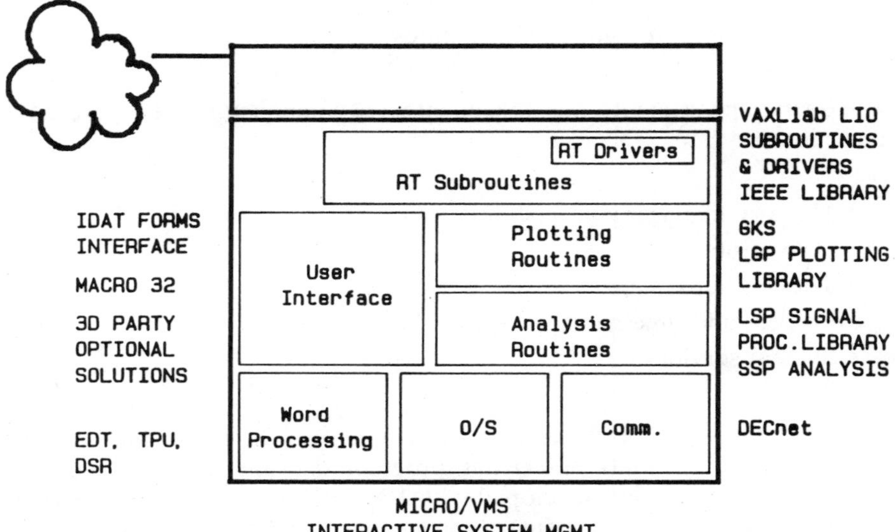

Figure 6.20 *VAX laboratory software.*

6.14.2 Q-bus

The Q-bus is the common communications path for the data, address, and control information that is transferred between the CPU, memory, and device interfaces. Each of the supermicrocomputers use only the Q-bus for these communications. The 22-bit Q-bus consists of 42 bidirectional and two unidirectional signal lines that are built into the backplane assembly. Logic modules are installed in the backplane and connected to these signal lines with backplane connectors. The signal lines are defined as follows:

- 16 multiplexed data/address lines,
- 2 multiplexed address/parity lines,
- 4 nonmultiplexed extended address lines
- 6 data transfer control lines,
- 6 system control lines, and
- 10 interrupt control and direct memory access control lines.

In addition to the data, address, and control signal lines, a number of power, ground, and spare lines have been defined for the 22-bit Q-bus (hereafter referred to as the Q22 bus). All communications on the bus are performed asynchronously to allow some devices to transfer at data rates greater than those of other devices. The bus operates with a *master/slave relationship*. When more than one device requests the use of the bus, the device with the highest priority gains access. It becomes the bus master and controls the data transfers until it releases the bus. In performing the transfers, it addresses another device that is designated as a slave.

The current data cycle is overlapped with the arbitration for the next cycle, enhancing the system performance. The upper eight Kbytes of address space are reserved for I/O devices. Some of the addresses are fixed within this space, and others are allowed to float, depending on the system configuration.

The bus transactions consist of initialization, arbitration, data transmission, and miscellaneous:

- The *initialization* lines of the bus provide the information required to start the processor after powering up and cause an orderly shutdown of the processor during power failures. In addition, they allow the processor to reset the I/O subsystem.
- The *arbitration* lines control access to the data transmission portion of the bus.
- The *data transmission* lines allow words or bytes to be moved about on the bus. Transmission of data is always accomplished with one device acting as master and the other acting as slave. The master controls the direction and length of transmission.
- The *miscellaneous* lines provide other functions, including processor control and memory refresh.

A master/slave relationship exists throughout each bus transaction. At any time, one device has control of the bus and is termed the bus master, and the other device is termed the slave. The bus master, which is typically the processor or a direct-memory access (DMA) device, initiates a bus transaction. The slave device responds by acknowledging the transaction in progress and by receiving data from, or transmitting data to, the bus master. The bus control signals transmitted or received by the bus master or the bus slave device must complete the sequence according to bus protocol.

The processor controls bus arbitration to determine which device becomes bus master at any given time. A typical example of this relationship is the processor, as master, fetching an instruction from memory, which is always a slave. Another example is a disk-drive device as master transferring data to memory as slave. Communications on the bus are interlocked so that, for certain control signals issued by the master device, there must be a response from the slave in order to complete the transfer. It is the master/slave signal protocol that precludes the need for synchronizing clock pulses.

Since bus-cycle completion by the bus master requires response from the slave device, each bus master includes a time-out error circuit that will abort the bus cycle if the slave device does not respond to the bus transaction within 10 microseconds.

6.14.3 Digital Network Architecture

Digital Network Architecture (DNA) is a set of hardware and software networking capabilities that support communications between Digital's systems, and between Digital's systems and other manufacturers' systems.

Digital-to-Digital communications are permitted through protocols, or rules, that are defined by the DNA. DNA protocols are based on the architectural models for open systems interconnection created by the International Standards Organization (ISO). These rules govern the format, control, and sequencing of message exchange among Digital computers.

Internet products provide a means for Digital's systems to communicate with systems built by other manufacturers. These products emulate common communications protocols and are data transfer facilitators rather than hardware emulators.

The lowest layer of the DNA structure, shown in Figure 6.21, is the *physical link layer*. This layer governs electrical and mechanical transport of information between systems that are connected. Computer systems can be physically connected by cables, fiber optic lines, microwave transmissions, or switched networks such as telephone lines. In addition to the physical connection, the electrical signals on the lines must be properly defined. The signal characteristics and data rates are all defined by the hardware comprising the interface module and the transmission link.

The next highest layer of the DNA structure is the *data link layer*. The data link layer can prepare messages for transmission according to a specified protocol, check the integrity of received messages, and manage access to the channel. The data link is usually implemented by hardware and software. For a simple asynchronous interface, the hardware contribution to the

<table>
<tr><th>ISO Seven Layers</th><th>DNA Layers</th><th colspan="3">DNA Functions</th></tr>
<tr><td rowspan="2">Application</td><td>User</td><td colspan="3" rowspan="3">File transfer
Remote resource access
Down line system load
Remote command file
Submission
Virtual terminals</td></tr>
<tr><td>Network management</td></tr>
<tr><td>Presentation</td><td>Network application</td></tr>
<tr><td>Session</td><td>Session control</td><td colspan="3" rowspan="2">Task to task</td></tr>
<tr><td>Transport</td><td>End communications</td></tr>
<tr><td>Network</td><td>Routing</td><td colspan="3">Adaptive routing</td></tr>
<tr><td>Data link</td><td>Data link</td><td rowspan="2">DDCMP
Point to point
Multipoint</td><td rowspan="2">X.25</td><td rowspan="2">Ethernet</td></tr>
<tr><td>Physical</td><td>Physical link</td></tr>
</table>

Figure 6.21 *Digital Network Architecture structure.*

data link is minimal. With other devices, such as the DEQNA Ethernet interface, almost all of the data link layer is implemented in hardware.

Because of the data link layer, the *routing layer* can rely on error-free connection to adjacent nodes. It addresses messages, routes them across intervening nodes, and controls the flow of messages between nodes. The routing layer and higher layers are implemented in software.

Because the routing layer establishes the path, the *end communications layer* can address the end machine without concern for route, and can perform end-to-end error recovery.

The *session control layer* manages the system-dependent aspects of a communications session. For instance, when the end communications layer reliably delivers a message from another manufacturer's system in the network, the session control layer interprets that message for acceptance by the system software.

The *network application layer* converts data for display on terminal screens and printers.

The *network management layer* monitors network operations by logging events and collecting statistical and error information. It also controls network operations by tuning network parameters and testing nodes, lines, modems, and interfaces.

The *user layer* provides services that directly support the user and application tasks such as resource sharing, file transfers, and remote file access.

REFERENCES

1. B. Souček, *Minicomputers in Data Processing and Simulation,* Wiley, New York, 1972.
2. G. Korn, *Minicomputers for Engineers and Scientists,* McGraw-Hill, New York, 1973.
3. C. Weitzman, *Minicomputer Systems,* Prentice-Hall, Englewood Cliffs, NJ, 1974.
4. J. Finkel, *Computer-Aided Experimentation,* Wiley, New York, 1975.
5. B. Souček, *Microprocessors and Microcomputers,* Wiley, New York, 1976.
6. P. Katz, *Digital Control Using Microprocessors,* Prentice-Hall International, London, 1981.
7. F. Jović, *Process Control Systems,* Kogan Page, London, 1986.
8. E. W. Dijkstra, The structure of the T.H.E. multiprogramming system, *Commun. ACM,* **11,** 341–346, 1968.

CHAPTER 7

High-Speed Neural Chips and Systems

INTRODUCTION AND SURVEY

Major advances in artificial neural networks are in the area of design of high-speed neural chips and systems. Digital and analog neural chips with remarkable features have become available. The characteristic feature of a digital neural chip is the small number of specific instructions, such as repeat, multiply, sum, and the inclusion of many simple processor slices within custom-designed memory chips. By eliminating inefficiencies in the movement and processing of data, we can readily achieve chips and modules performing billions of multiply-and-add operations per second.

The characteristic feature of an analog neural chip is direct simulation of intelligent processes, including learning and adaptation based on adaptive resonance theory, and silicon visual processing based on the model of retina system of higher animals. Leaders in the field believe that the ability to realize simple neural functions in silicon is strictly limited by an understanding of biological organizing principles and not by difficulties in realization.

The chapter ends with a description of the architecture of high-speed neural coprocessor.

7.1. GARTH SIMULATION-COMMUNICATION NEURAL CHIPS

According to Garth,[1] an appropriate machine for neural network simulations would be one with a very large address space, moderate power, and a few specific instructions that are dominant in any neural network (e.g., repeat, multiply, sum). A low-cost chipset has been designed by Texas Instruments with these features. This section is adapted from Garth.[1]

The overall system structure is shown in Figure 7.1. It consists of a collection of low-cost neural network simulator cards physically connected in an arbitrary three-dimensional array with a host computer acting as the system driver. Each network simulator card (NETSIM) is an autonomous element with sufficient local memory and processing to solve a network of typically 256 neurons with 256 synapses per neuron in less than 20 ms, yet sufficiently inexpensive that many such cards may be connected to form a system.

Each NETSIM card consists of communication and simulation elements. The processing is performed by a purpose-designed neural network solution engine integrated circuit. This chip acts as a coprocessor to a low-cost microprocessor and performs most of the high-speed neural network solution functions. Attached to the solution engine is the memory containing the synapse contents and input vectors. Synapses are stored as 16-bit integers, and I/O are 8-bit terms. Simulations have shown that this resolution is sufficient for a wide range of common neural network operations. Also attached to the local microprocessor is a three-dimensional serial communication chip. This enables messages to be passed to arbitrary locations in the system at a rate of up to 10 Mbit/s.

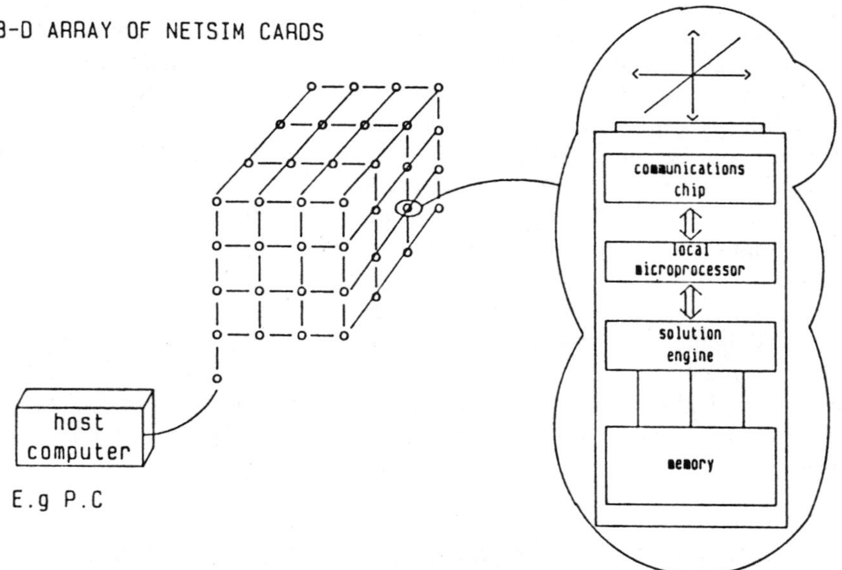

Figure 7.1 *The physical organization of the simulator. Each node in the simulator is a NETSIM card, capable of simulating a net of units. Arbitrary interconnection between the units is achieved by a serial message-forwarding system on each NETSIM card. (Reprinted by permission from Garth.[1]) Copyright © 1987 by IEEE.*

The solution engine performs the multiply-and-sum operations required for forward or backward propagation and the multiply-and-update operations required for synaptic update according to the error propagation algorithm. These operations are also appropriate in the solution of many other neural network algorithms. The local microprocessor performs the nonlinear function and determines the location to which an output term is sent (it defines the connectivity of the system). On completion of the simulation of each unit, the output value and the location of the data are loaded into the communication chip, which then passes the data packet along the shortest route to the destination net. On arrival, the receiving net's local microprocessor is interrupted and retrieves the data, storing it as an element in the new input vector. These operations may be pipelined such that the computation in the microprocessor and the communication of data add only minimal overhead to the solution time.

The solution engine consists of three principal sections: the math processor, address controller, and memory controller (Figure 7.2). The *math processor* is an 8-bit by 8-bit two's complement multiplier with 16-bit prescale. Simulations have shown that it is sufficient to multiply the input (or error) vector with only the top 8 bits of the synapse value in the solution phase. However, in the synaptic update phase, the full 16 bits of the synapse must be used to permit sufficiently small increments to the synapse value (failure to do this has, in simulation, been found to cause instabilities in the learning process). The prescale is used principally in the update mode to adjust the

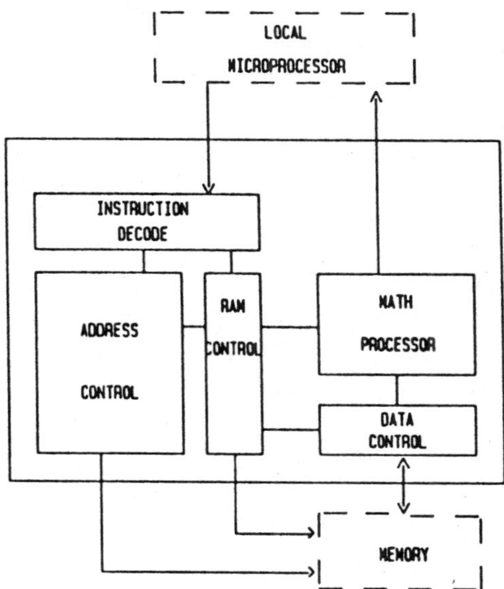

Figure 7.2 *Block diagram of the solution engine integrated circuit. (Reprinted by permission from Garth.[1]) Copyright © 1987 by IEEE.*

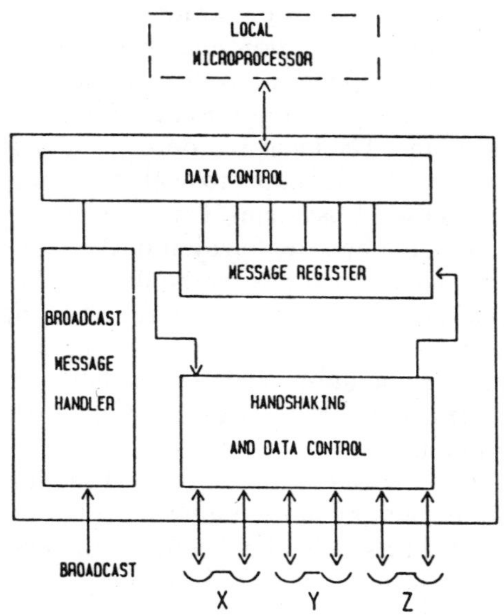

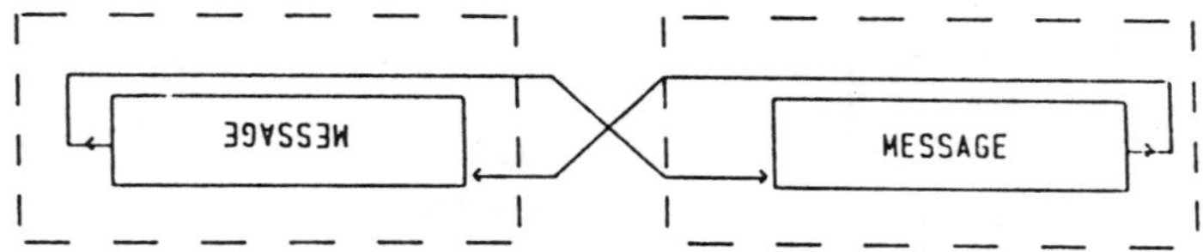

Figure 7.3 *Block diagram of the communication integrated circuit. Messages are passed serially in three dimensions, using a register-swapping architecture. (Reprinted by permission from Garth.[1]) Copyright © 1987 by IEEE.*

learning rate. The result of the computation is added to the sum register, a 24-bit register of which the top 16 bits are externally accessible.

The other major element in the NETSIM card is the communication handler chip (Figure 7.3). This consists of a 64-bit shift register in which the top 16 bits are dedicated to the chip address and the remaining bits to message data. The message length is programmable from 1 to 6 bytes of data. The message address is relative to the sending node and is capable of addressing ± 15 nodes in each of three dimensions (x, y, z)—i.e., a system of up to 27,000 nets.

Messages are transmitted on a first-come first-served principle with a priority system to arbitrate between multiple requests. The chips are organized such that three communication channels are declared to be master and three slave, the distinction being that master channels transmit a data clock and slave channels receive it.

The system may be used to simulate a wide variety of neural network algorithms, including error propagation and its derivatives. The solution time depends on several factors, including the details of the algorithm chosen and the power of the local microprocessor. The following are some typical performance figures for a net containing 256 units with 1024 inputs per unit.

Forward propagation time	(1024 × 256 × 250 ns)	70 ms
Back propagation time		70 ms
Synaptic update time		210 ms
Full cycle		350 ms

7.2. MORTON INTELLIGENT MEMORY CHIPS†

In most computers, large amounts of data are stored in memory chips. This data must be moved to a separate processor, only to have the results returned to memory.

Intelligent memory chips are matrix-vector multipliers. Multiple, simple, serial processor slices are placed within custom-designed, complementary metal-oxide semiconductor (CMOS) memory chips. Multiple chips work together in a small module to provide any matrix or vector precision desired. Inherently parallel, as more modules are used in a system, not only does the storage capacity increase but the amount of processing power directly increases as well. By eliminating inefficiencies in the movement and processing of data, these chips and modules provide systems that are 10 times more cost-effective than those previously available. Systems performing billions to trillions of multiply-and-add operations per second are readily achieved.

Applications include

Digital Signal Processing	Matrix Multiplications
Image processing	Three-dimensional graphs
Large, multiwindow convolution	Fixed- and floating-point supercomputing
Two- and three-dimensional FFTs	Pattern recognition
Adaptive filters	Artificial neural networks

† Sections 7.2 and 7.3 are adapted from *Intelligent Memory Preliminary Information*. Courtesy and copyright © 1988 by Oxford Computer.

According to Morton,[2] each module will provide 64 kbit to 1 Mbit of storage and 1.28 billion 8-bit multiplications and additions per second for image processing and pattern recognition, 40 million 32-bit multiplications and additions for two-dimensional FFTs and real-time three-dimensional graphics, or 80 million floating-point operations per second. Modules are designed to work together to provide ultrahigh performance.

7.2.1. Background

Conventional computers and parallel processors are very inefficient, which limits their ability to manipulate matrices in real time. The difficulty results from four factors: (1) the storage of matrices in conventional, semiconductor memory, where an entire row of hundreds of memory cells is accessed in each chip to transfer a single bit of information; (2) the need to repetitively move these matrices from memory to a separate processing unit over a low-capacity data path (the von Neumann bottleneck) in order to perform arithmetic operations; (3) the power and time required to move information between chips; and (4) the small fraction of time that many of the logic elements in each chip are active. These problems are made worse by the complexity of the real world, where one must quickly perform millions to billions of arithmetic operations on each update of each matrix. Therefore, manipulating complex three-dimensional graphics in real time, analyzing and simulating physical phenomena, realizing motion detectors and three-dimensional vision, controlling the motion of artificial limbs for humans and robots, recognizing cancer cells, continuous speech, handwritten zip codes on letters and dollar amounts on checks, manufacturing defects, complex character sets (e.g., Kanji) and many other patterns are far less capable and more expensive than many users require.

Intelligent memory chips remove these limitations by combining memory and simple processing logic into a single chip that is mostly memory by using information that is ignored in a conventional memory chip. Unlike "smart memories," such as video dynamic random-access memories (DRAMs) that operate independently and place shift registers, but little data processing capability, upon a memory chip, intelligent memory chips perform intense computations and work cooperatively. They solve many longstanding problems, providing "value-added memories" where a small amount of logic adds high value to a memory chip. Simply placing a 32-bit by 32-bit multiplier on a memory chip does not solve the problem—the poor yield of the multiplier greatly increases the cost of the underlying memory, the high number of pins required for interconnections greatly reduces the packing density, and it is difficult for many such chips to work together. Furthermore, one needs an architecture where only a small amount of logic is required on each chip so that the performance requirements for the logic are minimal and the amount of on-chip noise it generates is small. This allows high-density memory technology to be used—technology that is noise sensitive and decreases one's ability to build logic.

7.2.2. Focus on Matrix Multiplication

The generic intelligent memory chip set will break the von Neumann bottleneck for many computationally intense problems. Not only does the solution offer a 10- to 100-fold improvement in cost effectiveness over conventional solutions, where the amount of the improvement depends on the application, but it also simultaneously solves the widely different requirements for relatively low accuracy pattern recognition; conventional, high-accuracy DSP and three-dimensional graphics, including two-dimensional FFTs; and ultrahigh precision engineering and scientific computing, providing solutions to many pressing problems.

However, intelligent memories are not applicable to word processing, spreadsheets, and occasional numerical analysis, since they do not involve intense matrix manipulation. The future of the microprocessor as a general-purpose computing device is thus unchanged by this advance; rather, problems are solved that are not being solved well, if at all, today.

The solution is unlike analog optical and analog electrical approaches to artificial neural networks and matrix multiplication. These approaches have limited precision and stability and are unable to handle highly complex problems. The solution is fully digital, absolutely accurate, uses no numerical approximation techniques, will be built using readily available chip fabrication technology, and supports any precision and complexity of problem over commercial, as well as military, temperature ranges at low cost. Two simple twists have been added: a reorganization of the problem of multiplying matrices and a change in the sequence of performing floating-point operations.

This focus on multiplying matrices further results from the high efficiency obtained by summing multiple products simultaneously rather than by computing a single product and keeping a running sum. For example, when conventional hardware computes 256 products, each to M bits, and then sums them, $256M$ bits must be handled. However, intelligent memories handle only $M + \log_2(256) = M + 8$ bits to achieve exactly the same result. This allows the operation to be spread across many chips while using few interconnections.

Intelligent memory places tiny processors (actually, processor segments or "slices") on the same chip as the memory cell array in order to use most, or all, of the row of data. The resulting large number of connections is economical only within specially configured memory chips. Processors on multiple chips work together to provide the level of precision desired. Furthermore, partial mathematical operations are performed quickly and summed over time, rather than being completed in a single cycle, in order to further reduce the complexity and cost of each processor.

7.3. INTELLIGENT MEMORY CHIPS FOR MATRICES WITH HUNDREDS OF COLUMNS

The intelligent pattern recognition memory chip and the intelligent convolution memory chip (ICMC) operate on matrices with many rows and multiples of 256 columns. The ICMC is shown in Figure 7.4. It is a superset of the intelligent pattern recognition chip and handles not only pattern recognition but also convolution for motion detection and the spatial filtering of images.

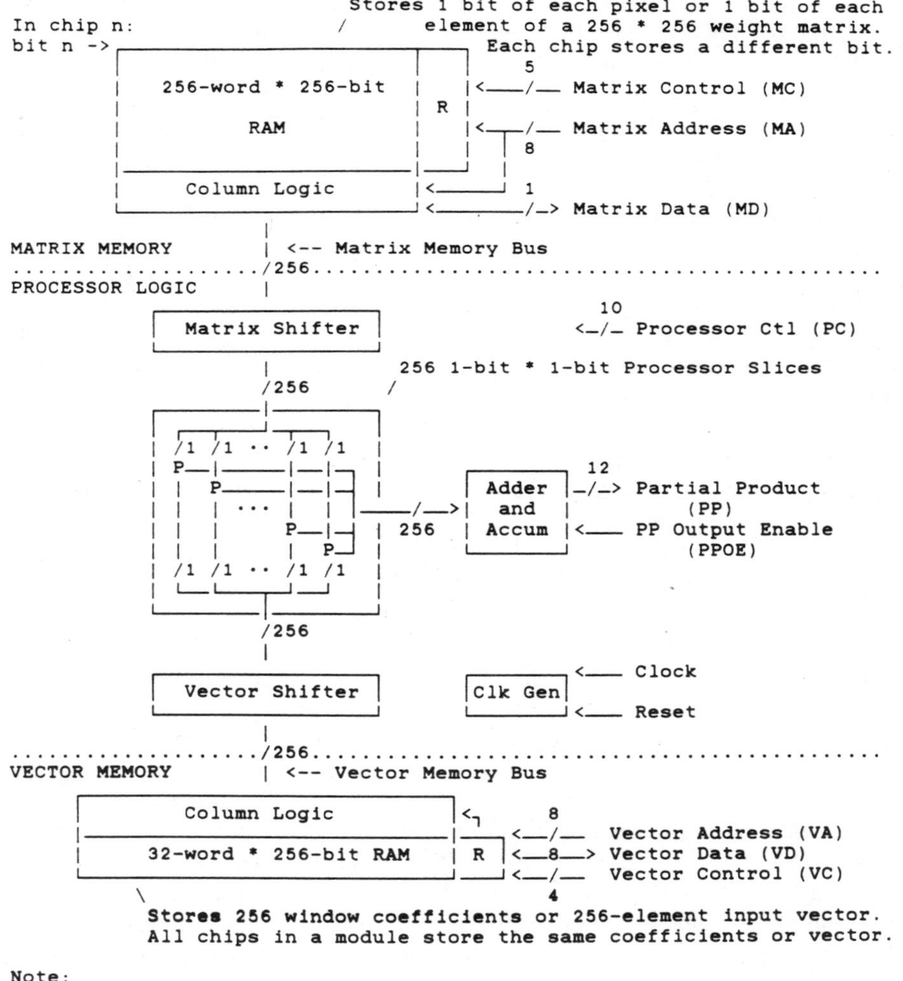

Figure 7.4 *Block diagram of the 64K 1-bit convolution memory chip. (Courtesy and copyright © 1988 by Oxford Computer.)*

On-chip shift registers allow arbitrarily large convolution windows to be implemented without any external shift registers. In addition, its flexible design allows the precision of the pixels, the precision of the coefficients, the number of points in the window and the throughput to be exchanged for one another. The size, such as 64K × 1-bit, refers to the number of bits (64K) of storage in the matrix memory and the number of connections (1) to the matrix data bus; later chips will have far higher capacity (1 Mbits) and more connections (4). Not shown in the figure are mask (or enable) logic to dynamically activate any combination of columns, and on-chip address generation logic to sequence through all or parts of the memories.

The target performance for the 64K × 1-bit ICMC memory chip is 10 billion bit operations per second when driven by a 40-MHz clock for internal operations. This is equivalent to one 16 × 16 bit, two 16 × 8 bit, four 8 × 8 bit, sixteen 8 × 2 bit, two hundred fifty-six 1 × 1 bit, and so on, multiplier/accumulators operating at 40 MHz. Data rates between chips to support this performance are 10 MHz or less, and the pin count is under 60, simplifying the use of the chip and reducing its package size and cost.

Although the chip shown in Figure 7.4 can provide multiple bits of precision of the input vector or window coefficients, a means is needed to provide multiple bits of precision of the weight matrix or pixels. Figure 7.5 shows an intelligent convolution memory block. Like ordinary memory chips, 8-bit precision of the weight matrix requires 8 mK × 1-bit ICMCs. An 8-bit block will be packaged as a SIMM (single in-line memory module), like common memory chips. To provide a simple engineering interface, each matrix element or pixel is loaded as though ordinary memory chips were being used, but with the constraint that a row of a weight matrix, or the pixels in a region of an image, is loaded into a physical row of memory cells. Unsigned or two's complement representation may be used.

The control chip provides sequencing operations based upon the size of the matrix, the required precision, and the representation. During computations, partial products are scaled and summed by a vector ACC chip to produce a full-precision product. The scaling accounts for the increasing weight of the bits of the matrix that are stored in the chips, where the partial product from the chip storing bit 1 has twice the weight of the partial product from the chip storing bit 0, and so on. Note that when two's complement notation of the matrix is used, the weight of the partial product from the most significant chip is negative.

A vector extension to the familiar "add-and-shift" multiply algorithm is used to multiply each matrix row vector by an input column vector. Serial arithmetic is used to multiply a pair of vectors rather than a pair of values. The number of ICMCs is equal to the precision of the matrix. The number of clock cycles per row of the matrix is equal to the precision of the vector. Each row of the matrix or region of an image is handled in turn. A total of 1.28 billion, 8-bit by 8-bit multiply/adds (or "connections" in neural network terms) per second, equivalent to 2560 millions of instructions per second

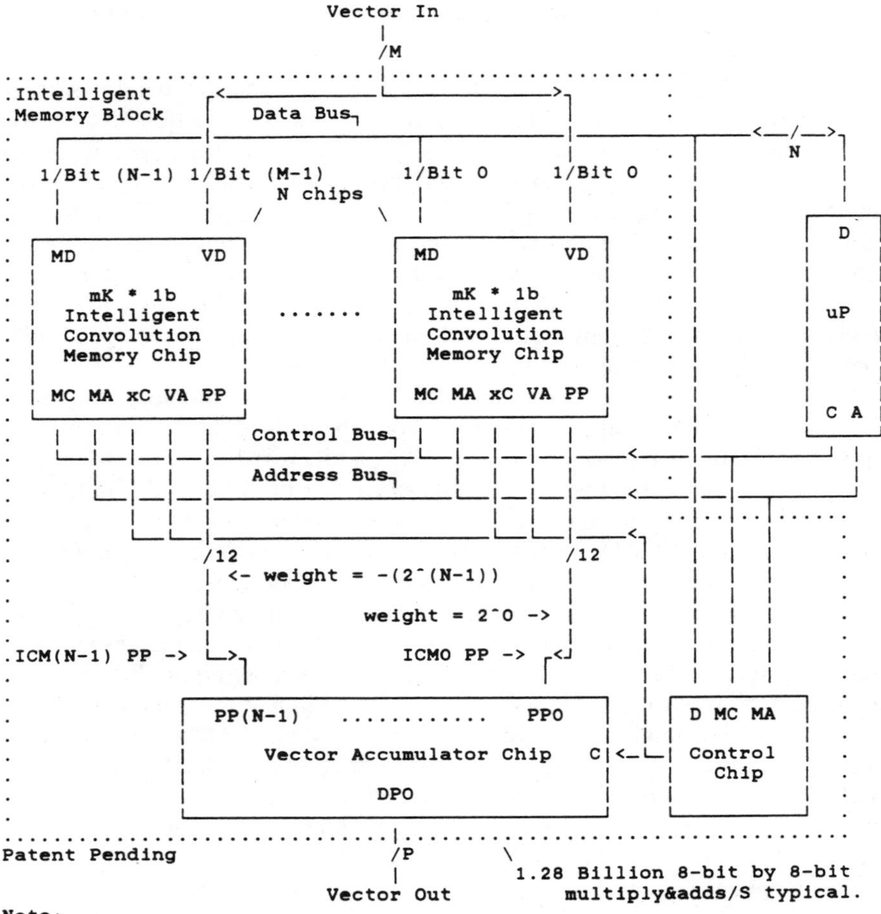

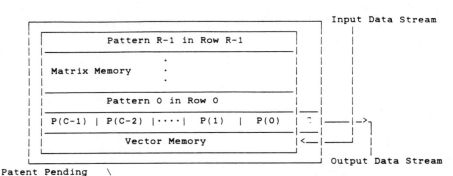

Note:
P = (log2 Matrix Rank) + M + N + 1, where M = number of bits of precision of vector.

Figure 7.5 *Block diagram of an Intelligent convolution memory block.* (*Courtesy and copyright © 1988 by Oxford Computer.*)

```
 ________________________________________________________   Input Data Stream
|  ____________________________________________________  |         |
| |              Pattern R-1 in Row R-1                | |         |
| |____________________________________________________| |         |
| |                               .                    | |         |
| | Matrix Memory                 .                    | |         |
| |                               .                    | |         |
| |____________________________________________________| |         |
| |              Pattern 0 in Row 0                    | |         |
| |____________________________________________________|_|_        |
| | P(C-1) | P(C-2) |····|   P(1)   |   P(0)           |   |______|->┐
| |____________________________________________________|__|      |  |
| |                 Vector Memory                      |<-|______|  |
| |____________________________________________________|  |         |
|________________________________________________________|  Output Data Stream
Patent Pending         \
                        Use multiple Intelligent Memory Modules per Block for
                           ultra high performance (10^9 - 10^10 mul&add/S).
```

Figure 7.6 *Intelligent memory block with stored patterns.* (*Courtesy and copyright © 1988 by Oxford Computer.*)

(MIPS), may be performed in a 10-chip module. Multiple logical intelligent memory blocks (IMBs), or physical intelligent memory modules may work together to increase the precision, the size of the problem in multiples of 256, or the performance.

Any form of densely connected neural network may be built efficiently by using ICMCs. There is no limit to the precision, accuracy, or dimensionality of the problem to be handled. Hierarchical systems may readily be built in layers, and adaptive systems may be built by using feedback.

Figure 7.6 shows an IMB with stored patterns. Each physical row of the matrix memory stores the parameters that represent each pattern. In signal processing terms, each set of parameters is "matched" to a particular pattern.

Figure 7.7 shows an associative memory or hierarchical network using intelligent memories. Since the essence of an associative memory is the repetitive multiplication of a state vector and a weight matrix, an IMB would store the weight matrix digitally and perform the computation. An interconnection block would feed back all of the outputs to the input, except when a stimulus vector is input.

An optional element is in series with the output of the IMB. The vector filter is a digital, programmable, multichannel filter that temporarily filters each element of the output vector from the IMB. This filtering controls the

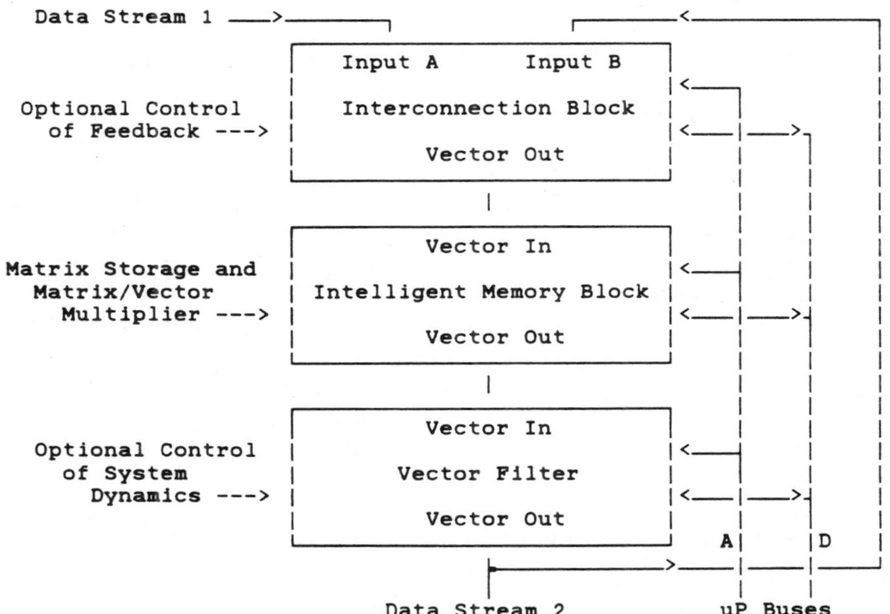

Figure 7.7 *Associative memory or hierarchical network using intelligent memories. (Courtesy and copyright © 1988 by Oxford Computer.)*

dynamics of the system, analogous to the effect of the frequency response of the amplifiers in the Hopfield network.

Note that all of the processing is provided within the IMB. The blocks are independent of one another, and as more blocks are used the total performance increases. A microprocessor that supervises the operation and changes the weights if desired is able to continue normal operation. Input data can thus be processed at a very high rate while the weights are being updated by software at a lower rate.

In a hierarchical network, the input to the IMB is a combination of outputs from a preceding block and the same block. A complex network may be implemented by multiple IMBs. A 1K × 1K fully interconnected weight matrix representing 1024 cells, each having 1024 inputs, may be built from sixteen 64-kbit IMBs. Each block handles a 256 × 256 weight matrix. In effect, all 1024 cells would receive 1024 inputs and be evaluated every 51.2 μs. Since all blocks operate simultaneously, this structure realizes 20 billion multiply/adds per second, which is equivalent to 40,000 MIPS. More parallelism can provide even higher performance.

Alternatively, a like size weight matrix may be implemented from a single block of 1M × 1-bit ICMCs. In effect, all 1024 cells would be evaluated every 819.2 μs—one-sixteenth the rate with one-sixteenth as many chips. Intermediate degrees of parallelism allow update periods between 51.2 and 819.2 μs to be obtained.

7.3.1. Intelligent Memory Chips for Matrices with Four Columns

The intelligent graphics memory chip (IGMC) and the intelligent floating-point memory chip (IFMC) are for matrices with multiples of four columns—befitting three-dimensional graphics, complex two-dimensional FFTs, and scientific and engineering computing. These matrices typically require 32-bit precision, whereas the matrices for image processing and pattern recognition typically require 8 or 16 bits and multiples of 256 columns, and the input data may have as little as 1 bit of precision.

Figure 7.8 shows the operations required to transform three-dimensional graphics matrices. The matrices may represent quantities other than graphics, but the principle is the same. Each of the many row vectors of the input matrix is multiplied in turn by a transformation matrix. Each column vector of the transformation matrix is applied in turn to each row of the input matrix. Note that, unlike the ICMC that operates upon one column vector at a time, the IGMC operates upon an entire 4 × 4 transformation matrix one column vector at a time. When the input image is composed of multiple objects and each object has a corresponding transformation matrix, then the transformation matrix must be changed when the processing of each object is complete.

```
     Input Matrix          Transformation      Output Matrix
                               Matrix

| A0 A1 A2 A3 |       | X0 X1 X2 X3 |       | a0 a1 a2 a3 |
| B0 B1 B2 B3 |   *   | Y0 Y1 Y2 Y3 |   =   | b0 b1 b2 b3 |
|      .      |       | Z0 Z1 Z2 Z3 |       |      .      |
|      .      |       | T0 T1 T2 T3 |       |      .      |
|      .      |                             |      .      |
                      └──── [B] ────┘
└──── [A] ────┘      (object-dependent)     └──── [C] ────┘

The operations on each row of [A] are equivalent to:

(|A0 A1 A2 A3| * | X0 | = | a0 |) + (|A0 A1 A2 A3| * | X1 | = | a1 |) +
                 | Y0 |                            | Y1 |
                 | Z0 |                            | Z1 |
                 | T0 |                            | T1 |

(|A0 A1 A2 A3| * | X2 | = | a2 |) + (|A0 A1 A2 A3| * | X3 | = | a3 |)
                 | Y2 |                            | Y3 |
                 | Z2 |                            | Z3 |
                 | T2 |                            | T3 |
```

Figure 7.8 *Multiplication of graphics matrices. (Courtesy and copyright © 1988 by Oxford Computer.)*

Since three-dimensional graphics typically require 32 bits of precision and it is convenient to place eight intelligent memory chips in a SIMM, each chip handles 4 bits of the input matrix. Each chip stores the entire transformation matrix. Unlike the intelligent convolution memory module, where the output of one module is fed to the input of the next, the intelligent graphics memory module (IGMM) stores its output (truncated to 32 bits) back within itself. The IGMM thus appears as a miniature array processor whose matrix memory is mapped into the memory of a host processor.

To reduce the amount of processor logic on each IGMC, the 32 bits of each element of the vector are handled in four cycles, with 8 bits being processed each cycle. The multiplier uses a combination of spatial (eight chips with 4 bits each) and temporal (four cycles at 8 bits per cycle) techniques. This partitioning requires the placement of a 4-bit by 8-bit multiplier, or only $\frac{1}{32}$ of a 32×32 multiplier, in each of four processor slices (one for each column of the matrix) in an IGMC. Thus for all four slices there is the equivalent of only an 8×16 bit multiplier on each chip.

Figure 7.9 is the block diagram of an ultrahigh performance graphics subsystem that is made possible by the use of intelligent memories. One or more IGMMs would be used in place of SRAMs. Assuming the use of 1 Mbit dynamic RAM (DRAM) technology for the IGMC, each module can store and process 64K three-dimensional vectors with 32-bit, fixed-point precision. Rather than requiring extremely fast SRAMs and a signal processor to perform three-dimensional transformations, the transformations may be performed within the IGMMs. An external processor would provide nonlinear

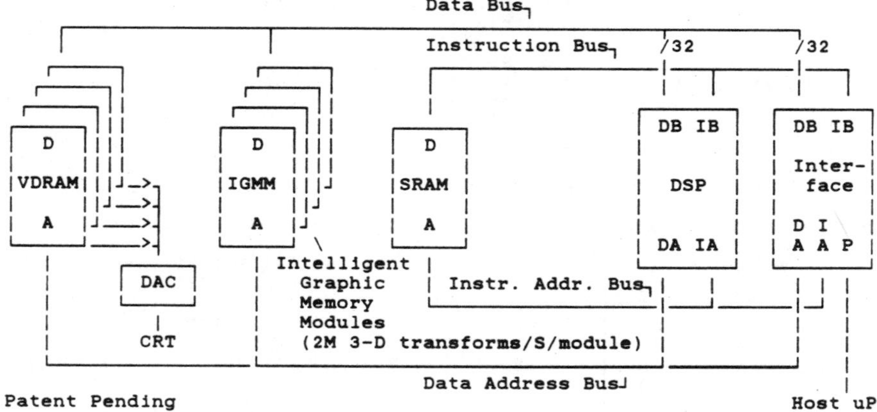

Figure 7.9 *Block diagram of an ultrahigh performance graphics subsystem.* (*Courtesy and copyright © 1988 by Oxford Computer.*)

functions, such as clipping, and transfer the results to the video DRAMs for display.

In addition, as more IGMMs are used, more vectors may be transformed per second. Unlike a conventional architecture where a single processor must handle all of the transformations, and where the more vectors are handled the lower is the number of updates per second, this modular architecture can maintain a constant 38-Hz rate, and removes the burden of transformation from the processor.

Two-dimensional, complex FFTs may be treated like three-dimensional graphics. A radix-2, complex FFT butterfly is represented by a 4×4 transformation matrix, and an image with complex data is partitioned into pairs of columns, giving row vectors with four elements. The matrix memory is partitioned into two buffers, one to provide the input data and the other to receive the transformed data. The roles of the buffers then reverse. The first pair of columns is processed with one butterfly, then the next pair of columns is processed with the appropriate butterfly, and so on. Transformed data are written into the matrix memory so that adjacent columns have the data that is input to each butterfly. As many passes over the image are made as there are stages in the FFT.

Thus in three-dimension graphics, two-dimension FFTs, scientific and engineering computing, expensive, very high speed, relatively low density SRAMs may be replaced by high-density, low-cost, intelligent DRAMs.

Floating-point arithmetic, rather than fixed-point as implemented by the previously described chips, will be implemented by the IFMC. This chip is a superset of the IGMC, providing both fixed-point and floating-point operations.

7.4. DENDROS NEURAL NETWORK ANALOG CMOS CIRCUITS†

DENDROS-1G, a monolithic CMOS integrated circuit, is an array of 22 dynamically modifiable synaptic connections plus one fixed connection to a single postsynaptic output. Figure 7.10 is a functional block diagram of DENDROS-1G. The input switches allow each connection circuit to be configured for feedforward (bottom-up) or feedback (top-down) operation. Tying the CONFIG pin to GND configures the modifiable connection circuits for feedforward operation; to V_{CC}, for feedback operation. The PWIDTH pin is a current input pin that controls how much the presynaptic pulse is extended. The extended pulse together with the postsynaptic pulse is used to modify the weight. Weight modification in the learning circuit employs a variant of the ART LTM equation. An external capacitor in the learning circuit is used as the LTM element. The sense of weight modification (positive or negative) is controlled by the deep-sleep (DSLEEP) pin. The LRATE and CLIMIT pins are current input pins that determine the learning rate and maximum storage capacitor charge, respectively. The learning circuit output voltage is used as the bias of a transconductance amplifier. This bias voltage determines the magnitude of current pulses supplied by the transconductance amplifier to the output (IOUT) pin. The fixed-weight connection consists of just the transconductance amplifier with externally adjustable current.

DENDROS-1G is designed for use in systems that incorporate the sleep-refresh mechanism for memory retention. This mechanism works in a manner analogous to DRAM, widely used in digital computers. Like its DRAM cousin, which has to be periodically refreshed, the sleep-refreshed capacitive memory (SRCM) has to be put to sleep regularly. The system-wide sleep state is entered by temporarily disconnecting all I/O and allowing the system to wander on its own.

DENDROS-1G utilizes a 68-pin PLCC package and operates over an ambient temperature range of -55 to $+125$°C.

Features of DENDROS-1G

- Designed for competitive-type, nonsupervised, multilayer networks;
- Incorporates sleep-refreshed memory retention mechanism;
- Configurable for both feedforward and feedback operation;
- Adjustable presynaptic input pulse width extender;
- Adjustable learning rate; and
- Adjustable weight limit.

† Section 7.4 is adapted from DENDROS Preliminary Information. Courtesy and copyright © 1988 by Syntonic Systems Inc.

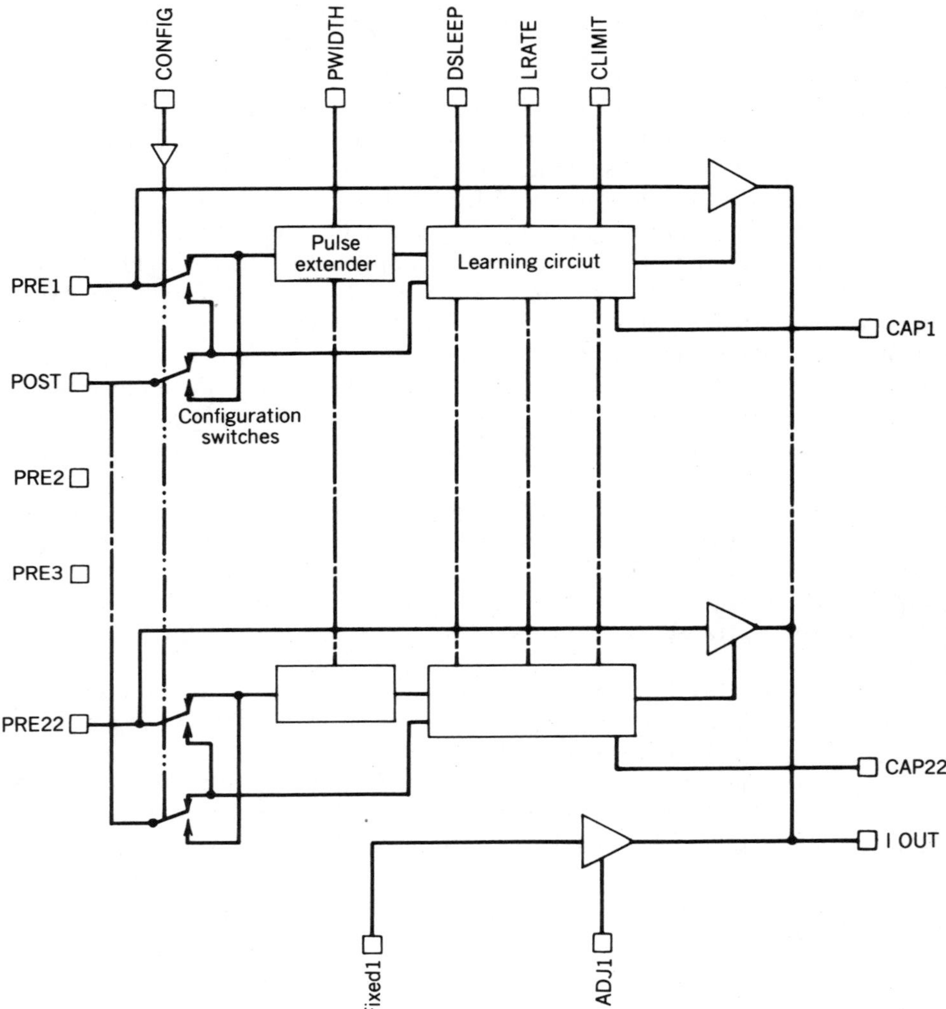

Figure 7.10 *DENDROS-1G, neural network analog CMOS circuit.* (*Courtesy and copyright © 1988 by Syntonic Systems Inc.*)

7.4.1. Typical Application

Figure 7.11 shows a typical competitive-type network. It consists of two layers: the input and the categorizer. Modifiable feedforward weights connect any node in the input layer to all nodes in the categorizer layer; and modifiable feedback weights connect any node in the categorizer layer back to all input nodes. DENDROS-1G houses 22 of either feedforward or feed-

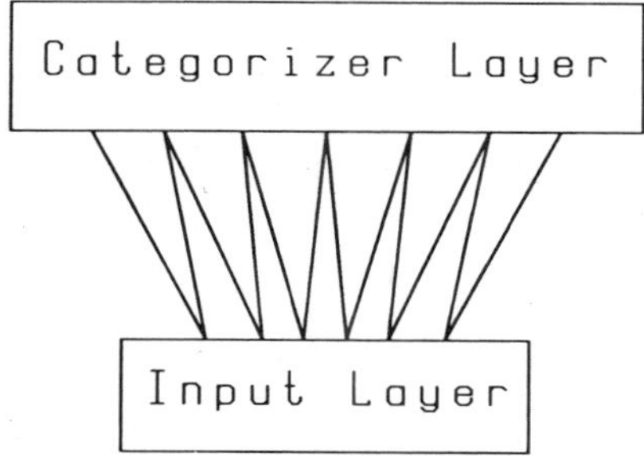

Figure 7.11 *A competitive-type network. (Courtesy and copyright © 1988 by Syntonic Systems Inc.)*

back weights; and DENROS-2 houses an input-categorizer node pair together with all support circuitry partly described below.

Inhibitory connections exist between nodes in the categorizer layer or in subsets of the layer called *clusters*. In the former case, only one node in the categorizer can fire at any moment (winner-take-all); in the latter case, two or more nodes may fire provided that such nodes are not in the same cluster (on-center, off-surround).

As data from the external world are presented to the input layer in the form of bilevel (or binary) signals, the categorizer layer automatically categorizes such input. Categorization is accomplished by assigning a node to represent each category. For example, if there are three nodes in the input layer and the system assigns categorizer node 1 to represent the input pattern 001, categorizer node 1 always fires whenever the same input pattern is presented to the system. The system assigns other categorizer nodes to other patterns possible with three binary bits (010, 011, 100, etc.).

As described above, there appears to be nothing different from the functionality of a typical two-layer network to that of a digital decoder circuit. A three-input, eight-category neural network that requires at least 22 DENDROS-1G and 11 DENDROS-2 chips can be implemented very simply by using a single 74LS138 digital chip. The big difference lies in the ability of the neural network version of the decoder to learn categories by itself. The digital version has to be prewired, and its reaction to environmental input is predetermined. If the environment in which the decoder has to work is suddenly changed (for example, if two categories suddenly need to be recognized as one, or a previously unobserved category suddenly comes into view), the digital version is unable to adapt to this change. The neural network version, on the other hand, thrives in a changing environment and is constantly on the lookout for regularities that it can categorize.

7.4.2. The DENDROS Architecture and the Deep-Sleep Cycle

Figure 7.12 illustrates part of the DENDROS architecture. As in Figure 7.11, input layer G and categorized layer F are heavily interconnected by feed-

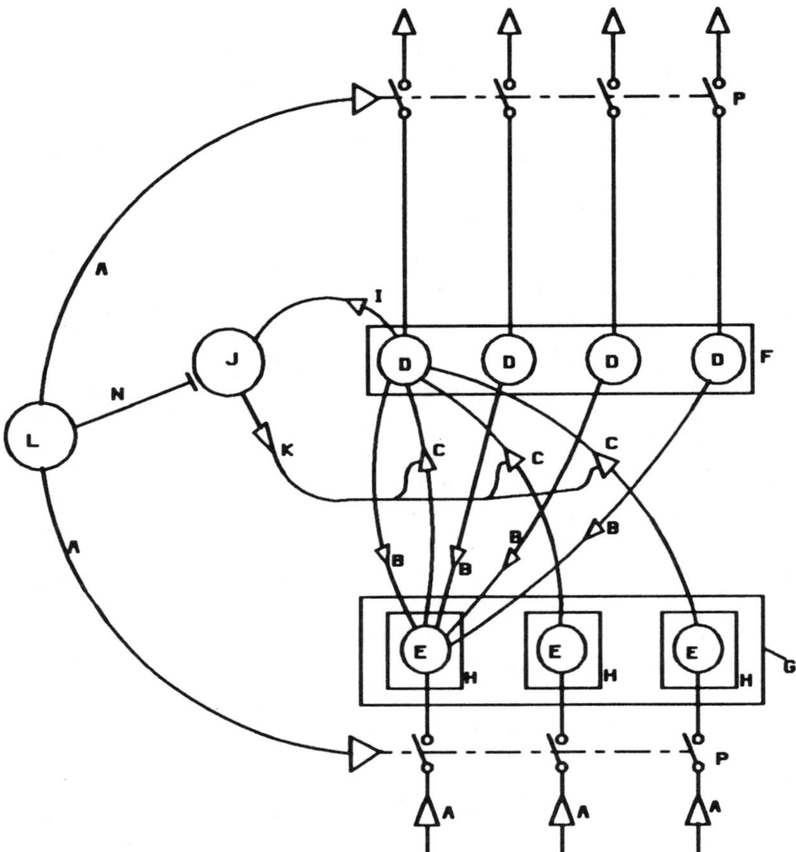

Figure 7.12 *DENDROS architecture. (Courtesy and copyright © 1988 by Syntonic Systems Inc.)*

forward weights C and feedback weights B. (Only one set of weights is shown for each layer). A sleep control node L to the left of the figure fires when the system is awake, and is quiescent otherwise. Such firing turns on all environmental switches P and allows the system to observe and react to its environment. The same firing, however, inhibits the deep-sleep nodes J (only one shown).

When the system is asleep for refresh, all environmental switches are turned off and the deep-sleep nodes J are enabled. (The deep-sleep nodes J do not fire until a deep-sleep condition arises, as explained later.) A nonspecific, constant signal is applied to all input nodes E. This constant signal allows the system to meander in its state space; that is, this signal causes oscillation such that the categorizer nodes resonate one after the other with the corresponding input nodes. A damper in each node raises its firing threshold whenever it fires so that a categorizer node is prevented from firing and resonating indefinitely. However, if a categorizer node has strong connections to and from the greatest number of input nodes, such a node could still dominate the systemwide oscillations. Such dominance simply means that that node fires more often than the rest of the categorizer nodes. This is called the *favored node syndrome* and results in all weights to and from the same favored node to grow at the expense of the weights to and from unfavored nodes. As the weights grow, so does the dominance. This continues until the favored node fires so often that it triggers its deep-sleep node L. When the deep-sleep node L fires, it sends a constant signal (through connection K) to all feedforward connections C that belong to the favored node. This deep-sleep signal reverses the learning of all those feedforward connections such that their weights are reduced instead of increased. Eventually, connections to the favored node are reduced to the point where it is no longer the favored node. The nodes then fire evenly for some time until another node starts to dominate the system, and the same deep-sleep cycle repeats. The deep-sleep cycle may occur several times during the course of sleep. Its overall effect is to enforce the so-called Weber law rule: given two categorizer nodes, if one has connections to more input nodes than the other, each of the feedforward weights to the former must be less in magnitude than each of the weights to the latter.

7.5. MEAD-MAHOWALD SILICON MODEL OF EARLY VISUAL PROCESSING

In the visual systems of higher animals, the well-known center-surround response to local stimuli is responsible for some of the strongest visual illusions. Illusion can also be traced to simple inhibitory interactions between elements of the retina. The high degree to which a perceived image is independent of the absolute illumination level can be viewed as a property of the mechanism by which incident light is transduced into an electrical signal. Mead and Mahowald[3] present a model of the first stages of retinal processing in which these phenomena are viewed as natural by-products of the mechanism by which the system adapts to a wide range of viewing conditions. The retinal model is implemented as a single silicon chip, which contains integrated photoreceptors and processing elements. This chip generates, in real time, outputs that correspond directly to signal observed in the corresponding levels of biological retinas. Because the model of retinal processing is implemented on a physical substrate, it has a straightforward structural relationship to the retinas of higher animals. This section is adapted from Mead and Mahowald.[3]

The key processing element is the triad synapse, which is found in the base of the photoreceptor. This synapse is the point of contact between the photoreceptor, the horizontal, and the bipolar cells. The computation performed by the model can be stated very simply in terms of these three elements. The photoreceptor takes the logarithm of the intensity. The photoreceptor output is spatially and temporally averaged by the horizontal cells. The bipolar cells' output is proportional to the difference between the photodetector signal and the horizontal cell signal. The center-surround computation is a result of the interaction of the photoreceptors, the horizontal cells, and the bipolar cells in the triad synapse.

The photoreceptor transduces an image focused on the retina into an electrical potential proportional to the logarithm of the local light intensity. The logarithmic nature of the response has two important system-level consequences:

1. An intensity range of many orders of magnitude is compressed into a manageable excursion in signal level.
2. The voltage difference between two points is proportional to the contrast ratio between the two corresponding points in the image, independent of incident light intensity.

The primary transducer in silicon retina is a photodetector (Mead[4]). This photodetector is a vertical bipolar transistor, which occurs as a natural by-product in the CMOS process used for implementing the analog processing elements. The exponential element is realized by two diode-connected MOS transistors in series. In the subthreshold range, corresponding to the current levels out of the phototransistor, the drain current of an MOS transistor is an exponential function of the gate-source voltage.

The Mead and Mahowald[3] silicon retina includes a hexagonal network of resistive elements, patterned after the horizontal cells of the retina. The network is constructed by linking each photoreceptor to its six neighbors with resistive elements, to form the hexagonal array shown in Figure 7.13. The CMOS technology does not include a resistor of sufficiently high value as an inherent part of the process. All circuit components (resistors, capacitors, etc.) are made out of transistors. As shown in Figure 7.13, the triad synapse consists of (1) a conductance through which the resistive network is driven toward the receptor output potential, and (2) an amplifier that senses the voltage difference across the conductance and thereby generates an output proportional to the difference between the receptor output and the network potential at that location.

According to Mead and Mahowald,[3] both biological and silicon resistive networks have associated parasitic capacitances. Integrated resistive elements have an unavoidable capacitance to the silicon substrate and, hence, provide the same kind of time integration as their biological counterparts. The effects of delays due to electronic propagation in the network are most apparent when the input image is suddenly changed.

The voltage stored on the capacitance of the resistive network is the space- and time-averaged output of the photoreceptors, each of which con-

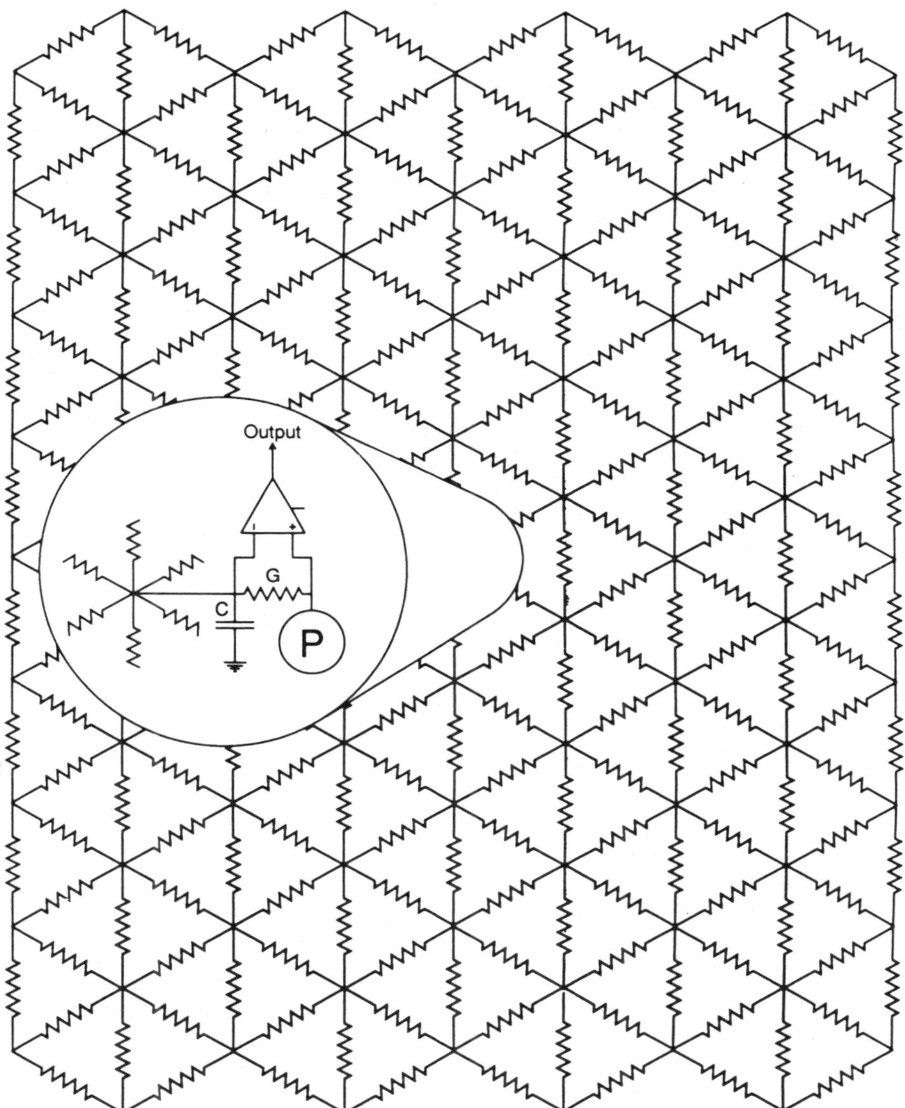

Figure 7.13 *The silicon retina. Diagram of the resistive network and a single pixel element, shown in the circular window. The silicon model of the triad synapse consists of the conductance (G) by which the photoreceptor drives the resistive network, and the amplifier that takes the difference between the photoreceptor (P) output and the voltage on the resistive network. In addition to a triad synapse, each pixel contains six resistors and a capacitor C that represents the parasitic capacitance of the resistive network. These pixels are tiled in a hexagonal array. The resistive network results from a hexagonal tiling of pixels. (Adapted by permission from Mead and Mahowald.[3]) Copyright © 1988 by Pergamon Press.*

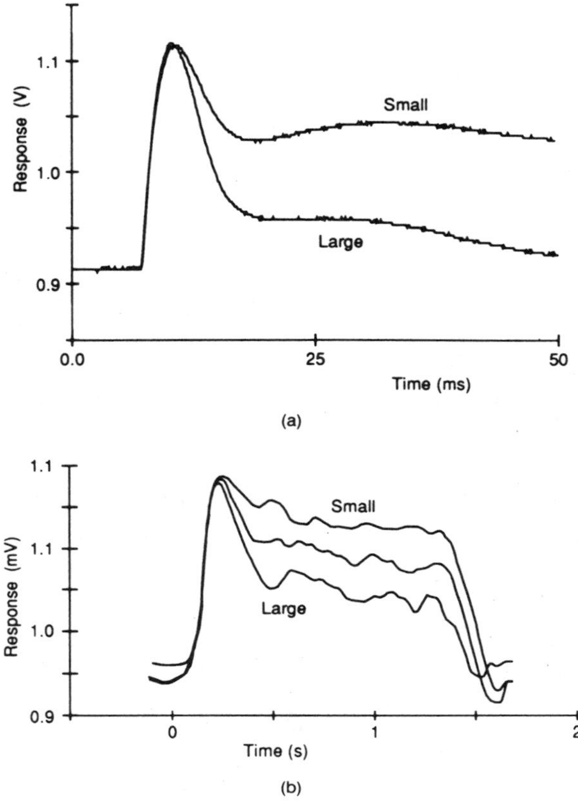

Figure 7.14 *Temporal response of a bipolar cell of the mudpuppy,* Necturus maculosus, *and of a pixel in the silicon retina, to different size test flashes. Test flashes of the same intensity but different diameters were centered on the receptive field of the unit. (a) Response of a pixel. Larger flashes increased the excitation of the surround. The surround response was delayed due to the capacitance of the resistive network. Because the surround level is subtracted from the center response, the output shows a delayed decrease for long times. This decrease is larger for larger flashes. (b) Response of* Necturus *bipolar cell. Data from Werblin.[5] (Adapted by permission from Mead and Mahowald.[3]) Copyright © 1988 by Pergamon Press.*

tribute to the average with a weight that decreases with distance. Figure 7.14 shows the response of a single output to a sudden increase in incident illumination. Output from a real bipolar cell is provided for comparison. The initial peak represents the difference between the voltage at the photodetector caused by the step input and the old averaged voltage stored on the capacitance of the resistive network. As the resistive network equilibrates to the new input level, the output of the amplifier diminishes. The final plateau value is a function of the size of the stimulus, which changes the average value of the intensity of the image as computed by the resistive network.

Silicon systems are very similar to those on neural systems. The design is fairly compact; Mead and Mahowald[3] can fit a 48 × 48 array of pixels on a $\frac{1}{4}$-cm^2 chip. As in the biological retina, density is limited by wire length. The chip operates at 100 μW of power, and the computation is performed in real time. Mead and Mahowald[3] believe that ability to realize simple neural functions is strictly limited by our understanding of their organizing principles, and not by difficulties in realization. If we really understand a system, we will be able to build it. Conversely, we can be sure that a system is not fully understood until a working model has been synthesized and successfully demonstrated.

7.6. DELTA FUNCTIONAL ARCHITECTURE†

The Delta floating-point processor (FPP) is a high-speed floating-point engine optimized for general digital signal processing algorithms and for neural network simulation. It is able to execute 32-bit floating-point multiply and accumulate instructions at clock speeds of approximately 11 MHz, which translates to 22 million floating-point operations per second peak rate. In a neural network simulation, it is necessary to calculate an activation value for each simulated neuron by multiplying each input synaptic weight by the activation value of the neuron which is driving the synapse and then adding up all of those weighted inputs. The Delta FPP processor can multiply two 32-bit numbers and add the result into a 32-bit running sum every 93 ns.

The Delta FPP supports IEEE STD 754 32 and 64-bit floating-point and 32- and 64-bit integer data types. Floating-point mode may be switched between IEEE and DEC F and G modes under software control by writing to a mode register. Most 32-bit instructions are executed at the rate of one instruction per clock cycle (93 ns). One additional clock cycle is required for 64-bit instructions to fetch, or store, the most significant half-word of the operand(s). The actual time required for the Delta FPP to perform an arithmetic operation is identical for all data formats except for divide and square root, which require one additional cycle for 64-bit operands.

The Delta FPP has 12 Mbytes of DRAM organized as three separate memories of 1 M words by 32 bits each. One of the memories is called *program memory,* although it can contain data as well. The other two memories are called *upper data memory* and *lower data memory* because of the manner in which they are connected to the two ports of the arithmetic chip set. The memory data paths make it possible for the Delta FPP to do multiply and accumulate operations by fetching one operand from one memory and another operand from the other memory, both in a single memory cycle.

There are four other memories in the Delta FPP architecture. There is a 1K × 32 bit register file whose first 16 locations are accessed as general

† Section 7.6. is adapted from Delta manuals, SAIC.

registers (R0–R15) and a 1K × 32 bit return stack. Both of these memories are implemented in a common set of SRAMs. A programmable read-only memory (PROM) provides 48-bit microinstruction words to control instruction execution, but it is not accessible to the user. Also there is a small PROM-based executive that manages host communication and diagnostics.

Another key feature of the Delta FPP architecture is its high-speed FIFO interface to the PC/AT compatible host. The PC sends packets of up to 512 words to the Delta FPP through one set of FIFO memories, and the Delta FPP sends similar packets of up to 512 words to the PC.

The Delta processor board is a full-size IBM PC/AT card with 17 standard daughtercard connectors plus a connector for I/O extension. Each daughtercard has 80 pins and is about 4 in long and 0.8 in high. Twelve of the daughtercards are memories with 1 Mbyte each. The other five provide address line drivers and latches, program counter and loop counter, instruction microcode, and file/stack SRAM. These daughtercards are on 0.25-in centers and use high-density surface mount circuitry, as does the motherboard itself. There are components on both sides of every board.

The Delta FPP processor includes an external power supply which supplies all operating power through a back-panel connector. Cooling is provided by two DC fans mounted in a shroud that ducts airflow over critical components and limits the maximum temperature of any component to 20°C above the ambient air temperature within the PC/AT.

The I/O extension connector near the far right edge of the board permits direct custom interfaces of the Delta FPP board to ADC, DAC, I/O cabling, or other peripheral equipment.

The Delta FPP is based upon pipelined instruction fetch, decode, and execution, using multiple parallel data paths, many of which are 32 bits wide. Figure 7.15 captures the logical flow of data through the Delta FPP. At the top is a bus, called the T bus, that is the main data highway in the processor. Almost everything in the processor is connected directly or indirectly to this bus. Solid bubbles in the figure represent hardwired connections, and non-solid bubbles represent buffered connections. All data pathways have been explicitly drawn.

At the far left (1) is the program counter, which supplies a 20-bit address to the program memory DRAM (2). This address is buffered into the program memory through 10-bit row and column buffers. The program counter can be pushed and popped via the return stack (3), and it is directly loaded from the U/L field of the instruction word during jump instructions. The 20-bit address is also sent to the executive PROMs, which supply the instruction stream for addresses less than 800 hex. These components, program counter, program memory DRAM and PROM, and return stack constitute the first stage of the instruction execution pipeline. When there is a jump or a return, the DRAMs are accessed with a full row address strobe/column address strobe (RAS/CAS) cycle. This also happens when the program counter increments through a 1K page boundary (or any other event that

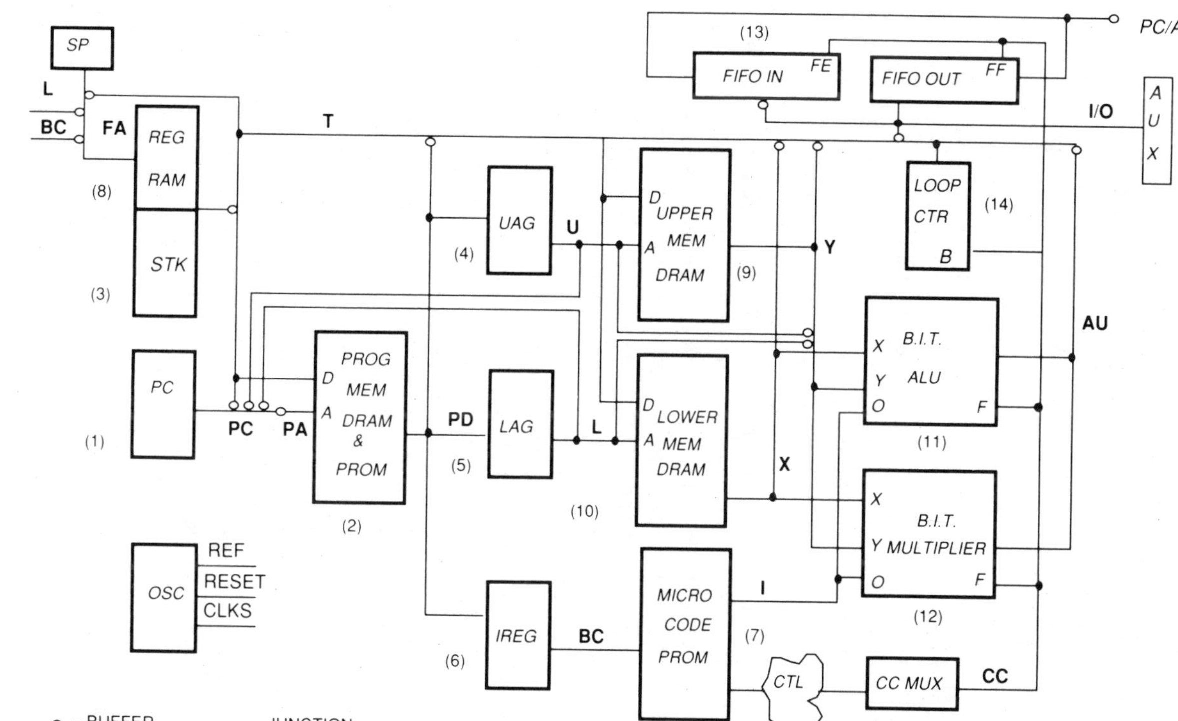

Figure 7.15 *DELTA functional architecture. (Adapted from DELTA Manuals, SAIC.)*

forces a full cycle). Otherwise, the DRAM is operated in static column mode, and address changes ripple through the DRAM, resulting in data changes.

In the second pipeline stage, the instruction is latched in several registers and decoded in order to set up the proper data memory addresses and data pathways. This is done in upper and lower address generators (4,5), the instruction register (6), and the microcode and control logic (7). The data memories are accessed for read or write. At the end of the second pipeline stage, everything is in place for the multiplier and the arithmetic logic unit (ALU) to perform an operation starting on the next clock cycle, which begins the third pipeline stage. This second pipeline stage is where many of the Delta FPP addressing modes have their influence.

The instruction word coming from the first pipeline stage consists of two or three parts, depending on the instruction type. The upper 12 bits are the opcode field. The lower 20 bits constitute either a full memory address, two 10-bit memory offsets, a 20-bit constant, or two 10-bit constants. The 12-bit opcode is latched in an instruction register that supplies the address to the microcode PROM. For those instructions that reference R0–R15, the four least significant bits (LSBs) of the instruction register supply the register address. The lower 20-bit field is latched in both the upper and the lower address generators in registers. If this memory cycle results in a RAS for random access to either DRAM, then the upper 10 bits of the full memory address will additionally be latched in a segment register in the corresponding address generator. Furthermore, both 10-bit fields can be latched in memory counters that can be used to autoincrement or autodecrement through either or both data memories. Finally, the 20-bit field can be passed through to the ALU chip as an immediate operand, fed back to the program counter as a jump address, or the 10 LSBs can be fed to the register file SRAM (8) as a scratch memory address.

A full data memory cycle is one that results in a RAS. This can be triggered by the use of a full 20-bit address for a random access, by explicitly loading the segment register, or by a jump or a return involving the program memory. It also occurs after a CAS-before-RAS refresh cycle in order to restore all memories to the proper segment. As with program memory, the data memories (9,10) can be accessed most of the time in static column mode for the most rapid access with only an occasional pause to change segments to access another block of 1024 words.

During this second pipeline stage while the memories are being accessed for a read or write, the microcode PROMs are supplying control signals throughout the Delta FPP board. These signals enable data paths, provide timing for various kinds of memory cycles, and specify the operation performed by the ALU and multiplier chip set. In combination, these signals ensure that the data get where they need to go in preparation for execution of this operation. The operation begins when the 8-bit operation code is optionally clocked into the ALU and multiplier chip set (11,12) in the final pipeline stage.

In this last pipeline stage, the ALU and multiplier chips register both data inputs and the operation to be executed. After a time delay that is specified in microcode, the results will be ready and can be stored by the next instruction, if desired.

To reiterate, while one instruction is being fetched, the last one fetched is being decoded to set up and/or store data, and the one before that is actually being executed by the ALU and multiplier chips. Normally these three things occur in parallel in the three-stage pipeline. However, certain instructions (such as unconditional jump) do not require the third pipeline stage, whereas other instructions (such as arithmetic conditionals) are interlocked to permit the pipeline to empty before execution.

The pipeline also operates in a special mode to execute multiply-and-accumulate (MAC) instructions. The ALU and multiplier chip set register both their inputs and their outputs. In a MAC instruction, this feature is used to effectively add another pipeline stage, yielding a four-stage architecture. While one chip multiplies two numbers, the other adds the previous product to an internally fed back running sum.

Other notable aspects of Delta FPP architecture are the I/O (13) and the loop counter (14). The loop counter is used by repeating instructions that do things like MAC or burst I/O. The borrow output is combined with other sources of branch condition codes to be used by the control logic to control instruction sequencing.

REFERENCES

1. S. C. J. Garth, A chipset for high speed simulation of neural network systems. *Proc. IEEE First Int. Conf. on Neural Networks,* San Diego, June 1987, Vol. III, 443–452.
2. S. G. Morton, Intelligent memory chips provide a leapfrog in performance for pattern recognition, digital signal processing, 3-D graphics and floating-point supercomputing. *Proc. Int. Neural Network Society Conf.,* Boston, 1988.
3. C. A. Mead and M. A. Mahowald, A silicon model of early visual processing. *Neural Networks* **1,** 91–97 (1988).
4. C. A. Mead, A sensitive electronic photoreceptor. *1985 Chapel Hill Conf. on Very Large Scale Integration,* 1985, 463–471.
5. F. S. Werblin, Control of retinal sensitivity. II. Lateral interactions at the outer plexiform layer. *J. General Physiology* **63,** 62–87 (1974).

CHAPTER 8

Concurrent Chips and Languages

INTRODUCTION AND SURVEY

A concurrent system is a set of relatively independent processes connected to each other through synchronized messages. The most advanced implementation of concurrent systems is the transputer family of chips supported by the OCCAM language. The OCCAM/transputer combination lets the designer identify the natural independent tasks in a system, program them, and distribute them among the transputers in the system.

This chapter outlines the functional features of T212, T414, T800, and C004 chips, and of OCCAM. Special attention is given to real-time programming. This involves the operation of timers, delays, generation of intervals, interleaving processing, scheduling, interrupts, and polling.

By maintaining the independence between the transputers and the tasks, the designer can increase the system performance simply by adding transputer chips. Many concurrent systems have been designed with remarkable features that cannot be achieved in single-processor systems.

This chapter also addresses OCCAM language, which is designed for parallel and real-time systems. The language consists of only five primitive processes: assignment, input, output, SKIP, STOP. OCCAM has been used in many parallel systems, as well as a language for teaching real-time programming. The ability to access the clock registers directly and recover from communication failures, coupled with the ability for true parallel execution of processes on different transputers makes OCCAM a powerful contender in any application that requires real-time control. These features are not available in traditional sequential languages, nor in their "parallel" extensions.

In OCCAM programming, we refer to the parts of a program as processes. A *process* starts, performs a number of actions, and then finishes. Processes communicate by using channels. *A channel* is a one-way point-to-point link from one process to one other process, on the same computer or on different computers. If an input process finds that no value is ready it will wait until one is supplied. In this way the timing problems are resolved by the system, simplifying the design and programming.

8.1. TRANSPUTER AND OCCAM

The IMS T212 transputer is a 16-bit CMOS microcomputer with 2 kbytes on-chip RAM for high-speed processing, an external memory interface, and four standard INMOS communication links. For example, a device running at 20 MHz achieves an instruction throughput of 10 MIPS.

The IMS T212 can directly access a linear address space of 64 kbytes. The 16-bit wide nonmultiplexed external memory interface provides a data rate of up to 2 bytes every 100 ns (20 Mbytes/s) for a 20-MHz device.

The IMS T414 transputer is a 32-bit CMOS microcomputer with 2 kbytes on-chip RAM for high-speed processing, a configurable memory interface, and four standard INMOS communication links. For example, a device running at 20 MHz achieves an instruction throughput of 10 MIPS.

The IMS T414 can directly access a linear address space of 4 Gbytes. The 32-bit wide memory interface uses multiplexed data and address lines and provides a data rate of up to 4 bytes every 150 ns (26.6 Mbytes/s) for a 20-MHz device. A configurable memory controller provides all timing, control, and DRAM refresh signals for a wide variety of mixed memory systems.

The IMS T800-20 is pin-compatible with the IMS T414-20, since the extra inputs used are all held to ground on the IMS T414. The IMS T800-20 can thus be plugged directly into a circuit designed for a 20-MHz version of the IMS T414. Software should be recompiled, although no changes to the source code are necessary.

The transputer is designed to implement the OCCAM language, but it also efficiently supports C, PASCAL, and FORTRAN.

The standard INMOS communication links allow networks of transputer family products to be constructed by direct point-to-point connections with no external logic. The IMS T800 links support the standard operating speed of 10 Mbits/s, but they also operate at 5 or 20 Mbits/s. Each link can transfer data bidirectionally at up to 2.35 Mbytes/s. Figure 8.1 shows an IMS T800 block diagram.

The INMOS communication link is a high-speed system interconnect that provides full-duplex communication between members of the INMOS

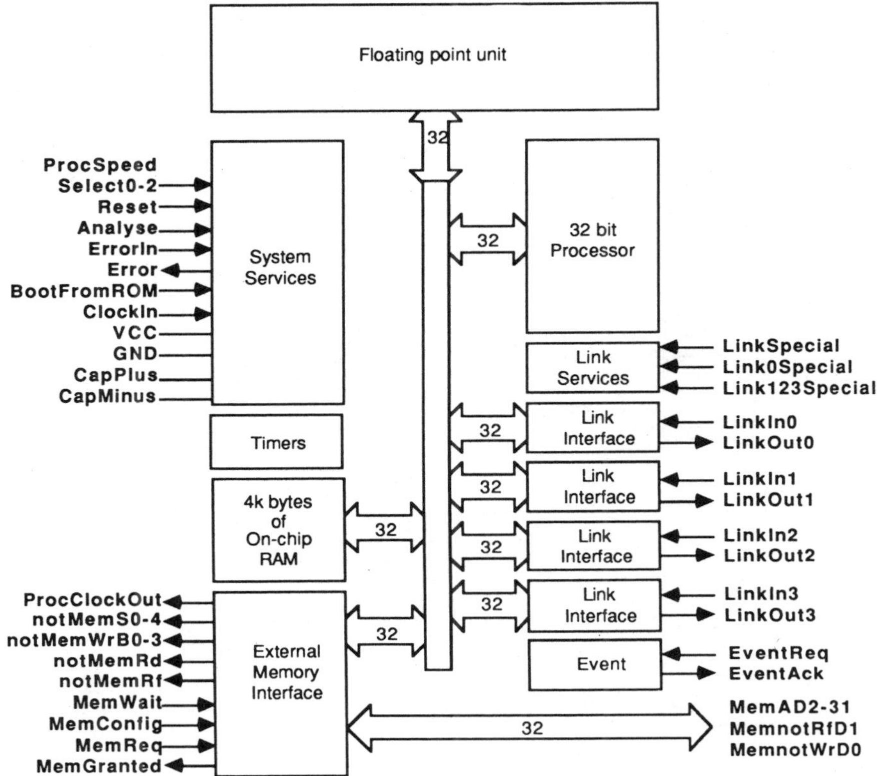

Figure 8.1 *IMS T800 block diagram. (Courtesy and copyright © 1988 by INMOS Group of Companies.)*

transputer family, according to the INMOS serial link protocol. The IMS C004, shown in Figure 8.2, a member of this family, is a transparent programmable link switch designed to provide a full crossbar switch between 32-link inputs and 32-link outputs. The IMS C004 will switch links running at either the standard speed of 10 Mbits/s or at the higher speed of 20 Mbits/s. It introduces, on average, only a 1.75-bit time delay on the signal. Link switches can be cascaded to any depth without loss of signal integrity, and can be used to construct reconfigurable networks of arbitrary size. The switch is programmed via a separate serial link called the *configuration link*. The IMS C004 is internally organized as a set of thirty-two 32-to-1 multiplexers.

OCCAM is the first language to be based upon the concept of parallel, in addition to sequential, execution and to provide automatic communication and synchronization between concurrent processes. In OCCAM programming, we refer to the parts of a program as *processes*. A process starts,

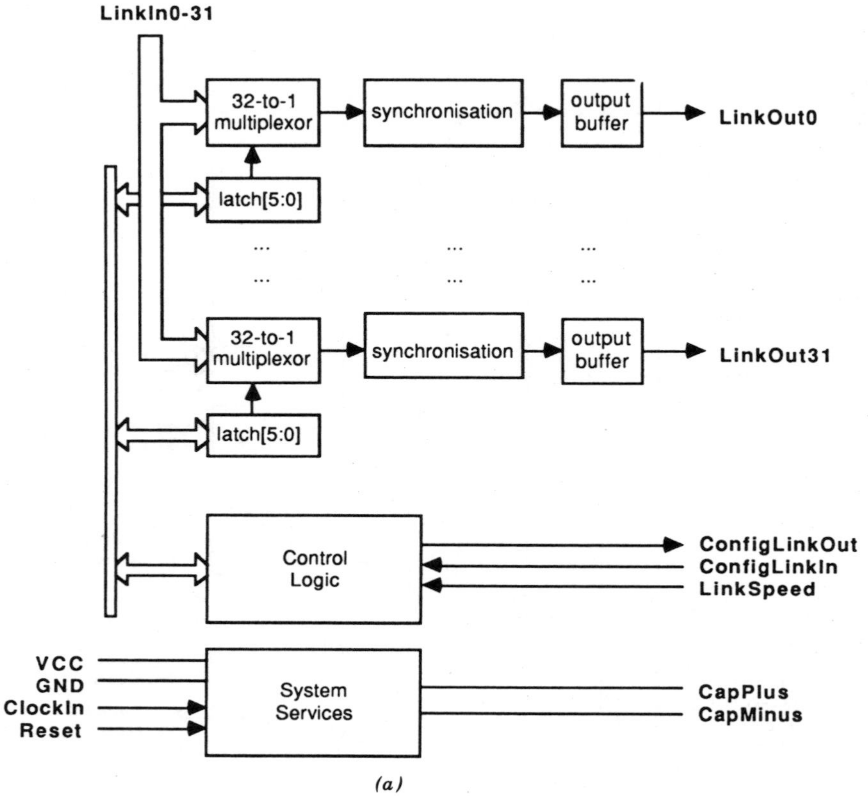

Figure 8.2a *IMS C004 block diagram. (Courtesy and copyright © 1988 by INMOS Group of Companies.)*

performs actions, and finishes. This definition fits an ordinary sequential program, but in OCCAM more than one process may be executing at the same time and processes can send messages to one another. More importantly, OCCAM does not mind whether the two programs that so communicate are running on different computers or are just two processes running concurrently on the same computer.

A *channel* is a one-way, point-to-point link from one process to one other process. Two novel features that distinguish channels from variables:

1. A channel can pass values either between two processes running on the same computer or between two processes running on different computers. In the first case, the channel would be just a location in memory, rather like a variable. In the second case, the channel could represent a real hardware link, such as a transputer link or other serial communication line. Both cases are represented identically in an OCCAM program.

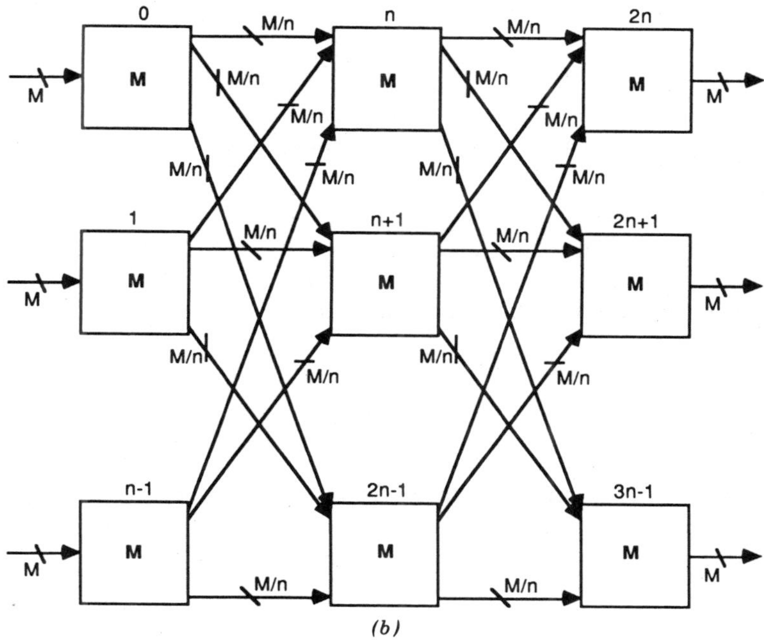

Figure 8.2b *Generalized link switch. (Courtesy and copyright © 1988 by INMOS Group and Companies.)*

An OCCAM channel describes communication in the abstract and does not depend on its physical implementation. You can thus write and test a program using channels without having to worry about exactly where the different processes will be executed. The program can be developed on a single-processor workstation; when it is finished and proved, you may decide to distribute various processes in the program onto different computers, and do so by making a few simple declarations at the beginning of the program.

2. Channels are patient and polite. If an input process finds that no value is ready, it will wait until one is supplied, without any explicit instruction from the programmer. Equally, an output will not send until the receiver is ready. This introduces the time factor into programming, but in a way that lifts much of the responsibility for "timekeeping" off the programmer's shoulders.

All OCCAM programs are built from combinations of three kinds of primitive process: assignment, input, and output.

An *assignment* process changes the value of a variable, just as it would in most conventional languages. The symbol for assignment in OCCAM is :=.

So the assignment process

```
fred := 2
```

makes the value in variable `fred` two. The value assigned to a variable could be an expression such as

```
fred := 2 + 5
```

and this expression could contain other variables:

```
fred := 5 - jim
```

Be sure not to mix up = and :=. In OCCAM, = means a test for equality, not an assignment.

An *input* process inputs a value from a channel into a variable. The symbol for input in OCCAM is ?. The input process

```
chan3 ? fred
```

takes a value from a channel called `chan3` and puts it into variable `fred`. Input processes can only input values to variables. It is quite meaningless to input to a constant or to an expression. An input process cannot proceed until a corresponding output process on the same channel is ready. As an aid to memory, think of the question mark as meaning "Where's my value?"

An *output* process outputs a value to a channel. The symbol for output in OCCAM is !. The output process

```
chan3 ! 2
```

outputs the value 2 to channel `chan3`. The value output to a channel can be anything that you could assign to a variable, so it may be a variable or an expression, and the expression may contain variables. An output process cannot proceed until a corresponding input process on the same channel is ready. As an aid to memory, think of the exclamation mark as meaning "Here's your value!"

Several primitive processes can be combined into a larger process by specifying that they should be performed one after the other or all at the same time. This larger process is called a *construction,* and it begins with an OCCAM keyword that states how the component processes are to be combined. The simplest construction to understand is the `SEQ` (pronounce it "seek"), short for sequence, which merely says "do the following processes one after another." Here is an example:

```
SEQ
  chan3 ? fred
  jim := fred + 1
  chan4 ! jim
```

This says, "do in sequence, input from `chan3` to `fred`, assign `fred + 1` to `jim`, and output `jim` to `chan4`". In sequence means, to be more precise, that the next process does not start until the previous one has terminated. A `SEQ` process therefore works just like a program in any conventional programming language; it finishes when its last component process finishes.

The `PAR` construction, short for parallel, says "do the following processes all at the same time" (i.e., in parallel). All the component processes of a PAR start to execute simultaneously. For example:

```
PAR
  SEQ
    chan3 ? fred
    fred := fred + 1
  SEQ
    chan4 ? jim
    jim := jim + 1
```

says, "at the same time, input from `chan3` to `fred` and then add 1 to the result, while inputting from `chan4` to `jim` and then adding 1 to the result."

Channels are all of the type CHAN OF *protocol*. It is necessary to specify the data type and structure of the values that they are to carry. This is called the channel *protocol*. For now, we regard channels as able to carry single values of a single data type, rather like variables.

A channel that carries single integer values would be specified by

```
CHAN OF INT chan3 :
```

where the INT specifies the type of values that may pass along chan3. The type of `chan3` is CHAN OF INT. In general, the protocol of a channel is specified by CHAN OF *protocol*.

Communication between parallel processes is the essence of OCCAM programming. At its simplest, it requires two processes executing in parallel and a channel joining them:

```
INT x :
CHAN OF INT comm :
PAR
  comm ! 2
  comm ? x
```

This trivial program merely outputs the value 2 from one process and inputs it into the variable `x` in the second. Its overall effect is exactly as if we had a single process that assigned 2 to `x`.

In OCCAM, choice has an extra dimension lacking in ordinary programming languages. We can make choices according to the values of variables in a program using `IF`. But we can also make choices according to the state of channels. This is made possible by the `ALT` construction, whose name is short for alternation. Like `IF`, `ALT` joins components into a single construction, but the component parts of an `ALT`, called *alternatives,* are more complicated than `IF` choices.

The simplest kind of `ALT` has as each alternative an input process followed by a process to be executed. The `ALT` watches all the input processes and executes the process associated with the first input to become ready. Thus `ALT` is basically a first-past-the-post race between a group of channels, with only the winner's process being executed:

```
CHAN OF INT chan1. chan 2. chan3:
INT x:
ALT
  chan1 ? x
    ... first process
  chan2 ? x
    ... second process
  chan3 ? x
    ... third process
```

If `chan2` were the first to produce an input, then only the second process would be executed. Here choice is being decided in the time dimension, the inputs causing the program to wait until one of them is ready.

8.2. REAL-TIME PROGRAMMING

Timing in OCCAM is provided by declaring named objects of the type `TIMER`. A timer behaves like a channel that can only provide input. The value input from a timer is, not surprisingly, the current time represented as a value of type `INT`.

The simplest kind of timer process looks like

```
TIMER clock:
INT time:
clock ? time
```

Delays can be added to a program by using a delayed input. This is an input from a timer that cannot proceed until the time reaches a stated value. The operator AFTER followed by an expression representing a time is used to cause the delay.

The crude delay procedure is

```
PROC delay (VAL INT interval)
  TIMER clock :
  INT timenow :
  SEQ
    clock ? timenow
    clock ? AFTER timenow PLUS interval
```

An instance of this procedure, say delay (6000), would pause for 6000 ticks before terminating.

A delayed input could be used in an ALT to provide a real-time wait:

```
TIMER clock :
VAL timeout IS 1000 :
INT timenow :
SEQ
  clock ? timenow
  INT x :
  ALT
    input ? x
      ... process
    clock ? AFTER timenow PLUS timeout
      warning ! (17 •: "Timeout on input!")
```

This process will send the timeout warning message if input does not produce an input within the prescribed time of 1000 ticks.

AFTER can also be used as a comparison operator that returns a truth value; x AFTER y is equivalent to (x MINUS y) > 0. In other words, AFTER subtracts y from x, modulo the largest INT, and sees if the result is positive. Modulo arithmetic must always be used for times, hence the use of PLUS instead of + in the two preceding examples.

In both a PRI ALT and a PRI PAR, the component processes are assigned a priority according to the textual order in which they appear in the program—the first has highest priority and so on. In a PRI ALT, when two inputs become ready simultaneously, the component process with the higher priority will be executed.

A special example of the use of a PRI ALT is this routine to guarantee that a channel carrying an important signal will be looked at:

```
WHILE cycling
  PRI ALT
    quit ? any
```

```
      cycling := false
    TRUE & SKIP
      ... main cycle
```

The TRUE & SKIP option is always ready, and if used in an ordinary ALT this path could be taken at every cycle without quit ever getting a look in. The PRI ALT however forces the program to inspect the channel quit because it has a higher priority and thus guarantees that the cycle can be broken when desired.

In a PRI PAR, processes with a lower priority will be executed only if no higher-priority process can proceed. So in

```
PRI PAR
  SEQ
    input1 ? x
    output1 ! x
  SEQ
    input2 ? y
    output2 ! y
```

the second SEQ cannot proceed, even when input2 is ready, unless the first (higher-priority) SEQ is waiting on its input or output.

If PRI PAR is used, the question of buffering may well arise. It is pointless to run a process at high priority to service an impatient device if, while servicing that device, it can be kept waiting to communicate with another process. A high-priority process of this kind should have all such communications with other processes buffered so that data can be sent without delay. The size of buffer needed would be tuned to the actual timings of the processes involved.

In any OCCAM implementation, there will be I/O channels that can be used by programs. These channels may in some cases lead directly to the hardware via driver programs that the OCCAM compiler links to your program. In other cases, they may lead to the operating system of the host computer, which then handles I/O on behalf of OCCAM.

A typical OCCAM system will at least support channels for a video display unit (VDU) screen, a keyboard, and a filing system. These channels are given numbers, which can be found in the manual for the particular OCCAM implementation.

Let us suppose that the "hard" channels are numbered as follows: (1) output to screen, (2) input from keyboard. These numbers are associated with the channel names used in an OCCAM program as follows:

```
PLACE screen AT 1 :
PLACE keyboard AT 2 :
```

Inside the program these channels can all be input to and output from in the usual fashion. So

```
VAL message IS "Hello world!" :
SEQ i = 0 FOR SIZE message
  screen ! INT message [i]
```

would display the message on a VDU screen, and

```
keyboard ? x
```

would input the code for a single character typed at the keyboard into variable x.

8.3. GENERATING EVENTS AT REGULAR INTERVALS

A program that must perform a task at regular intervals cannot do so simply by means of a fixed delay between processing, as in the previous example. If a simple delay were used, then the time at which the task happens will slip gradually because the delay does not account for the time taken by the task itself (which may vary), and this error accumulates. This is illustrated in Figures 8.3 and 8.4.

To make this more explicit, assume the task must be scheduled every millisecond and will execute for 10 μS. The task executes and is then descheduled for 1 ms (plus the time required to reschedule the process). The interval between tasks is therefore at least 1.01 ms, and this error will accumulate, so after 1 s the task will have been executed only 990 times instead of 1000 times. It would be possible to adjust the delay to take the processing time of the task into account, but this implies that the processing time is known and fixed, unlikely in a real system. Consider the following example:

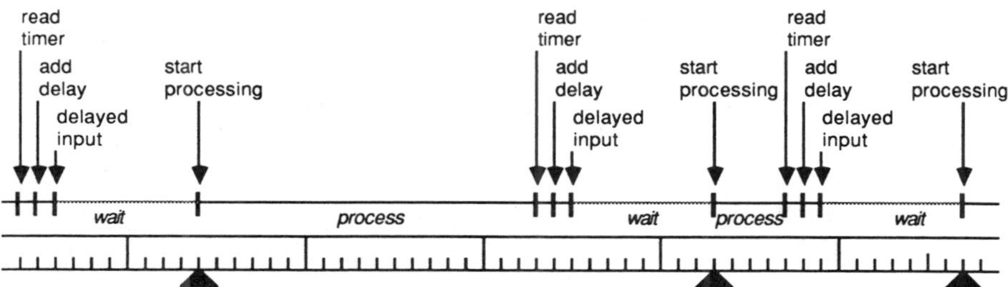

Figure 8.3 *Using timers to generate delays between processes. (Courtesy and copyright © 1988 by INMOS Group and Companies.)*

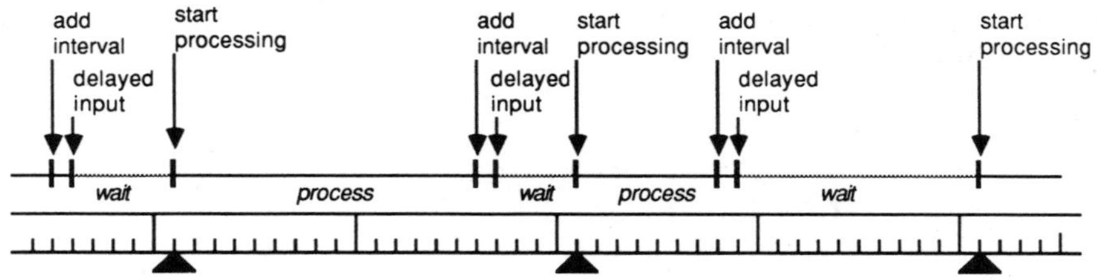

Figure 8.4 *Using timers to perform processing at fixed intervals.* (*Courtesy and copyright © 1988 by INMOS Group of Companies.*)

```
TIMER clock :
INT time :
SEQ
  WHILE active
    SEQ
      ...  perform process P at intervals
      -- wait for 'delay' clock ticks
      clock ? time
      clock ? AFTER time PLUS delay
```

The time taken to execute the loop is the delay time plus the execution time of process P. Any variation in the processing required in P will vary the frequency at which it is executed.

A far more accurate way to achieve the desired effect is as follows:

```
TIMER clock :
INT time :
SEQ
  clock ? time
  WHILE active
    SEQ
      ...  perform process P at regular
intervals
      -- add interval to the time the process
started
      time := time PLUS interval
      -- and wait until it is time to execute
the process again
      clock ? AFTER time
```

The important point to note here is that the value of the timer is only read once, before the loop is entered. After that, the time is updated by adding a constant increment to the current value. This ensures that the delayed input always waits *until the desired starting time* rather than for a fixed delay. This prevents any drift in the timing of the processing.

To take the previous example of a task being scheduled every millisecond, we can see that the task is initiated at (or shortly after, because of scheduling latency) the time specified by the value of `time`. When the task is completed, a constant amount is added to the value of `time` to calculate the time for which the task should next be scheduled. This time is independent of the time taken by the task. The possible variation in the time taken to schedule a process may introduce some jitter into the timing of the task, but will not cause it to slip.

8.4. USING TIMERS IN ALTs

Delayed timer inputs are often used in alternative constructs.

8.4.1. Interleaving Processing

An alternative may be used to interleave processing at fixed times with processing performed when data are received. As an example, a data logging process may need to record data received from a channel and, at suitable intervals, insert a time stamp in the recorded data. This could be written with an `ALT` very simply:

```
TIMER clock :
INT time, data :
SEQ
  clock ? time
  WHILE active
    SEQ
      time := time PLUS one.second
      PRI ALT
        clock ? AFTER time
          ...   insert time stamp in file
        in ? data
          ...   store data in file
```

Note that the delayed input is prioritized with respect to the channel input; this ensures that, even if the channel `in` is always ready, the time-stamping process will be selected when it becomes ready.

8.4.2. Time-Outs on Channels

Another use of delayed inputs in alternatives is to provide some sort of time-out on channel communication. This may be to execute a process, if no user command is received, or to detect an error condition. For example, a disk controller may wish to "park" the heads (i.e., move them to a safe position on the disk) if no commands are received within a time limit:

```
WHILE active
  SEQ
    clock ? time
    ALT
      (headsNotParked) & clock ? AFTER time
PLUS timeout
        ...   move heads to shipping track
      in ? command
        ...   execute command from file system
```

8.4.3. Multiple Delayed Inputs

An alternative may contain several delayed inputs with different delays. This may be useful if it is necessary to handle a number of devices at different, fixed intervals. For example, if the processor needs to be scheduled to service two peripherals at different periods, then an ALT can be used to correctly interleave the handling of these devices (Figure 8.5):

```
TIMER clock :
INT timeA, timeB :
VAL intervalA IS 96 :
VAL intervalB IS 42 :
SEQ
  clock ? timeA
  clock ? timeB
  WHILE active
    ALT
      clock ? AFTER timeA
        SEQ
          timeA := timeA PLUS intervalA
          ...   handle device A at fixed
```

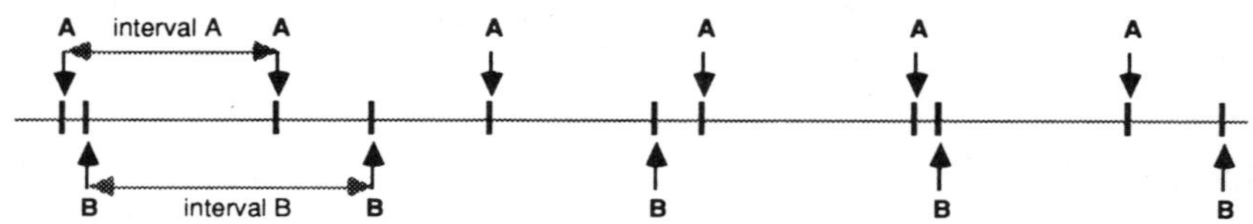

Figure 8.5 *Scheduling processes A and B at different intervals. (Courtesy and copyright © 1988 by INMOS Group of Companies.)*

```
intervals
      clock ? AFTER timeB
        SEQ
          timeB := timeB PLUS intervalB
          ...   handle device B at fixed
intervals
```

Only times that are within half a timer cycle can be compared by AFTER, so, if several times are being compared, they must all be within half a cycle of one another. If an ALT contains more than one delayed input, then *all* of the times involved (including the present timer value) must be within half a cycle of one another. A simpler, but sometimes more restrictive, rule is to ensure that all times in the delayed inputs are within a quarter of a cycle of the current timer value.

8.4.4. Transputer Implementation of Timers

The transputer has hardware and microcode support for OCCAM timers. This allows timer instructions to be fast and, more importantly, delayed inputs to be *nonbusy* (i.e., to consume no processor time while waiting). There are two timer clocks, with the same word length as the device, that tick periodically. One timer is accessible only to high-priority processes and is incremented every microsecond. The other can only be accessed by low-priority processes and ticks every 64 μs, giving exactly 15,625 ticks per second. The cycle time of these timers depends on the word length of the device. The approximate cycle times, for the current range of 16- and 32-bit transputers, are shown in the table:

Transputer Type	Priority High	Priority Low
IMS T800 & IMS T414	1.2 h	76 h
IMS T212 & IMS M212	65.5 ms	4.2 s

It is important to have a resolution of 1 μs for precise timing. However, on a 16-bit processor, this means a cycle time of only 65 ms—too short for many applications. To provide both high resolution and a long cycle time, two timer rates were introduced. The same method was used on the 32-bit processors, so the timers behave similarly on all transputer types.

Timers are local to each processor, so the absolute time values read by processes on different transputers in a network will be different. However, the rates of the timers on each transputer will be the same, independent of processor speed, etc.

Although timers can be shared between parallel processes, this can appear rather odd if a timer is shared between processes at different priorities. This would have the effect of a single timer producing different values in each process. To make it clear which timer is being used within a process it is good practice to declare timers local to each priority; for example:

```
PRI PAR
  TIMER hiClock :
  SEQ
    ...  high priority process
  TIMER loClock :
  SEQ
    ...  low priority process
```

8.4.5. Scheduling Latency

The transputer has a microcoded scheduler that enables concurrent processes to be executed together, sharing processor time. Processes that are descheduled, waiting for a communication or delayed input, do not consume any processor time. The scheduler supports two levels of priority.

The latency between the time a process becomes ready to execute and the time it begins processing depends on the priority at which it is executing. Low-priority processes are executed whenever there are no high-priority processes ready to execute. A high-priority process runs until it has to wait for a communication or timer input, or until it has completed processing.

8.4.6. Low-Priority Processes

Low-priority tasks are periodically time-sliced to provide an even distribution of processor time between computationally intensive processes. If there are n low-priority processes, then the maximum latency is $2n - 2$ time-slice periods. The latency will generally be much less than this because processes are usually descheduled for communication or by a delayed input before the end of their time-slice. The time-slice period is approximately 1 ms.

High-priority processes run whenever they are able to, interrupting any currently executing low-priority process if necessary. If a high-priority process is waiting on a timer input and no other high-priority processes are running, then the interrupt latency is typically 19 processor cycles (0.95 μs with a 20-MHz processor clock). The maximum latency depends on the processor type as shown in the table:

Transputer Type	Maximum Interrupt Latency Processor Cycles	Microseconds (at 20 MHz)
IMS M212, IMS T212	53	2.65
IMS T414	58	2.9
IMS T800 (FPU in use)	78	3.9
IMS T800 (FPU not in use)	58	2.9

These times indicate that a transputer can handle many tens of thousands of interrupts per second, even while engaged in computationally intensive tasks involving floating-point calculations.

8.5. INTERRUPTS

Interrupts are the usual way of handling devices that require infrequent but fast servicing. Interrupt handlers are notoriously difficult to write and debug, they are usually only supported by programming in assembler and this is often very difficult to integrate with other code written in a high-level language. OCCAM and the transputer support both internal and external interrupts in a very simple and efficient way. An example of an internal interrupt is a communication or delayed input; external interrupts can be generated from the transputer's links or the *event* input. A transition on the `EventReq` pin behaves just like a channel communication and can be used to synchronize with an OCCAM process. It is, therefore, very easy to write an OCCAM process that handles events—it simply has to perform an input from the channel mapped on to `EventReq` and, when both the event channel and the process are ready, the process is scheduled. The following example shows how a UART,† which has its *data received* interrupt connected to the transputer's event input, would be handled in OCCAM.

```
{{{  event handler
CHAN OF BYTE error :
PLACE event AT 8 : -- event channel control
word
BYTE sync :
WHILE active
```

† Universal asynchronous receiver-transmitter: A peripheral device that controls a serial communications port, such as an RS-232 interface.

```
  SEQ
    event ? sync        -- wait for input from
EventReq
    read.data (char)    -- read data from UART
    to.buffer ! char    -- output to waiting
process
}}}
```

If this process is run at high priority, it can interrupt a low-priority process:

```
PRI PAR
  ...  event handler
  PAR
    ...
    ...    low priority (background) processes
    ...
```

Interrupts can have various disadvantages. With multiple sources of interrupts, there is inevitably a cost in determining which device generated the interrupt. This may be extra hardware to encode and prioritize the interrupts, or software to poll the devices on receipt of an interrupt to see which are ready.

8.6. POLLING

The main disadvantage of polling is that it is *busy;* i.e., it consumes processor time. In the transputer, this can have a wide impact on performance because it will affect the scheduling of processes. Low-priority processes are time-sliced to ensure that all processes get a fair share of processor time. However, in most real OCCAM programs, processes are frequently descheduled before the end of the time-slice period because they perform some communication. A process that is continuously polling a memory-mapped device, for example, can get a disproportionate amount of the processing resource simply because other processes are descheduled more frequently for communication purposes. If a process in parallel with the polling process is transmitting individual bytes down a link, then each communication may appear to take several milliseconds, because the polling process will be scheduled between each byte transfer and not be descheduled for one or two time-slice periods.

If a peripheral device must be polled, then it is much more efficient to use a delayed input to control exactly when and how often polling takes place. In most cases, this can be done with no degradation in the performance of the device, since the maximum rate at which data can arrive is known. There is no point in polling the device more frequently than this because the data will not be there. An example of this is polling a UART. The maximum rate at which characters arrive is (baud rate)/10 characters per second (assuming 8 data bits, 1 start bit, and 1 stop bit). In the following example, the value `interval` is set to be slightly less than the shortest possible time between received characters (i.e., 10/(baud rate) − Δ).

```
SEQ
  clock ? time
  WHILE active
    SEQ
      -- wait until a character might be ready
      time := time PLUS interval
      clock ? AFTER time
      {{{  poll and read data from UART
      data.ready (ready) -- check UART status
register
      IF
        ready
          SEQ
            read.data (char)
            to.buffer ! char
        TRUE
          SKIP
      }}}
```

This loop only consumes processor time while it is actually reading the UART registers. After a character has been received and passed on, it is descheduled until just before the next character is ready, freeing the processor for other work.

This example can be readily extended to allow mixing of data from the serial port and from an OCCAM channel:

```
SEQ
  clock ? time
  WHILE active
    SEQ
      time := time PLUS interval
      PRI ALT
        clock ? AFTER time
          ...  poll and read data from UART
        source ? char
          -- insert character from channel
into buffer
          to.buffer ! char
```

Another simple example is a program communicating with a transputer system, emulating a terminal, and simultaneously checking the error flag of the system. The system error flag only needs to be checked occasionally, say 10 times a second, to give the impression of instant response to an error. The following code shows how the two data sources and the error flag are all handled in a single loop:

```
SEQ
  clock ? time
  WHILE active
    SEQ
      ALT
        clock ? AFTER time
          SEQ
            ...  check error pin
            time := time PLUS interval
        keyboard ? char
          ...  send character to system
        link ? char
          ...  display character on screen
```

This process is only scheduled when data arrive (from the keyboard or the transputer system) or it is time to check the error flag.

It is worth noting why this code is structured as a single `WHILE` loop rather than three parallel processes:

```
PAR
  ...  check error flag
  ...  copy data from keyboard to system
  {{{  copy data from system to screen
  WHILE active
    SEQ
      link ? char
      ...  display character on screen
  }}}
```

Although this approach appears simpler, it introduces the problem of causing three concurrently executing loops to terminate correctly. The solution that would usually be adopted is for each process to have an extra input channel and to terminate when a message arrives on that channel. This then means that each loop requires an `ALT`, and the initial simplicity of this approach disappears.

REFERENCES

1. IMS T800 Preliminary Data, INMOS Group of Companies.
2. IMS C004 preliminary Data, INMOS Group of Companies.
3. D. Pountain, A tutorial introduction to OCCAM programming. INMOS 72OCC04307, 1987.
4. J. Backer, Simpler real-time programming with the transputer. INMOS 72TCH05100, 1988.

CHAPTER 9

Concurrent System Design and Applications

INTRODUCTION AND SURVEY

This chapter describes hardware and software issues in the design of concurrent intelligent real-time systems. Different multiprocessor topologies and distributed operating systems are examined. Concrete examples and applications are presented, including transputers in speech, in image processing, and in robot arm control.

Computer-generated two- and three-dimensional images and interactive concurrent graphics hardware and software are shown. A genuine piece of application code written in OCCAM for three-dimensional transformation is described. The operations of translation, rotation, concatenation, projection, shading, and clipping are explained.

The chapter ends by describing large-scale concurrent systems: multiuser on-line flight simulators, with users connected in a ring; parallel PROLOG machine for high-speed execution of expert systems; and control system organization of flexible manufacturing cells. The configuration of a flexible manufacturing cell contains robots, machine tools, milling machine, transporters, and sensors.

9.1. MULTIPROCESSOR SYSTEM TOPOLOGY

Major reasons for multiprocessor architectures are high system throughput, modular extension, and high availability. The degree of possible parallelism is shown in Figure 9.1. Comparative analysis of parallel structures, based on

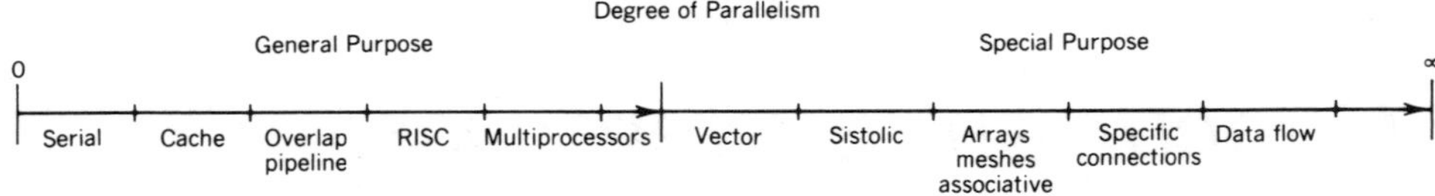

Figure 9.1 *From serial to data flow machines. (Following Brajak.[1])*

Brajak,[1] is given in Figure 9.2. The structures are divided into two groups:

1. Master/slave configuration: One central processor unit (CPU) (master) performs all I/O scheduling and system functions, and other CPUs (slaves) execute user applications. Typically, master/slave configurations support less than 10 CPUs.
2. Symmetrical configuration: All CPUs can execute both user applications and all I/O system service functions. Systems with many CPUs have been constructed. A job can be assigned to a CPU (static assignment) or to the next available processor (dynamic assignment).

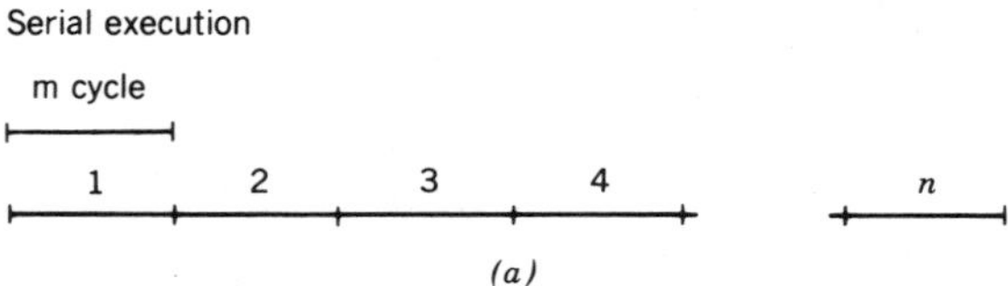

(a)

Each line represents a metacycle. An m cycle is an abstract representation of a full instruction cycle: fetch, decode, fetch operands, and execute operations. We assume that m cycles are identical for all instructions. A serial execution of n instructions, takes n m cycles of program execution.

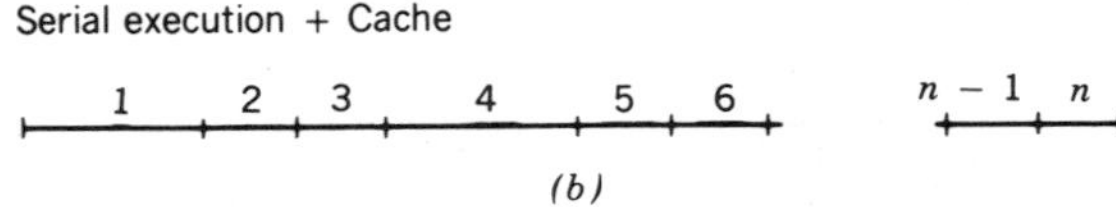

(b)

Some m cycles shortened because some instructions and operands reside in cache, which has a shorter access time. Not all m cycles shorten, because of cache miss effects.

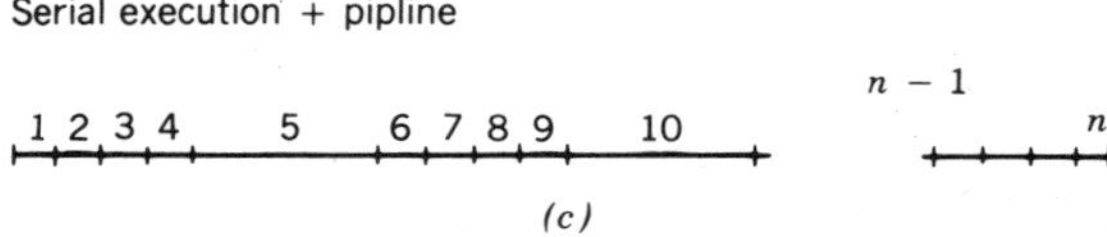

(c)

A processor has a multifunctional capability: while it is fetching instruction i, it is simultaneously decoding instruction i-1, fetching operands for instruction i-2, and executing instruction i-3. Degradations are due to jumps and interrupts in the program.

Figure 9.2 *Degree of parallelism. (Following Brajak.[1])*

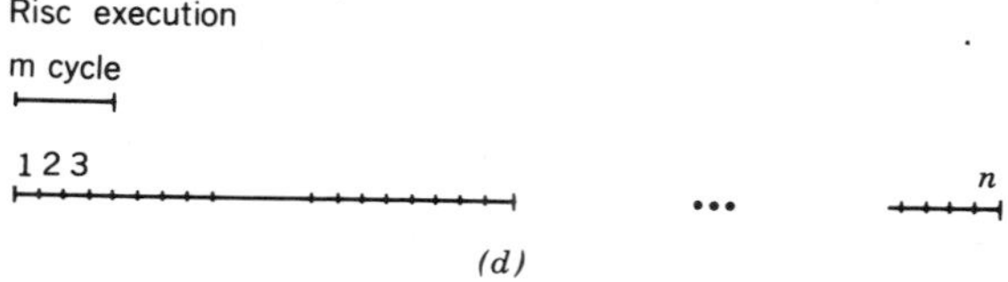

(d)

The overall computation shortens because

1. m cycles are shorter, due to higher technology (m′ cycle):
2. Pipelining is optimized by using many fast registers and silicon compilers.

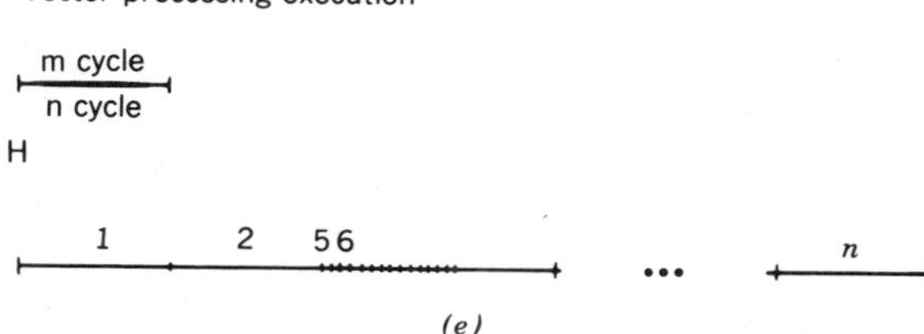

(e)

The overall computation is a combination of m cycles and n cycles. When a machine is in a serial mode of operation, it executes with the speed of m cycle. However, when the machine is in a vector mode, computation is faster (n cycles).

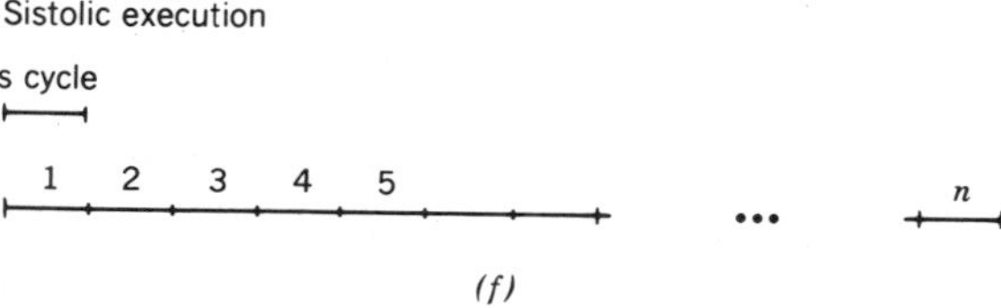

(f)

If we define s cycle as a cycle of each sistolic cell, and if all cells have identical operations, the speed of the overall computation is determined by the speed of the slowest cell, provided that enough problem uniformity is supplied.

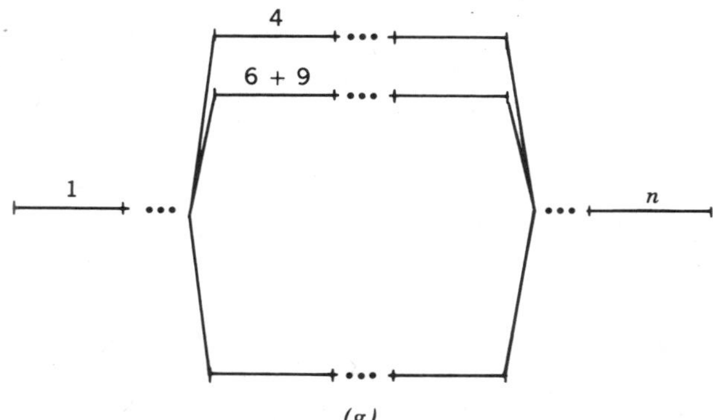

(g)

Data is distributed among the processors in such way that each processor gets specific data and works on it simultaneously with the other processors. Instructions come from the master processor and each processor executes the same instruction, but using different data set.

Figure 9.2 (*Continued*)

Data flow machines

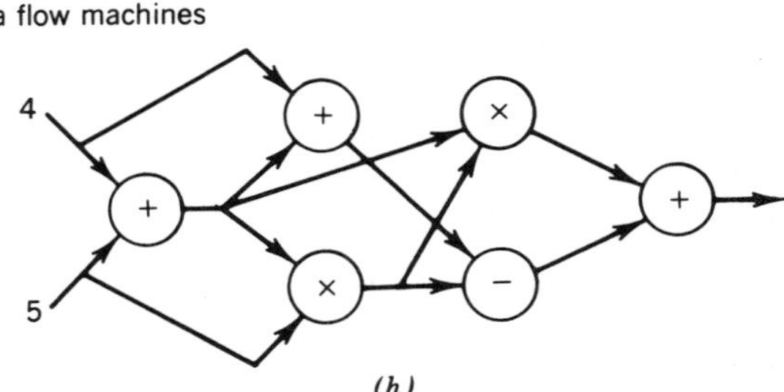

(*h*)

This is the richest possible parallelism. Each processor represents a program instruction. All processors can work in parallel, provided that all operands are available to each processor.

Multiprocessors

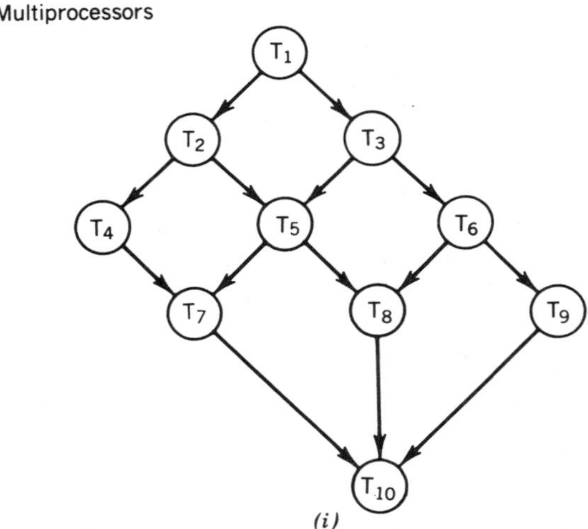

(*i*)

This is a combination of serial and data flow execution. Parallelism is on a level of tasks. The overall speed is determined by the successfull program decomposition into large number of independent tasks.

Figure 9.2 (*Continued*)

In multiprocessor structures, each processor alternates between two states:

1. *Computation,* with variables stored in its own memory;
2. *Communication,* to exchange information with other processes in the systems (e.g., exchanging addressed messages among the processors).

Individual message transportation time would depend on whether the source and destination nodes are directly connected. In addition, each intermediate node must take active part in relaying the messages.

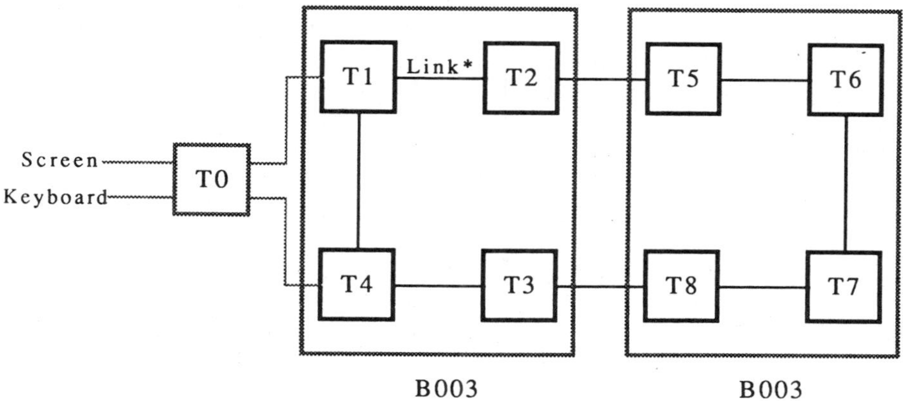

Figure 9.3 *Physical connections for unidirectional loop. (Reprinted by permission from Das and Fay.[2]) Copyright © 1988 by Elsevier Science Publishers.*

Das and Fay[2] studied the performance of eight transputer systems in view of message communication in different architectural configurations. The simplest transputer network is a unidirectional loop, as shown in Figure 9.3. For an N-transputer system, the worst-case distance between a source and a destination is $N - 1$, and an average distance is $N/2$.

A bidirectional loop is shown in Figure 9.4. The worst-case and average distances would be $N/2$, and $N/4$, respectively.

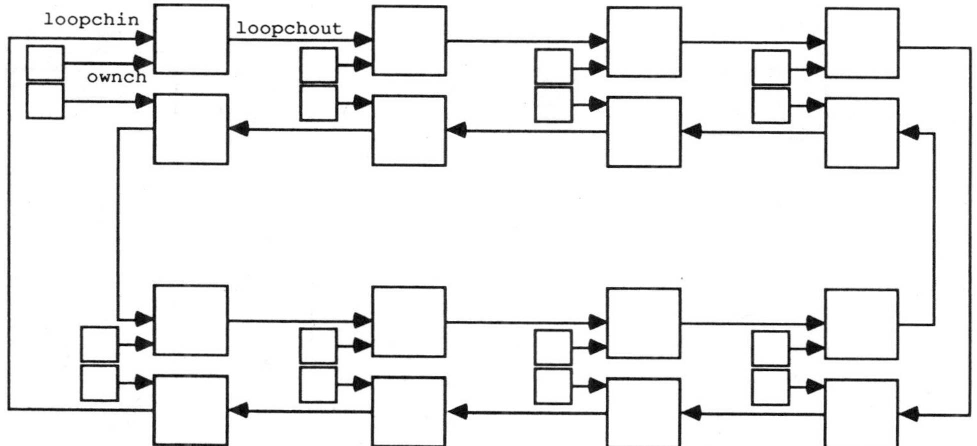

Figure 9.4 *Logical connections in Bidirectional loop. (Reprinted by permission from Das and Fay.[2]) Copyright © 1988 by Elsevier Science Publishers.*

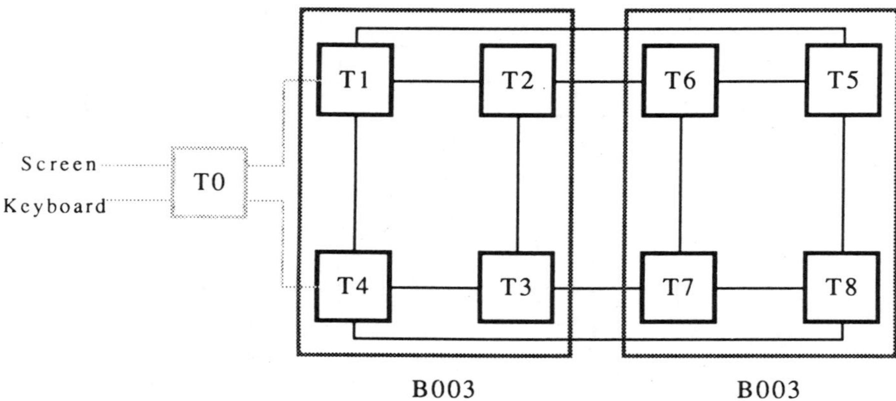

Figure 9.5 *Physical connections for binary cube. (Reprinted by permission from Das and Fay.[2]) Copyright © 1988 by Elsevier Science Publishers.*

A binary n-cube system is shown in Figure 9.5. The worst-case and average distances would be n and $n/2$ respectively, where $n = \log_2 N$.

A dynamic switched-link configuration is shown in Figure 9.6. The additional transputer T9 has two switchable links, L0 and L1, each connected to any of four links at once. A router process running on T9 continually scans all nodes and, on obtaining a message, performs a link switching at either L0 or L1, depending on the specified destination in the message header, and transmits it to the destination node. Since processors T1 through T8 never take part in any message transactions other than those originated by or

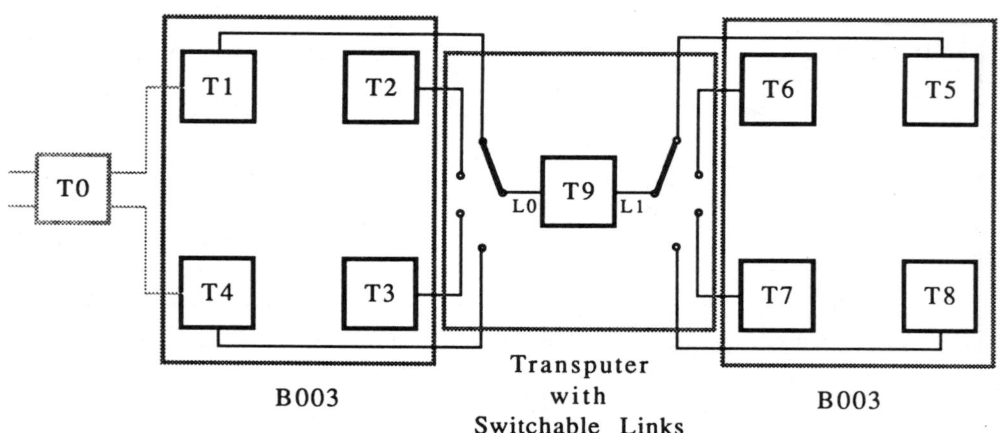

Figure 9.6 *Physical switched link configuration. (Reprinted by permission from Das and Fay.[2]) Copyright © 1988 by Elsevier Science Publishers.*

addressed to themselves, the communication processes at these nodes are inherently much simpler and free of deadlocks.

Das and Fay[2] show that the switched-link architecture performs significantly better in almost all respects than does static architecture (unidirectional, bidirectional, and cube). Also, switched-link architecture simplifies programming.

9.2. DISTRIBUTED OPERATING SYSTEM

Operating systems make maximum use of the computer's extensive resources. Early operating systems were large and monolithic, composed of a kernel and a set of user or application processes. With the transputer as a base, the system already provides the basic services, such as processes and message passing. The development of an operating system is simpler and depends on the application. Here we discuss the issues in the design and implementation of a distributed operating system for a general-purpose interactive program development environment. The operating system, called Wisdom, was developed by Murray and Wellings.[3]

Wisdom is composed of modules that interact with themselves and with user modules to create a general and easy to use programming environment. Interprocess and intermodule communication is shown in Figure 9.7. Figure 9.8 shows the layers of a Wisdom system. The kernel is the combination of the three modules: routing, naming, and load balancing.

The *routing module* allows any processing node to talk to any other. The *naming module* provides the interface between the router and other processes. Without some form of naming system, it is impossible for different

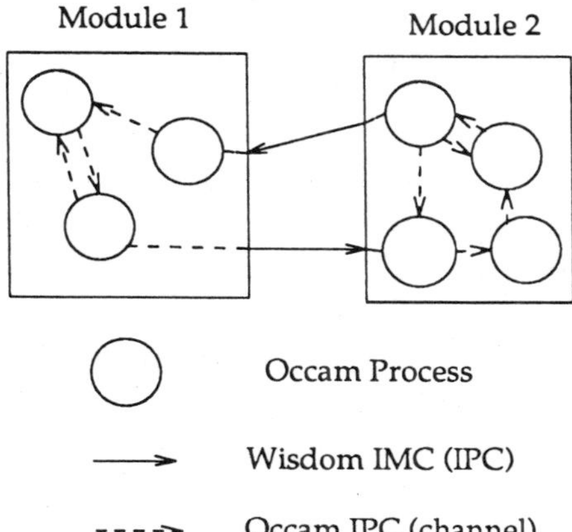

Figure 9.7 *Interprocess and intermodule communication. (Reprinted by permission from Murray and Wellings.[3]) Copyright © 1988 by Elsevier Science Publishers.*

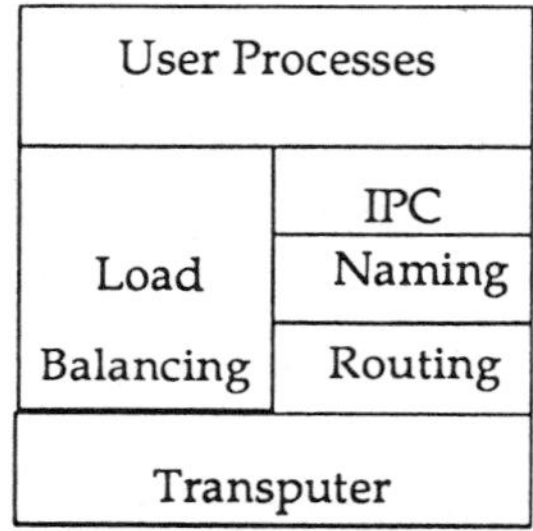

Figure 9.8 *Wisdom hierarchy. (Reprinted by permission from Murray and Wellings.[3]) Copyright © 1988 by Elsevier Science Publishers.*

programs to communicate in a truly dynamic fashion. The *load balancing* module shares the workload as evenly as possible between the available processors.

The routing, naming, and balancing modules create a simple, well-structured system, out of which it should be simple to build any services needed. Murray and Wellings[3] propose changes to OCCAM to enable both dynamic processes and the transmission of channel variables in messages.

9.3. TRANSPUTERS IN SPEECH PROCESSING

Many people are deaf through disorders of the cochlea, the sensory organ in the ear. If the central nervous system and auditory nerve are intact, it is possible to create a sensation of sound by direct electrical stimulation of the auditory nerve. The model in Figure 9.9 appears promising in the development of acoustic prostheses that will enable the generation of sensation that constitutes a fascimile of normal sound sensation.

The model, developed by Adamson, Donnan, and Black,[4] has the following units:

Gain: multiplies a value passing through it by a constant;

Adder: adds the values on its input lines;

Delay: suspends the progress of a value until the next or subsequent values are available; and

Junction: disperses a value along two or more lines.

All of the features identified in the model of the filter become distinct procedures in OCCAM. There will therefore be four types of procedures: gain, adder, delay, and junction. The connection of procedures is achieved by declaring channels and matching them appropriately so as to model the lines on the filter diagram. For the low-pass section in Figure 9.9, five procedures

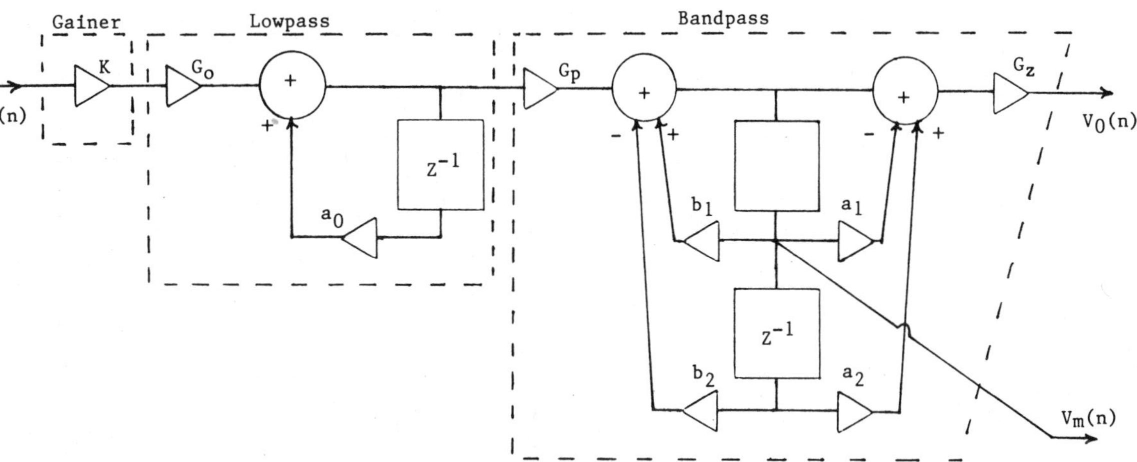

Figure 9.9 *Digital filter model of the cochlea. (Reprinted by permission from Adamson, Donnan, and Black.[4]) Copyright © 1988 by Elsevier Science Publishers.*

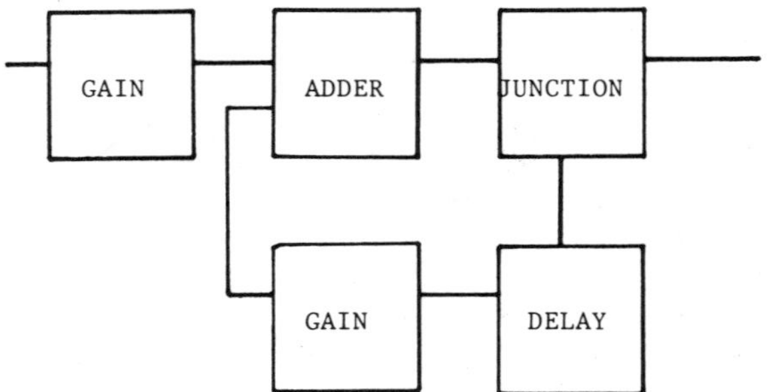

Figure 9.10 *Transputer procedures forming a lowpass filter of the cochlea. (Reprinted by permission from Adamson, Donnan, and Black.[4]) Copyright © 1988 by Elsevier Science Publishers.*

are necessary, as shown in Figure 9.10: gain (K), gain (G_0), adder, junction, and delay.

According to Adamson, Donnan, and Black,[4] this research could be of direct interest in the design of speech recognition systems, the development of natural-sounding speech synthesizers, and the development of acoustic prostheses (i.e., artificial cochlea implants).

9.4. CONCURRENT SYSTEM FOR HOUGH TRANSFORM IN VISION

The Hough transform[5,6] is a popular pattern extraction technique for computer vision. Implemented on transputers, it operates in real time and can be used in industrial vision for factory automation. The Hough transform extracts low-level features, such as straight lines and arcs, from an edge image map.

For a straight line, the Cartesian coordinates (x, y) can be translated into polar coordinates by the equation

$$r = x \cos \theta + y \sin \theta \tag{9.1}$$

The sinusoidal curves produced by plotting Equation 9.1 for edge point of a line in (r, θ) space intersect at a point that represents the parameters of the line (for explanation see Souček and Souček[6]).

Sandler and Eghtesadi[7] use a network of eight transputers, shown in Figure 9.11, to obtain a high-speed real-time Hough transform. Each transputer receives a copy of all edge points from the master. A look-up table is used to replace calls to sin and cos library functions. Each variant implements a single serial process on each transputer. Experiments with 4000 edge points in 256 × 256 image have been performed. It has been shown that even a network having only eight transputers can perform transformation at a rate of a few image frames per second.

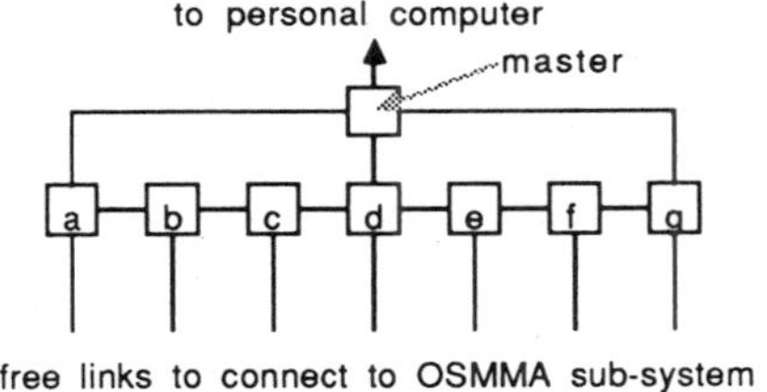

Figure 9.11 *Transputer-based implementation of the Hough transform. (Reprinted by permission from Sandler and Eghtesadi.[7]) Copyright © 1988 by Elsevier Science Publishers.*

9.5. A MULTIPROCESSOR ARCHITECTURE FOR ROBOT ARM CONTROL

The purpose of the robot arm position controller is to maintain a prescribed motion for the hand along a desired trajectory by applying the necessary torques and forces to the joint motors. The real-time computation of applied torques and forces in nonlinear and strongly coupled multilink systems is complicated and time-consuming.

Katbab[8] presents a massively parallel architecture for the control computation, based on transputers and OCCAM. The system is organized on a dataflow concept. The dataflow model deals only with values, not with the addresses of the values. An instruction is executed when and only when all required input values become available. Because many instructions may be available for execution at the same time, concurrent computation is a natural solution for the dataflow concept. The whole system for a six-link arm consists of 1834 processing elements. For illustration, Figure 9.12 shows the transputer-based implementation of one block of elements and the corresponding OCCAM program. A controller for a six-link robot, which consists of 1834 processing elements, will require 1.5 ms to compute the torques for the six links. The system can be implemented by fewer processing elements at the expense of speed. If only one transputer is used, the system is slowed down by a factor of 36. By using a moderate number of transputers and a pipeline organization, we can build a system fast enough for real-time control application.

9.6. COMPUTER GRAPHICS†

Computer-generated images, particularly interactive graphics, is one of the fastest-growing and most important application areas for high-performance computing systems. A brief introduction to some of the techniques and terminology used is given.

† Sections 9.6, 9.7, and 9.8 are adapted from INMOS Manuals.[9,10] Courtesy and copyright © 1988 by INMOS Group of Companies.

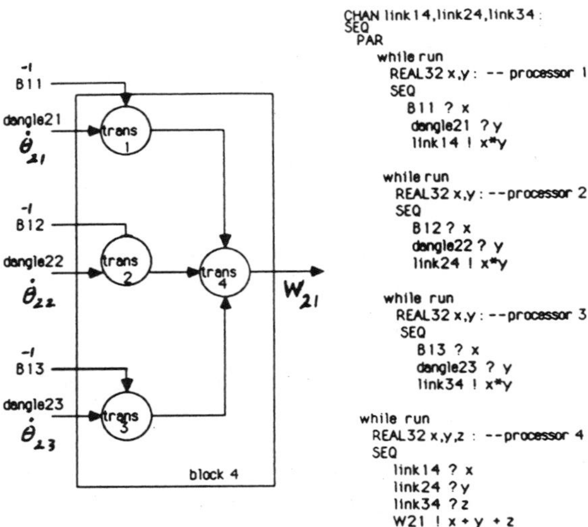
-1
B11
dangle21
$\dot{\theta}_{21}$
trans 1
-1
B12
dangle22
$\dot{\theta}_{22}$
trans 2
trans 4
W_{21}
-1
B13
dangle23
$\dot{\theta}_{23}$
trans 3
block 4
CHAN link14,link24,link34 :
SEQ
PAR
while run
REAL32 x,y : -- processor 1
SEQ
B11 ? x
dangle21 ?y
link14 ! x*y
while run
REAL32 x,y : --processor 2
SEQ
B12 ? x
dangle22 ? y
link24 ! x*y
while run
REAL32 x,y : --processor 3
SEQ
B13 ? x
dangle23 ? y
link34 ! x*y
while run
REAL32 x,y,z : --processor 4
SEQ
link14 ? x
link24 ?y
link34 ?z
W21 ! x + y + z

Figure 9.12 *Robot arm control. Transputer-OCCAM implementation of the part of a process. (Reprinted by permission from Katbab.[8]) Copyright © 1988 by Elsevier Science Publishers.*

9.6.1. Modeling Objects

To render or generate images of an object, some way of modeling the object in the computer is needed. A convenient primitive to use as the basis of modeling objects is the polyhedron. By an increase in the number of faces, the shape of any solid object can be approximated, although at the cost of having more data to manipulate. An arbitrary polyhedron can be modeled by defining its faces; each face is then a polygon that can be defined by an ordered list of vertex coordinates.

Each polygon will have other attributes associated with it, such as color and orientation. The orientation is represented by a line or vector perpendicular to the surface. This is called the *surface normal* and can be calculated from the coordinates of three vertices. The surface normal is closely related to another attribute, the plane equation of the face. A plane is represented by four numbers (a, b, c, d) so that $ax + by + cz + d = 0$ is true only if the point $[x \quad y \quad z]$ lies in the plane. If a point does not lie in the plane, then the sign of the expression $ax + by + cz + d$ indicates which side of the plane the point is located on. By convention, points in front of the plane have positive values of $ax + by + cz + d$. The components of the normal vector are given by the plane equation; the vector is $[a \quad b \quad c]$. The plane equation and normal vector are very important for visibility and shading calculations.

9.6.2. Transformation

Geometric transformations play an important role in generating images of three-dimensional scenes. They are used (a) to express the location and orientation of objects relative to one another and (b) to achieve the effect of different viewing positions and directions. Finally, a perspective transformation is used to project the three-dimensional scene onto a two-dimensional display screen.

Transformations are implemented as matrices that are used to multiply a set of coordinates to give the transformed coordinates. All rotations, translations, and other transformations to be performed on data are combined into a single matrix that can then be applied to each point being transformed. Transformations may be nested, like subroutine calls, so that parts of a model can be moved independently but still take on the global movement of the model or the viewpoint.

9.6.3. The Homogeneous Coordinate System

The coordinates of points are represented by using homogeneous coordinates. Any point in three-dimensional space can be mapped to a point in four-dimensional homogeneous space. The fourth coordinate, w, is simply a scaling factor, so a point with the homogeneous coordinates $[x \quad y \quad z \quad w]$ is represented in 3-space as $[x/w \quad y/w \quad z/w]$. This representation simplifies many calculations and, in particular, means that the division required by perspective transformation can be done after clipping when there may be many fewer points to process.

The value of w is arbitrary as long as x, y, and z are scaled by the same amount. Generally, when converting from three-dimensional to homogeneous coordinates, it is simplest to make $w = 1$ so that no multiplication of x, y, and z is necessary. After being transformed, the value of w may have changed, so at some point the x, y, and z coordinates must be divided by w. This can be done when scaling to physical screen coordinates.

The transformation matrices used are 4×4 matrices for the transformation of homogeneous coordinates and are designed to have the desired effect on the point in ordinary 3-space. When implemented on a computer, coordinates and transforms will generally use floating-point representation for maximum accuracy and dynamic range.

9.6.4. Translation

Translation, or movement of a point in space, is simply achieved by adding the distance to be moved in each axis to the corresponding coordinate:

$$x' = x + t_x$$

$$y' = y + t_y$$

$$z' = z + t_z$$

where t_x, t_y, and t_z are the distances moved in x, y, and z, respectively. This can be represented as a matrix multiplication:

$$[x' \quad y' \quad z' \quad w'] = [x \quad y \quad z \quad w] \begin{bmatrix} 1 & 0 & 0 & 0 \\ 0 & 1 & 0 & 0 \\ 0 & 0 & 1 & 0 \\ t_x & t_y & t_z & 1 \end{bmatrix}$$

9.6.5. Rotation

Three-dimensional rotations can be quite complex. The simplest form is rotating a point about an axis that passes through the origin of the coordinate system and is aligned with a coordinate axis. For example, rotation about the z axis by an angle θ is written as

$$x' = x \cos \theta + y \sin \theta$$
$$y' = -x \sin \theta + y \cos \theta$$

This can be represented as a matrix multiplication as shown:

$$[x' \quad y' \quad z' \quad w'] = [x \quad y \quad z \quad w] \begin{bmatrix} \cos \theta & -\sin \theta & 0 & 0 \\ \sin \theta & \cos \theta & 0 & 0 \\ 0 & 0 & 1 & 0 \\ 0 & 0 & 0 & 1 \end{bmatrix}$$

To perform rotations about an arbitrary point, we translate the point to the origin, perform the rotation, and then translate the point back to its original position. Rotations about axes that are not aligned with the coordinate system can be performed by concatenating simpler rotations.

9.6.6. Concatenation

The successive application of any number of transforms can be achieved with a single transformation matrix, the concatenation of the sequence. Suppose two transformations M_1 and M_2 are to be applied to successively to the point v. First v is transformed into v' by M_1; this is then transformed into v'' by M_2:

$$v' = vM_1 \qquad v'' = v'M_2$$

Substituting the first equation into the second gives

$$v'' = (vM_1)M_2 = v(M_1M_2)$$

Therefore the concatenation of a sequence of transformations is simply the product of the individual transform matrices. Note that, because matrix multiplication does not commute, the order of application of the transformations must be preserved.

9.6.7. Perspective Projection

The most realistic way of displaying three-dimensional objects on a two-dimensional screen is perspective projection. There is a simple transformation that distorts objects so that, when viewed with parallel projection (orthographically), they appear in perspective. This defines a viewing volume, a truncated pyramid, within which objects are visible (see Figure 9.13). This transformation preserves the flatness of planes and the straightness of lines and simplifies the clipping process that follows. The perspective transform uses three parameters: the size of the virtual screen onto which the image is projected; the distance from the viewing position to this screen; and the distance to the farthest visible point. The result of the perspective transform is to normalize all coordinates so that values range between -1 and $+1$, the center of the image is at the point $(x, y) = (0,0)$. To display these on a real device, the coordinates must be scaled by the screen resolution of the display.

The perspective transform used in the programs is based on Sutherland and Hodgman.[11]

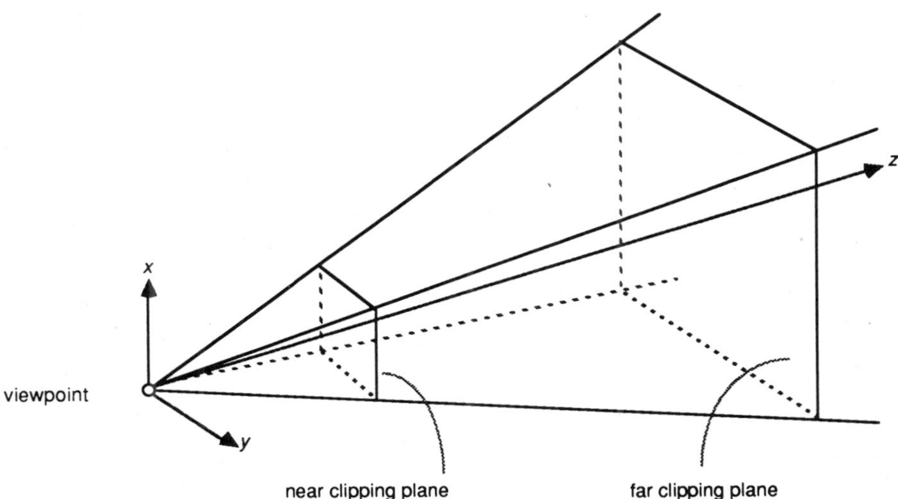

Figure 9.13 *Viewing objects in perspective. (Courtesy and copyright © 1988 by INMOS Group of Companies.)*

9.6.8. Scan Conversion

Raster displays are the most commonly used output device for computer graphics systems. They represent an image as a rectangular array of dots or pixels. The image to be displayed is stored in a frame buffer, an area of memory where each location maps onto one pixel. The main advantages of raster displays are low cost and their ability to display solid areas of color as easily as text and lines.

To display objects that are represented as polygons, it is necessary to scan-convert the polygons. This involves finding all the pixels that lie inside the polygon boundaries and assigning them the appropriate color. A shading model is used to calculate the color of each pixel. Techniques for scan conversion generally take advantage of coherence; since visibility and color of adjacent pixels is usually very similar, there are only abrupt changes at polygon boundaries. This allows incremental methods, using only integer arithmetic, to be used.

9.6.9. Shading

To generate realistic images, we must assign the correct colors to the various parts of the model. This means shading the objects to represent lighting conditions. The apparent color of a surface depends on the nature of the surface (its color, texture, etc.), the direction of the light source, and the viewing angle. A realistic shading model may require a large amount of floating-point arithmetic to multiply the vectors representing surface orientation (the surface normal), direction of the light source, etc.

Where objects are represented as a number of polygons, the faceted appearance can be reduced by using a smooth shading model. There are two simple and reasonably effective techniques. *Gouraud shading* simply interpolates the surface color across each polygon. This can, however, introduce anomalies, for example, in the shape of highlights and the way shading changes in moving sequences. Many of these problems can be relieved by using a technique developed by Phong, but at the expense of increased calculation. *Phong shading* interpolates the surface normals across the polygons and reapplies the shading model at each pixel.

9.6.10. Clipping

Clipping is necessary to remove points that lie outside the viewing volume and to truncate lines that extend beyond the boundaries. Clipping can be done more simply after the perspective transformation. However, clipping in the z axis must be done before the division by depth, which the full-perspective projection requires, since this destroys the sign information that determines whether a point is in front of or behind the viewer. Points with a negative value of z are behind the viewer.

Clipping to the x and y coordinates need only be performed to screen resolution. This has led to many clever, although not always simple, techniques using fast integer arithmetic to clip lines quickly. The availability of fast floating-point hardware means that more straightforward methods can be used.

The use of homogeneous coordinates and perspective projection simplifies clipping. Because the points can be viewed in parallel projection, x and y values that are inside the viewing pyramid are in the range -1 to 1 and z values are in the range 0 to 1. The use of scaled, homogeneous coordinates means that the tests that have to be applied are

$$-w \leq x \leq w \qquad -w \leq y \leq w \qquad 0 \leq z \leq w$$

These limits correspond to the six bounding planes of the truncated viewing pyramid.

9.6.11. Hidden Surface Removal

To generate realistic images, we must remove from an image those parts of solid objects that are hidden. In real life these would be obscured by the opaque material of the object. In computer graphics, the visibility of every point must be explicitly calculated.

Hidden surface algorithms are classified as either object space or image space. An *object-space* algorithm uses the geometrical relationships between the objects to determine the visibility of the various parts and so will normally require at least some floating-point arithmetic. An *image-space* method works at the resolution of the display device and determines what is visible at each pixel. This can be done most efficiently with integer arithmetic. The computation time of object-space techniques tends to grow with the total number of objects in the scene, whereas image-space computation will tend to grow with the complexity of the displayed image.

9.7. THREE-DIMENSIONAL TRANSFORMATION ON THE IMS T800

One of the main uses for a floating-point processor in a computer graphics system is for calculating three-dimensional transformations. This will include both generating a transformation matrix and applying this transformation to sets of coordinates. Here, a four-element vector is multiplied by a 4×4 matrix, to give a four-element result:

$$[x' \quad y' \quad z' \quad w'] = [x \quad y \quad z \quad w] \begin{bmatrix} a & b & c & d \\ e & f & g & h \\ i & j & k & l \\ m & n & o & p \end{bmatrix}$$

This can be expanded as

$$x' = ax + ey + iz + mw$$
$$y' = bx + fy + jz + nw$$
$$z' = cx + gy + kz + ow$$
$$w' = dx + hy + lz + pw$$

Hence, multiplying the vector by the matrix requires 28 floating-point operations (16 multiplications, 12 additions), which pipelines very efficiently on the IMS T800. The following OCCAM procedure multiplies the vector by the matrix and stores the result.

```
PROC vectorProdMatrix ([4]REAL32 result,
                       VAL [4]REAL32 vec,
                       VAL [4][4]REAL32 matrix)
  VAL X IS 0 :
  VAL Y IS 1 :
  VAL Z IS 2 :
  VAL W IS 3 :
  SEQ
    result[X] :=  (vec[X]*matrix[0][X])
                + ((vec[Y]*matrix[1][X]) +
                  ((vec[Z]*matrix[2][X])
                + ((vec[W]*matrix[3][X]))))
    result[Y] :=  (vec[X]*matrix[0][Y])
                + ((vec[Y]*matrix[1][Y]) +
                  ((vec[Z]*matrix[2][Y])
                + ((vec[W]*matrix[3][Y]))))
    result[Z] :=  (vec[X]*matrix[0][Z])
                + ((vec[Y]*matrix[1][Z]) +
                  ((vec[Z]*matrix[2][Z])
                + ((vec[W]*matrix[3][Z]))))
    result[W] :=  (vec[X]*matrix[0][W])
                + ((vec[Y]*matrix[1][W]) +
                  ((vec[Z]*matrix[2][W])
                + ((vec[W]*matrix[3][W]))))
:
```

Analyzing the statement

```
result[X] :=  (vec[X]*matrix[0][X])
            + ((vec[Y]*matrix[1][X]) +
```

```
        ((vec[Z]*matrix[2][X])
      + ((vec[W]*matrix[3][X]))))
```

we see that all vector offsets are constant and will be folded out by the compiler into very short instruction sequences. Furthermore, all floating-point operations are fully overlapped with subsequent address calculations. The statement compiles into only 27 instructions, most of which are only a single byte.

The entire vector matrix multiplication operation, including the call to the procedure, takes less than 19 μs on the IMS T800-20, allowing a single transputer to perform three-dimensional transformation on over 50,000 points per second. This is a genuine piece of application code, and the inner loop of all three-dimensional transformations.

9.7.1. The INMOS Distributed Z-Buffer

The Z-buffer is a general solution to the computer graphics hidden surface problem. When presented with the primitives that constitute a scene, the Z-buffer will output the scene as viewed by the observer, with hidden or partially hidden surfaces correctly obscured.

The core of the Z-buffer program is the distributed scan converter, which allows the processes of scan conversion and Z-buffering to be distributed over a number of transputers. For each pixel on the screen, a record is kept, in a depth or Z-buffer, of the depth of the object at that pixel that lies closest to the observer, and the color of that pixel is kept in a separate frame buffer. As each new object is scan-converted, the depth of each pixel generated is compared with the value currently in the Z-buffer; if this pixel is closer than the previous one at that position, then the depth and frame buffers are updated with the values for the pixel. When all polygons (and other primitives) have been scan-converted into the Z-buffer, the frame buffer contains the correct visible surface solution.

In pseudocode the Z-buffer algorithm is essentially

```
for each polygon
  {
  for each (x,y) on the screen covered by this
polygon
    {
    compute z and color at this (x,y)
    if z < zbuffer[x,y] then
      {
      framebuffer[x,y] := color
      zbuffer[x,y] := z
      }
    }
  }
```

So for each polygon, the `z` value and the `color` must be computed at each screen position covered by that polygon. For maximum speed, the values of `z` and `color` for each pixel are usually computed by using only simple integer arithmetic at each step.

The architecture of the Z-buffer system is simple, but flexible and easily extended (see Figure 9.14). An INMOS IMS B004 board (a) is used as a data base, file interface, and user interface. It sends transformation matrices, polygons, and spheres to the geometry system. The geometry system consists of four transputers on a single IMS B003-2 transputer evaluation board, which has been modified by replacing a IMS T414-20 with an IMS T800-20. This transputer (b) performs all the floating-point computation, performing three-dimensional transformation, z clipping, and conversion to screen coordinates. Two IMS T414's (c and d) then perform x and y clipping. A final IMS T414 (e) preprocesses ("cooks") polygons and spheres into a form suitable for the scan converters: the polygon vertex format is converted to edge format and edge slopes are computed; coefficients are calculated for the sphere shading equation.

The cooker outputs its processed polygons and spheres to the Z-buffer array (f through m). Note the link usage—polygons are passed through the emboldened vertical links, independently of the horizontal links that pass pixels to the graphics card (n). This separation of polygon flow and pixel flow allows a finished frame to be passed to the graphics card while the next frame is being computed, pipelining work efficiently for animated sequences. This organization also takes maximum advantage of the autonomous link engines on each transputer. The graphics card used is an IMS B007 evaluation board, which has two banks of video memory, allowing the next frame to be read in without disturbing the currently displayed image. When the complete frame

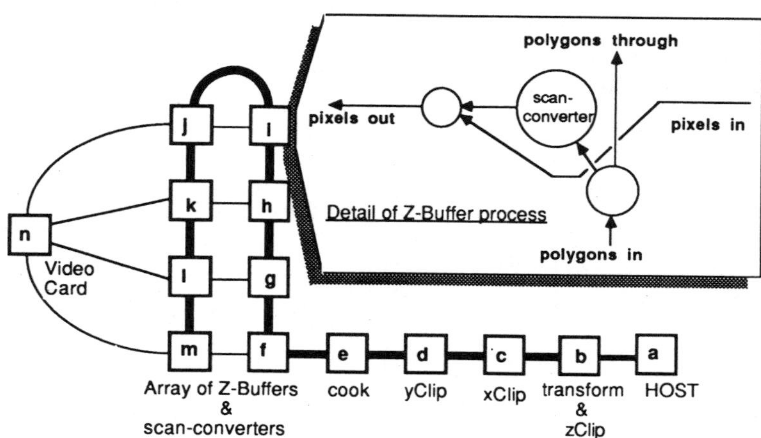

Figure 9.14 *Distributed Z-buffer architecture. (Courtesy and copyright © 1988 by INMOS Group of Companies.)*

has been received, the two memory banks are swapped by writing to a control register. This must be synchronized with the frame flyback of the display to avoid distracting visual artefacts.

The Z-buffer is fully interactive, and on existing models image generation speeds range from over 10 frames per second down to around 1 frame per second.

9.8. MULTIUSER FLIGHT SIMULATOR

A flight simulator system must be able to portray the outside world in sufficient detail (both graphically on the windshield, and numerically using instruments), and possibly simulate the motion of the vehicle using a motion platform, such that the pilot feels that he is really flying the aircraft. Such a system consists of very high performance subsystems, such as a display system, motion controller, and a data base system that can maintain a model of the world (and any objects that may appear in it), and environmental data (rain, clouds, etc.) that must be accessed during the simulation. All this data must be displayed fast (and realistically) enough to give the impression of real flight. To get a frame rate of 20 to 30 frames per second, most of the work is currently done in hardware, which explains the high cost of this system.

With a multiuser simulator, each node must be able to access the data and display it in accordance with the current position of the craft at that node. Also needed is a knowledge of where all other users in the system are, so they can also be displayed (if visible). This implementation of a flight simulator allows users, each with their own simulation engine, to interact. Each user gets a view of the world as if looking through the cockpit window. The world is made of polygons displayed at a rate of approximately 17 frames per second (at about 200 polygons per frame). This frame rate is limited by the design of the graphics board used in the current system. To avoid visual artefacts, one must wait for frame flyback before updating the display. Since there are only two display banks on the IMS B007 graphics board, this has the effect of holding up link communications with the shader processors for up to one frame time (1/50 s). If the wait for frame flyback is removed, the frame update rate is increased to approximately 22 frames/s, since the buffered image can be displayed as soon as it is received. An enhanced graphics board is currently being designed at INMOS, which has up to four frame buffers, allowing higher frame rates (as the $(n + 1)$st frame can be read while the nth frame is waiting to be displayed) with frame flyback.

All users are connected in a ring. Any part of the world that needs to be distributed is passed around to each user in turn, who can read it, modify it, or ignore it, and then pass it on to the next user. Objects can be dynamically added to this network (such as missiles that have been fired) and taken out when no longer needed. The ring architecture allows any number of users to be included in the system, and the software has been written with this feature in mind.

The program is written entirely in OCCAM, and the hardware used in the implementation consists of transputer variants (T212, T414, and T800) all running on standard INMOS transputer evaluation boards. These boards are connected by the INMOS links, allowing complex systems like this to be built with relative ease (approximately 10 min to wire a four-player implementation of the simulator).

The architecture for a single-user system is shown in Figure 9.15. The system has been subdivided into the most logical processes that occur in a simulator (e.g., the core simulator, three-dimensional transformation, clipping). Note that this is the software model for such a system and not the hardware implementation. The system has been designed to allow any number of flight simulators to be connected in a ring. Messages are passed around the ring defining the position and orientation of objects in the simulation. Figure 9.16 shows an example of four such systems connected in a ring.

The ring control process handles all ring communications, and interaction with the pilot controls. From these information sources, a description of the next visible scene for this user can be derived.

Objects are described as a set of polygons, and these polygons are stored in a large data base. To display an object, these polygons must be output such that the near faces of the object obscure those further away. The data base process takes care of this hidden surface algorithm. The polygons described in the data base are not suitable to be written directly to the screen. Each polygon must undergo a transformation to convert it to a displayable form. In the following sections, reference will be made to model, world, eye,

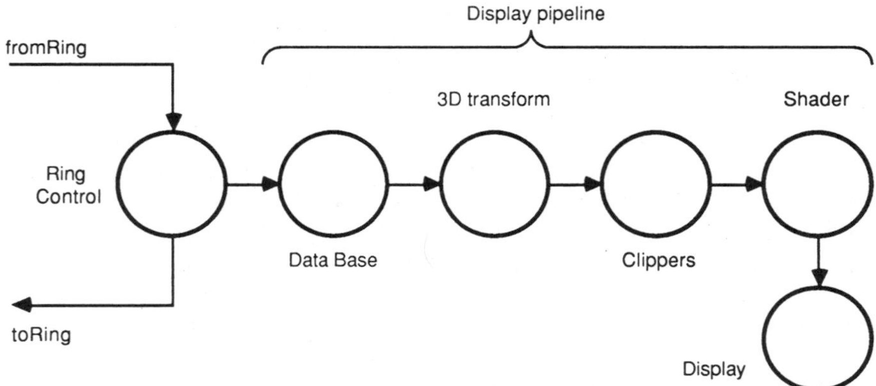

Figure 9.15 *Architecture for one player.* (*Courtesy and copyright © 1988 by INMOS Group of Companies.*)

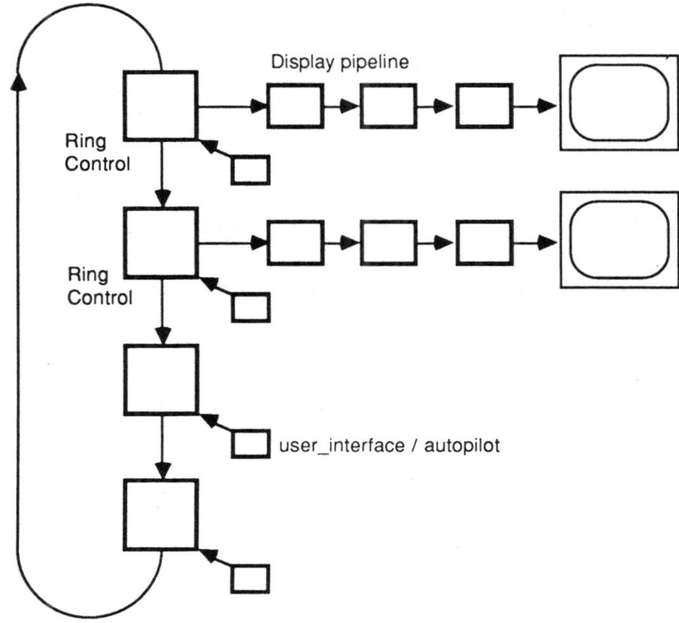

Figure 9.16 *A two-player, two-autopilot example. (Courtesy and copyright © 1988 by INMOS Group of Companies.)*

and screen coordinate systems. Figure 9.16 shows an example of how these different coordinate systems relate. Converting between coordinate systems requires the coordinates (of a polygon, for example) to be transformed by using matrix multiplications. The transformations can be rotations about an axis, scaling, and translation along an axis. For example, the transform from model to world space requires a 90° rotation about the Y-model axis.

The front end of the system (the ring controller and transforming processes) are floating-point intensive and are placed onto IMS T800 processors. Other processes, such as the x and y clippers, do not use the floating point unit of the IMS T800, but take advantage of the higher link bandwidth available (all links are run at 20 Mbits/s and use overlapped acknowledge packets).

As well as interfacing to the joystick modules, the IMS T212 processors run an autopilot process, which cuts in if the joysticks are not touched for a certain time.

The system hardware is standard INMOS transputer evaluation boards, and all the software (written using the INMOS transputer development system) was written in under three weeks. We believe this is a record for such a system.

9.9. PARALLEL BACKTRACKING PROLOG ENGINE

Forward-backward chaining of knowledge is the basic operation in rule-based expert systems. If an expert system uses a large set of rules, chaining takes a long time. The system is slow and cannot be used in a real-time environment.

De Blasi et al.[12] introduced a parallel architecture for an efficient execution of backtracking in expert systems. The architecture is intended as a processing system dedicated for PROLOG, and is connected to the host computer. The architecture is composed of a bidirectional ring of transputers shown in Figure 9.17. Each transputer controls its unification processor.

Unification is carried out in two distinct sequential phases. In the first phase, the terms are interpreted in such a way as to obtain a descriptor-level representation; in the second phase, the true unification takes place on these descriptors, using the terms only when needed, so that the unification can be performed more efficiently.

The architecture is strictly related to the depth-first fashion resolution strategy of PROLOG.

9.10. CONTROL SYSTEM OF THE FLEXIBLE MANUFACTURING CELL

Flexible manufacturing cells present the basis of modern industry. Jocković[13] describes the cell used for automatic production of metal parts with specific dimensions. The configuration is shown in Figure 9.18, and it contains robots R1 and R2, machine tools (NC1—milling machine, NC2—lathe, NC3—press), two auxiliary buffers (B1 and B2), incoming (T1) and outgoing (T2) transporters, bin for rejected parts, visual TV system, and a set of sensors, including S1 and S2 (or robots R1 and R2), which indicate whether the robot has grasped a part, positional sensors in machines SP1–SP3, tightening sensors of parts in machines (SM1–SM2), and distance-indicating sensor SI1.

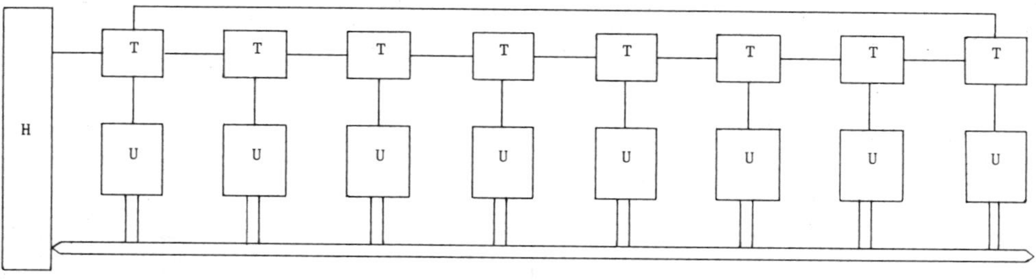

Figure 9.17 *Architecture of parallel backtracking prolog engine: T = transputer; U = unification processor; H = host system. (Reprinted by permission from De Blasi, Gentile, Lopez, and Franco.[12]) Copyright © 1988 by Elsevier Science Publishers.*

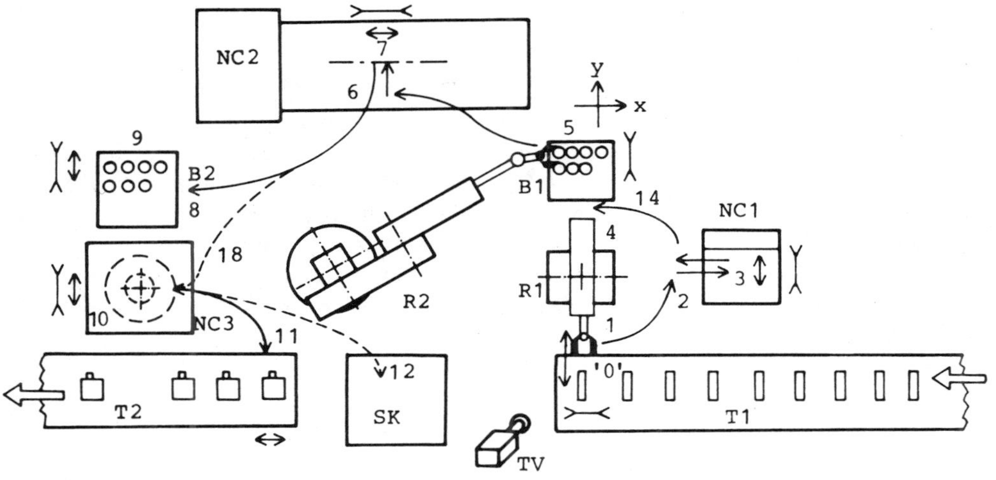

Figure 9.18 *Flexible manufacturing cell: ↔ release (open), ⤚ grasps (closes). SK-ruined part store. (Reprinted by permission from Jocković.[13]) Copyright © 1988 by Elsevier Science Publishers.*

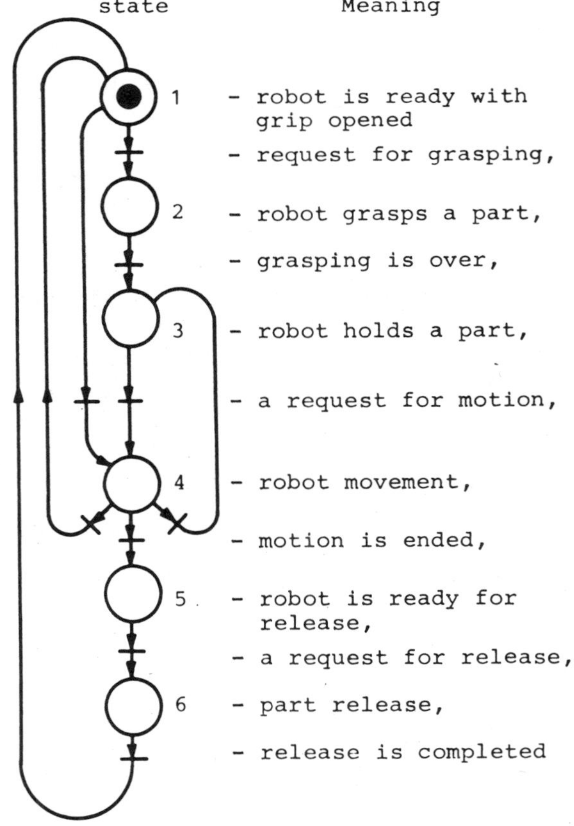

Figure 9.19 *Model of robot Petri net. (Reprinted by permission from Jocković.[13]) Copyright © 1988 by Elsevier Science Publishers.*

The need for manufacturing cell flexibility dictates the possibility of combining tasks, defined by sequence sets. The program solution[14] is realized by assuming parallel work of machines NC2 and NC3 served by robot R2 and machines NC1 served by robot R1. Introducing the net learning process results in improved performance. A model of the robot R1 in the form of a Petrinet is shown in Figure 9.19. A changeover from one system state to another is based on data from sensors and on information from lower levels.

A flexible manufacturing cell is a top-level complex intelligent real-time system.

REFERENCES

1. P. Brajak, Designing a reconfigurable intelligent memory module (RIMM) for performance enhancement to large scale, general purpose parallel processor. *Informatica* **1,** 19–53 (1987).
2. P. K. Das and D. Q. M. Fay, Performance studies on multitransputer architectures with static and dynamic links. *Microprocessing and Microprogramming* **24,** 281–290 (1988).
3. K. A. Murray and A. J. Wellings, Issues in the design and implementation of a distributed operating system for a network of transputers. *Microprocessing and Microprogramming* **24,** 169–178 (1988).
4. K. Adamson, G. Donnan, and N. D. Black, Simple transformation rules in the application of transputers to the physiological processing of speech. *Microprocessing and Microprogramming* **24,** 397–402 (1988).
5. P. V. C. Hough, Method and means for recognizing complex patterns. U.S. Patent No. 3069654 (1962).
6. B. Souček and M. Souček, *Neural and Massively Parallel Computers: The Sixth Generation,* Wiley, New York, 1988.
7. M. B. Sandler and S. Eghtesadi, Transputer based implementations of the Hough transform for computer vision. *Microprocessing and Microprogramming* **24,** 403–408 (1988).
8. A. Katbab, A multiprocessor architecture for robot-arm control. *Microprocessing and Microprogramming* **24,** 673–680 (1988).
9. P. Atkin and J. Packer, High performance graphics with the IMS T800. INMOS 72TCH03700 (1988).
10. P. Atkin and S. Ghee, A transputer based multi-user flight simulator. INMOS 72TCH03601 (1988).
11. I. E. Sutherland and G. W. Hodgman, *CACM* **17**(1) (1974).
12. M. De Blasi, A. Gentile, G. Lopez, and A. Franco, Parallel backtracking Prolog engine. *Microprocessing and Microprogramming* **24,** 607–612 (1988).
13. M. Jocković, An application of Petri-net in the control system of the FTC. *Microprocessing and Microprogramming* **24,** 681–686 (1988).
14. M. Vukobratović, D. Stokić, R. Krtolica, M. Jocković, D. Mamula, and V. Devedžić, *A Software Model for Simulation and Control of Flexible Manufacturing Systems,* Institute M. Pupin, Belgrade, 1987.

CHAPTER 10

Transputer-Based Computing Surface, Clusters, and Hyperclusters

INTRODUCTION AND SURVEY

The computing surface and clusters use interprocessor communications to split a computing task into many parallel subtasks. These subtasks exchange data and control information over a large number of dedicated, point-to-point communication channels, thereby avoiding the bottlenecking inherent in a bus architecture. The architecture is modular, so more clusters can be added, increasing the system's speed.

The cluster is based on the T800 transputer, which has four communications channels. Transputers are grouped in clusters of 16 and linked through a network-configuration unit. Each cluster has a pair of 16-channel communications lines. The clusters, in turn, are grouped in units of four, linked through two network-configuration units, to make the basic 64-processor Supercluster.

Each unit has workstation interfaces and a system services cluster, which houses the disk-drive filing system, host facilities, and some application-specific modules. Larger superclusters can be formed by connecting two or more basic units through the communications channels emanating from the basic cluster's two network-configuration units.

The basic supercluster's 64 processors together handle 640 million instructions/s and 96 million floating-point operations/s in scalar computations. The model 256's four supercluster units hit 2560 Mips and 386 Megaflops. A faster transputer model considerably boosts performance: The 64-processor cluster offers 960 Mips and 144 Mflops in scalar operations.

Supercluster price is about one-tenth the price of a conventional supercomputer. A key reason for the price/performance advantage is that the interprocessor–communications scheme facilitated by the transputer breaks the bottleneck imposed by conventional bus-based or other memory-coupled designs. This is accomplished by organizing a system in a number of local computing nodes. These nodes exchange control information and data via the fast communications channels.

Adding more nodes means adding channels, and therefore communications bandwidth, so the overall balance of computing power and communication bandwidth is always maintained. Theoretically, at least, the supercluster can expand infinitely, with overall throughput increasing proportionately to the number of processors. Among other things, that greatly extends the life of the system. After a few years, users can outgrow a supercomputer with a conventional architecture, but a supercluster system stays up to date with processor technology and user requirements.

In addition to its virtually unlimited expansion capability, the supercluster has built in host facilities making it independent of front-end computers. Also, standard workstations may be connected to a supercluster via fast communication channels so that each workstation application can get access to a user-defined partition of the system.

The hypercluster is a reconfigurable multitransputer architecture. Many application specific topologies like ring, torus, hypertree, and so on can be configured with the network configuration unit, which consists of a 96 by 96 switch. This chapter ends with the description of a Helios operating system.

10.1. COMPUTING SURFACE†

To gain the power of the computing surface will inevitably involve concurrency, but there is a wide spectrum of approaches which are tractable. Since every single standard computing element is a significant computer in its own right, it can be treated as such. A simple view to take is that of the computing surface as a 'processor farm' operated as a multitask environment with a separate independent task per computing element. A single element will perform many existing applications outright with virtually no modification.

An example is numerically intensive simulation. Often, many simulations have to be performed on the same data set, but with differing starting or operating conditions. This set of simulations is the overall task, but conventionally it is the performance of an individual simulation which is measured and optimised. If each one of the set of simulations is performed simultaneously with the others, with no interactions between tasks, a linear decrease in elapsed time for the overall task will be enjoyed.

The other end of the spectrum is the truly distributed implementation involving a completely fresh look at the problem in question, or indeed

† Section 10.1 is adapted from Meiko manuals.

tackling a problem which hitherto was looked upon as infeasible with conventional computers.

A computing surface is formed by networking many computing elements in an application specific topology. Each computing element is a self-sufficient independent hardware process, with processor, memory and high performance point-to-point communications channels. The size, and therefore the power of a computing surface, is determined by the quantity and mixture of computing element types.

The computing surface has no personality. Users impart their own flavor to the machine. They are not constrained by arbitrary choices made by the developers, however intelligent. Truly optimal configurations can be developed. Most important, they can be fine-tuned as more is learned about an application. Therefore there is no block diagram for a computing surface. Each user develops his own.

Figure 10.1 shows the computing surface configured as a distributed rendering engine in which an image is shared between many processors, each one rendering a patch, or number of rasters, and then forwarding its contribution to a display element ready for the next frame. Systems such as this provide ideal examples of how load balancing in concurrent implementations can be achieved; small patches are served on demand to the processors

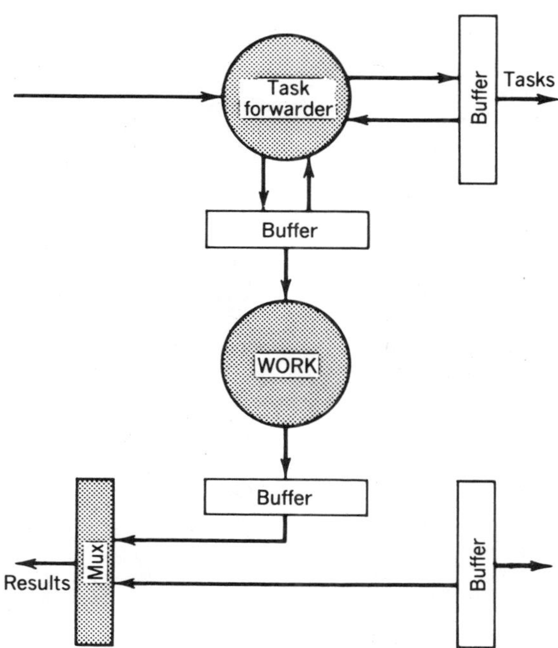

Figure 10.1 *One node of a load balancing task server. Adapted from Meiko manuals, 1989.*

which will require differing amounts of time to render them, depending on the image complexity within the patch.

The computing surface is about flexibility. Freedom for implementers to control their own solution space. The support infrastructure which makes this tractable underpins the whole machine. A local host is capable of building a physical map of the entire computing surface. Using this map and electronic configuration it wires a machine to a high level specification derived from the application program which is being loaded.

A computing surface may be configured as a general purpose computing resource or be optimised to a specific function. A mixture of boards or subsystems is chosen to populate computing surface modules and create a customised solution to a computing problem. A subsystem contains one or more function specific computing elements depending on the physical space occupied by an individual element.

All computing elements conform to the same generic model, (shown in Figure 10.2) giving the important property that they provide a logically consistent interface to the application programmer. The same tools, interfaces and conventions are used with each, for configuration, programming, communication and debugging. This results from their each being based on a transputer with its own interface to the global supervisor bus, and with a quantity of additional private local memory and specialist function unit appropriate to the subsystem.

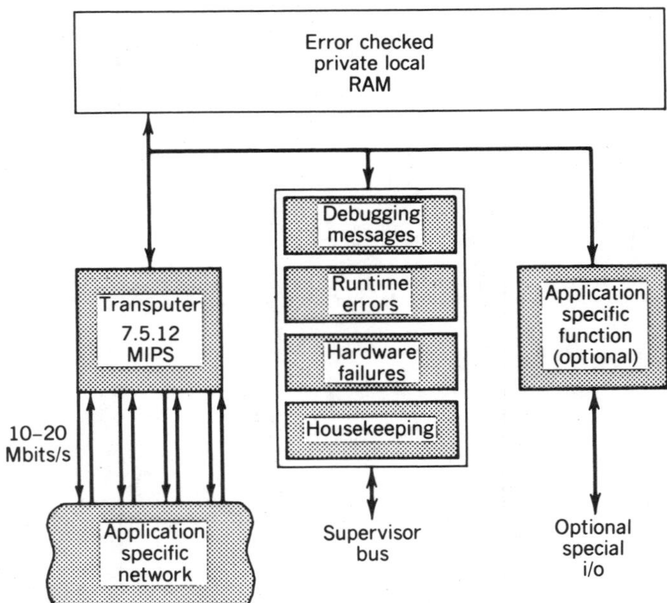

Figure 10.2 *Generic computing element. Adapted from Meiko manuals, 1989.*

Every element has eight high speed communication channels which are capable of direct memory access for high speed, low latency message passing to or from other computing elements. Each channel can transfer data at up to 10M bits per second.

The message passing latency is remarkably low for several reasons. The point-to-point communication channels are dedicated, always ready, and contention free. Also there is exceedingly little time spent in the scheduling operations commonly associated with message passing since the computing element performs message passing as a single instruction, in which the appropriate process scheduling is achieved in an efficient microcode sequence as opposed to a software kernel scheduling function commonly found in distributed systems.

Software is no longer used solely to specify the application program; now it is also used to specify the machine in which the application is executed. The boundaries between hardware and software, processor and memory have been dissolved. OCCAM specifies connections, communications and computations in one consistent formally based notation. The transputer is the optimal vehicle to implement the occam model and execute OCCAM code. The computing surface is the optimal vehicle to deliver transputers and support application development.

10.2. THE MEGAFRAME MODULE FAMILY†

According to Kübler,[1,2] in context of small systems, using a bus to connect parallel processors is sufficient. Of course, the bus will be the bottleneck for greater applications. So, all currently available parallel bus coupled multiprocessor computers incorporate only from two to approximately eight processors. Even advanced techniques like extensive caching have little effect on further increase of performance while adding processing modules.

Thinking of very large systems with dozens or even hundreds of processors is impossible with a bus system. The same applies with systems that have no fixed size to match variable requirements. Instead, the VME bus will be used for local interconnection within subsystems. The global system design will no longer be based on the bus but on a message passing oriented architecture. On this area the transputer is already an industrial standard.

For building multitransputer networks, the processors are connected via the four links in a point-to-point manner. Via those links, the processors interchange data at 20 Mbit/s while simultaneously proceeding with processing. Changing the network topologies can be realized by simply reconfiguring the link connections. Thus a lot of different network architectures are possible and easy to realize.

† Sections 10.2 and 10.3 are adapted from Parsytec manuals. (Courtesy and copyright © 1989 by Parsytec.)

Figure 10.3 shows an example for a distributed transputer system that is built up from several system units. The different system units are connected by standard MEGAFRAME linkcables for distances up to 10 meters. Thus processors are able to communicate at the same speed as they would when residing on the same board. The interfaces to the standard based outside world are implemented by bus bridges, (e.g., for VME). An extremely high speed interface, (e.g., to custom hardware) is implemented by the dual 16-bit parallel interface of the VTF module enabling data transfers of up to 50 Mbyte/s for each channel.

Implementing such systems for design engineers, industrial applications are as easy as possible, with MEGAFRAME system family of transputer-based multiprocessing components.

To enable the transputer user to make quick efficient use of application knowhow in completed systems, certain features are provided in the system:

- Flexible extendability because of bus-free multitransputer architecture;
- Mapping of tasks from design, through software, to hardware by means

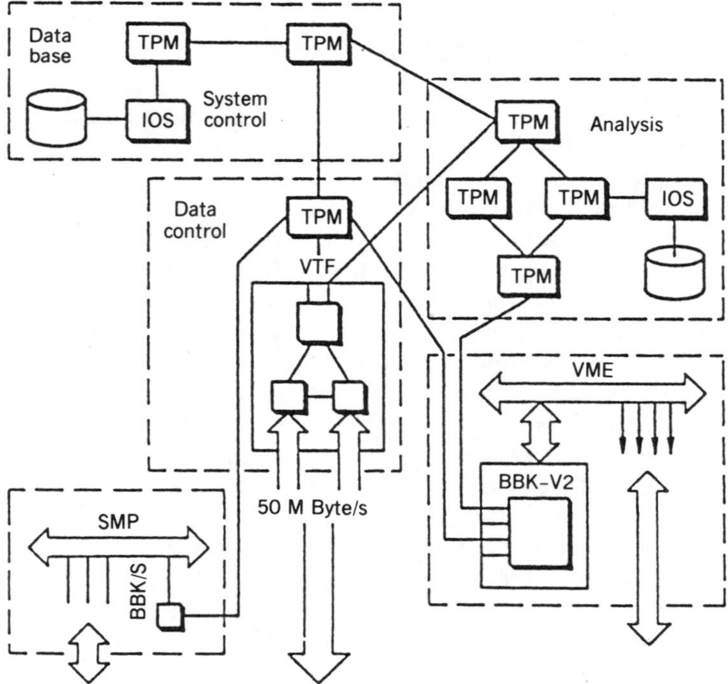

Figure 10.3 *The MEGAFRAME module family application example. (Courtesy and copyright © 1989 by Parsytec.)*

of freely determinable topology made by simply plugging in modules to establish interconnections;

- Ease to use any of the whole range of standard peripherals from VME-bus, SMP and ECB systems or from IBM PCs or to combine them within a single complex system; and
- A complete system can be divided into physically separate units without losing information-processing power or reliability.

The modules are in the extended single Euroformat or VMEbus format and can be used in standard 19-inch systems, either as target system or as a desktop model and as an autonomous development system, or connected to IBM-PCs by adapters specially developed for this purpose. The systems are absolutely bus-free. The modules communicate within system units as well as between separate subsystems via plug-in standard link cable with the use of these differential-driven cables, signals are transmitted in both directions at a speed of 20 Mbit/s over a distance of up to 10 m. The cables also provide the dynamic reset and programmed reload of the modules with program code. At present, optical waveguide interfaces are in preparation which will convey signals up to 1000 m with the same bandwidths and even despite interference.

The designer can, for example, select from the second row of modules in Figure 10.4 the desired corresponding processing power for each task in a subsystem. For each module this might mean up to 4 transputers, 4 Mbytes, 40 Mips, 3 Mflops or 8 million Whetstones. Compared with conventional computer architecture this is an absolutely incredible performance which can be multiplied simply by using more modules. Because the architecture is purely communication-oriented, any combination of modules can be made with the single plug-in links. In this way, topology, the number of active parallel processes and local memory size for each processor can be chosen individually. A variety of busless modules can be used in the same way as the VMEbus based modules VMTM, BBK-V1, or BBK-V2. The interconnection between all processor nodes also can be configured under software control by using the MEGAFRAME/XBAR crossbar switch.

In addition, from the third row of modules, the VTF module (versatile transputer frontend) can be connected by means of high-speed parallel data interfaces to customized hardware. The transputer can transfer data in program-controlled mode up to 10 Mbytes/s via an address window and even up to 50 Mbytes/s in burst mode if under external DMA control.

The third row of Figure 10.4 shows a module family that has been specially developed for the integration of standard systems. Bus bridges for SMP and ECB systems are capable of masterslave processing and deal with bus protocol by means of local intelligence. So, for instance, from the point of view of a SMP-I/O card the transputer connected by the link seems to be directly connected to the bus, whereas from the point of view of the transputer there is an intelligent, message-oriented device connected in, which is

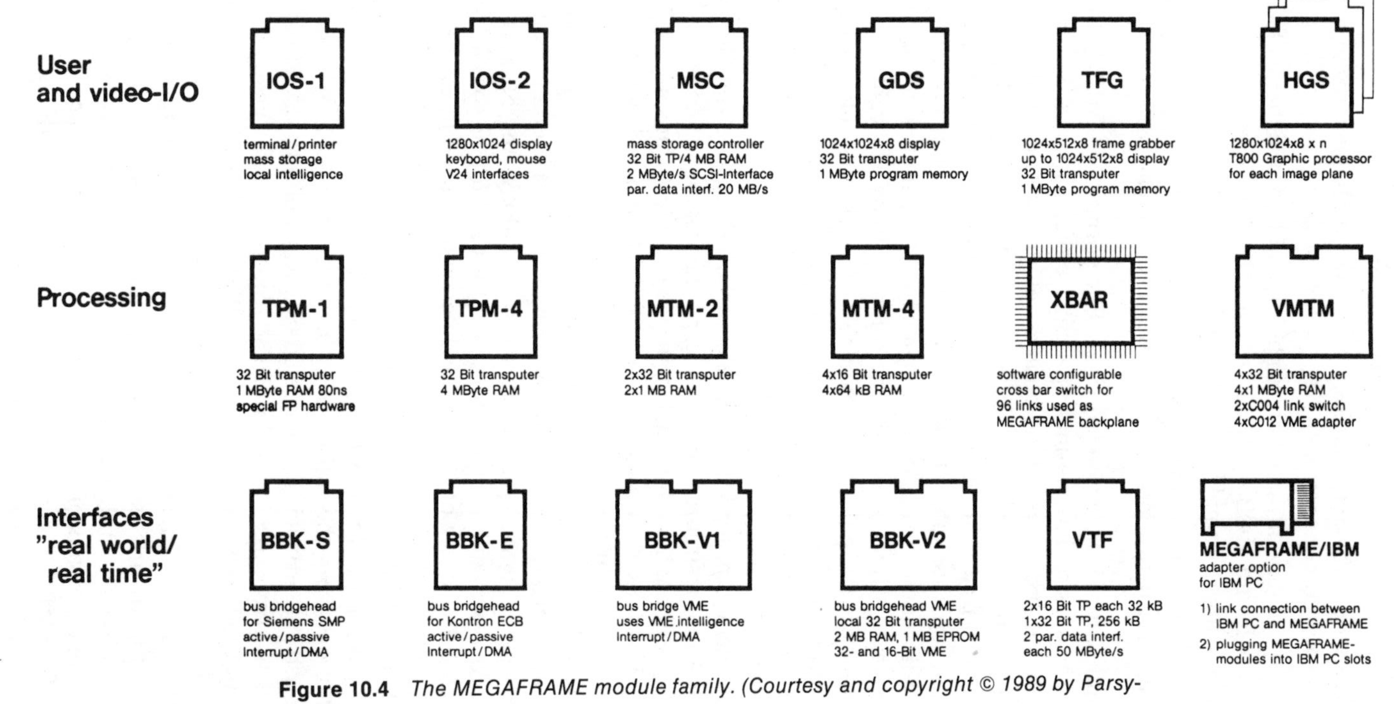

Figure 10.4 *The MEGAFRAME module family. (Courtesy and copyright © 1989 by Parsytec.)*

driven by data and interrupt messages. When the designer wishes to include VMEbus-systems, she can choose between two options. The BBK-V1 bridge hooks up to "intelligence" already available in a VMEbus system, whereas the BBK-V2 brings its own high performance transputer system, capable of supporting multimaster configurations into the VMEbus where it handles the local processing either alone, or together with further BBK-V2 or VMTM modules, or even together with conventional intelligence that is already there.

Finally, the IBM-PC integration module is a speciality which can take on a multiple function in a system. It can be directly plugged into a "slot" of an IBM-PC or a compatible computer and connected by means of a standard link cable to a MEGAFRAME module, for example in a physically separate system unit or in a VMEbus system. In this way, the PC processor can perform the same fast exchange of data—either program controlled or interrupt-driven—as the other modules of the BBK-line can provide. It is also possible to connect any of the transputer processing modules already mentioned to the integration module plugged into the PC. Together they form a long plug-in module so that the PC, enhanced by a transputer, has considerable preprocessing power and link-based data transfer capacity.

The modules of the first row helps to further extend the flexibility for the MEGAFRAME user by providing access to different peripherals. It provides fast SCSI-based mass storage control systems as well as graphics modules and a transputer based frame grabber for image recognition systems.

In addition, the software of such an interconnected network of multiprocessors can be loaded into the system from any node via the links which are later on used for data communication, as long as the node has access to mass storage. This can be done by a MEGAFRAME system unit with an I/O subsystem (IOS), or by a VMEbus subsystem with one of the BBK bridges or by a PC connected by a link cable.

Special configuration software generates a code file which already contains all the initial program loaders and routers to load all the processors and which has to be fed into the system only via a link. It has never been so easy to work with a multiprocessor system.

Apart from OCCAM-2 as a dedicated language to develop parallel system, C, Pascal and Fortran are also available. By using standard languages as subprocesses, OCCAM enables the system programmer to make use of existing software libraries.

The development of large parallel system is aided by the vision-windowing debugger. The system provides a logical terminal for each process, independent of the mapping to logical processors. The programmer has access to any logical terminal from any node, as if it were directly connected to this process or processor. All inputs and outputs to this logical terminal are transparently routed to the physical terminal which is connected and disconnected to the host node. The designer can connect any logical terminal to any physical window on the screen by pressing the corresponding keys. In this way, he has complete control over the program flow in each subprocess of the system.

Figure 10.5 demonstrates an image processing system that may already exist in conventional technology and is to be expanded in processing power. The conventional CPU on the VMEbus, oftenly a 68000 or 68020 processor, is controlling the local image data acquisition. Via the bus bridge BBK-V1 and under the control of the local CPU image data are transferred at 20 Mbit/s to an eight-transputer array built-up by two MTM-4 modules.

There within an analyzing process, they are transferred to object oriented informations and fed further on to a control system. The VMEbus processing unit needs only to initialize the transfer as it is then done autonomously by the DMA hardware of the BBK-V1. More complex levels of interaction can be implemented by a bidirectional software handshake, where the transputer via the link generates an interrupt on the VMEbus to which the local CPU responds appropriately. System integration is very easy, as the whole program code of the transputer network may be downloaded from VME mass storage via the BBK-V1.

Figure 10.6 is evolved from Figure 10.5 showing the same application but in a much more powerful configuration. The example incorporates the BBK-

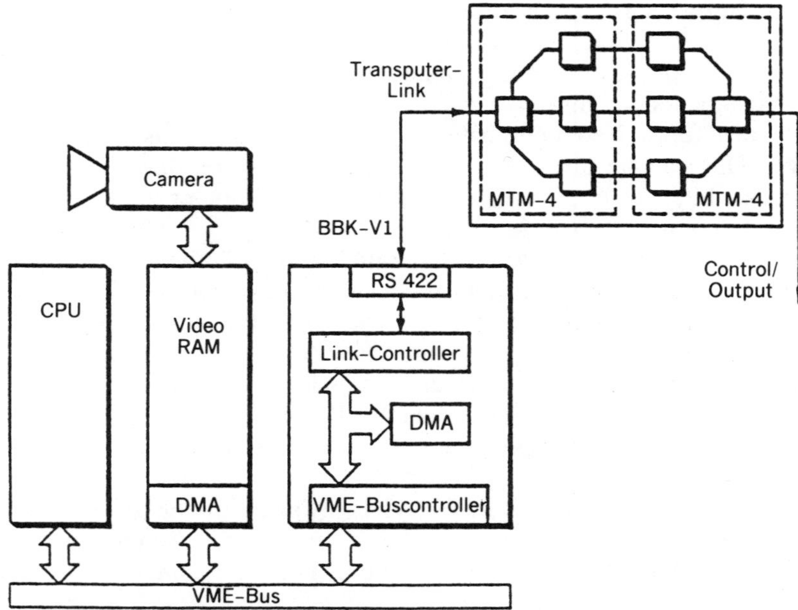

Figure 10.5 *A VMEbus based image processing system. (Courtesy and copyright © 1989 by Parsytec.)*

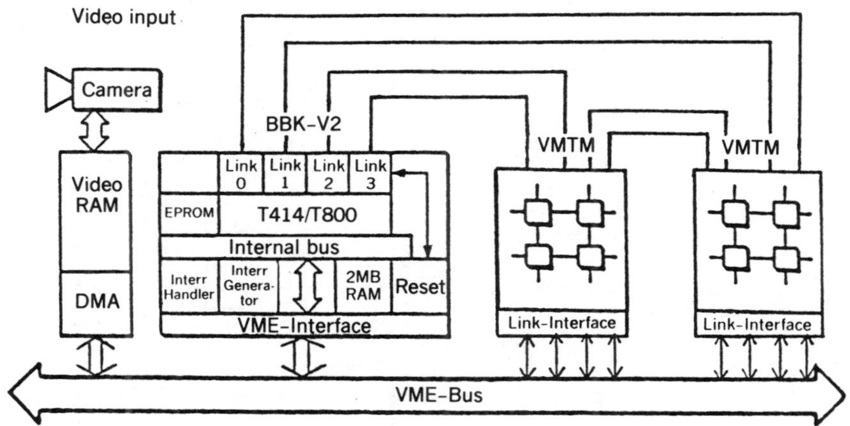

Figure 10.6 *VMTMs for image processing. (Courtesy and copyright © 1989 by Parsytec.)*

V2 as main VMEbus-processor having full access to all VMEbus peripherals and some VMTM modules as additional computing devices. Each VMTM has four transputers with 1 MByte local memory per processor node thus providing 40 Mips respectively 6 Mflops. The link connections can be switched under software control. The VMTM also provides unique multiuser transputer development facilities when connected to UNIX or OS-9 systems (Figure 10.7).

The program code of the whole distributed system may be loaded automatically out of the PC. If the system implementor wishes to be independent of mass storage devices it also may be loaded out of the 1 Mbyte EPROM area of the BBK-V2.

The example of Figure 10.8 also is aimed at demonstrating the power, flexibility and easiness of building complex overall systems even out of subsystems that normally are not to be combined like VME, IBM, and industrial busses like the SIEMENS SMP.

The highly integrated system of Figure 10.8 uses the communication concept of the MEGAFRAME systems family to easily integrate the overall system from subsystems, which are built up from different system standards choosing the optimal technique for each subsystem. Image data acquisition again is based on the VMEbus but this time from the beginning on it is implemented as a high performance subsystem with its own transputer. The T800 or T414 on the BBK-V2 module (Figure 10.9) is controlling the camera autonomously. There may be a separate image memory on the VMEbus or the image data are transferred directly via DMA into the VME memory of the module. Because of the multi master capabilities of the BBK-V2 there may also be more than one module on the bus enabling overlapped data

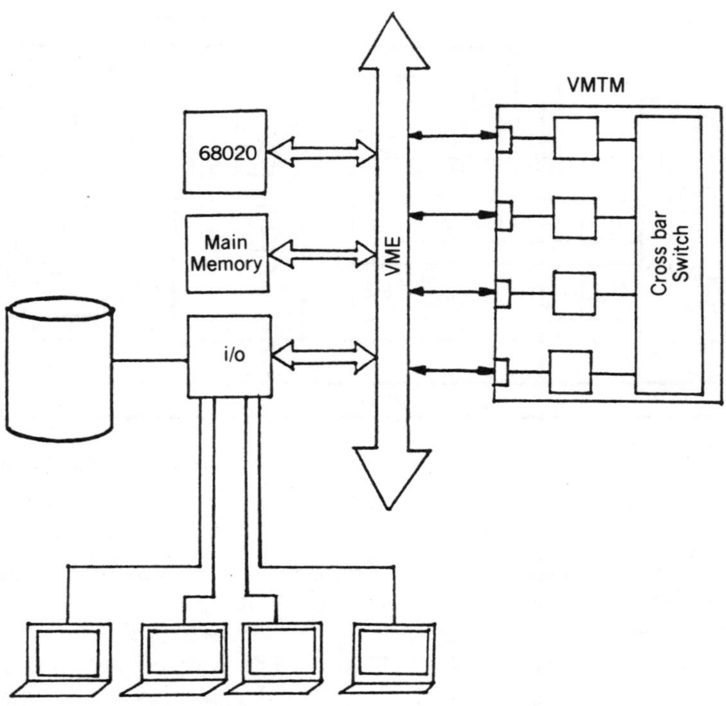

Figure 10.7 *UNIX based multiuser transputer development system (e.g., SUN-3). (Courtesy and copyright © 1989 by Parsytec.)*

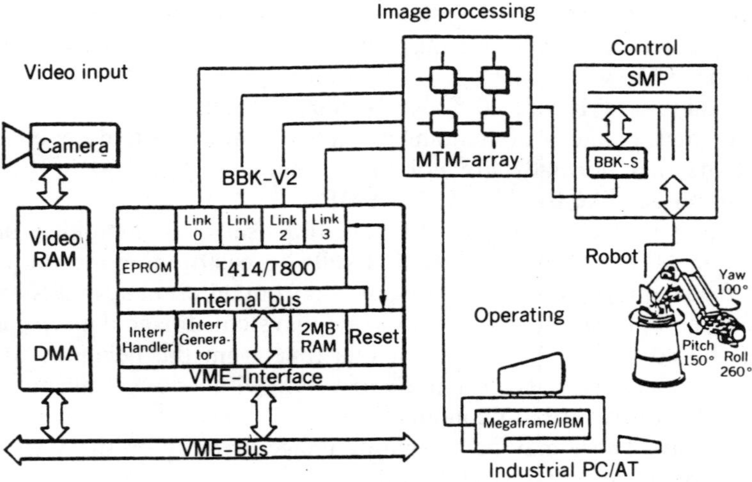

Figure 10.8 *Embedded system with transputers and VMEbus. (Courtesy and copyright © 1989 by Parsytec.)*

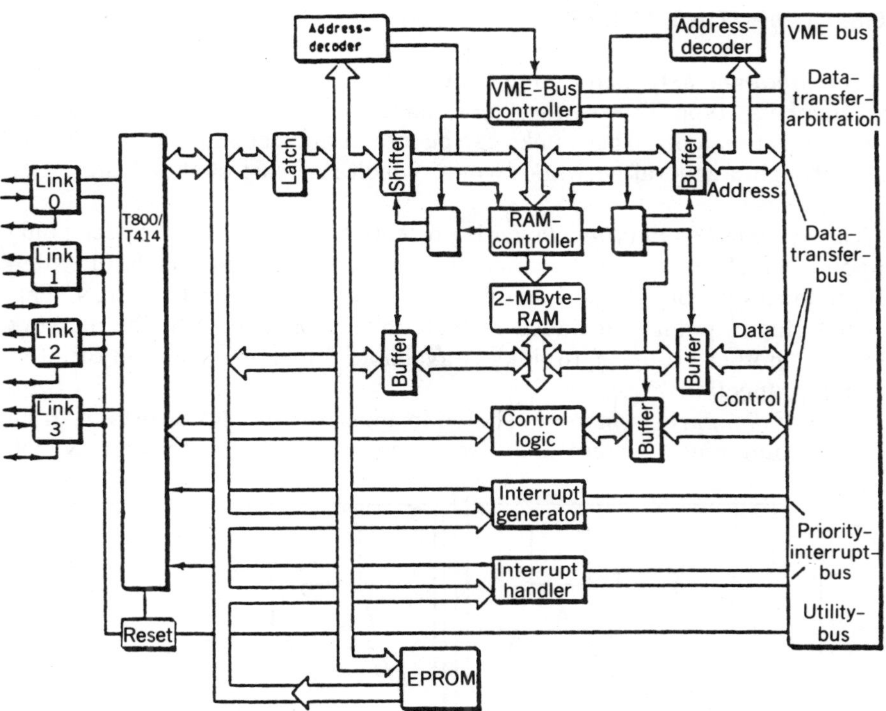

Figure 10.9 *BBK-V2 block diagram. (Courtesy and copyright © 1989 by Parsytec.)*

acquisition for extremely high performance requirements. 10 Mips or 1.5 Mflops for each module enable substantial preprocessing before feeding data via four links at 80 Mbit/s total to a processing network built up from TPM, MTM, or VMTM modules. Via another of those standard link cables one of the network modules may control a Siemens-type motion control system interfacing with a BBK-S bus bridge.

The full flexibility of the systems architecture may be visible looking at the number of options from which a system implementor can choose for operator control and user interface. One possibility is to implement it directly on the VMEbus or to build it up with the appropriate module of the MEGAFRAME systems family, (e.g., the GDS, graphics display system). With the same degree of easiness one also could use an industrial PC, which additionally may be used by the operator for further applications. The connection to the transputer system simply is done with the MEGAFRAME/IBM adapter module and a standard link cable. If necessary the PC may get substantial local transputer power by simply plugging a TPM or MTM module onto that adapter.

10.3. COMPUTING CLUSTER

The *computing cluster* is presented in Figure 10.10. It consists of 16 processing elements, type T800 with a local memory of 1 Mbyte and with four communication links. These links can be interconnected into various topologies through a general network switch, which is a part of the cluster, (see Figure 10.11).

The *extended computing cluster* is presented in Figure 10.12. Special plug in point in a cluster provides connection to a compression processor with 4 Mbyte local memory, or peripheral module for graphics, or to a LAN. This special plug-in point is included in the connection schema of the network switch. Another group of 16 links is available for implementation of inter-cluster connections.

A *quad computing cluster* is shown in Figure 10.13. It consists of three normal computing clusters and one extended computing cluster, which

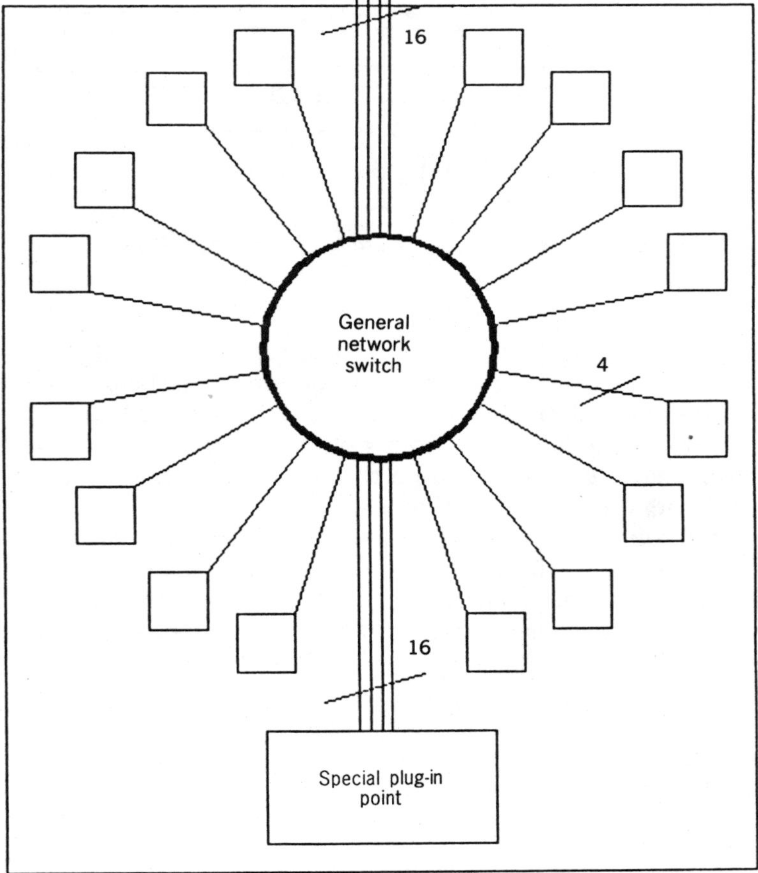

Figure 10.10 *Computing cluster. (Courtesy and copyright © 1989 by Parsytec.)*

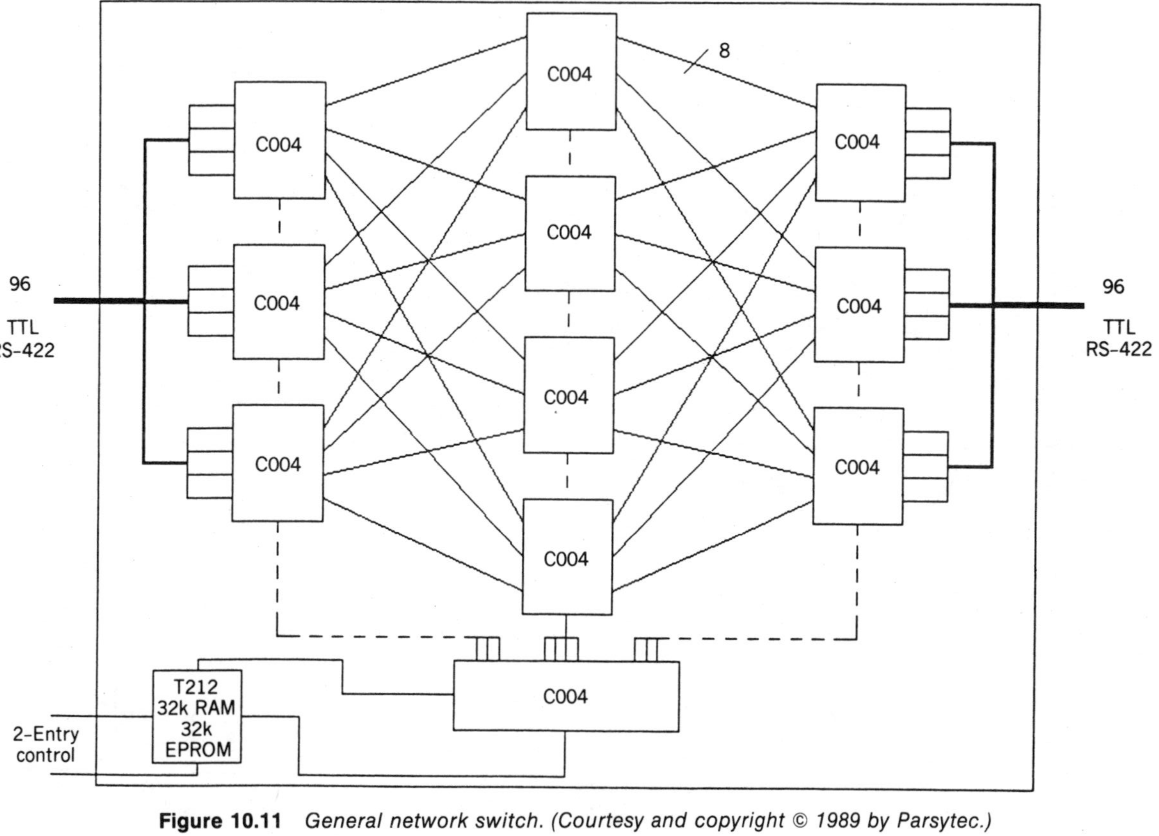

Figure 10.11 *General network switch. (Courtesy and copyright © 1989 by Parsytec.)*

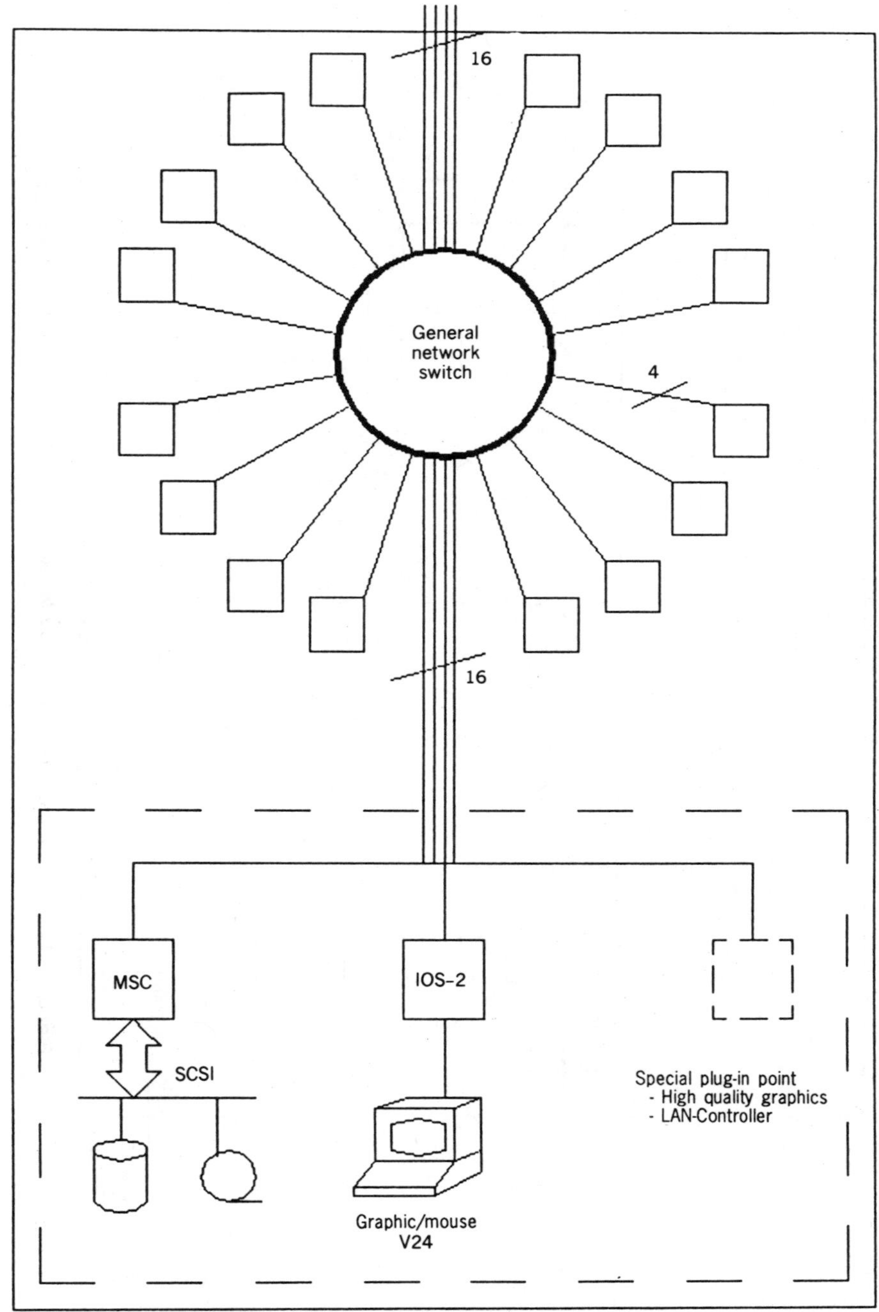

Figure 10.12 *Extended computing cluster. (Courtesy and copyright © 1989 by Parsytec.)*

Computing Cluster

Computing Cluster

32

16

16

General Network Switch

16

16

Computing Cluster

Extended Computing Cluster

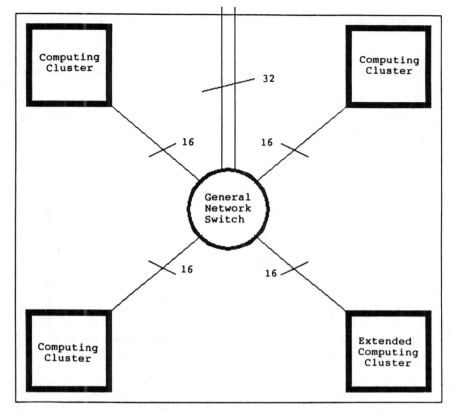

Figure 10.13 *Quad computing cluster. (Courtesy and copyright © 1989 by Parsytec.)*

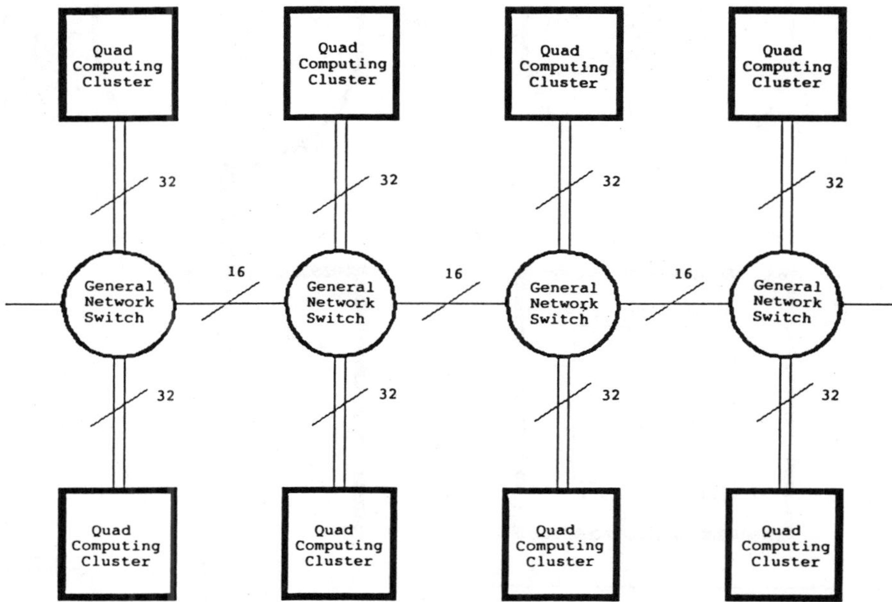

Figure 10.14 *Complex system. (Courtesy and copyright © 1989 by Parsytec.)*

serves as a host. A general network switch of 4 by 16 links connects the four clusters and also provides up to 32 links for connections with additional quad clusters.

Figure 10.14 shows a large system consisting of eight quad computing clusters. These are connected through four general network switches. Figure 10.15 shows an example of a 32 by 16 network. Figure 10.16 shows two binary tree structures composed of 255 and 511 processors, respectively.

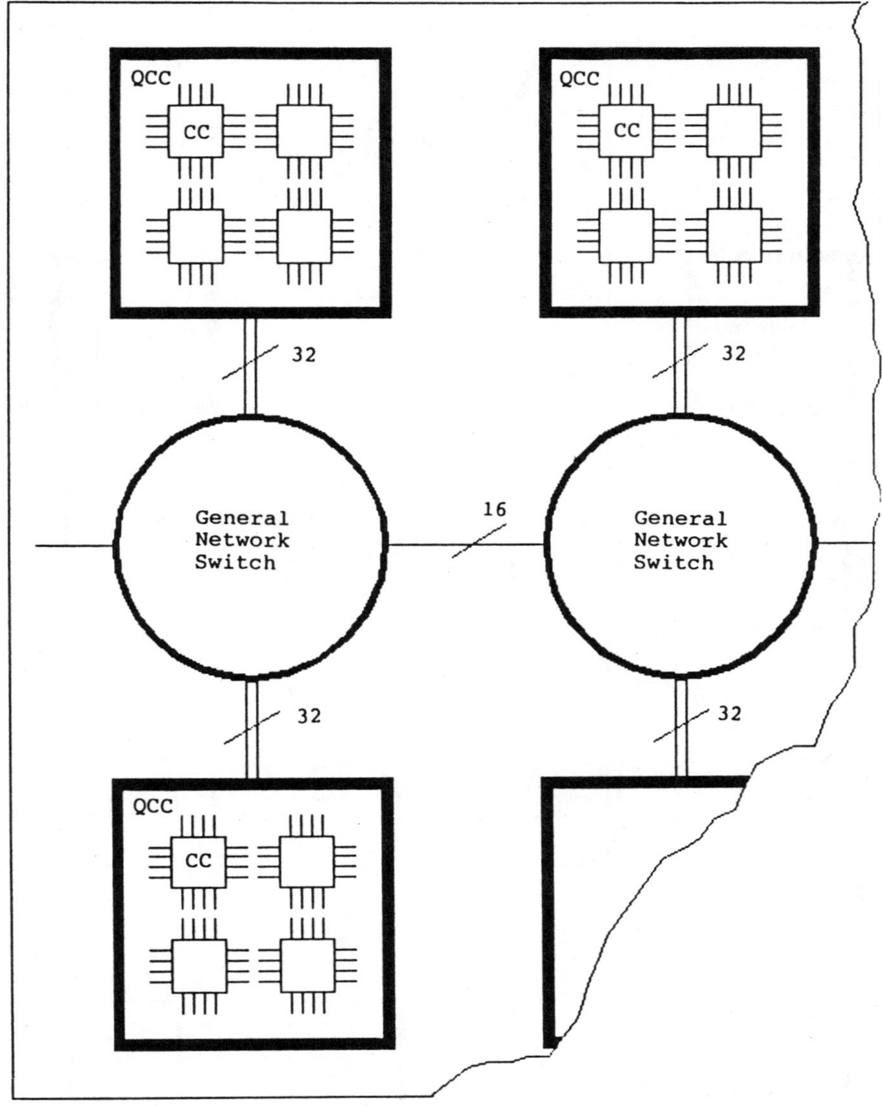

Figure 10.15 *Grid 32 by 16. (Courtesy and copyright © 1989 by Parsytec.)*

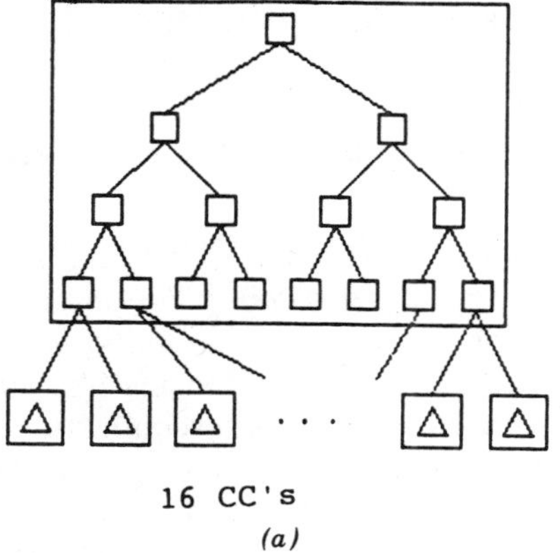

(a)

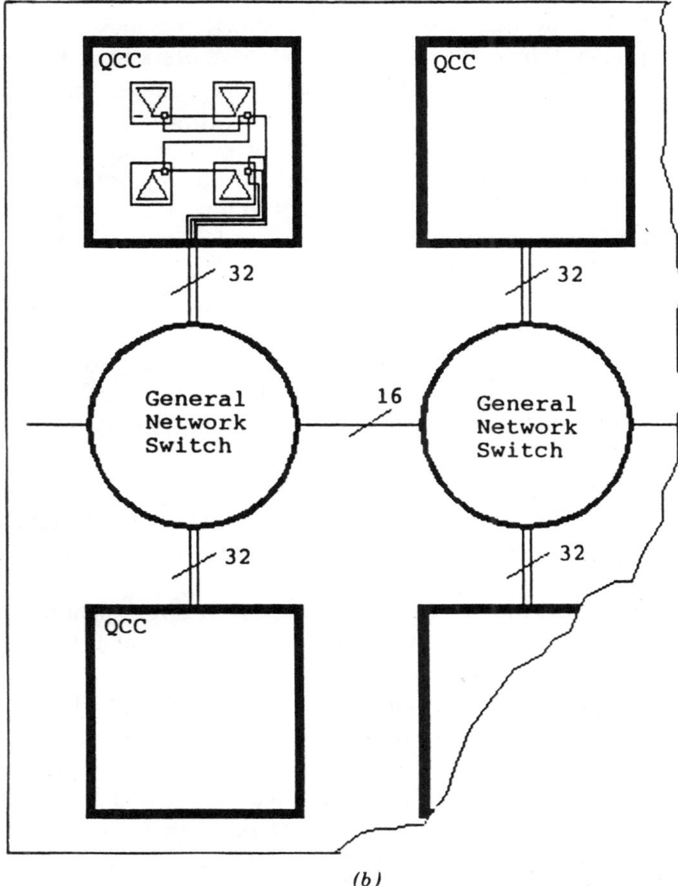

(b)

Figure 10.16 *Tree structures. (a) 255 processors, 8 levels, 128 processors in the base level. (b) 511 processors, 9 levels, 256 processors in the base level. (Courtesy and copyright © 1989 by Parsytec.)*

10.4. MÜHLENBEIN–KRÄMER–PEISE–RINN MEGAFRAME HYPERCLUSTER†

10.4.1. A Reconfigurable Architecture for Massively Parallel Computers

The MEGAFRAME hypercluster is a reconfigurable multiprocessor architecture based on the INMOS transputer family. The interconnection network consists of distributed network configuration units, each of which is a 96 × 96 switch. Many application specific topologies like ring, torus, hypertree and so on can be configured with this interconnection network. The power of the architecture is demonstrated with applications which have been implemented on a 64-processor system. They run with high efficiency in comparison to systems which use reconfiguration on the level of system software. Two implementations, parallel genetic algorithms for combinatorial optimization and neural networks are shortly discussed.

Many efforts on designing large parallel computers have been reported[4]. They are based on three different architecture configurations: a point-to-point topology such as the hypercube for the connection machine[5], multistage networks used in the BBN Butterfly processor,[6] and bus-based architectures[7] like the Cm* and SUPRENUM[8]. Multistage interconnection networks and bus-based architectures attempt to link all the nodes as a pseudocomplete graph and are viable for medium sized system with a few hundreds of nodes. The point-to-point topology is more favorable due to direct communication paths, expansion of the communication bandwidth with growing system size and simpler communication protocols.

The INMOS transputer is a building block for point-to-point networks. Each chip consists of a microprocessor with four bidirectional communication links. With the transputer element one can easily build network topologies where the connectivity of each node is at most four.

These network topologies are restricted to one specific class of applications. In general, different applications need different topologies. So systems are needed, where the topology is configurable by a crossbar like switch system.

Unfortunately the size of the switch system is direct proportional to the square of the communication links. This is not acceptable for big systems, (e.g., more than thousand nodes).

A compromise is a cluster-oriented architecture, which has a general connectivity within the cluster and is slightly restricted between clusters.

Several reconfigurable parallel architectures have been proposed. Most notable are the TRAC and CHiP. In TRAC, processors and memories are separate and connected by a banyan network.[9] In CHiP, the processing elements are connected to a programmable switch lattice.[10]

† Section 10.4 is based on Mühlebein, Krämer, Peise, and Rinn reports. (Courtesy and copyright © 1989 by Mühlenbein, Krämer, Peise and Rinn.)

We present a system called "hypercluster" which is based on the INMOS transputer chip and a network configuration unit (NCU) which consists of a 96 by 96 switch. Systems are constructed recursively. Sixty-four links of an NCU are connected to a lower level and 32 links go to higher levels in the hierarchy. The system has been successfully applied to a number of applications. A switched cluster of transputers has also been developed within the european supernode project.[11]

10.4.2 The Basic Elements Of The Architecture

The first three layers of the system are called cluster, supercluster and hypercluster.

The *cluster* consists of 16 transputers T800 (see Figure 10.17). Their 64 communication links are connected to the network communication unit (NCU) which contains a 96 by 96 switch. In addition to the 64 internal links, there are 32 external channels.

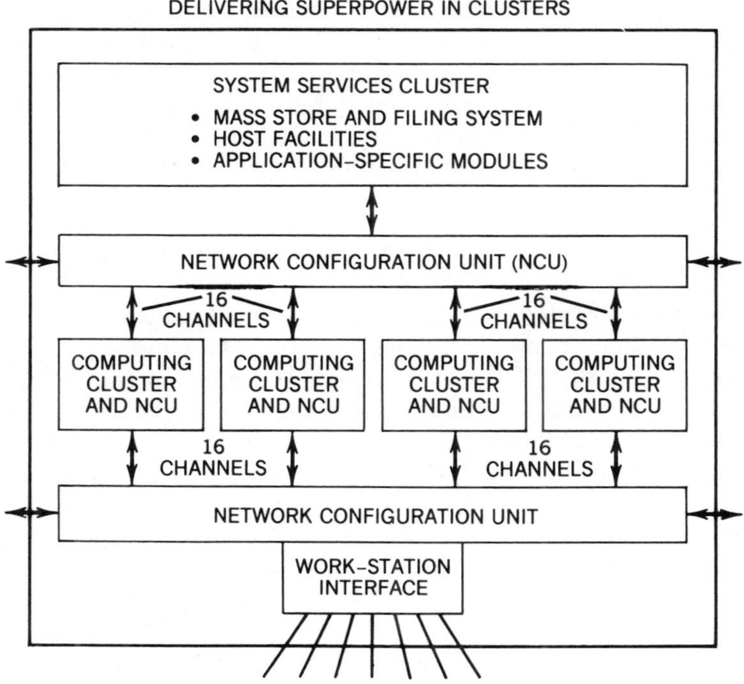

The Megaframe Supercluster groups 16 transputer-based processors in each of four clusters that are linked through a network-configuration unit.

Figure 10.17 *The MEGAFRAME supercluster system. (Courtesy and copyright © 1989 by Mühlenbein et al.)*

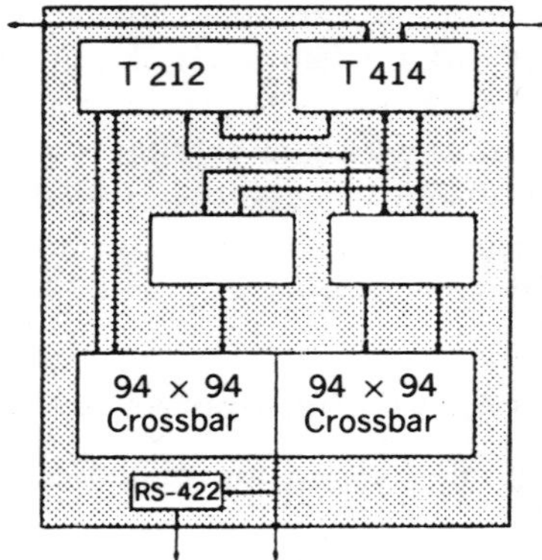

Figure 10.18 *Network configuration unit (NCU). (Courtesy and copyright © 1989 by Mühlenbein et al.)*

Four of these clusters are connected in a *supercluster* system, which has 64 external connections. (see Figure 10.17.) The supercluster contains system services like disks and interfaces to connect workstations. *Hyperclusters* are built out of superclusters and NCUs. Figure 10.18 shows two 96 by 96 crossbar switches. One is for communication and the other to switch the reset system according to the specified architecture. The peak performance of the supercluster system with 64 nodes and a hypercluster with 256 nodes is shown in Table 10.1. Both systems are available with the transputers T800 or T801.

10.4.3. Hypercluster Networks

The basic elements of the architecture—clusters and network configuration units—can be taken to construct larger systems. Many different topologies for interconnecting the NCUs are possible. The problem can be stated as follows: How to construct a connection topology in a simple way that almost any graph of degree of four or less can be switched?

Two different architectures are proposed.

TABLE 10.1: Peak Performance.

	Supercluster		Hypercluster	
	T800	T801	T800	T801
Main memory	256 Mbyte		1 Gbyte	
Instructions per second	640 MIPS	960 MIPS	2.56 GIPS	3.84 GIPS
Scalar flops	96 Mflops	144 Mflops	384 Mflops	575 Mflops
Communication bandwidth	230 Mbyte/s		920 Mbyte/s	

Hypercluster Network B. In network B bigger systems are constructed out of two subsystems. Each of them has 64 external connections, but an arbitrary number of internal nodes. The connection is done by two additional NCUs, such that the whole system has again 2 × 32 external links. This is shown in Figure 10.19, where squares are clusters and circles represent NCUs. Each connection is a bundle of 16 transputer links. In this network, there is a communication bottleneck between the two subsystems. They are arrays connected by 64 links.

The NCU is designed to provide a full permutation switch between 96 input and 96 output links. It is realized by using the INMOS C004, which is a programmable 32 by 32 switch.

A digital switch has been selected because it can easily be cascaded and it has a high signal quality. The drawback of course is that digital switches have a propagation delay.

The INMOS communications protocol requires acknowledge packets to be sent for the purpose of synchronization. The T800 links are capable of sending overlapped acknowledges and do not have to wait until the data packet has been received. One byte of data is transmitted in 11 bits, the acknowledge is 2 bits.

Measurements have shown that at a link speed of 20 Mbit/s data are transmitted at about 1.5 Mbyte/s in each direction. In using one NCU we got a speed of about 1.1 Mbyte/s and with three pipelined NCUs 0.7 Mbyte/s (data bytes).

In big systems the intercluster connections can bridge long distances. Noise immunity and high signal quality can be achieved by using buffer methods according to RS422 specifications. These differential driven lines can be used up to 30m at 10 Mbit/s or 10m at 20 Mbit/s.

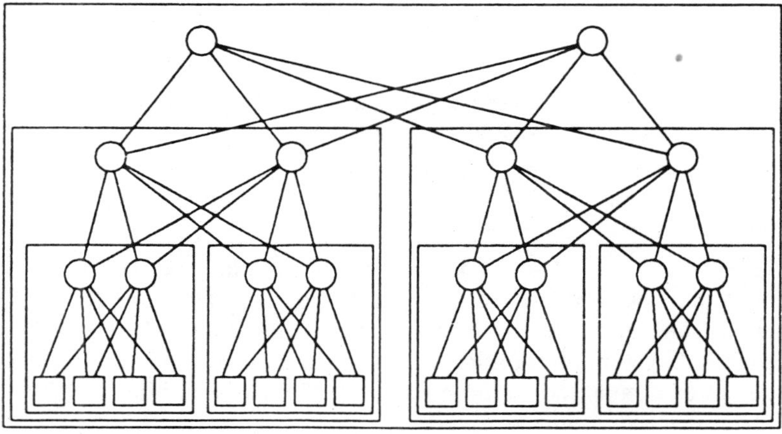

Figure 10.19 *Supercluster network B with 256 nodes. "B" stands for binary. (Courtesy and copyright © 1989 by Mühlenbein et al.)*

TABLE 10.2. Propagation Delays (worst case)

Unit	Delay
Gate	7 *ns*
Buffered output	10 *ns*
C004	100 *ns*
NCU	128 *ns*
3 NCUs	450 *ns*

Table 10.2 gives the propagation delays of the major components.

There are many methods to realize a larger crossbar switch out of smaller ones. The most general way is to use a matrix of C004 switches, which results in a pipeline of switches for each connection. This increases the propagation delay of all channels and reduces the communication bandwidth. For a 96 by 96 crossbar these would be a propagation delay of three C004 chips.

In point-to-point networks the switching of one to many processors (broadcast) is not necessary. If the crossbar is restricted to switching of permutations only, a simpler realization of the 96 by 96 crossbar is possible.

The hypercluster 96 by 96 switch is realized using 10 INMOS C004 chips. One switch is used to configure the other nine switches, which interconnect the 96 channels. They are combined in some combinatorial logic and work in parallel. Therefore the 96 by 96 switch has only one C004 propagation delay. The NCU of the hypercluster series consists of one processor node for control and for communication with other NCUs.

Hypercluster Network Q. In network Q four identical modules are taken to build the next larger system. The system is defined recursively by the following rules. The number of transputers is denoted by T, the number of NCUs on the highest level by N.

Basic System (Level 1). Basic system is the supercluster with $T_1 = 64$ transputers and $N_1 = 2$ NCUs on the highest level.

Level L. A level L hypercluster system is built of four systems of level $(L - 1)$. It has $T_L = 4\ T_{L-1}$ Transputers and has $N_L = 2\ N_{L-1}$ global NCUs.

NCU Connections. The NCUs of the subsystems are connected to the NCUs of the next higher level similar to a shuffle. The NCUs of each level L are numbered from 1 to N_L. Also the bundles of external links in each subsystem are numbered from 1 to $2\ N_{L-1} = N_L$. So each bundle becomes connected to the NCU with the same number.

Figure 10.20 shows a hypercluster system wit 256 nodes. The number of external links grows with a factor of two if the number of nodes increases by a factor of four.

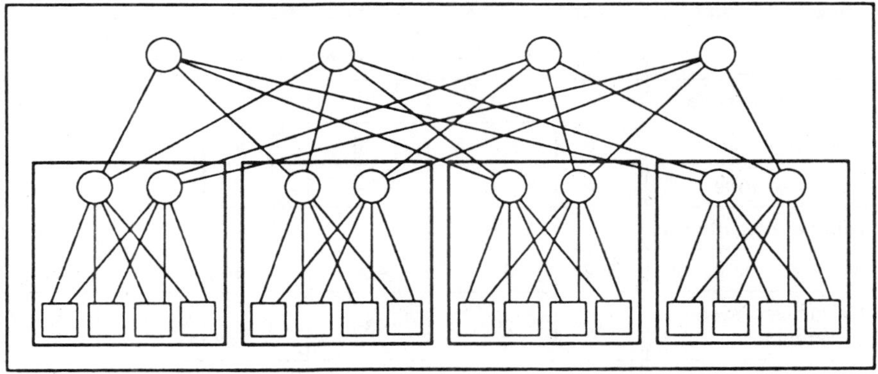

Figure 10.20 *Hypercluster network Q with 256 nodes. "Q" means quadruple. (Courtesy and copyright © 1989 by Mühlenbein et al.)*

Evaluation. Now we compare the hypercluster networks B and Q with other topologies. The Torus, Hypertree[12], Hypernet[13] and Banyan interconnection network have been selected because they have the property that the number of links for each node is restricted to four.

Table 10.3 compares the following features.

Max distance	maximal number of hops between a pair of nodes (diameter)
Average distance	average number of hops between a pair of nodes
Max ports per node	maximal number of port per node
Number of switches	total number of switching elements
Number of links	total number of links
Normalized average distance	average distance/max ports per node
Message density	number of nodes · average distance/number of links.

TABLE 10.3. Comparison of Different Networks with *n* Nodes

	Torus	Hypertree	Banyan	B	Q
Max distance	$\sqrt{n}$	$\frac{3}{2}$ ld $(n) - \varepsilon$	ld $(n) + 1$	2 ld $(n) - 8$	ld $(n) - 2$
Average distance	$\frac{1}{2}\sqrt{n}$	$\frac{5}{4}$ ld $(n) - \varepsilon$	ld $(n) + 1$	$O(\text{ld } n)$	$O(\text{ld } n)$
Max ports per node	4	4	2	4	4
Number of switches	—	—	$\frac{1}{2}n$ ld n	$\frac{1}{8}(n - 16)$	$\frac{1}{8}(n - 2\sqrt{n})$
Number of links	$2n$	$3n - \varepsilon$	$n(\text{ld } (n) + 1)$	$8(n - 16)$	$8(n - 2\sqrt{n})$
Normalized average distance	$2\sqrt{n}$	5 ld $(n) - \varepsilon$	2 ld $(n) + 2$	$O(\text{ld } n)$	$O(\text{ld } n)$
Message density	$\frac{1}{4}\sqrt{n}$	$\frac{5}{12}$ ld n	1	$O(\text{ld } n)$	$O(\text{ld } n)$

TABLE 10.4. Comparison of Different Networks with 256 Nodes

	Torus	Hypertree	Hypernet	Banyan	B	Q
Maximal distance	16	10	15	9	8	6
Average distance	8	7.4	9	9	6.4	5.4
Ports per node	4	4	4	2	4	4
Number of switches	—	—	—	1024	30	28
Number of links	512	381	460	2304	1920	1792
Normalized average distance	32	29.6	36	16	25.6	21.6
Message density	4	4.97	5	1	0.85	0.77

For systems consisting of 256 nodes this gives the values in Table 10.4. The maximal and average distance in the network Q grows logarithmic and is better than the banyan network, which is the best of all other systems. This is achieved with a linear amount of links and switches! The message density of both hypercluster networks is below 1; (i.e., when all nodes communicate with four randomly chosen partners, only 77 percent (85 percent) of the available links are used). This shows the redundancy in the communication network.

The hypercluster networks will now be analyzed in more detail.

Number of Paths. The number of (shortest) paths between a pair of transputers increases exponentially when the distance between the transputers grows (see Table 10.5). This is a result of the great flexibility in each NCU. One of 32 external links can be chosen to realize the connection to a higher level. This feature of the hypercluster networks is very important concerning fault tolerance.

Distance. The maximum distance for a pair of CPUs in the hypercluster network grows in $O(\text{ld}\ (n))$, where n is the number of transputers.

In network B the maximal distance increases by 2 when the size of the system is doubled, while in network Q only a four times bigger system enlarges this distance by 2. The maximum and average distances in both networks are shown in Figure 10.21.

TABLE 10.5. Number of Shortest Paths for the Hypercluster Networks

Distance d	2	4	6	8	d ($d \geq 4$)
B	16	8192	2^{23}	2^{33}	$\frac{1}{128}2^{5d}$
Q	16	8192	2^{22}	2^{31}	$\frac{1}{32}2^{9d/2}$

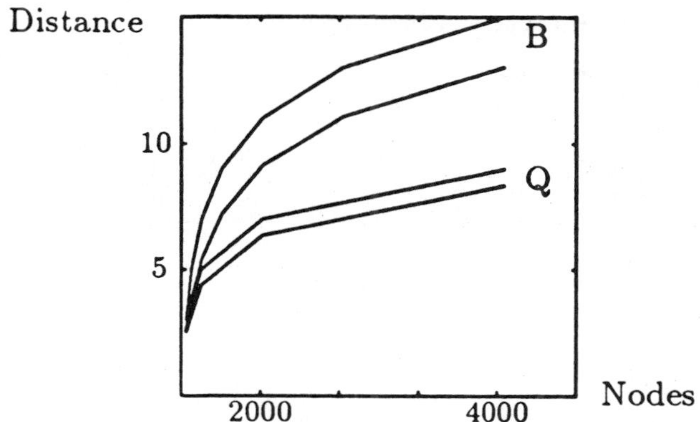

Figure 10.21 *Maximal and average distance in the hypercluster networks. (Courtesy and copyright © 1989 by Mühlenbein et al.)*

10.4.4. Configuration of Application Topologies

The task of the hypercluster network is to allow the configuration of different topologies for different applications. Consider the typical topologies ring, torus, and hypertree, and investigate whether these topologies can be switched.

Since connections which use more NCUs have a larger delay than connections using only one NCU, the object of the configuration is to minimize the average number of NCUs per link. Minimal possible distance between a pair of transputers is 2, the connection in a cluster by the cluster internal NCU.

A random chosen pair of nodes in the Hypercluster systems has an expected distance shown in column "random" of Tables 10.6 and 10.7. For an optimal imbedding of a ring, torus, and hypertree only short connections can be used. So the average distances in the so configured system is far less than this values and are near to 2, the minimal distance in the system. The values for the hypertree have only been computed for the supercluster.

TABLE 10.6. Average Distances and Throughput for Hypercluster B Configurations

	Average Distance				Average Throughput in Mbytes/s			
B	Random	Ring	Torus	Hypertree	Random	Ring	Torus	Hypertree
64	3.52	2.13	2.5	2.39	0.78	1.08	1	1.02
256	6.39	2.18	2.88	—	0.51	1.08	0.97	—
1024	10.13	2.18	3.13	—	0.31	1.08	0.96	—
4096	14.03	2.2	—	—	0.2	1.08	—	—

TABLE 10.7. Average Distances and Throughput for Hypercluster Q Configurations

Q	Average Distance				Average Throughput in Mbytes/s			
	Random	Ring	Torus	Hypertree	Random	Ring	Torus	Hypertree
64	3.52	2.13	2.5	2.39	0.78	1.08	1	1.02
256	5.39	2.16	2.75	—	0.56	1.08	0.98	—
1024	7.35	2.17	2.88	—	0.43	1.08	0.97	—
4096	9.34	2.17	2.94	—	0.32	1.08	0.97	—

In network B the number of available links between the two units is always 64. This implies that topologies where the minimal number of links between two parts exceeds 64 cannot be configured.

For example, a ring of length n has a minimal cut of 2, so that the network B can always be configured to a ring. The minimal cut of a $l \times l$ torus contains $2l$ channels. This implies that a hypercluster B network with more than 1024 transputers cannot be configured to a torus.

The hypercluster network can easily configure a torus. Almost any graph of degree at most four can be configured with the hypercluster network Q.

10.4.5. Hardware Model

The structure of the hypercluster system can be described by the following mathematical model.

T	Set of transputers	
N	Set of NCUs	
$\mathcal{T}$	Transputer incidence function	$\mathcal{T}: T \rightarrow N$
$\mathcal{N}$	NCU incidence function	$\mathcal{N}: N \rightarrow N$

The fixed parameters of the configuration are: 16 Transputers with 64 links are connected to one NCU. Each NCU has 96 links, 2 by 16 are used for the connectivity with higher levels.

Now we can describe the class of process graphs which can be realized by the hypercluster system. Necessary conditions are the following:

Condition 1 Number of Nodes. The number of nodes is less or equal to the number of transputers.

Condition 2 Node Degree. The node degree is less or equal to 4.

Condition 3 Clustering. The graph must be partitionable into $|T|/16$ parts, each with no more than 16 nodes. The number of edges leaving each part must not exceed 32.

10.4.6. Configuration Schemes

The system can be configured

- Explicit by the programmer,
- By using a library of topologies (ring, torus, tree, . . .),
- Automatic.

The explicit configuration is done in the following way. In order to switch a permutation the NCU needs the adjacency list of the permutation as input. Out of this information it then creates configuration messages for the C004s. The following scheme defines a pipeline (Figure 10.22).

All NCUs are connected by their control processor in a pipe. The configuration of a supercluster is done by a network configuration manager (NCM), which resides in the first NCU. It takes as input the global adjacency list, divides it into six parts and sends the remaining five parts to the other NCUs of the supercluster.

Standard topologies, also for bigger hypercluster systems are switched by library functions in the above manner.

The automatic configuration facility of a supercluster takes as input the user program, where the process graph of the application is defined. Processes are grouped together in separately compiled units (SC). This information is extracted from the program and a one-to-one mapping of a SC to a physical processor is done. The mapping tries to minimize the intercluster connections. Therefor the mapping problem is equal to the graph partitioning problem. Several new algorithms which are based on genetic algorithms have been developed.

For the hypercluster network a more general tool is in development. It works in two steps:

Step 1 Process Placement. The placement of the processes onto the transputers is done by a top-down approach. The whole graph is partitioned into the number of subsystems (i.e. two for network B and four for Q). This problem, known as the "graph partitioning problem" is solved by a heuristic which minimizes the number of channels between the parts. Each subgraph

```
SEQ i = 0 FOR 96                 _ Each switch position
  adlist [i] := (-1)             _ Gets an initial value

SEQ i = 0 FOR 14                 _ Each transputers
  adlist [(i*4)+2] :=              link number 2
  ((i+1)*4)                      _ Is connected to
                                   neighbor link 0
```

Figure 10.22 *Configuration of a 16-stage pipeline. (Courtesy and copyright © 1989 by Mühlenbein et al.)*

gets assigned to an own subsystem. This procedure is repeated recursively for each part, until the level of clusters is reached. In each clusters the assignment of processes to processors is done arbitrary. In each partitioning step the number of channels leaving a part is computed. Whenever this number exceeds the number of available links of the according subsystem the algorithm tries to find a better partitioning. When no feasable solution can be found, the algorithm stops without success. In this case the configuration must either be done by hand, or a one-to-one mapping is impossible. For this case a runtime system which supports multiplexing and routing is needed.

Step 2 Switch Setting. The switch setting is done straightforward because the process placement done in the previous step ensures that the number of links is sufficient to realize all channels between different transputers. For each channel a shortest path between the partners is switched.

10.4.7. Fault Tolerance

We distinguish between two kinds of fault tolerance. In the first kind we try to reconfigure a system topology invariant. Figures 10.23 and 10.24 show how a ring is reconfigured after a CPU fault and a link fault. The reconfigured network is still a ring.

The second kind of fault tolerance can be defined as the connectivity of the interconnection network. A fault in a network communication unit of a cluster cannot be handled since all connections are realized exclusively by this NCU. NCU faults in higher levels can be handled, since the communication system provides alternative routes.

The number of links which can be damaged such that the system remains connected are

- Three of 4 links to a transputer
- Fifteen of 16 links of each bundle.

This shows that the network structure of the hypercluster is very robust against link failures since only 75 percent to 94 percent of the links are sufficient to keep the system running.

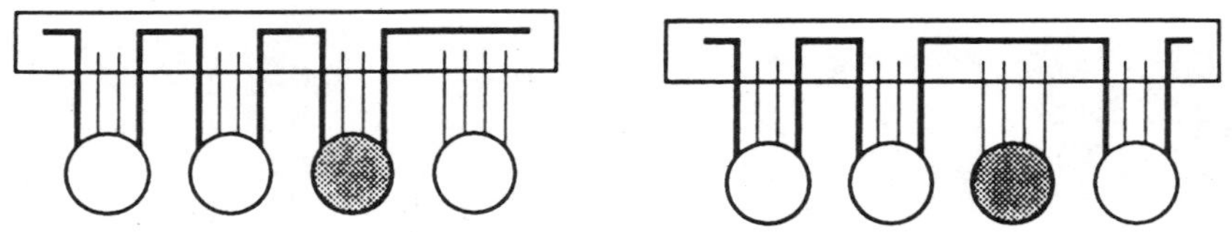

Figure 10.23 *Reset network at CPU-fault. (Courtesy and copyright © 1989 by Mühlenbein et al.)*

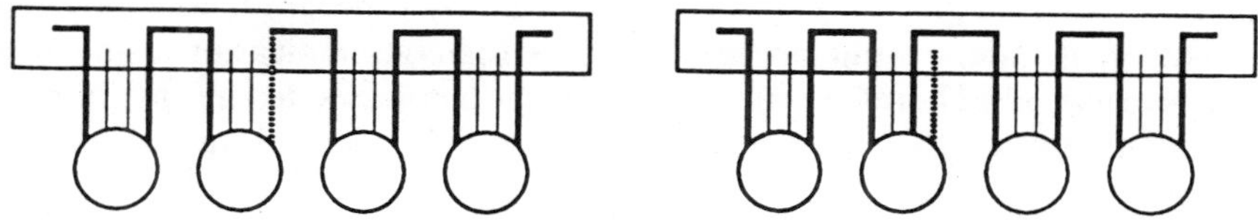

Figure 10.24 *Reset network at link-fault. (Courtesy and copyright © 1989 by Mühlenbein et al.)*

10.4.8. Hardware versus Software Reconfiguration

The hardware reconfiguration of the hypercluster has to be traded-off against the more general software reconfiguration. The transputer processor family supports low level operating system functions like process scheduling and communication in hardware. Therefore, applications whose process graph can be mapped on to the hypercluster do not need any operating system support. Process graphs that cannot be mapped need a runtime system with multiplexing, buffering, and routing facilities.

More general operating systems for the transputer family are also available, like Helios which provides the illusion to the application programmer, that each process can be connected to each other process, regardless on which processor they are placed.[14]

The greater flexibility on the application layer is accompanied by less flexibility on the hardware interconnection topology and a loss in efficiency. The operating systems assume a fixed topology and can not take advantage of the configuration facility of the hypercluster.

The efficiency is shown in the following Table, where the end-to-end delay for one byte for a point-to-point connection is shown:

Implementation	Time
firmware	12 μs
runtime system	90 μs
Helios	500 μs

The power of the hypercluster system therefore shows up with applications which can be mapped onto the architecture.

We are now studying how the reconfiguration facility of the hypercluster can be used by the Helios operating system. The idea is that different users get different partitions of the hypercluster which will be configured application dependent.

10.4.9. Applications

So far our applications are based on *natural parallelism*. This paradigm sees the applications as a community of entities which communicate with each other. This paradigm can easily be supported by a programming paradigm consisting of independent processes, ports for communications, and message passing.[15,16] Therefore in many applications a one-to-one mapping of the application to the implementation is possible. So far we have implemented

- Distributed discrete event simulation,[17]
- Parallel genetic algorithms,[18]
- Neural networks,[19] and
- Immune system simulations.

The parallel implementation leads often to new algorithms which is demonstrated by neural network implementations and our parallel genetic algorithm for combinatorial optimization. The basic parallel genetic algorithm works as follows:

Step 1: Give the problem to n processes.
Step 2: Each process computes a local solution.
Step 3: Each process selects partners in the neighborhood for mating.
Step 4: An offspring is created using genetic operators mutation and recombination.
Step 5: Continue with step 2.

The main difference of this parallel genetic algorithm to sequential genetic algorithms are:

- Partners mate not randomly, but only in a neighborhood.
- Partners mate asynchronously; there are no generation steps.

In the hypercluster we often used the neighborhood in Figure 10.25.

The results of this algorithm are more than encouraging. On a 64 processor supercluster we have computed the best solution found by a heuristic for one of the biggest traveling salesman problems with 532 cities[20]. Moreover, often the parallel genetic algorithm has a superlinear speedup: 64 processes get the same quality of the solution as the 16 processes in less than a fourth

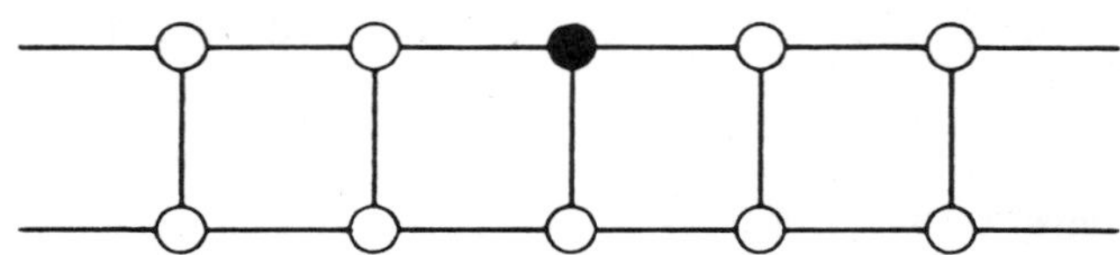

Figure 10.25 *Neighborhood for a parallel genetic algorithm. (Courtesy and copyright © 1989 by Mühlenbein et al.)*

of the time. The parallel genetic algorithm has been applied with equal success to a number of combinatorial optimization problems, like the quadratic assignment problem and the graph partitioning problem.[18,21]

Neural networks have been implemented on the hypercluster with two different approaches. In the first approach the implementation is tailored to a specific kind of network (e.g., Hopfield or back-propagation). The second approach supports general user defined networks. A neural network executive has been implemented which can deal with neural networks specified by a general network language. This language is based on the Rochester connectionist simulator.[22] The implementation uses a torus like interconnection.[23]

10.5. OPERATING SYSTEM KERNEL ON THE CHIP

The transputer does not need an operating system, at least not in typical real-time and control applications. As already indicated, everything that is handled conventionally by a real-time multitasking operating system kernel, (i.e., the management of all computational resources, like scheduling of tasks, communication, etc. with the transputer) is done completely and much more efficiently than by software by built-in on-chip hardware and microcode. Communication, loading, and starting of processes when using the conventional sequential languages are included in easy-to-use library routines, with parallel languages implicitly contained in dedicated statements and the configuration software.

Apart from the structural flexibility of the hardware, there is a further characteristic of the transputer, that enables the programmer to choose implementation strategies not feasible on conventional processors, thus having a significant impact on application design. This characteristic is support for virtual parallelism even when using only a single physical transputer. Whereas, standard processors use run-time management of the computational resources (i.e., scheduling and communication is done by a multitasking operating system kernel in software), in transputer, this is done completely in hardware and microcode. So the effective process switch time, (e.g., with a 68020 running under PSOS is approximately 50 microseconds) is reduced by nearly two orders of magnitude: it is a mere 800 nanoseconds.

10.6. HELIOS OPERATING SYSTEM

Apart from its success in real-time and control applications the transputer has been used increasingly for scientific computing, number-crunching, and other kinds of general-purpose data processing. In these areas an operating system gets other responsibilities because it has to insert an additional software layer between the application and physical computer system, in order to shield the properties of the hardware from the programmer and allow the same program to run on different types of hardware. So for these types of applications, the operating system question had to be answered a second time.

The Helios operating system, although having just entered the marketplace in 1987, has become a de facto standard in the transputer world. This is evident by the fact that both Commodore and Atari are using it as the standard operating system for their transputer-based workstations due out in 1989.

The main reasons for this degree of acceptance can be seen in its concept. Helios is a truly distributed operating system fully based on the transputer's superior message passing concept of parallelism; supports Unix-based portability; is hardware-independent by using the client-server concept; achieves basic fault tolerance on system level; and provides load balancing and automatically scales itself to the system size. Helios[14] is a new operating system designed specifically for the next generation of parallel processing computers. It provides:

- Multitasking system sympathetic to transputer architecture,
- Support for multiple processors,
- Interprocessor communication via messages down links,
- Support for parallel programming,
- A true-distributed operating system,
- A multiuser system which includes a capability-based protection scheme,
- All codes automatically shared,
- Familiarity to Unix users,
- Fault tolerance,
- Graphics support under X-windows V11, and
- Language support including C, Fortran and OCCAM.

Helios blends the power of a network of INMOS transputers with the familiar feel of single processor operating systems such as Unix. It provides a multitasking environment for multiple users, spread over many different processors.

Unlike existing operating systems, programs running under Helios may make use of parallel programming techniques to distribute their processing load over different processors. This can lead to dramatic improvements in performance. Helios passes information between processes using messages; these processes may be in different processors but this is transparent to the calling program.

Helios is designed for many different applications. The multiuser design ensures that it is suitable for large supercomputers, while the transparent inter-processor message passing scheme ensures that it is also suitable for a distributed workstation environment. The message passing allows for failures in the communication medium after which Helios automatically tries to find an alternative route for the message to reach its destination. This fault tolerant behaviour is essential in process control applications.

Helios is an operating system designed to be sympathetic to the architecture of the transputer whilst remaining familiar to users of Unix. The transputer provides in hardware many of the items often implemented in existing systems software such as process creation, process switching, timeslicing, and interprocess message passing. Helios uses these primitives as the basic building blocks for an operating system that is designed to run on multiple processors. It is also a true distributed operating system; there are no central services upon which the whole system relies. This results in increased system reliability since the failure of any processor, or the partitioning of the network, will not cause unrelated parts of the system to fail (although they may continue at a somewhat reduced capacity). The distributed nature of Helios is transparent both to the user at his terminal and to programs running within the system which need never be aware of the exact location of any services. This feature differenentiates Helios from a network operating system where the distributed nature is more explicit.

Helios is intended to be an open system architecture where parts may be added, removed, modified or replaced transparently to suit specific purposes. In many ways Helios is simply a set of conventions, or codes of practice, for the behavior of programs. It may be thought of as a "software backplane," providing an infrastructure for processes to locate and communicate with each other. Helios presents a low level interface that will be familiar to programmers who have worked on Unix. Each user runs a number of tasks, which can communicate between themselves using a simple message passing protocol. A message may be transferred between two tasks in the same machine or between tasks in different processors; in each case the call is identical and the message is copied rather than passed by reference.

The design of Helios is based on the client–server model, where application tasks request services from system provided server tasks. These server tasks may be present in any or all of the processors available, although each processor must run the bare minimum of the name server, which identifies the location of other services. Other servers include file handlers, window managers, date servers, spoolers, and so on. All servers respond to a general server protocol which is designed so that servers may be stateless and hence unaffected by crashes and communication losses. This mechanism allows a wide choice in the way in which servers are implemented: for example, floppy disks are written using the MS-DOS format whereas Winchester disks use a format similar to Unix. A sophisticated protection scheme is implemented using capabilities. This is used to protect processors from unauthorized use (each processor is allocated to a single user) and to control access to the filing system.

According to Kübler and Cochran[1,2,24] the Helios can run on a single processor, a processor network with a transputer-based host, a standard workstation-based host, or on the combined networks of many individual users. A typical structure of the latter is shown in Figure 10.26. Each individual processor runs a Helios-kernel to provide system services. Helios is a truly distributed operating system in the sense that an application, transparent to the programmer can run distributed on to multiple nodes of the combined network, and resources available somewhere in the network automatically are made available to the whole network without the application having to know where it is. Resources, for example may be system-supplied, file servers or graphic servers, but also can be user-supplied services or just computing nodes.

Helios is independent of the transputer, and ports to other processors are currently under way, but the transputer's specific on-chip hardware support for virtual parallelism and communication is fully exploited with the Helios's concept of communicating via message ports and support of threads/tasks. So the transputer's effective process switch time of just 800 nanoseconds allows virtually no overhead even for extensive implicit or explicit system or user multitasking. In a similar way the communication within the processor network becomes extraordinarily efficient.

According to Kübler and Cochran[1,2,24] Helios ports most of the Unix standards to message-passing oriented parallel processing familiar user interfaces like the C-shell and to program interfaces for which a Posix-compatible library is supplied. Thus the porting of existing applications becomes easy and straightforward. Implementations of X-Windows V11 and a BSD 4.3 compatible filing system for parallel processing make the transputer's outstanding expandable performance available for demanding applications. With portability, Helios even goes beyond what was possible with conventional Unix: Unix never gave more than source-code portability, providing that a port was tried within the same "dialect" of Unix. The best pieces of software usually are created by people, who afterward want to get their investment back from the market. So for most packages source-code portability does not help because it is available only as object. Helios addresses this by giving the transputer world a full object-code portability. This encourages third-party software developers to offer standard application packages, which have been developed on one brand of hardware so they can be sold for all transputer-based machines, provided they fulfill some very basic requirements. This characteristic of Helios may be one of the main reasons for its fast-growing acceptance as a de facto standard.

Both portability and message passing are best reflected by the Helios's consequent usage of the client-server concept. Having already been accepted in the community as an adequate vehicle for software engineering

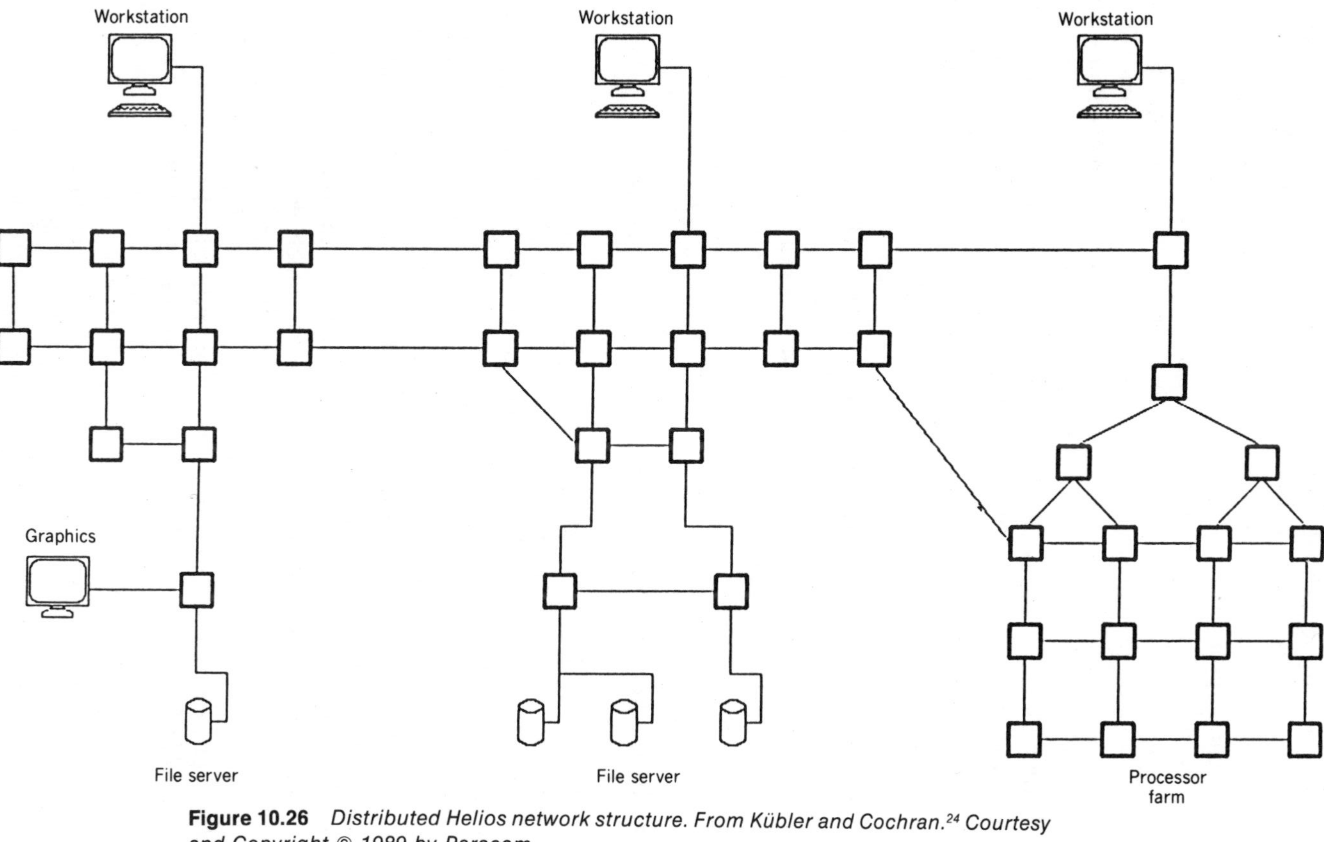

Figure 10.26 *Distributed Helios network structure. From Kübler and Cochran.*[24] *Courtesy and Copyright © 1989 by Paracom.*

even on standard sequential systems (e.g., with X-Windows), the client-server concept with the message-passing facilities of transputer networks makes it possible to hide the physical properties of a given system to the user and application programs, as illustrated in Figure 10.27. A client process can access a system- or user-supplied service, like the file server in the example, without knowing where it is located within the network. At the first access a "locate" is done, by which a transparent to the application via each Helios nucleus in the network the server is searched, and then a permanent physical communication path is established. This path uses the transputer link as a basic communication backbone. An application is not affected if a different user system has a totally different hardware structure. The application doesn't even need to know whether the used-service is running on a transputer node at all. In the example, it may have been implicitly assumed that the file server in order to match with the application processors performance runs on a transputer (e.g., Paracom's MSC module); even this is hidden to the application. It could also be running on a host's I/O system, for example a SUN running Unix or a PC/AT running DOS, connected to the transputer network via a bus bridge. The overall network even can contain all three different systems at the same time, making them all available in a uniform way to the application.

10.7. PROBLEM-ADAPTED TRANSPUTER STRUCTURE

According to Kübler and Cochran,[1,2,24] it is the simplicity and cost efficiency of communication which allows the system designer with its implementation structure to flexibly follow the original problem structure. (Not the other way around as is often necessary with more conventional data processing systems!) Sometimes engineers are surprised to see how easily they can build systems of any structure and size just by plugging together computing and I/O-nodes as building blocks, and that this works in reality and is not just an euphemistic allegory. As Paracom's Megaframe series of industrial transputer boards and systems contain an implementation of the link channels (the Megalink interconnection standard), which without any further provision allow the distance between processors to be up to 30 feet (selectively setting down the link speed by 50% allows 100 feet), the structures problem can even be distributed as illustrated in Figure 10.28. Here, different transputer nodes are distributed according to a problem structure into different system units (e.g., some parts of the system acting as a background computing- and data-server for analysis, some acting as a central system supervisor with graphical user interfaces, and some acting as frontend I/O-controllers).

The system designer is not forced to use the same type of node for all different tasks; but choosing from a palette of roughly 30 different modules, he can allocate to each function within the system to choose the optimally suited module for processing or special purpose I/O. He can even continue

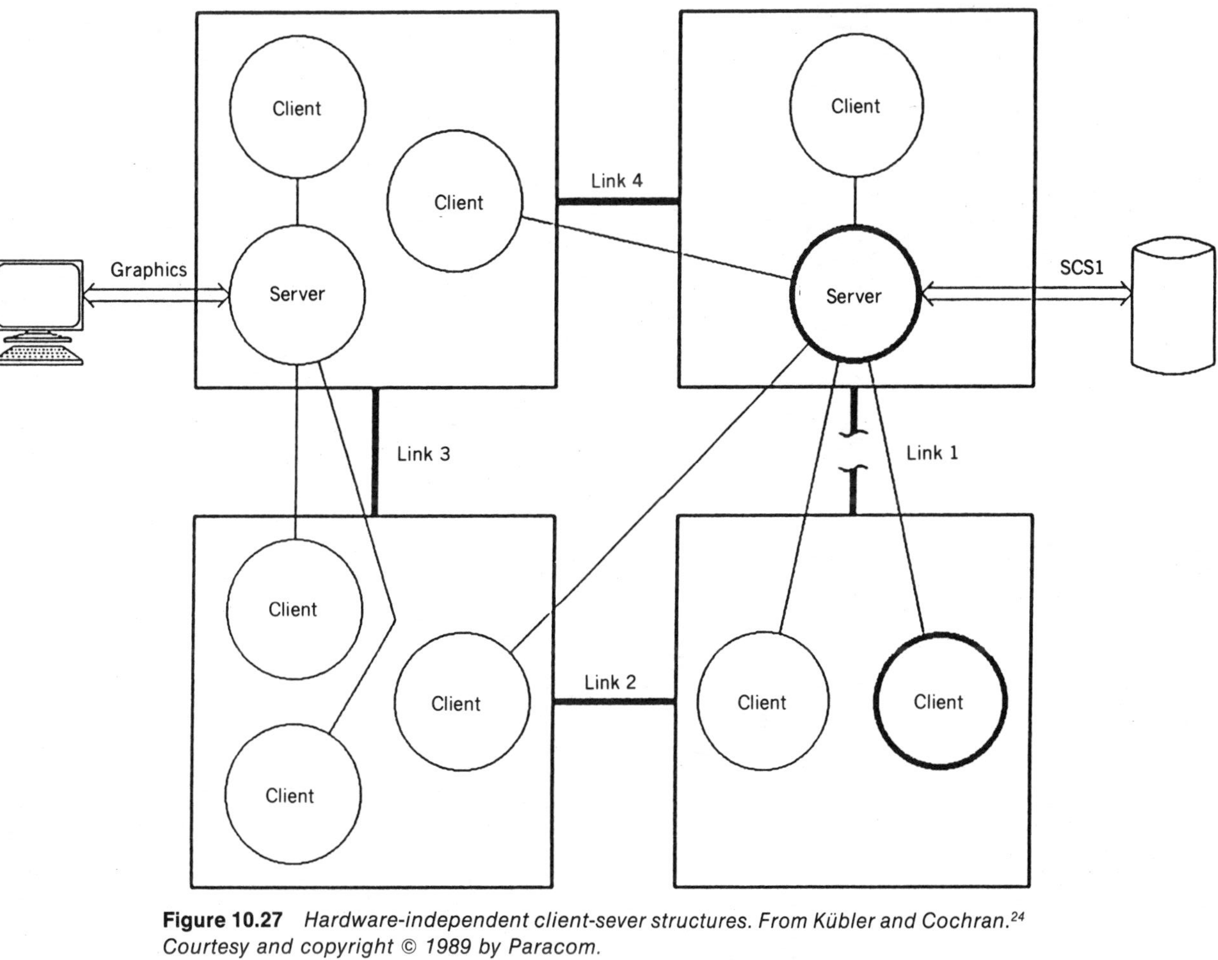

Figure 10.27 *Hardware-independent client-sever structures. From Kübler and Cochran.[24] Courtesy and copyright © 1989 by Paracom.*

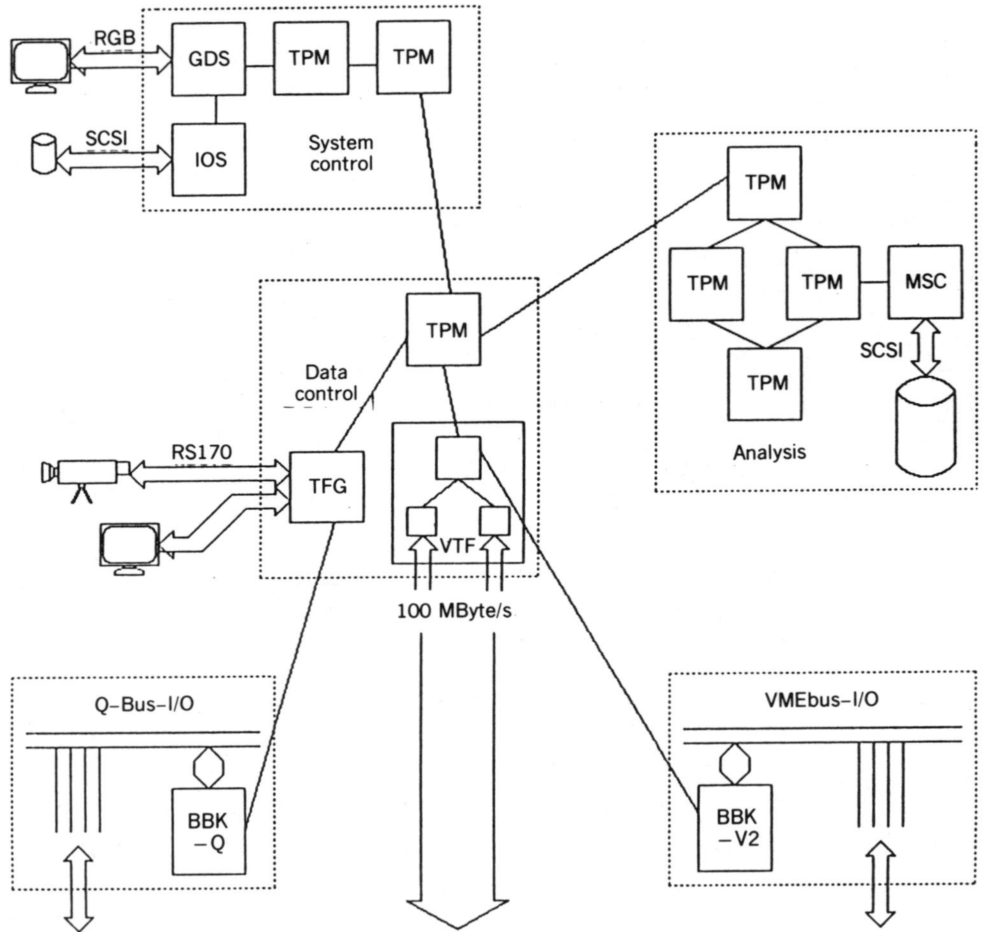

Figure 10.28 *Problem-adapted transputer structure. From Kübler and Cochran[24] Courtesy and copyright © 1989 by Paracom.*

to use standard bus-based peripheral interfaces, I/O subsystems, or host systems. They all can be flexibly integrated into the application by means of unique bus bridges available for all major standard bus structures like VME, PC/AT, PS/2, Q-Bus, SUN, Multibus, and others.

10.8. EASY AND EFFICIENT SCALABILITY

Cochran[25] discusses the issue of scalability from the VMEbus level to a fully distributed structure in the following way.

The examples take an image processing application which might have been developed initially without having the transputer in mind. As shown in

Figure 10.29, it consists of a WME bus system with a conventional processor and some standard VME bus peripherals including a frame grabber. Typically the CPU controls the I/O done by the frame grabber, does the image analysis after the frame is read, and then does further system control using additional peripherals (e.g., a motion control system). This whole application may have been developed and working satisfactorily for some time.

Taking into account ever increasing application demands, after some time a new image recognition algorithm may require more computational power than can be delivered, even by using a faster-clocked CPU. Under normal conditions this would impose a difficult situation for the engineer because a major redesign of his application would need to be done, most probably implying redoing most of the development.

Not so, using transputers! One of the main purposes of Paracom's line of transputer support modules for standard bus systems is to help the developer keep as much of already existing hardware and software as possible. So the designer keeps the VMEbus-CPU initially choosen. He also keeps all the peripherals and other environments of the initial development. Even a substantial part of the application software can be kept, for example, the whole user interface that has been programmed, the I/O programming of the frame grabber and, the overall system control of the other peripherals. What changes in this example is that now the computationally intensive part of the image analysis is given to a parallel processing transputer array. The standard CPU, after having acquired an image from the frame grabber splits the whole image into eight subimages and sends these to eight transputer processors residing additionally on the VMEbus as shown in Figure 10.29. The transputers work in parallel to the image analysis while the conventional CPU may continue to do some further system housekeeping. After that, it gets the eight subimages back and continues with the preexisting part of the application.

Each VMTM module in the example contains four T800 transputer processors each having 1 Mbyte of local memory. The 16 communication channels inside a VMTM are built by transputer links running at 20 Mbit/sec and are configured to the best-suited connection structure by on-board configuration hardware under software control. Four of those transputer links can be switched to the VMEbus. The conventional CPU can read/write to/from these links via I/O mapped registers in a fashion fairly similar to serial ports, but three orders of magnitude faster! The application software running within this slave network is loaded into the transputer under control of the VMEbus CPU via the same links using presupplied library calls. It may have been developed in standard languages like C, Fortran, or Pascal or in special purpose parallel-processing languages. The transputer development system runs under the familiar VMEbus environment of the main CPU, like OS-9 or Unix, but also can be done on an outside workstation like SUN, PC/AT, PS/2, Mac II, or micro-Vax, and then subsequently downloaded onto the VMEbus system.

Apart from retaining as much of the existing environment as possible, one

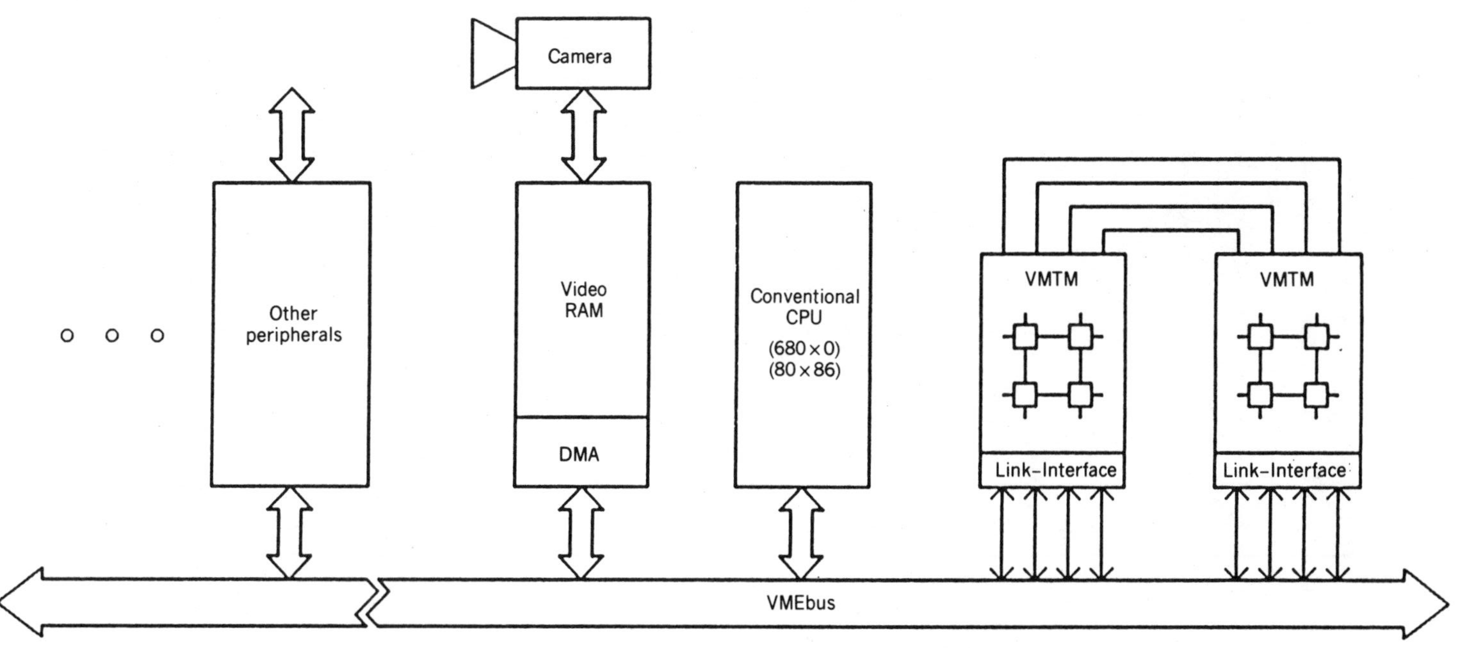

Figure 10.29 *Conventional implementation of VMEbus image processing (left) and transputers as accelerators for existing applications (right). From Cochran.[25] Courtesy and copyright © 1989 by Paracom.*

further benefit of the structure in Figure 10.29 is its scalability. Depending on the amount of computational power required, the developer may start with a single VMTM module contributing four transputers (40 MIPS, 16 million Whetstones!) but with increasing demands he simply can add further modules if and when its necessary. The transputer's software tools allow the software typically to be developed in a way that additional processors do not need recoding just reconfiguration. Regardless of the number of processors, the VMEbus' communication bandwidth no longer is a limiting factor because all interprocessor communication is done by the transputer's dedicated links as indicated in Figure 10.29. Only the transfer of the I/O data is still done via the VMEbus.

As shown in Figure 10.30, the developer gradually can go even further. If she wants to also use the transputer's power for the VMEbus master processor, she can use a BBK-V2 module substituting the conventional bus-master. With the BBK-V2, the on-board transputer has direct access to the VMEbus and can do everything possible with a conventional CPU-card on the VMEbus. So in Figure 10.30, it may set up for example the control registers of the frame grabber's DMA-controller, then have the image frames directly transferred into its dual-ported local memory, where it may be preprocessed before being sent via the BBK-V2's own link channels to the other transputers in the system. This structure again uses the VMEbus strictly for I/O-transfers, and relieves it from all other communication. Contrary to the previous example, it does not need a conventional CPU responsible for I/O data transfer. But as the BBK-V2's transputer is capable of running in a multimaster environment, if desired it could also still coexist with the conventional CPU which might continue to run once-existing user interface or other software.

The easy and efficient scalability even goes beyond the VMEbus environment. From some number of processors, it might no longer be desired to plug additional transputer modules into the VMEbus system because its physical capacity is exhausted. In this case the developer can expand its application system to a fully distributed structure. (See Figure 10.31.)

The VMEbus system continues to operate as a local I/O subsystem but most of the processing power is now concentrated in a busless transputer network with Paracom's TPM or MTM modules. This can accommodate any number of processors in dedicated 19-inch racks or in reconfigurable supercluster systems with multiples of 64 processors. Paracom's standard link-cable technology allows the same link channels, which in the previous example have been used for the local processor interconnection within the VMEbus rack, now to be used for the interconnection of the processors over distances of up to 100 feet.

Paracom's implementation of the transputer's link channels and the support of a variety of standard bus structures allow the user to construct an application as a fully distributed system gaining flexibility and power. With the example in Figure 10.31, the central busless transputer system can use the same link-cable technology, which it is using for data transfers from the

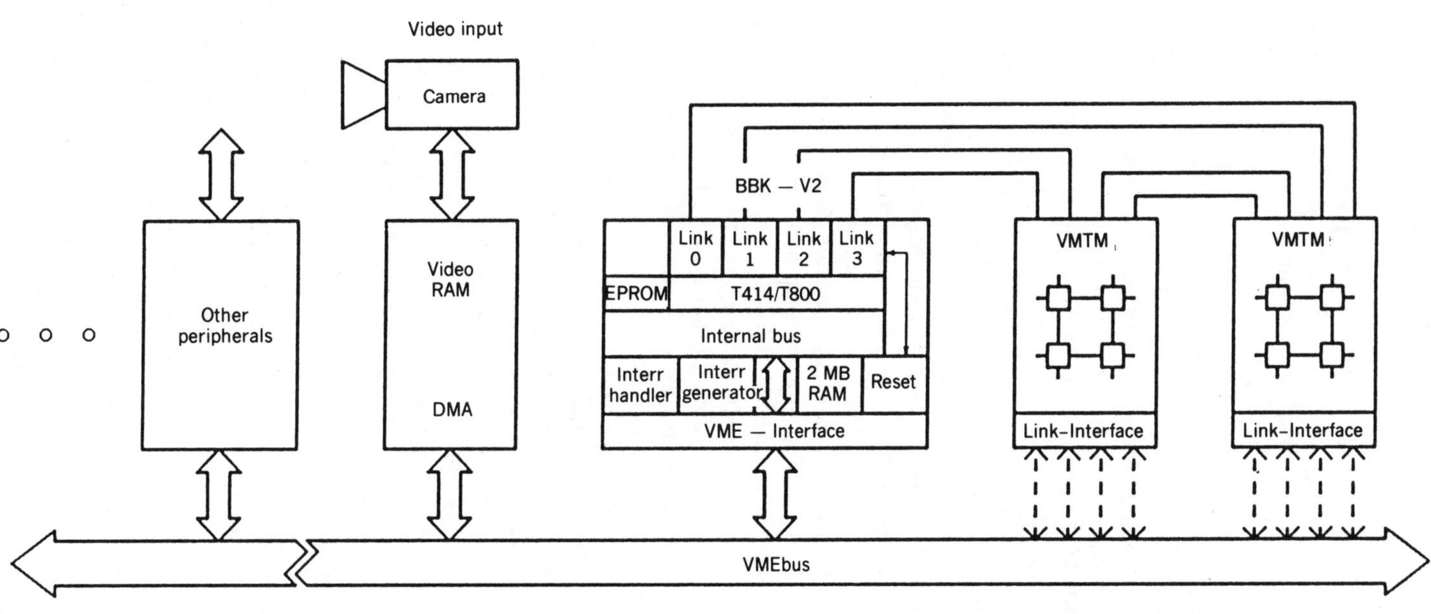

Figure 10.30 *Transputer as VMEbus master processor. From Cochran.*[25] *Courtesy and copyright © 1989 by Paracom.*

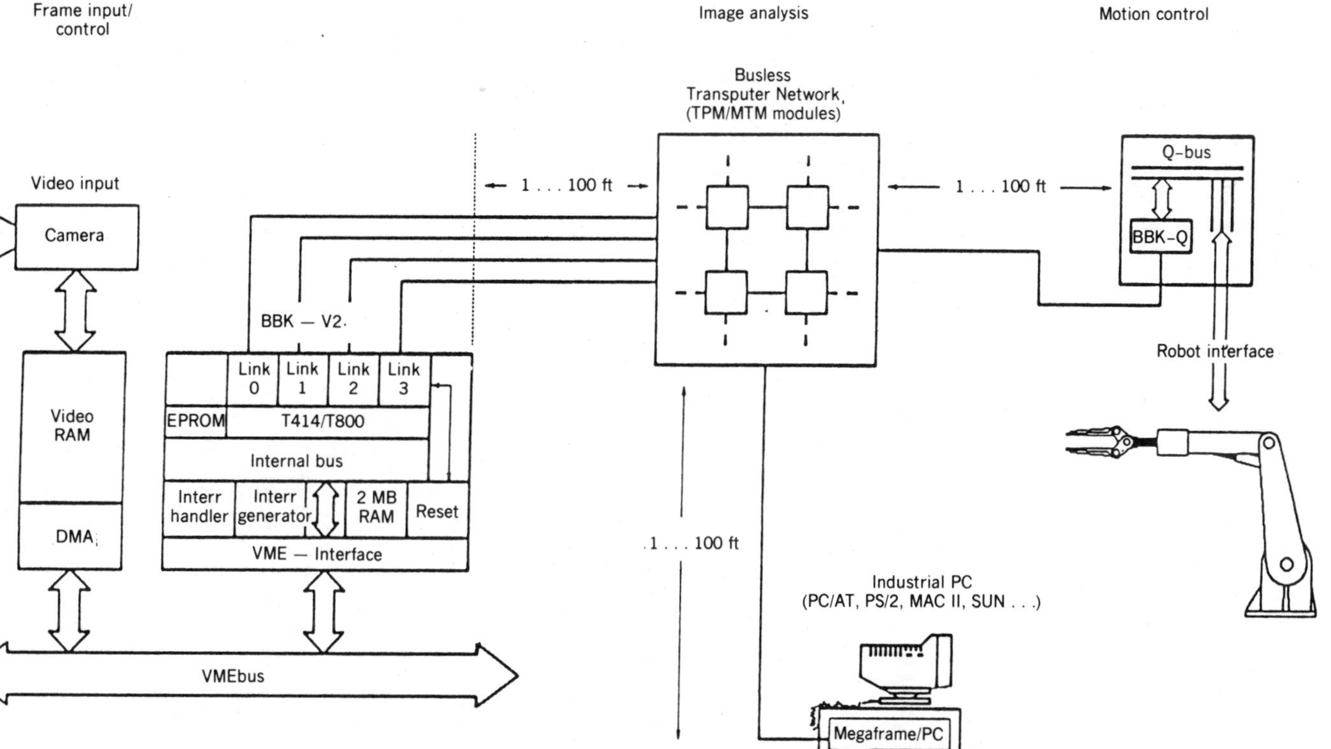

Figure 10.31 *Expanded and distributed system using VMEbus subsystem. From Cochran.*[25] *Courtesy and copyright © 1989 by Paracom.*

VMEbus subsystem, to control a motion-control system and connect to a standard PC- or workstation-based user interface. Every single-link connection is running at 20 Mbit/sec and while giving a fairly tight coupling of the individual subsystems, it provides at the same time a means of independence and exchangeability not at all possible with conventional technology. If for example, during the lifecycle of the application the user interface is exchanged from using a PC to using a Macintosh or a SUN, then simply this part is updated by exchanging the bus-interface module, the whole rest of the application remains unchanged and thus unaffected. The same applies to the motion-control system and also to the initial VMEbus system acquiring the image data.

10.9. NUCLEAR MAGNETIC RESONANCE COMPUTER TOMOGRAPH

Figure 10.32 shows an actual transputer-based application in the medical field. A computer tomograph (CT) writes its output to a bank of Winchester disks. Each hard disk has a transputer-based mass storage controller (MSC-module) that can transfer data at up to 4 Mbytes/sec from the SCSI storage disk. The MSC transfers this data in parallel to a processor farm, which computes new views from the previous cross section that were generated by the CT. The processor farm analyzes the raw data and passes it to the GDS module, which displays the latest brain gean picture on a high-resolution monitor, for evaluation by the physician.

In this application, an Apple Macintosh II acts as the host system.

10.10. INDUSTRIAL APPLICATION

Figure 10.33 shows a typical transputer application from the industrial world. This installation consists of a video camera, a transputer frame grabber (TFG) module, a transputer-based processor array, and a VMEbus-based system (equipped with a BBK-V2 bus bridge) to control the robot's actions. The TFG module converts the analog video signals into a digital format and sends it on the parallel processing array. The transputer structure performs the computationally intensive image processing functions and passes the results to the VME-based control system via the BBK-V2 bus bridge. The VME system then issues the insructions that direct the robot's actions. This system provides a substantial amount of flexibility since there are no performance limitations on the processor farm and computational power may be added or subtracted from the system to suit the particular application requirements. In this example, the host system is an IBM PC/AT linked to the transputer network via a BBK-PC link adapter.

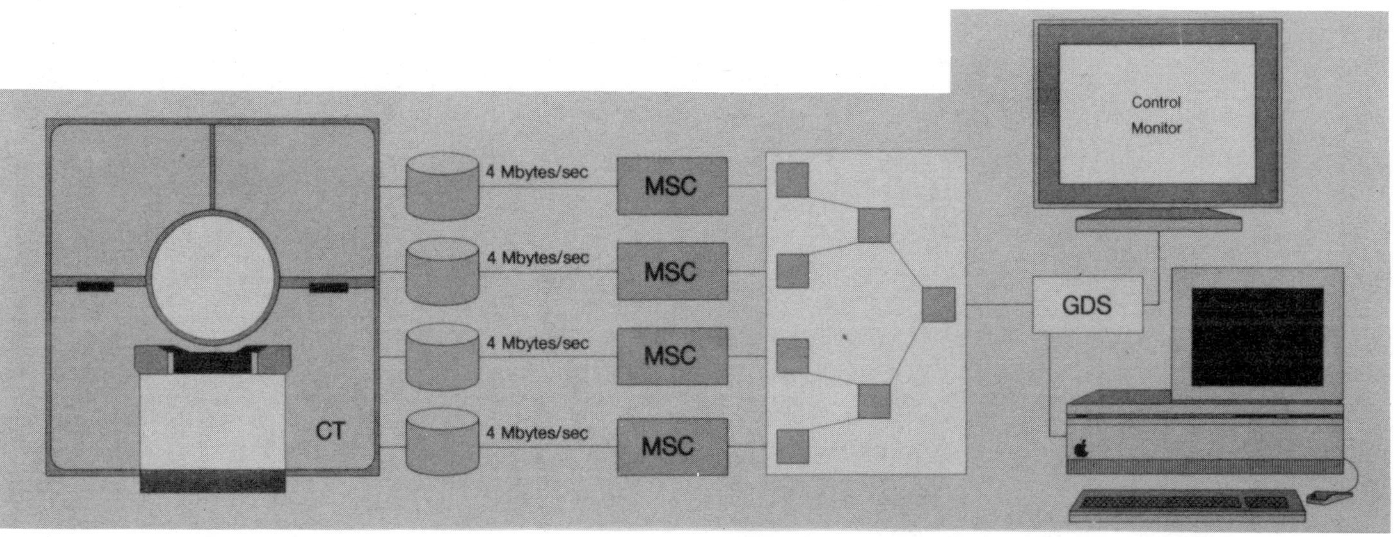

Figure 10.32 *Nuclear magnetic resonance computer tomograph. From Paracom manuals, 1989.*

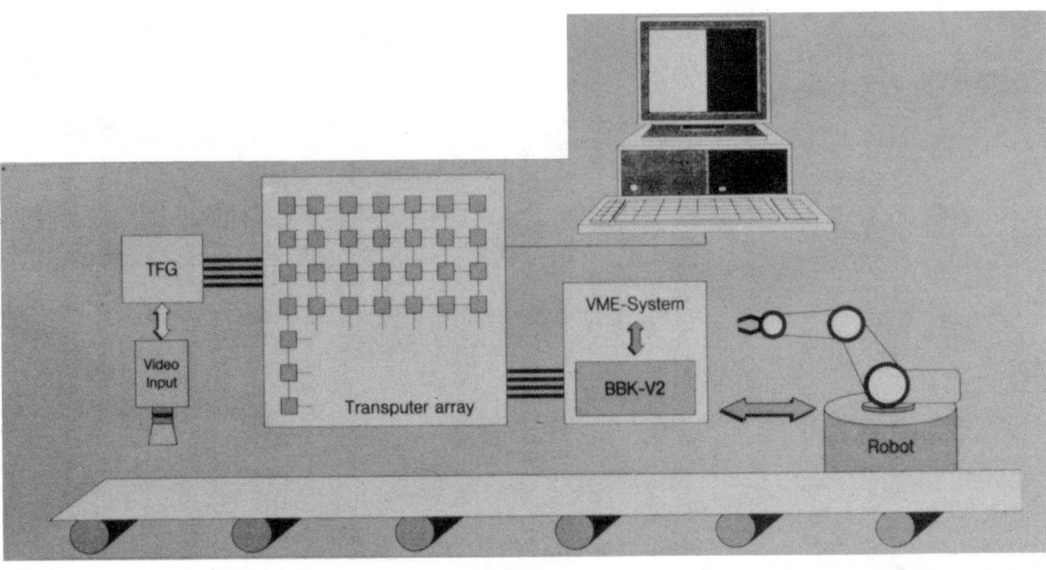

Figure 10.33 *Transputers in industrial application. From Paracom manuals 1989.*

REFERENCES

1. F. D. Kübler, *Transputers and Their Application in VMEbus Systems*, Parsytec Report, 1989.
2. Hochleistungs-Parallelrechnersystem zur Netzwerk-Programmierung aus Transputer-Basis, Parsytec Report, 1989.
3. H. Mühlenbein, O. Krämer, G. Peise, and R. Rinn, *The Megaframe Hypercluster,* Gesellschaft für Mathematic und Datenverarbeitung-Parsytec Report 1989.
4. R. W. Hockney, "MIMD Computing in the USA—1984." *Parallel Computing*, 2:119–136, 85.
5. D. W. Hilis. *The Connection Machine, The MIT Press Series in Artificial Intelligence,* MIT Press, Cambridge, 1985. Ph.D. Thesis.
6. BBN. *Butterfly Products Overview.* Technical Report, BBN Advanced Computers Inc., October (1987).
7. E. F. Gehringer, D. P. Siewiorek, Z. Segall. *Parallel Processing, The Cm* Experience.* Digital Press, (1987).
8. P. M. Behr, W. K. Giloi, and H. Mühlenbein. "SUPRENUM: The German Supercomputer—Rationale and Concepts." In *IEEE Internat. Conference on Parallel Processing,* (1986).
9. M. C. Sejnowski et al. "An overview of the Texas reconfigurable array computer," In *AFIPS Conference Proceedings,* pages 631–642, 1980.
10. L. Snyder. "Introduction to the configurable, highly parallel computer," *Computer*, 47–56, January (1982).
11. C. Jesshope. "Transputers and switches as objects in OCCAM," *Parallel Computing,* **8**(1–3), 19–30, October (1988).
12. J. R. Goodman, and C. H. Séquin. "Hypertree: A multiprocessor interconnection topology," *IEEE Transactions on Computers,* **C-30**(12), 923–933, December (1981).
13. K. Hwang, and J. Ghosh. "Hypernet: A communication-efficient architecture for constructing massively parallel computers," *IEEE Transactions on Computers,* **C-36**(12), 1450–1466, December (1987).
14. Perihelion, *Helios Technical Manual.* Technical Report, Perihelion Software Ltd., June 1988.
15. "MUPPET: A programming environment for message based multiprocessors," *Parallel Computing,* **8**(1–3), 201–221, October (1988).
16. H. Mühlenbein, T. Schneider, and S. Streitz. "Network programming with MUPPET," *Journal of Distributed and Parallel Computing,* **5**, 641–653, (1988).
17. H. Ashoff, and K. Hanno. Verteilte Simulation diskreter Ereignisse. Diplomarbeit, Univerisität Bonn, April (1988).
18. H. Mühlenbein, M. Gorges-Schleuter, and O. Krämer. "Evolution algorithms in combinatorial optimization." *Parallel Computing,* **7**(1), 65–88, (1988).
19. J. Kindermann, C. Lischka. *Workshop Konnektionismus.* Arbeitspapier der GMD 329, GMD, August (1988). (Ed.).
20. M. W. Padberg, and G. Rinaldi. "Optimization of a 532-city symmetric traveling salesman problem by branch and cut," *Operations Research Letters,* **6**, 1–7 (1987).

21. H. Mühlenbein. "The dynamics of evolution and learning-towards genetic neural networks." *Int. Conf. Connectionism in Perspective,* Zürich, in press.
22. N. Goddard. *The Rochester Connectionist Simulator.* Technical Report, Dept. of Computer Science, University of Rochester, 1987.
23. J. Kindermann, H. Mühlenbein, and K. Wolf. *Implementierung von Neuronalen Netzen.* Technical Report, GMD, 1988.
24. F. D. Kübler and R. Cochran, *Developing Parallel Processing Applications with Transputers,* Paracom Report, 1989.
25. R. Cochran, *Parallel Processing Adds Performance and Flexibility to VMEbus,* Paracom Report, 1989.
26. ——, *Performance by Paracom. The Power of Parallel Processing,* Paracom Manual, 1989.

CHAPTER 11

Market and Trends

INTRODUCTION AND SURVEY

Commercialization of neural networking technologies, of new concurrent systems, and of intelligent real-time systems has grown rapidly. In the early 1980s, there were only a few companies worldwide. Today more than 100 different concerns actively pursue products, applications, chips, systems, training, consulting, and research that focuses on neural, concurrent, or intelligent systems. Government funding organizations were drawn into biologically based computing. Investments and capital funding from banks and from venture capital flow into this new market.

This chapter describes three market segments: reconfiguration of established technologies, to make them intelligent; new neural, concurrent, and intelligent technologies that minimize the bottlenecks of software production, knowledge acquisition, and analytical system design; and the merger of new technologies with neurobiology and behavior.

The market covers numerous application areas, including pattern recognition in signals and in images, speech, vision, robotics, industrial process control, knowledge data bases, on-line simulation and decision making, intelligent artificial organs, and psychology software and services. Productivity and quality through research and development in intelligent systems enhances competitiveness in the world market.

11.1. SIXTH-GENERATION INTELLIGENT SYSTEMS

Souček and Souček[1] define three levels of man-made intelligence:

1. Artificial intelligence (AI) is based on logic and provides rule-based software packages called expert systems.
2. Brain behavior intelligence (BBI) mimics intelligent behavior in man and in animals and approximates some of the brain functions.
3. Molecular intelligens (MI) deals with the molecular level of cognition and information processing that could result in an interface between biological and technological information devices.

Computers can be used for data processing, knowledge processing, and intelligence processing. We could therefore define computer generations in the following way:

First to fourth generation: data processing;

Fifth generation: knowledge processing, based on AI; and

Sixth generation: data, knowledge, and intelligence processing, combining AI, BBI, and MI.

The sixth-generation computers emulate information processing in the brain and in neural networks. Their features include massive parallelism, machine learning, adaptability and self-organization, goal-directed processing, intelligent processor/memory elements, concurrency, and event trains. Intelligent real-time systems present an important segment of the sixth-generation technology and market.

Sixth-generation computers penetrate the market in three ways:

1. Established technologies are being reconfigured. Consumer goods and services, as well as industrial hardware and software receive the feature of intelligence.
2. New technologies are being created. They bypass present-day bottlenecks, such as software development, knowledge acquisition, and analytical approach to signal processing, process control, and robot systems, and data delivery. According to Hecht-Nielsen,[2] because of the potential development and implementation cost and time savings, 10 years from now neurocomputing may become the information processing paradigm of choice in every application where it can be used.
3. Neurobiology receives new artificial organs and new intelligent services. According to Mead,[3] analog very large scale integration (a neural network-based chip-making approach) will do for neurobiology what gene splicing did for genetics. First results are very promising. See Section 7.5 (Mead-Mahowald[4] silicon retina) and Section 9.3 (Adamson-Donnan-Black[5] transputer-based model of artificial cochlea). The market for neuroware has been born.

11.2. TRENDS IN MASSIVELY PARALLEL COMPUTERS

Intelligent behavior requires enormous computational power. A massively parallel computing architecture is the most plausible way to deliver such power. Parallelism, rather than raw speed of the computing elements, seems to be the way that the brain gets such jobs done. According to Souček and Souček[1], massively parallel architectures present the basis for brainlike, sixth-generation computers. According to Fahlman, Hinton, and Sejnowski[6] massively parallel architectures could be classified by the type of signals that are passed among the computing elements into three classes: message-passing, marker-passing, and value-passing systems.

Message-passing systems are the most powerful family. They pass around messages of arbitrary complexity and perform complex operations on these mssages. Concurrent systems described in Chapters 7 to 10 belong to this class. The future will see more and more systems of this kind, in computing, simulation, communication, instrumentation, robotics, and process control.

Marker-passing systems pass around single-bit markers. Each processor has the capacity to store a few distinct marker bits and perform simple Boolean operations on stored and marker bits arriving from other elements. An example of such a system is CLIP, (cellular logic image processor). CLIP is a large-scale integrated circuit array using a semiconductor chip specially designed for its application and comprising eight processors. It is used to process a picture of 96 × 96 cells.

Duff[7] describes the basic features of CLIP 4 cell, shown in Figure 11.1, in the following way.

Consider, for the sake of simplicity, that the image making up the input has been "thresholded" so that the image elements entering the cells is either a 0 or a 1: that is, the elements are in binary form. At the core of the

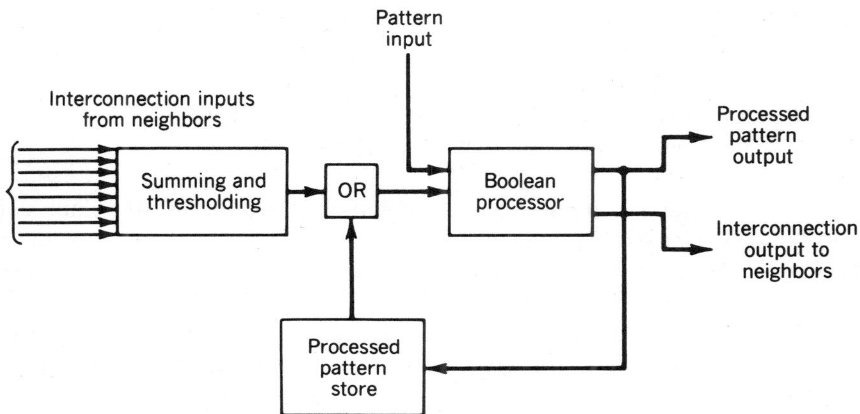

Figure 11.1 *Schematic logic system of the CLIP-4 cell. Adapted from Duff[7].*

cell there is a Boolean processor, which accepts two binary inputs and transforms them to give two independent binary outputs. Clearly, the two inputs can present any of four possible combinations of elements: 00, 01, 01 and 11. For each of these there are four possible output combinations, depending on the particular function the processor performs. This gives a total number of 16 possible output states. It is easy to show that the number of possible transformations from input to output is equal to the number of output states raised to the power of the number of input states (4^4 or 256). The transform function is selected by appropriately setting eight control lines entering the processor. (Eight lines are needed: 256 is 2^8).

One of the two outputs is regarded as a new pattern element and is loaded into a store. The other fans out to each of the neighboring cells, and it is these signals that after gating, and OR-ing go to form one of the binary inputs to the Boolean processors in the cells. Each signal is compared in an OR gate with a pattern element from the cell's store. (When one or both the inputs to an OR gate are 1, it passes an element 1, but when both inputs to it are 0, it gives an output element 0).

Marker-passing systems of this kind are powerful computing tools. However they require a radically new approach to programming and to signal, image, and data processing. Innovative architectures and packing technologies are now available for the design of large-scale marker-passing systems.

Value-passing systems pass around continuous quantities or numbers and perform simple arithmetic operations on these values.

Marker-passing and value-passing systems have a form of a uniform array of identical cells in an n dimensional space. Such arrays are known by the name *cellular automata*.

Figure 11.2. shows a two-dimensional array. Each cell communicates only with its nearest neighbors. Cellular automata can be characterized by four basic properties. These are the cellular geometry, the neighborhood specification, the number of states per cell, and the computation rule under which the cellular automation computes its successor states.

Figure 11.2. shows a case with two possible states: 0 and 1. The computation rule defines the state of the cell in cycle $t + 1$ in the following way:

State is 1, if the sum of states of four neighbors is even
State is 0, if the sum of states of four neighbors is odd.

The most popular computation rule is called the game of life. Each cell could have two possible states: dead and alive. An initial configuration of states is stored in the array. Each cell is connected to its eight neighbors. The computation rule is as follows:

If the cell is alive, it will stay alive in the next cycle only if two or three cells in the neighborhood are alive. If the cell is dead, it will become alive only if exactly three neighbors are alive. In all other cases the cell will stay

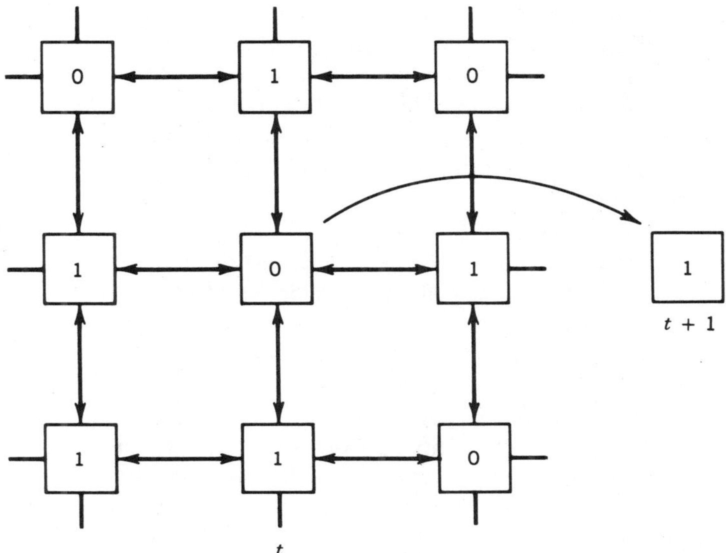

Figure 11.2 *Two-dimensional cellular array.*

dead or it will die. The system resembles microorganisms that swim, reproduce, eat, and die.

Cellular automata have been demonstrated by many researchers to be good computational models for physical systems simulation. For instance, a cellular automaton can readily simulate crystal growth as illustrated by the growth of a snowflake, simulated with the simplest of cellular automata.

The study of cellular automata was initiated by John von Neuman in the 1950s. Three major factors have resulted in the revival of interest in the behavior of cellular systems. First, the development of powerful computers and microprocessors have made possible the rapid simulation of cellular automata in a serial, parallel, and/or cellular mode of operation. Second, the use of cellular automata to simulate a variety of physical systems has generated much interest in the scientific community. Third, the advent of VLSI as an implementation medium has focused attention on the communication requirements of successful hardware algorithms.

The extension of cellular automata is a *cellular neural network*. The basic circuit unit of cellular neural networks is called a cell. It contains linear and nonlinear circuit elements, which typically are linear capacitors, linear resistors, linear and nonlinear controlled sources, and independent sources. The structure of cellular neural networks is similar to that found in cellular automata; namely, any cell in a cellular neural network is connected only to its neighbor cells. The adjacent cells can interact directly with each other. Cells not directly connected together may affect each other indirectly because of the propagation effects of the continuous-time dynamics of cellular neural networks.

Cellular neural networks share the best features of both worlds: its continuous time feature allows real-time signal processing found waiting in the digital domain and its local interconnection feature makes it tailor made for VLSI implemetation.

Wolfram[8] shows that despite their simple construction, some cellular automata are capable of complex behavior. Based on investigation of a large sample of cellular automata, Wolfram[8] suggests that many (perhaps all) cellular automata fall into four behavior classes. Cellular automata within each class exhibit qualitatively similar behavior. The small number of classes implies considerable universality in the qualitative behavior of cellular automata and implies that many details of the construction of a cellular automaton are irrelevant in determining its qualitative behavior. Thus complex physical and biological systems may lie in the same universality classes as the idealized mathematical models provided by cellular automata. Knowledge of cellular automaton behavior may then yield rather general results on the behavior of complex natural systems.

According to Wolfram[8], cellular automata may be considered as discrete dynamical systems. In almost all cases, cellular automaton evolution is irreversible. Trajectories in the configuration space for cellular automata therefore merge with time, and after many time steps, trajectories starting from almost all initial states become concentrated onto "attractors." These attractors typically contain only a very small fraction of possible states. Evolution to attractors from arbitrary initial states allows for "self-organizing" behavior, in which structures may evolve at large times from structureless initial states. The nature of the attractors determines the form and extent of such structures.

Parallel computers present natural tools for implementation of cellular automata (connection-machine, and transputer-based computing surfaces and clusters). NCR delivers a special purpose cellular chip called GAPP (Geometrical Arithmetic Parallel Processor) which has 72 processors in a 6×12 grid. Each processor has a small 132-bit memory, and four bit-serial links to the neighbors. Using connection-machine, transputer-based systems or a collection of GAPP chips it is now possible to investigate cellular automata with 100,000 cells, or more. Applications include simulation, neural networks, image processing, pattern recognition, intelligent behavior, and related research.

Kanerva[9] investigates a special kind of massively parallel systems, called *sparced distributed memory* (SDM). SDM is a random-access memory for very long words with approximate addressing. An item is stored by distributing copies of it in many storage locations. Kanerva[9] defines the SDM in the following way.

The memory will be built of addressable storage locations. A location is activated whenever a read or write address is within a certain number of bits of the location's address. For storing information, a storage location has n counters, one for each bit position.

Information is stored by incrementing a counter to store a bit that is 1 (and possibly decrementing a counter to store a bit that is 0).

Information is retrieved by pooling the contents of the storage locations activated by the read address and then finding, for each bit, whether zeros or ones are in the majority.

Let us start with address decoding. A storage location should be accessible from anywhere within r_p bits of the location's address. That means that (linear-threshold) neurons can be used for address decoding. The threshold of each address-decoder neuron would be set permanently to r_p units below the neuron's maximum weighted sum.

Reading at x is done by pooling the contents of the locations accessible from x and finding the average word $W(x)$. The average can be computed from n bitwise sums, and hence a storage location (one associated with an address decoder—a hard location) can be realized as n counters, the ith one counting bits in the ith position.

A bit location should have three lines or connections: one coming to it from an address decoder for selecting the location, one leading away from it to allow its contents to be read, and—this is important—one leading to it to allow its contents to be updated. Activity on the address-decoder line activates the location for a read or write operation, but it alone cannot effect the writing into the location. For that, we need the data-input lines.

Since many bit locations are pooled to form a single bit of output from memory, they must be connected to a common output line. Then, storing the data, calls for a matching network that takes one input line and distributes it to the very bit locations that are pooled for a single bit of output. In computer memories, the same wire can be used for both input and output; however since neurons conduct in one direction only, neuron memories must have separate input and output lines. What is significant is that input and output lines should correspond to one another, one for one, and therefore they should run in matched pairs.

SDM, as described by Kanerva[9], works with long vectors of bits. These vectors can be thought of as patterns of binary features. For example, an object viewed from slightly different angles and distances will produce a set of similar patterns. Each pattern is stored with itself as the address. Consequently, many similar addresses will be used in writing into the memory, and they will select many common locations. An object occupies a region of the pattern space with poorly defined boundaries. Kanerva[9] suggests that SDM might be relevant in explaining the operation of the brain, as well as the base for the design of fuzzy intelligent systems.

11.3. TRENDS IN RISC PROCESSORS

11.3.1. Benchmarking

The market is presently focused on high-speed RISC (Reduced Instruction Set Computer) processors.

How can these systems be evaluated? Computer performance is often measured in terms of Mflops (millions of floating-point operations per second) and Mips (millions of machine instructions per second). A benchmark is supposed to be a standard measure of performance that enables one computer to be compared with another. Benchmarking intends to indicate the relative performance of various machines under the same workload. By definition, a computer benchmark is a set of key programs or sections of key programs that are executed for timing purposes. The best known benchmarks are: the Whetstone, the Savage, and the Dhrystone.

The Whetstone benchmark program[10] was constructed to compare processor power for scientific applications. It includes integer arithmetic, array indexing, procedure calls, conditional jamps, and elementary function evaluations. These are mixed in proportions carefully chosen to simulate a typical scientific application program.

The Savage benchmark[11] is a benchmark of elementary function evaluation only. It tests both speed and accuracy.

The Dhrystone is a synthetic benchmark[12] designed to test processor performance on systems programs. It was originally published in Ada, but the most widely used version is a translation into C, distributed over USENET.

It is likely that the wide variety of possible architectures for RISC and for parallel machines will render benchmarking impractical. The timing information that benchmark releases, reflects only the relative performance on one problem area, and not an overall performance of a computer system. Overall performance includes high system throughput, modular extension, high availability, high-level language support, memory management and virtual memory support, support for multiprocessing and concurrent processing, input/output, compilers, operating system, and utility software. The choice of a computer system will be based on the compromise between many features, and not only on Mflops and Mips.

The market has become crowded with new RISC processors. These include:

- SPARC chip set used in the new SUN SPARC station.
- MIPS processor used in the Silicon Graphics Personal IRIS station.
- Motorola 88000 used in Opus, Everex, and Data General stations.
- IBM RISC CPU used in IBM's RT PC.
- INMOS TRANSPUTER, aimed at concurrent systems.

- INTEL 80486 general purpose chip.
- INTEL 80860, aimed at supercomputing.

11.3.2. Transputer-Based Concurrent Systems

The transputer presents an important component in designing concurrent systems. It has six "engines" that operate simultaneously: central processing unit, floating point unit and 4 communication channels. Result is: 10 million machine instructions per second; 2 million floating point operations per second; 20 million bits per second on each of four input/output channels. In short, T800 on a chip could be compared in power with machines of the category VAX 8600.

The transputer is the first one chip machine designed for direct execution of a parallel high level language, OCCAM. OCCAM follows the doctrine of the philosopher Guillaume d'Ockham, 1270–1349: "Entia non sunt multiplicanda praeter necessitam" ("Do not multiply entities beyond the necessary level"). OCCAM follows the strict formalism for the specification and design of parallel systems, developed on Oxford University by Hoare and his group.

European Strategic Programme for Research and Development in Information technology, ESPRIT, supports the research and development of very powerful machines called Super Nodes, based on T800. Computing modules based on transputers have been developed and delivered to the market from many sources: INMOS, MEIKO, PARSYTEC, Computer Systems Architects, Gemini Computer Systems, Niche Data Systems, Transtech, Perihelion, Sension, Quintek, Simtech, Levco, Mechanical Intelligence, Ergonomics, Smith Associates, CGEE, and others. The modules could be used on VMEbus; as accelerators for IBM-PC, Macintosh, Atari, Sun, Apollo; or for the design of special machines and supercomputers.

The Edinburgh team is working towards the machine with 1000 transputers and 1000 million floating point operations per second, which is comparable with Cray Supercomputer Y-MP. At the same time, project ESPRIT, Geselschaft für Mathematic und Datenverarbeitung and also PARSITEC offer the solutions in the form of smaller but dynamically reconfigurable machines: the configuration follows the structure of the problem, aiming at 575 Mflops.

At this moment, transputer-based multiprocessor systems exist in the area of picture analyzing, graphics, simulation, fluid dynamics, real-time processing, neural networks, robotics, artificial intelligence, and evolution algorithms. Further developments include database systems, molecular simulation, flight simulation, and highly sophisticated parallelization tools.

11.3.3. INTEL 80860: A Supercomputer on a Chip

Intel designed the 80860 with a million transistors on a chip. Everything, including the memory caches, is on a single chip. Internal 128-bit wide pathways enable transfer rates of more than a billion bits per second. The 80860 chip is designed to do three things at once: integer math, floating-point addition, and floating-point multiplication. As a result, at a 50 MHz version that will be available in the future, the 80860 will theoretically produce as many as 120 million results per second (105,000 Dhrystones per second; 17 millions floating-point operations per second).

Special three-dimensional graphics hardware is included on a chip, and it provides functions like z-buffering and shading. Z-buffers store information of each pixel in an image and allow high-speed three-dimensional imaging. The chip is planned in 33 MHz to 50 MHz versions.

Intel 80860, standing alone or in parallel configurations, will grab a share of the market in graphics, workstations, real-time, personal computers, and minisupercomputers.

11.4. TRENDS IN VMEBUS

Standardized buses are becoming faster, more sophisticated and more specified. We explain this trend with the VMEbus.

The VMEbus specifications define an interfacing system used to interconnect data processing, data storage, and peripheral control devices in a closely coupled hardware configuration. The VME specification consist of four buses: data transfer, arbitration, priority interrupt, and utility.

11.4.1. Data Transfer Bus (DTB)

DTB allows master devices to direct the transfer of binary data between themselves and slave devices. DTB lines can be grouped into three categories: addressing lines, data lines, and control lines.

Addressing Lines. The smallest addressable unit of storage is the byte location. Master devices use address lines A02–A31 to select one 4-byte group. Four additional lines—DS0, DS1, AO1, and LWORD—are then used to select a byte location within the group. Address modifier lines, AM0–AM5, allow the master device to pass additional addressing information to the slave device.

Data Lines. VMEbus provides either 16 data lines, D00–D15, allowing to access two byte locations simultaneously, or 32 data lines, D00–D31, allowing up to four byte locations to be accessed.

Control Lines. The following signal lines are used to control the movement of data over the data transfer lines:

AS	Address Strobe
DS0	Data Strobe Zero

DS1	Data Strobe One
BERR	Bus Error
DTACK	Data Transfer Acknowledge
WRITE	Read/Write

11.4.2. Arbitration Bus

The VMEbus arbitration subsystem schedules requests from multiple master devices for optimum bus use. It prevents simultaneous use of the bus by two master devices. The arbitration subsystem detects the requests coming from several boards, and grants the bus to one board at a time, using one of the three scheduling algorithms: prioritized, round robin, and single level.

Prioritized arbitration assigns the bus according to a fixed priority scheme where each of four bus request lines has a priority from highest, BR3, to lowest, BR0.

Round-robin arbitration assigns the bus on a rotating priority basis. When the bus is granted to bus request line BR(n), then the highest priority for the next arbitration is assigned to bus request line BR($n - 1$).

Single-level arbitration only accepts requests on BR3 and relies on BR's bus grant daisychain to arbitrate the requests.

11.4.3. Priority Interrupt Bus

Priority interrupt bus provides the signal lines needed to generate and service interrupts. Interrupt subsystems can be classified into two groups: single handler systems and distributed systems.

In a single handler system, all interrupts are received by one interrupt handler and all interrupt service routines are executed by one processor. The single handler system is well suited to machine or process control applications, where a supervisory processor coordinates the activities of dedicated processors. The supervisory processor receives interrupt requests, servicing them in a prioritized manner.

In a distributed system, two or more interrupt handlers are included, each servicing only a subset of the bus interrupts. The distributed system is well suited to architectures with multiple, co-equal processors executing the application software. Each processor services only these interrupts directed to it, establishing dedicated communication paths among all processors.

The priority interrupt bus consists of seven interrupt request signal lines, IRQ1 to IRQ7, one interrupt acknowledge line, IACK, and one interrupt acknowledge daisychain, IACKIN/IACKOUT.

11.4.4. Utility Bus

This bus includes signals that provide timing and coordinate the power-up and power-down of VMEbus.

11.4.5. VMEbus and Future Architectures

The concept of VMEbus is related to Motorola's development of the 68000 microprocessor systems in 1970s. In 1983, the IEEE standardized VMEbus and gave it the name IEEE PO14. The VMEbus International Trade Association (VITA) Technical Committee studies proposals for next-generation architecture requirements. VITA requirements are listed in Tables 11.1 and

TABLE 11.1 VITA Next-Generation Architecture Requirements

Requirement 1: Architectural upwards compatibility with VME
- Minimize the impact on software (i.e., define a shared memory architecture)
- Mechanically compatible with VME (i.e., stay as close as possible to IEC-297)
- Fully specify a bridge to VME (i.e., provide the necessary hooks that will allow a VME subsystem to coexist within the system)

Requirement 2: High performance
- Burst data rates 10 times those on VMEbus (100 m transfers/sec)
- High performance over transaction mix

Requirement 3: Native support for copy-back caches
- Protocols to ensure data coherency in multiprocessor systems
- Extendable to multicrated systems
- Does not preclude the implementation of systems that require data security

Requirement 4: Dynamic configuration and reconfiguration
- Geographical addressing
- Standard control and status registers
- Standard self-test procedures

Requirement 5: High integrity
- Detection & reporting of transfer errors
- Sufficient number of power and ground pins
- Standards for noise immunity, crosstalk, emc, reflections, and so on

Requirement 6: Technology independent
- Processor independent
- Accommodate new technologies easily and efficiently

Requirement 7: Cost effective
- Price performance ratio < VME
- Scalable interface, from 32 to 64 to 128 to 256 bits
- Siliconable using today's technologies
- Practical

Requirement 8: Maintainable/support fault tolerance
- Error and fault containment
- Support hot swap
- Support hardware redundancy
- Support test and maintenance (T&M) bus

Requirement 9: Message transport layer
- Optional, but fully defined

Requirement 10: Other
- Specify two board sizes: 6U × 160 and 9U × 400
- Many user-defined I/O pins available (at least 128)
- Allow extensions
- Military version

Development of document: Use the IEEE 896.1-87 as a basis and participate in the P896.1, P896.2 and P1156 working groups to influence their development to accommodate the requirements formulated by the NGAWG

11.2 (published in *VME Business,* March 1988). VITA announced the selection of IEEE 896.1-1987 as the basis of its Next Generation Architecture (NGA). The U.S. Navy Space and Naval Warfare Systems Command and Intel also announced the selection of IEEE 896.1-1987 as the basis of their bus architecture beyond MMII. According to VITA, these events are pivotal for the direction of the whole computer industry, discouraging proprietary buses from springing up. International standardization improves chances for software compatibility and for freedom of movement, and it lowers overall costs. VITA reports a weighted average growth of VME business of approximately 37 percent in 1988, and predicts a 27 percent increase in 1989.

TABLE 11.2 VITA's Requirements from a Next-Generation Bus Compared to the Features of the 896.1 and the Proposed Futurebus

Feature	Requirement for NGAbus	Documented in 896.1-1987	Proposed for Futurebus
Data bus width	32/64/128/(256)	32	32/64/128/256
Burst data rate	1990—≥25 Mxfrs/sec 1992—≥50 Mxfrs/sec 1994—≥100 Mxfrs/sec	≈25 Mxfrs/sec	TBD
Address width	32/64	32	32/64
Byte ordering	By lane	By lane	By lane
Transfer protocols	Compelled asynch Uncompelled	Yes No	Yes Yes
Types of cycles (and no others)	Block transfer Single address as P/O blt Locked access Address only Slave induced broadcast Intervention (split access)	Yes No Yes Yes No Yes No	Yes Yes Yes Yes Yes Yes TBD
Parity	Yes	Yes	Yes
Tag bit	Yes	Yes	Yes
Geographical address	≥4 ≥ 5 bits	5 bits	Yes
Arbitration	Fast Distributed	No Yes	TBD Yes
Asynchronous events	7 Interrupts Power failure System failure	No No No	TBD TBD TBD
Extension mechanism	Yes	Yes	Yes
Power	+5 VDC ±12 VDC +3.3 VDC (−5.2 VDC)	Yes No No No	Yes No Yes Yes

TABLE 11.2 (*Continued*)

Feature	Requirement for NGAbus	Documented in 896.1-1987	Proposed for Futurebus
Connectors/bus	1/≥64-bit bus	1/32-bit	TBD
#User-defined pins	1 connector	168 pins	TBD
Hot swap	Yes	Yes	Yes
Board sizes	6U × 160 9U × 400	No No	Yes Yes
Serial bus	Yes	IEEE P1394	IEEE P1394
Secondary bus	Yes	Same	Same
Redundant bus	Yes	Same	Same
Intercrate bus	Yes	IEEE P896.2	TBD
Cache coherency	Moesi model	IEEE P896.2	IEEE P896.2
CSR standards	Fully specified	IEEE P896.2	IEEE PXYZ
Message transport	Fully specified	IEEE P896.2	IEEE P896.2
Environmental specs	Fully specified	No	IEEE P1156
Military version	Fully specified	No	IEEE P1156
Test bus	Yes	No	IEEE P1156

11.5. NEURAL NETWORK MARKET

Companies dealing with adaptive and learning-based computing were first formed during the 1960s and 1970s, among which are Adaptronics, Memister, and Nestor. In the early 1980s, government funding organizations were drawn into biologically based computing, among them the Defense Advanced Research Project Agency (DARPA), Office of Naval Research (ONR), Air Force Office of Scientific Research (AFOSR), National Aeronautics and Space Administration (NASA), Jet Propulsion Laboratories (JPL), National Science Foundation (NSF), and Strategic Defense Initiative Office (SDIO). As a result, many new and existing companies started the research, development, and production of neural networks. Most of the carry products were software-based simulations of neural networks. Finally, in 1986 and 1987, neurocomputing hardware products began to reach the marketplace. The TRW MARK III artificial neural network simulator was the first to debut, and was followed soon after by HNC's ANZA neurocomputer.

Neural software products available on the market include AINET by AI-WARE, SIMNET by Blair House, Netwurkz by DAIR Computer Systems, Neurosoft by HNC, GOSPL by Texas Instruments, ANS kit by SAIC, Neural Works by Neural Ware, Awareness by Neural Systems, Syspro by Martingale Research, and Mactivation by JOLY Group/U.

Neural network application products available on the market include handwritten data entry by Nestor and HNC, airline marketing by BehavHeuristics; expert system design by Neuraltech, EKG analysis by Nestor and HNC, data base management system by Savvy, and process and robot control by HNC and AI-WARE.

Neural chips, accelerator boards, and workstations are offered by TRW, HNC, SAIC, TI, AI WARE, Human Devices, Syntonic, Oxford Computer, and others.

A list of manufacturers is given in the appendix.

Figure 11.3 shows the topology of the neural network market developed by HNC.

11.6. MARKET FOR NEURAL AND CONCURRENT REAL-TIME SYSTEMS

11.6.1. Pattern Recognition

Pattern recognition means detecting simple forms and features from signals, images, handwritten text, weather maps, and speech spectra. Neural and concurrent real-time systems are capable of learning elementary features and functions. In this way, the system self-organizes itself without heuristic programming. Due to massive parallelism, the systems operate at high-speed, thus opening new application areas in remote sensing, medical image analysis, industrial computer vision, process control, robot vision, and input devices for computers. The key to expanding the market outside of its current applications is integrating robotics systems and visual recognition systems. This must be done by (a) providing highly intelligent visual systems that will interface with products in the robotics market, and (b) reducing system costs. This type of visual recognition system would increase the accuracy of robots by incorporating real-time location sensing, and would save time by minimizing the amount of extraneous robot movement.

11.6.2. Knowledge Data Bases

A large memory capacity and stored selected knowledge frames present the base for intelligent system design. In real-time systems, knowledge is stored in two ways: expert systems and artificial neural networks.

An *expert system* is a computer software program that incorporates a knowledge base and an inference engine. A *knowledge base* contains all of the information about a specific subject or domain. An *inference engine* is a structured program that contains rules of logic for associating the informa-

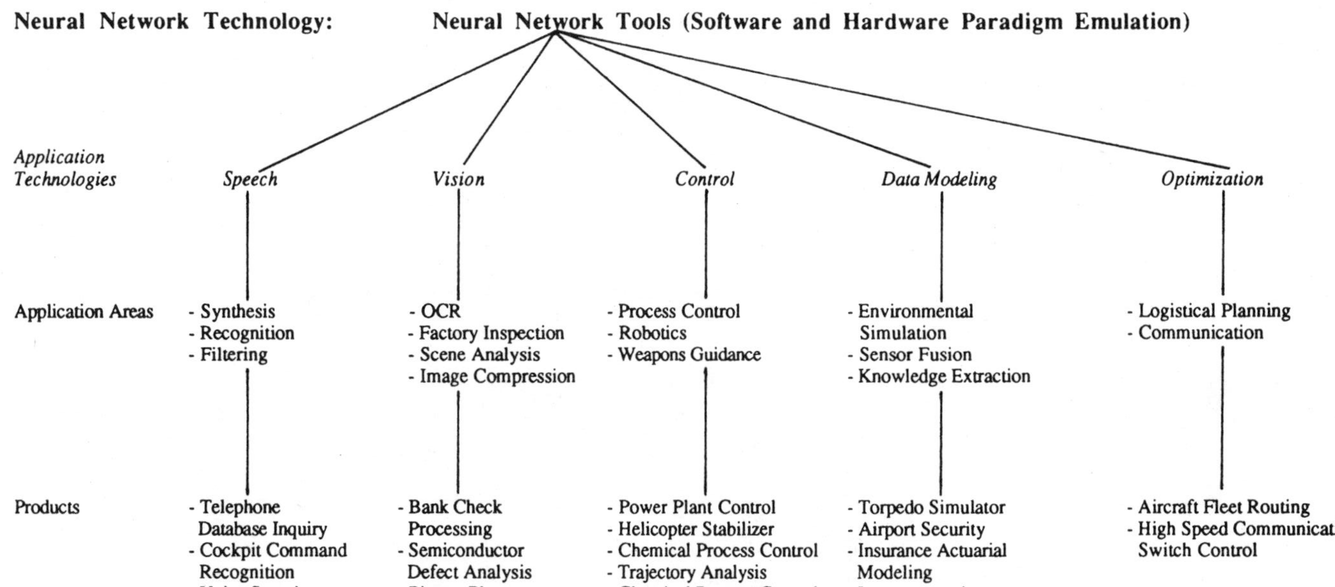

Figure 11.3 *Neural network market topology, following Hecht-Nielsen Neurocomputer Corporation.*

tion in the knowledge base through a series of cross-references or by using If-Then rules.

In artificial neural networks, storage elements are analog devices, and their matching can only be defined with relatively low accuracy. As a consequence, a neural network will accept an incomplete question, and it will find an answer through the process of network relaxation. The answer will correspond to some kind of energy minimum, global optimum, or local optimum of the network. Although the answer might not be complete, it will be an acceptable solution in practice, available in real time.

The market for expert systems and neural networks in knowledge bases include military, manufacturing, mission planning, encryption, deciphering, medical diagnosis, oil and mineral exploration and analysis, electronics testing and development, robot and process control, signal and image processing, and fuzzy reasoning.

11.6.3. Robot and Process Control

Neural and concurrent systems bring new blood to robot and process control. The trend from programmed systems toward adaptive intelligent systems is expected.

In *programmed systems,* sequences of commands, coordinates, and parameters are stored in memory. A time-consuming analytical procedure is necessary to program the system. The resulting system is rigid and could easily fail.

In *adaptive intelligent systems,* actions and behavior area learned from experience. The designer tells the system the goals of the operation, not *how* to reach those goals. The system learns how to behave through interaction with the environment. Sometimes a high degree of learning is necessary. According to Kohonen,[13] learning locomotion in an unknown environment is a task that can hardly be formalized by logic programming. Coordinating complex sensory functions with motor ones cannot be solved in analytical form. Neural computers provide elegant, self-adaptable solutions (see Chapter 4).

Presently, hybrid, programmed intelligent systems dominate the market. Such systems could be easily developed with concurrent processors (see Chapter 9). The market includes home appliances, automobile and aircraft industry, shipbuilding, instruments, tools, industrial hardware, entertainment, and communication.

11.6.4. On-Line Simulation and Decision Making

Here again, programmed, adaptive, intelligent, and hybrid solutions are available. Some examples are presented in Chapter 9. The complex performance of hybrid systems is partially programmed and partially learned from examples. Programmed rules are stored in the if-then form. The knowledge established automatically through learning exists in implicit form as the collective states of the adaptive interconnections.

The market for on-line simulation and decision making includes data delivery systems, multiuser flight simulators, electronic games, interactive high-speed simulation, computer-aided design and manufacturing (CAD/CAM), computer-aided instructions (CAI), optimization computations, and advisory systems.

Corporations have traditionally spent over $3 billion per year on management and employee training aids (U.S. Training and Census Report), and the military has implemented training tools into almost all of its divisions. With the advent of neural and concurrent processors and with systems that see, hear, speak, and touch, on-line simulation and decision making has become a fast-growing market. The market includes tutorials (a simplified teacher/textbook on-line guide), simulation (real-situation interaction with the user), drill/practice (utilizing repetition as a learning aid), ''psychology software'' (CAI focused on self-motivation and management skills; this is an example of a market for psychoware), administration (programs that test and record the user's knowledge and learning pace on a given subject), and on-line encyclopedia (giga- and tera-bit knowledge/intelligence base with mixed text, sound, and image on video disk).

11.7. MARKET FOR INTELLIGENCE AND SENSATION

From the 1920s to the 1980s, world industry and business have been dominated by motor vehicles and petroleum refining. The world's largest industrial corporations produce motor vehicles or refine petroleum for these vehicles. Driving a car and travelling are convenient, pleasurable, and helps business. There are also side effects: polluted air and water, dead forests, and depletion of energy resources.

The second leading group of industries includes computers, electronics, office equipment, telecommunication, and electronic appliances. Several corporations in this area have achieved sales revenues from $20 to $50 billion per year (IBM, ATT, General Electric, Matsershita Electric, Hitachi, Siemens, Philips, and others). American firms have maintained world leadership in computers and telecommunication. Japan and Germany follow.

The vehicle and petroleum industry is peaking and cannot grow forever. Computers, electronics, and telecommunication industries are far from saturation, and they exhibit a fast growth rate. These industries use little energy and raw material, and they do not pollute. Their products present the infrastructure for the world's economy. They are used within vehicles and refineries, for cleaner and more effective operation. These products also give pleasure to the user. The pleasure is in the area of human hunger for knowledge, curiosity, communication, happenings, sensation, and intelligence. This is especially true for new products and services based on a two-way exchange of knowledge.

Combining these industries and related services with neurobiology and behavior provides one of the driving forces for the economy of the 1990s and of the twenty-first century. The market for intelligence and sensation constantly grows.

Figure 11.4. presents a prediction for the European Common Market, for 1990 and 2000 and notes the following:

1980:	Oil and chemistry	100
	Automobile	48
	Electronics	25
2000:	Electronics	170
	Oil and chemistry	160
	Automobile	70

Obviously, Europe is strongly emphasizing the electronics industry. Several projects are in progress, such as Esprit and JESSI—the Joint European Submicron Silicon (estimated at $4 billion). Large corporations, such as Siemens, Philips, SGS-Thomson, and INMOS are involved. One of their goals is a 64-Mbit memory chip.

Japan is even more oriented toward electronics. Toshiba expects to have a 64-Mbit memory chip by early 1990s. Mitsubishi, with revenues of $200 billion and other Japanese giants are closing in on a world monopoly in electronics.

Companies like Intel, Motorola, and TI are in the lead with microprocessors and are strongly pushing forward. As we head toward the year 2000, chips, computers, and intelligent systems will dominate the world market (See Figure 11.4.).

11.8. NOBEL LAUREATES IN INTELLIGENCE RESEARCH

The brain and intelligence are among the most complex areas in science. Many different disciplines are needed to attack these problems. Several Nobel laureates have devoted their time and energy to intelligence research. Here we name only a few:

Hodgkin-Huxley: physiological model of propagation of electrical signals along the axon of a neuron;

Katz: all-or-none model of synaptic junction;

Hubel and Wiesel: feature-extraction model of visual cortex;

Eccles: brain physiology, brain/mind relations;

Tinbergen: goal-directed behavioral models;

Simon: theory and model of the brain, and general problem solver;

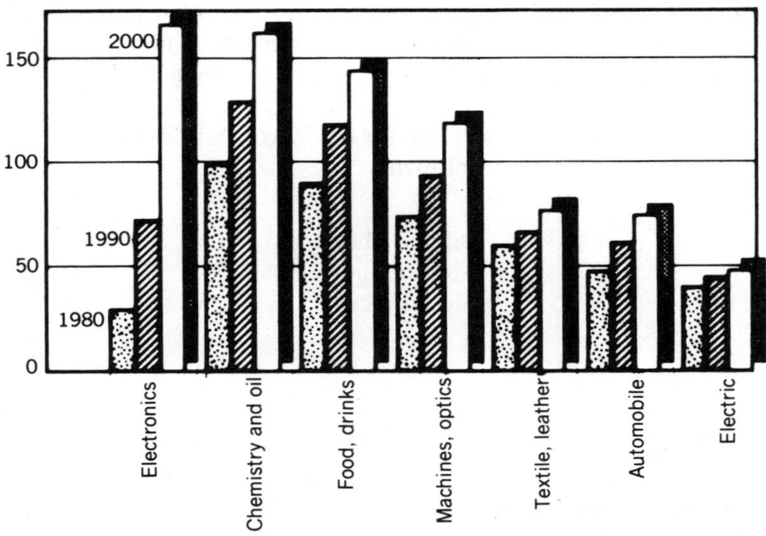

Figure 11.4 *Trends in major industries, in billions of Ecu (European currency unit).*

Feynman: nanotechnology as a base for intelligent system design, and thinking machines;

Lederberg: expert systems, including DENDRAL;

Cooper: pattern recognition in artificial neural networks;

Binning, Rohrer: scanning tunneling microscope.

Lorenz: human and animal behavior. Modern man is still governed by destructive intelligence and aggressive instincts genetically inherited from the stone age;

Lwoff, Jacob, Monod: Genetic code; and

Prigogine: Self-organization and dissipative systems. (New Alliance);

Intelligence research now gives results that inspire the design of new tools and devices and open new services. Feynman proposed the construction of nanomachines, nanotools, molecular-scale robots, and computers. These kinds of machines are referred to as *Feynman machines*. Feynman machines directly manipulate matter of submicron to nanometer size. They could be used for repairing human tissue, for modification and interaction with existing organisms, or for building extremely large and fast computer memories. In general, Feynman machines open the road toward MI (see Souček and Souček[1]). The Binning-Rohrer scanning tunneling microscope combined with nanoscale manipulators might provide the necessary tool for implementing nanoscale MI machines.

According to Hameroff[14], Drexler[15] and Clarkson[16] the dividing line between the microscopic and the molecular is 1 μ. Below that, the difference is no longer merely a matter of scale, it is a matter of domain as well. Below microscopic level electricity no longer exists as a mass phenomenon, and electrons must be treated as individuals. Electrons can shift from one atom in one part of a molecule to an atom somewhere else. The shifting of electrons can change the fundamental properties of the molecule, such as its ability to conduct electricity or to absorb light of a certain wavelength. These could be the base to design molecular electronic devices and molecular computers. The United States and Japan are working to build a molecular computer but it may be several years before we see products based on molecular electronics appearing on the market.

Cooper believes that neurocomputing is an important segment for science with great commercial potential. He formed a new company dealing with neurocomputing. Among other things, he developed a pattern recognition system capable of recognizing complex handwritten characters, including Kanji characters widely used in Japan, China, and other Asian countries.

Intelligence research and development become important segments of science and industry. The products of intelligence research influence all segments of traditional markets and create new markets with new products and services.

According to Prigogine, each event in the nature is unique and it cannot be predicted in a deterministic way, as it was believed by Newton and his followers. All living and some nonliving systems present dissipative structures. These structures are unstable and flexible and they reorganize in the direction of increased flow of matter and energy. Hence biological and other structures properly treated, could increase their complexity. This is the basis for new science, technology, and economy: Nature is not static; it behaves as a living organism following the laws of selection, genetic mutation, entropy, and intelligence.

Prigogine and Stengers[17] define a *new alliance* between men and nature, based on *experimental dialogue* and not on experimental observing. The goal is to understand the nature and to *modify* the nature. The modifications include new biotechnologies, genetic engineering and creation of new forms of life and intelligence. According to Lorenz, Rifkin[18], and others, the modifications should not go beyond the point of no return.

Wolters[19] claims that intelligent computers, instruments, and robots present the key for the new economy and industry. Production chains and services should follow the laws of biocybernetics and should keep the balance with nature. Short times between discovery and commercial application open new businesses. Flexible manufacturing cells enable industry to produce new goods by changing only the software in the production line, keeping the same industrial hardware.

Kahn, Brown, and Martel[20] predict a future of abundance through new technologies. The balance between technologies, nature, and human life asks for a high level of intelligence.

11.9. NOBLE INTELLIGENCE

It could be argued that one of the chief aims of technological innovation is to emulate and eventually improve upon man's natural capabilities, including intelligent behavior. Manmade devices can now certainly detect light and sound with greater sensitivity than the retina of the eye or the ear. The impressive calculating speeds of electronic computers make it possible to complete, in a few seconds, computations which would have taken many years without computers. Many computers and their programs are exhibiting some kind of intelligence, involving the solution of problems, prediction and ability to learn. To make more intelligent computers, it would help to know more about the brain.

We know very little about the brain's detailed microcircuitry on neural network, cellular, and molecular levels. In some cases, each cell can be considered to be an oscillator, and the entire network a system of coupled oscillators. (See the Brain Window Theory, Souček and Souček[1].)

It seems that natural neural networks are not rigid hard-wired circuits. They are flexible circuits that can be modified by the actions of chemical, hormonal, and electrical modulators. Circuits can adapt not only be changing synaptic strength but by altering virtually every physiological parameter available to it. Bullock[21] composed a comprehensive list of physiological parameters with numerous variables. From this list, we take only two examples:

1. Synaptic transmission:
   Chemical or electrical,
   Excitatory or inhibitory,
   Polarized or unpolarized, and
   High gain or low gain;
2. Postsynaptic response:
   Potential change or conductance change,
   Monophasic or biphasic,
   Slow or fast,
   Only passive or partly active,
   With increased or decreased conductance, and
   Facilitating, antifacilitating, or neither.

According to Silverston[22], only a small number of the preceding parameters have been considered so far in designing artificial neural networks and intelligent systems.

Further computational efforts must be grounded on empirical data. In the same time theoretical modeling should serve as a quide for the experimenta-

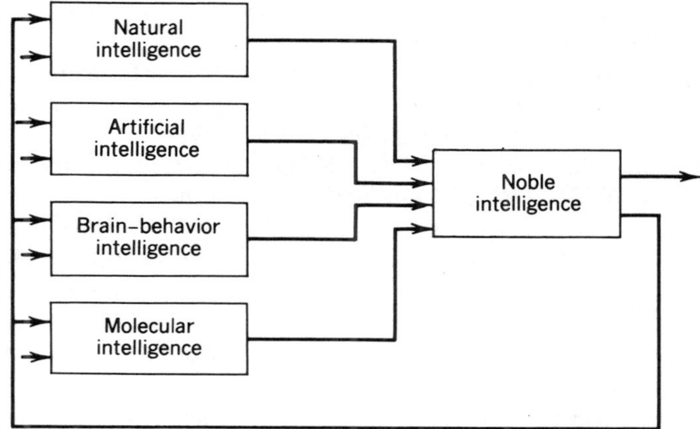

Figure 11.5 *Noble intelligence, from individual to the global level, is the driving force of the sixth-generation technology and services.*

list in acquiring meaningful data. This means that the research in natural intelligence and in man-made intelligence present one single domain of science, as shown in Figure 11.5. We define name for this science: *noble intelligence*. Noble intelligence should provide the base for new highly efficient economy and business in combination with nature, a healthy environment, and a happy life. It should generate new jobs, products, services, applications, and markets. According to Fiddler,[23] an isolated computer will become a thing of the past, with most computers being used primarily as ports to access a network. Geographical distance will decrease once people, machines, information, homes, offices, and vehicles are linked together conceptually. Even time will blur as worldwide communications improve. Noble intelligence should be able to solve complex problems in a multidimensional space, outlined by science, technology, business, environment and people.

Real-time systems are an integral part of this scenario. Robots, factories, vehicles, houses, and many other machines will inevitably be networked. Real-time data acquisition and control serve as an essential window between networks and real world events.

REFERENCES

1. B. Souček and M. Souček, *Neural and Massively Parallel Computers: The Sixth Generation,* Wiley, New York, 1988.
2. R. Hecht-Nielsen, Neurocomputer applications. *Proc. 1987 IEEE Asilomar Signal and System Conf.,* IEEE Press, 1988.
3. C. A. Mead, A sensitive electronic photoreceptor. *1985 Chapel Hill Conf.* on Very Large Scale Integration, 1985, 463–471.

4. C. A. Mead and M. A. Mahowald, A silicon model of early visual processing. *Neural Networks* **1,** 91–97 (1988).
5. K. Adamson, G. Donnan, and N. D. Black, Simple transformation rules in the application of transputers to the physiological processing of speech. *Microprocessing and Microprogramming* **24,** 397–402 (1988).
6. S. E. Fahlman, G. E. Hinton and T. J. Sejnowski, *Massively Parallel Architectures for AI: NETL, THISTLE and BOLTZMANN machines.*
7. M. J. B. Duff, "Seeing machines." In J. E. Hayes and D. Mickie, (eds.), *Intelligent Systems,* Ellis Horwood Ltd., Halsted Press, Wiley, New York, 1984.
8. S. Wolfram, Universality and complexity in cellular automata, *Physica* **10 D** 1–35, (1984).
9. P. Kanerva, *Sparce Distributed Memory, A Bradford Book,* The MIT Press, Cambridge, 1988.
10. H. J. Curnow and B. A. Wichmann, A syntetic benchmark, *Computer Journal,* **19**(1) February (1976).
11. B. Savage, *Dr. Dobb's Journal,* p. 120, September (1983).
12. R. P. Weicker, Dhryston: A syntetic systems programming benchmark, *Communications of the ACM,* **27**(10), October (1984).
13. T. Kohonen, *Self Organization and Associative Memories,* Springer-Verlag, Berlin, 1988.
14. S. R. Hameroff, *Ultimate Computing: Biomolecular Consciensness and Nanotechnology,* Elsevier, New York, 1987.
15. K. E. Drexler, *Engines of Creation,* Doubleday, New York 1987.
16. M. A. Clarkson, The quest for the molecular computer, *Byte,* **14**(5), 268–273, May (1989).
17. I. Prigogine, I. Stengers, *La Nouvelle Alliance,* Metamorphose de la science.
18. J. Rifkin, *Entropy, A New World View,* Viking Press, New York, 1980.
19. M. F. Wolters, *Die Fünfte Generation, Der Schlüssel zum Wohlstand durch Industrieroboter und Intelliggente Computer,* Wirtschaftsverlag Langen Müller/Herbig, 1984.
20. H. Kahn, W. Brown, L. Martel, *The Next 200 Years,* William Morrow, New York, 1976.
21. T. H. Bullock, In search of principles in neural integration. In Fentress (ed.), *Simpler Networks and Behavior,* Sinauer Associates, Sunderland, MA, 1976.
22. A. I. Silverstone, A consideration of inverterbrate central pattern generators as computational data base. *Neural Networks* **1,** 109–117 (1988).
23. J. Fiddler, The Future of Networking, *Vx World* **1**(4), 1989.

LIST OF MANUFACTURERS

Company	Product
ADAPTICS 16776 Bernardo Center Drive Suite 110 B, San Diego, CA 92128	Neural networks, consulting, and training
AI WARE Inc. 11000 Cedar Avenue Cleveland, OH 44106	Manufacturing process control via a neural net. Load advisor system, neural software
AP Laboratories Inc. 4411 Morena Blvd. Ste. 150 San Diego, CA 92117	Programmable I/O subsystems for real-time
Applied Intelligent Systems 110 Parkland Plaza Ann Arbor, MI 48103	Visual recognition systems
ASEA Robotics 16250 West Glendale Drive New Berlin, WI 53151	Vision systems
ATM Heinzelova 70 A 41000 Zagreb, Yugoslavia	Sensors, actuators, process control systems
Automation Intelligence Inc. 1200 West Colonial Drive Orlando, FL 32804-7194	Vision systems

Company	Product
Automatix 1000 Technology Park Drive Billerica, MA 01821	Robotic and artificial vision systems
Bridge Communications, Inc. 2081 Stierlin Road Mountain View, CA 94043	Communication/Networking Servers
Cognex Corporation 72 River Park Street Needham, MA 02194	Visual recognition systems
Cognitive Software Inc. 703 E. 30th Street Fall Creek Building, Suite 7 Indianapolis, IN 46205	Cognition neural network simulator for Macintosh and transputer boards
Control Automation, Inc. P. O. Box 2304 Princeton, NJ 08540	Visual recognition systems
Corollary Inc. 17881 Cartwright Rd. Irvine, CA 92714	Multiprocessing, C (cache) bus
Digital Equipment Corporation CFO 1-2/M92 200 Baker Avenue West Concord, MA 01742	Real-Time systems; Networks; Computers: Expert systems
Dragon Systems Inc. Chapel Bridge Park 55 Chapel Street Newton, MA 02158	Speech processing
Everett/Charles Automation Systems 2887 North Towne Avenue Pomona, CA 91767	Machine vision and robots
Excalibur Technologies 122 Tulane S.E. Albuquerque NM 87106	Savvy neural net, pattern, image, text, signal recognition

Company	Product
General Electric Intelligent Vision Systems Operation Highway 441 North Plymouth FL 32768	Visual recognition systems
Gesellschaft für Mathematik und Datenverarbeitung mbH POB 1240, D-5205 St. Augustin Germany	Transputer based reconfigurable hyperclusters
Global Holonetics Corporation P.O. Box 1305, 1900 W. Stone Fairfield, IA 52556	Optical-neural manufacturing inspection
Hecht-Nielsen Neurocomputer Corporation 5501 Oberlin San Diego, CA 92121	ANZA neural processors and boards. Neural software and applications, signals, robots, control
Hewlett-Packard Co 3495 Deer Creek Road Palo Alto, CA 94304	Real-time systems; Networks; Instruments; Computers; Expert systems
INMOS Group of Companies 1000 AZTEC WEST Almondsbury Bristol BS 124SQ, England	Transputer family of chips and boards, OCCAM language
INTEL Scientific Computers 15201 N.W. Greenbrier Parkway Beaverton, OR 97006	Hypercube-based parallel computers
Institute Mihajlo Pupin Volgina 15 11000 Belgrade, Yugoslavia	Robots, Control Systems
Institute Ruder Bošković Bijenička 54 41000 Zagreb, Yugoslavia	Intelligent instrument, Data Acquisition Systems
IntelliCorp 707 Laurel Street Menlo Park, CA 94025-3445	Knowledge engineering environment (KEE)

Company	Product
International Robomation/ Intelligence 2281 Las Palmas Drive Carlsbad, CA 92008	Robotic vision systems
Interstate Voice Products 1001 East Ball Road P.O. Box 3117 Anaheim, CA 92803	Voice recognition systems
Kurzweil Applied Intelligence 411 Waverley Oaks Road Waltham, MA 02154	Voice recognition devices
Machine Vision International Corp. 325 East Eisenhower Parkway Ann Arbor, MI 48104	Visual recognition products
MARK Ware Associates 96 Queens Road Bristol BS81NS, England	Transputer boards and software
Meiko Incorporated 6201 Ascot Drive Oakland, CA 94611	Transputer-based computing surface
Microelectronics and Computer Technology Corporation 9430 Research Boulevard Echelon Building 1, Suite 200 Austin, TX 78759-6509	Developing advanced technologies for use by U.S. corporations
Microwave Systems Co. 1900 N.W. 114th Street Des Moines, IA 50322	Real-time operating system UniBridge = Unix: 0S9
Micro Way P.O.B. 79 Kingston, MA 02364 or 32 High St. Kingston-Upon-Thames UK	Transputer development system, monoputer, software, boards
Mitek Systems 2033 Chennault Drive Carrollton, Texas 75006	Network Server Products

Company	Product
Mizar Inc. 1419 Dann Drive Corrollton, TX 75006	Real-time processors and application systems, VMEbus boards
NEC America Inc. 8 Old Sod Farm Road Melville, NY 11747	Speech recognition equipment
Nestor Inc. One Richmond Square Providence, RI 02906	Pattern recognition neural systems for industrial and financial applications, including image, signal, speech, character, and process control
Network Research Corporation 2380 N. Rose Avenue Oxnard, CA 93030	Network software
Network Systems Corporation 7600 Boone Ave. No. Minneapolis, MN 55428-9990	Network systems hardware and software products; Hyper-channel
Neural Systems Inc. 2827 West 43rd Ave. Vancouver, BC Canada V6N3H9	Neural robot control, software package awareness
Neuralware Inc. 103 Buckskin Court Sequickley, PA 15143	Neural software, character recognition, professional development environment
Neuronics Inc. One Kendall Square Suite 2200 Cambridge, MA 02139	McBrain family of neural products for research, education, and application generation
Object Recognition Systems, Inc. 440 Wall Street Princeton, NJ 08540	Visual recognition systems
Octek Inc. 7 Corporate Place South Bedford Street Burlington, MA 01803	Visual recognition systems

Company	Product
Olmstead and Watkins 2411 East Valley Parkway Suite 294 P.O. Box 3751 Escondido, CA 92025	Neural network simulation packages
Oxford Computers 39 Old Good Hill Road Oxford, CT 06483	Intelligent memory chips for neural networks and computer vision
Paracom Inc. Bldg. 9, Unit 60 245 W. Roosevelt Rd. West Chicago, IL 60185	Transputer-based VME boards and parallel systems
PARACOM Juelicher Str. 338 D-5100 Aachen, W. Germany	Transputer-based VME boards and parallel systems
Parsytec GmbH Juelicherstrasse 338 D-5100 Aachen Germany	Transputer based parallel systems, clusters and superclusters
Perceptron Inc. 23855 Research Drive Farmington Hills, MI 48024	Visual recognition systems
Rade Končar Falerovo Šetalište 22 41000 Zagreb, Yugoslavia	Real-Time systems
Robotic Vision Systems Inc. 425 Rabro Drive East Hauppauge, NY 11788	Visual recognition systems
SAIC, Artificial Neural Systems Division 10260 Campus Point Drive MS/71 San Diego, CA 92121	Delta/Sigma neural processor and boards. ANSpec neural language. Neural software for robotics and control. GINNI neural system development tool
Schwartz Associates 1470 Wildrose Way Mountain View, CA 94043	Consulting, training, marketing in neural networks

Company	Product
Scott Instruments Corp. 1111 Willow Springs Drive Denton, TX 76201	Voice recognition systems
Sistemi za Energetiko Tržaška cesta 2 61000 Ljubljana Yugoslavia	Real-time systems for process control
Symbolics 11 Cambridge Center Cambridge, MA 02142	MACSYMA, powerful general-purpose mathematical software. Plexi neural network system
Syntonic Systems, Inc. 20790 N.W. Quail Hollow Drive Portland, OR 97229	Analog CMOS neural chips
Texas Instrument Co. Manton Lane, Bedford, MK417PA, England	Signal and neural network chips and systems
3L Ltd. Peel House, Ladywell Livingston EH54 6AG, Scotland	Parallel Pascal compiler for transputers
Topologix Plaza la Reina Office Tower Suite 439 6033 West Century Blvd. Los Angeles, CA 90045	Board level parallel processing based on transputers
Transputer Systems Group Center for Industrial Research Box 124, Blindern, 0314 Oslo 3, Norway	Transputer cards for IBM AT
TRW One Rancho Carmel San Diego, CA 92128	Mark family of neural workstations. Neural hardware, software, and applications
U-Microcomputers Ltd. 12 Chetham Court Calver Rd, Windwick Quay Warrington, Cheshire WA2 8RF, UK	Graphics for transputers

Company	Product
Verbex/Exxon Two Oak Park Bedford, MA 01730	Voice recognition systems
Vesta Technology Inc. 7100 W 44th Ave, Suite 101 Wheatridge, CO 80033	Custom design for control computers
Voice Control Systems, Inc. 16610 Dallas Parkway Dallas, TX 75248	Voice recognition systems
Votan 4487 Technology Drive Fremont, CA 94538	Voice recognition and generation systems
Wind River Systems Inc. 1351 Ocean Ave. Emeryville, CA 94608	Real-time software
The Wollongong Group 1129 San Antonio Road Palo Alto, CA 94303-4374	Communication/networking software
Alpha Products 242 B West Avenue Darien, CT 06820	Adapters/cards for process control
California Scientific Software 160 E. Montecito, #E Sierra Madre, CA 91024	Neural networks
Capital Equipment Corp. Burlington, MA 01803	IEEE 488 control for PC/XT/AT
Cesius Ltd. Southgate Whitefriars Lewins Mead Bristol BS1 2NT U.K.	Transputer boards and software for PC/XT/AT
Flagstaff Engineering 1120 Kaibob Lane Flagstaff, AZ 86001	Trainable OCR reader

Company	Product
I/O Tech Inc. 25971 Cannon Road Cleveland, OH 44146	IEEE 488 interfaces
Micro Devices 5643 Beegs Rd. Orlando, FL 32810	CMOS fuzzy set neural chip
National Instruments Corp. 12109 Technology Blvd. Austin, TX 78727-6204	Data acquisition boards
Parex Polanškova 8 61231 Ljubljana Yugoslavia	CIM, Real-time, Unix, vision, expert systems
Perihelion Ltd. 33 Bridge Street Cambridge CB2 1UW U.K.	Parallel processing by transputers
Pinacle Micro 15265 Alton Parkway Irvine, CA 92718	Removable, erasable, optical storage
Ward Systems Group Inc. 228 West Patrick Street Frederick, MD 21701	Neural networks

AUTHOR INDEX

SUBJECT INDEX